D0804743

Christological
Perspectives

For Barbara Turner

from

Robert F. Buerkey

REMOVED FROM THE
ALVERNO COLLEGE LIBRARY

Photo by Fred M. Dole

Harvey K. McArthur

Christological Perspectives

Essays in Honor of Harvey K. McArthur

EDITED BY

Robert F. Berkey and Sarah A. Edwards

232
C 556

The Pilgrim Press

NEW YORK

ALVERNO COLLEGE LIBRARY
MILWAUKEE, WISCONSIN

Copyright © 1982 The Pilgrim Press
All rights reserved

No part of this publication may be reproduced, stored in a retrieval system, or transmitted in any form or by any means, electronic, mechanical, photocopying, recording, or otherwise (brief quotations used in magazines or newspaper reviews excepted), without the prior permission of the publisher.

Biblical quotations marked RSV are from the Revised Standard Version of the Bible, copyright 1946, 1952 and © 1971 by the Division of Christian Education, National Council of Churches, and are used by permission. Scriptural verses from *The New English Bible* are © The Delegates of the Oxford University Press and the Syndics of the Cambridge University Press, 1961, 1970, and are used by permission.

The text of the *Testamonium Flavianum* in chapter 14 is from Josephus, *Antiquities* 18.63–64, Loeb Classical Library, vol. 9, ed. Louis H. Feldman, Harvard University Press, London, 1965. Copyright 1965 by the President and Fellows of Harvard College. Used by permission.

Library of Congress Cataloging in Publication Data
Main entry under title:

Christological perspectives.

    Includes bibliographical references.
    1. Jesus Christ—Person and offices—Addresses, essays, lectures. 2. McArthur, Harvey K.
I. McArthur, Harvey K. II. Berkey, Robert F.
III. Edwards, Sarah A., 1921–
BT202.C544   232   81–21013
ISBN 0–8298–0491–9   AACR2
ISBN 0–8298–0606–7 (pbk.)

The Pilgrim Press, 132 West 31 Street, New York, NY 10001

Harvey King McArthur

This volume is a testimony to Harvey K. McArthur. His life and career are detailed in the "vita" which follows, but we the editors want to add our personal expressions of gratitude and esteem for this unusual scholar, teacher, pastor, and friend. The thoroughness of his scholarship is unmistakably clear in the things he has written; the depth of his perception and understanding have overwhelmed many generations of theological students at both the seminary and graduate level; the *Word* of the Gospel has been the very fabric of his life and work. *Our lives,* and the lives of thousands of students, parishioners, and colleagues, bear witness to the purpose for which this collection is set forth.

Harvey King McArthur was born May 9, 1912, in Billingsville, Missouri, the son of United Presbyterian Church missionaries to India (now Pakistan) who were home on furlough. Part of his boyhood was spent in what is now Pakistan.

1925–29	High school on Bainbridge Island, in the state of Washington.
1929–31	Tarkio College, Tarkio, Missouri.
1931–33	Wheaton College, Wheaton, Illinois. Ph.B. degree.
1933–37	Westminster Theological Seminary, Philadelphia, Pennsylvania. Certificate received.
1937–38	Study in Germany at the Universities in Berlin and Tübingen (Frank H. Stevenson Fellowship for study abroad, from Westminster Theological Seminary).
1939–41	Study at the Hartford Seminary Foundation, Hartford, Connecticut in the field of New Testament. Master of Sacred Theology (1940), Doctor of Philosophy (1941). Both years on Jacobus fellowships.
1941–44	Pastor of Blackstone Federated Churches, Blackstone, Massachusetts (Baptist and Congregational).
1944–46	Chaplain, U.S. Army in the European Theater (75th Infantry Division), with a semester at the Divinity School, Glasgow University, Scotland after the end of World War II.

1946–47	Study at Union Theological Seminary in New York City and, in spring 1947, substitute Instructor in New Testament at Bangor Theological Seminary, Bangor, Maine.
1947–48	Instructor in Department of Biblical History, Wellesley College, Wellesley, Massachusetts.
1948–78	Faculty member in New Testament at The Hartford Seminary Foundation, Hartford, Connecticut (1948–53 Associate Professor; 1953–60 Professor; 1960–78 Hosmer Professor of New Testament; 1976–78 Acting President, the Hartford Seminary Foundation).
1961–62	Sabbatical in Heidelberg, Germany on Fulbright Senior Fellowship.
1967–68	Sabbatical in Cambridge, England with American Association of Theological Schools Fellowship.
1975–76	Sabbatical in Oxford, England and in Israel.
	Ordained minister of the United Church of Christ (ordained 1942 in Blackstone, Massachusetts).
	Married Elizabeth R. Dimock in 1941; three children: Harvey (1951), John (1952), Pamela (1955).
	Retired to Wilmington, Vermont in 1978. Address: Box 128, Wilmington, Vermont 05363.

Publications

Books
Editor &
Contributor:
New Testament Sidelights. Hartford, CT: Hartford Seminary Foundation Press, 1960.
In Search of the Historical Jesus. New York: Charles Scribner's Sons, 1969. British edition: London: SPCK, 1970.
Author:
Understanding the Sermon on the Mount. New York: Harper & Bros., 1960. British edition: London: Epworth Press, 1961.
The Quest Through the Centuries. Philadelphia: Fortress Press, 1966.

Articles
"Liberal Concessions to Fundamentalism." *Religion in Life* 14, no. 4 (1945): 535–44.
"Mark XIV 62." *New Testament Studies* 4, no. 2 (1957–58): 156–58.

"The Dependence of the Gospel of Thomas on the Synoptics." *Expository Times* 71, no. 9 (June 1960): 286–87.

"The Irrationale of Capital Punishment." *The Torch* 24, no. 3 (July 1961): 7–10, 22.

"Paradise" and "Parousia." *The Interpreter's Dictionary of the Bible*. Nashville: Abingdon Press, 1962.

"The Problem of Authority: A Protestant View." *Christianity and Crisis*, May 27, 1963, pp. 96–98.

"Basic Issues: A Survey of Recent Gospel Research." *Interpretation* 17, no. 1 (January 1964): 39–55.

"The Earliest Divisions of the Gospels." *Studia Evangelica* 3, Texte und Untersuchungen 88, ed. F.L. Cross. Berlin: Akademie-Verlag, 1964. Pp. 266–72.

"The Eusebian Sections and Canons." *Catholic Biblical Quarterly* 27, no. 3 (July 1965): 250–56.

"Computer Criticism." *Expository Times* 76, no. 12 (September 1965): 367–70.

"A Further Note on Paul and the Computers." *Expository Times* 77, no. 11 (August 1966): 350.

"Ethical Teaching of St. Paul," "Sermon on the Mount," "Mammon," "Household Codes," "Jesus' Ethical Teaching," "Golden Rule," and "Kingdom of God," in *Dictionary of Christian Ethics*, ed. John Macquarrie. Philadelphia: Westminster Press, 1967.

"*Kai* Frequency in Greek Letters." *New Testament Studies* 15, no. 3 (1968–69): 339–49.

"From the Historical Jesus to Christology." *Interpretation* 23, no. 2 (April 1969): 190–206. Condensed version in *Theology Digest* 18, no. 1 (Spring 1970): 29–35.

"The Burden of Proof in Historical Jesus Research." *Expository Times* 82, no. 4 (January 1971): 116–19.

"The Parable of the Mustard Seed." *Catholic Biblical Quarterly* 33, no. 2 (April 1971): 198–210.

"On the Third Day." *New Testament Studies* 18, no. 1 (1971–72): 81–86.

"Current New Testament Issues." *The Unitarian Universalist Christian* 27, no. 2 (Summer 1972): 43–53.

"Son of Mary." *Novum Testamentum* 15, no. 1 (1973): 38–58.

"The Origin of the 'Q' Symbol." *Expository Times* 88, no. 4 (January 1977): 119–20.

Contents

ix

Preface

Christological Perspectives seems to be an appropriate title for these essays in honor of Harvey King McArthur, since Christology was the unifying theme of his scholarly work. The historical-Jesus problems, the implicit theology of the Sermon on the Mount, the reality of the resurrection, the debate over the Son-of-man occurrences—all these have been recurrent topics of far-reaching importance in New Testament investigation during McArthur's career, and to these issues his teaching and writing have been creatively addressed. The christological studies presented here voice the gratitude of many colleagues and students whose careers and ministries have been enhanced beyond measure by this exceptional person. The distinction of those who have contributed to this volume is a semeion of the quality and, in the best sense of the word, the class that marked Harvey K. McArthur's work.

Christology is the "theological interpretation of the person and work of Christ."[1] In these essays the terms "Christology" and "christological" are used not only in the narrow sense to describe Jesus as the Christ-Messiah, but also in the broadest sense to include the historic roots of messianic thought in Judaism and to express the mystery and meaning of Christ Jesus as Lord.

By "perspective" we mean "the capacity to view things in their true relations or relative importance."[2] No one person, no one church, no one faith has the capacity to comprehend the fullness of Christ. In the New Testament itself Jesus is viewed in many perspectives. The special experience of the apostles, the treasured traditions of the evangelists, and the cumulative understanding of the early Christian communities constantly open up new capacities for theological affirmation.

The title "Christological Perspectives" celebrates the significance of every way in which Jesus is authentically viewed. The picture of Jesus Christ in the New Testament—and our picture—is ever developing, ever beckoning, ever incomplete. That is the fascination of biblical studies.

The editors wish to thank Hartford Seminary for its encouragement and support in the publication of this volume, which reflects some of the best of its life and scholarship. We would like to express our appreciation to Ms. Marion M. Meyer of The Pilgrim Press for many helpful suggestions, tactful criticisms, and undaunted perseverance in getting this book through the works. We also wish to thank the Faculty Grants Committee of Mount Holyoke College for the financial support made available to Dr. Berkey to work on this project.

Robert F. Berkey
Sarah A. Edwards

PART I

Christological Perspectives: Introductory and Methodological Considerations

CHAPTER 1

Christological Perspectives:
The Context of Current Discussions

Robert F. Berkey

There is no question about the importance of christological affirmations in the New Testament and about their significance for the ongoing theological stream that has continued to flow from those twenty-seven books that emerged in late antiquity. Surely no issues of Christian thought have gone through more thorough analyses in this century than those problems pertaining to the New Testament affirmations of the unique, unprecedented, once-for-all character of the person of Jesus, affirmations appropriately designated under the general rubric of Christology. Indeed, any pilgrimage into the subject of Christology will of necessity carry the traveler back through the decades of modern New Testament criticism, as well as out through the broader fields of contemporary New Testament interpretation.

Asking christological questions invariably confronts the inquirer with some of the most probing historical and literary questions relating to Christian beginnings and leads with equal deliberation into the vastly complicated and variegated world of Christian theology in all its cultural, social, and ecumenical relationships. The essays in this collection focus on these christological issues relating to the historical and literary makeup of the New Testament itself; Harvey K. McArthur's career surely dictates that this should be the case. Yet that same career is also a powerful reminder of the urgency for interpretation and reflection, for dialogue and understanding, for involvement and commitment, for tolerance and reconciliation when dealing with issues and affirmations that are so central to the whole community of faith. Attempting therefore to be faithful to the McArthur paradigm as well as to contemporary biblical scholarship, this collection includes, by deliber-

Robert F. Berkey received his Ph.D. from the Hartford Seminary Foundation in 1958 with Harvey K. McArthur as *ordinanus*. He is currently Professor of Religion at Mount Holyoke College, South Hadley, Massachusetts.

ate design, essays reflecting wider theological and cultural perspectives, as well as discussions focusing on additional perspectives from outside the Christian community of faith.

The purpose of this introductory essay is simply to set forth in broad terms the general context in which christological discussions proceed in our time, and consequently the context in which the essays in this collection have taken shape. If one were to return to the mainstream of liberal Protestant biblical and theological interpretation existing at the beginning of this century, one might find it difficult to understand how Christology, at least in its two-nature Chalcedonian dress, could ever have survived in serious discussion through this final quarter of the twentieth century. The story of nineteenth-century critical analysis of the New Testament, especially as that analysis relates to christological issues, does not need to be retold here. Simply recalling the work of so important a historian/theologian as Adolf von Harnack will be sufficient to recover what was a dominant mood among critical scholars when Harnack gave his now famous lectures in Berlin, published in 1900, under the title *Das Wesen des Christentums*. For Harnack, historical criticism had clearly established a picture of Jesus, not so much in transcendent christological terms but as a kind of spiritual genius: "Jesus is convinced that he knows God in a way in which no one else ever knew him before, and he knows that it is his vocation to communicate that knowledge of God to others by word and deed—and with it the knowledge that men are God's children."[1] Or one also recalls that statement so frequently cited as expressive of Harnack's antichristological bias: "The Gospel as Jesus proclaimed it has to do with the Father only and not with the Son."[2] And although Harnack actually ended up crediting Paul's theologizing as that which happily released the historic message of Jesus from the limitations of its Jewish setting, he nonetheless saw Christology always as a kind of threat to the "majesty and simplicity of the Gospel," indeed, as a "perverse proceeding to make Christology a fundamental substance of the Gospel."[3]

Harnack's reconstruction of the "essence" of Christianity carried with it the general outlook that "enlightened" theology of the nineteenth century embraced so enthusiastically, namely, the conviction that the Pauline and subsequent interpretations *about* Jesus, especially as these were eventually defined and articulated in a non-Jewish, Hellenistic environment, constituted a distortion of the earlier, simpler, and more acceptable (rationally more understandable?) ethical and spiritual *message* of the historical Jesus. In one sense, attempts thus to redefine Christianity in terms of Jesus' own inner spiritual consciousness, historically demonstrated and proven, might well have placed an even stronger emphasis on the *person* of Jesus (Christology?). In fact, however, such

4

interpretations *about* the person gave way finally to an emphasis on ethical and spiritual truths generally affirmed and appropriated, while traditional messianic, universal, transcendent declarations were either radically redefined or set aside entirely. What was universalized was the *message* rather than the *person*, all of which was a fundamental denial of Christology as it had been biblically and dogmatically defined.

Even a cursory glance at the world of New Testament interpretation makes it clear that the Harnackian model did not prevail and that transcendent Christology did not collapse in the face of historical criticism. One need only recall that when the World Council of Churches was organized in 1948 in Amsterdam its member churches declared their common acceptance of Jesus as "God and Savior." Here were Christian communions, representing in some ways the very fruits of Enlightenment theology, less than half a century removed from Harnack's Berlin lectures, affirming an explicitly christological claim that a Harnack and those of his persuasion could only have rejected outright. From the vantage point of the last quarter of the twentieth century, it is clear that the whole climate, christologically speaking, has undergone dramatic changes. And while Roman Catholic theology never underwent the radical redefinition that is represented in Harnack's reconstruction of Christianity's "essence," it should be pointed out that Catholic thought, too, has experienced a revival of christological interest and affirmation.[4] Much diversity continues to dominate the exegetical, theological, and dogmatic discussions, whether in Protestant circles or Catholic circles, but the point to be pondered here is the very survival of christological interest as it has survived the onslaught of nineteenth-century attempts to "spiritualize" or "ethicize" New Testament christological affirmations.

Harnack's *Das Wesen des Christentums* is surely not the context in which christological discussions now take place. In fact, even as Harnack was addressing his Berlin audience, new christological breezes were beginning to blow across the field of New Testament investigation and interpretation, although only the most sensitive and well-informed observer might have noticed. What were some of the parameters of this christological revolution that was beginning to take shape? To answer that question fully would require a far more detailed discussion than can be attempted here, but a few observations are important in order to sense something of the present context in which christological reflection continues.

Lying at the very center of this shift away from Harnack's "dechristologizing" was the dilemma posed by Johannes Weiss in *Die Predigt Jesu vom Reiche Gottes*, a book written in 1892, though only recently made available to English readers.[5] Weiss's conclusions, later expanded and

5

popularized in the work of Albert Schweitzer,[6] called attention to what were viewed as the somewhat embarrassing results of modern critical and historical analyses of the New Testament, namely, that the figure of Jesus ultimately exposed by critical investigation was an apocalyptic fanatic declaring the end of the age, the beginning of the kingdom of God. Gone from the center of this reconstruction was Harnack's underlying assumption that the Jesus of history must or can by definition be found compatible with "enlightenment" spirituality. And while these notions of Weiss and Schweitzer seemed devastating in certain respects, the very loss of Harnack's spiritual paradigm had the opposite effect of forcing New Testament critics to turn now with renewed vigor to the *person* of Jesus, which from the earliest layers of Christian tradition occupied the center of theological/christological affirmation. In short, although the Weiss/Schweitzer conclusions about the figure of Jesus were clearly destructive to the assumptions of enlightened criticism, they also carried the seeds of a revived interest in Christology. Anyone who by 1900 had read Weiss's *Die Predigt* found ample reason to question the historical validity of Harnack's spiritualized, nonchristological picture of Jesus, and it was that line of questioning which has in fact been pursued with utmost seriousness during the twentieth century.

There were other factors beginning to emerge at the same time. A fundamental and still-unanswered question was raised in 1901 with the publication of William Wrede's *Das Messiasgeheimnis in den Evangelien*.[7] In this work Wrede pointedly raised the issue of the "messianic secret" inherent in Mark's reconstruction of the life of Jesus, a motif generally adhered to in the other two synoptic Gospels as well. That issue in turn raised again a whole series of questions about what, if any, christological affirmations were made by Jesus himself. Martin Kähler's earlier work, *Der sogennante historische Jesus und der geschichtliche biblische Christus*,[8] sharply defined the underlying question of whether the "real" Jesus could be recovered from the christologically controlled Gospels, a question which was to be a central problem dealt with by the later form critics.[9] One central assumption with which criticism had worked—namely, that investigation *could* make available an accurate reconstruction of the historical Jesus—was beginning to be eroded. All this was destined to redirect attention to the essentially christological framework and substance of the New Testament.

Moreover, by the 1920s the whole theological mood was changing, as European Protestants in particular were being introduced to Karl Barth's "strange new world within the Bible."[10] In that "new world" we were confronted with Jesus not so much as a spiritual "teacher" but as the *Word* made flesh, as revelation and judgment, as reconciliation and salvation. In addition to all this was the form-critical dilemma that the

Gospels themselves were ultimately determined and shaped by that Word of salvation (kerygma), and of no small importance was the 1936 publication of C.H. Dodd's *Apostolic Preaching and Its Development*, making the case for a consistently unified kerygma (christological raw materials!) running through the entire New Testament: Acts, Gospels, Epistles.[11] In short, theological and exegetical discussions were adding up to a new and revitalized awareness of the christological character of the New Testament, and it is within that same "strange new world" that contemporary christological discussions are pursued. Such a climate would certainly have been at best only vaguely apparent when Harnack was describing his "essence" of Christianity in 1900.

There is no attempt here to make any systematic survey of recent christological studies, although readers can benefit from the many surveys that have already appeared.[12] And the reader will not find here any comprehensive analysis of the constituent titles of christological discourse in the New Testament. Two important works along these lines are by contributors to this very volume.[13] The focus, much more modest in scope, is on certain areas that constitute some of the major stress points within the whole range of New Testament christological discussion, whether approached historically and exegetically, or interpretively and theologically.

Still it appears that the most important unresolved issue in the christological debate can be named with the fundamental question "Where did it all begin?" Is Christology essentially a product of the postresurrection Christian community? Or did Christology have its birth in Jesus' historic self-awareness? The remainder of this essay therefore centers around the question of christological origins, both because of its widespread importance in recent discussions and, even more important, because the major issues of christological inquiry ultimately carry us back to that fundamental problem.

The contemporary phase of this debate proceeds from the important conclusions reached by the late Rudolf Bultmann, a position so well known that it need not be repeated here in any detail. Bultmann's point of view can be best summed up in the opening line of his *Theology of the New Testament*: "The message of Jesus is a presupposition for the theology of the New Testament rather than a part of that theology itself."[14] Hence, for Bultmann, Christology is wholly a product of the postresurrection Christian community, a position which Bultmann reached only after a rigorously and consistently applied form-critical analysis of the Gospel records,[15] an analysis which left him with continuing and fundamental reservations about what can be known with certainty of the historical Jesus. Already in his introductory comments to *Jesus and the Word,* Bultmann reminded his readers that it is only

7

through a critical analysis of the many-layered synoptic tradition that finally "an oldest layer is determined," though even there "we have no absolute assurance that the exact words of this oldest layer were really spoken by Jesus."[16] Bultmann's refusal to locate Christology within Jesus' own self-disclosure is rooted both in such strong reservations about the gospel traditions, and in his continued insistence that the very nature of the kerygma is confirmed not in historical proof but in the faith of the resurrection.[17] Bultmann's insistence on that fundamental distinction between the proclamation *of* Jesus and the proclamation *about* Jesus was never compromised in his later works. It is a stance both well known and fundamentally accepted among many contemporary New Testament scholars in Germany and, to a lesser degree, in Great Britain and America. At least two of the contributors included in this volume have worked out their Christologies from that same form-critical framework,[18] and Harvey K. McArthur himself remains essentially a Bultmannian on these issues. In a 1969 essay, after a brief survey of the various ways of understanding the historical materials in the Gospels, McArthur said:

> In the historical area I reject as largely unprofitable the theories that the Gospels contain substantial quantities of eyewitness material or that they are the end product of a professionally controlled oral tradition. On the other hand, I stand on the boundary between the more radical form critics and those who hold that by the eclectic use of a variety of criteria a relatively substantial sketch of the teaching of Jesus, and perhaps of his ministry, may be made probable. In my judgment there is, unfortunately, no reason to believe that these sketches will ever be sufficiently stable to serve as a foundation for the construction of a traditional Christology.[19]

There has indeed been some tendency in recent years for Bultmannians to place more stress in one way or another on the christological importance of what *can* be recovered of the historical Jesus. Sometimes labeled as the "post-Bultmannians," this ambiguously defined group has presumably modified Bultmann's insistence on the fundamental break between the historical Jesus and the preached Christ. This movement is usually said to have begun with a 1953 Marburg lecture given by Ernst Käsemann, "The Problem of the Historical Jesus,"[20] and these "new questers," as they are now commonly called, were reviewed sympathetically at an early stage by James M. Robinson.[21] Perhaps best known among the original "post-Bultmannians," at least in the English-speaking world, is Günther

Bornkamm, whose full-length "life" of Jesus has been available in translation now for twenty years.[22] But this group has not resorted to the older attempt to probe the inner consciousness of Jesus in order to uncover some degree of christological awareness, nor has it parted company in any decisive way with the methods of Bultmannian form-criticism. In fact, the sum of what these post-Bultmannians have isolated as "historical" is not much greater than what Bultmann himself consistently accepted as carrying a high degree of historical probability in its favor. The difference is far more subtle, with these modified Bultmannians essentially emphasizing certain lines of continuity they see between the historical Jesus and the proclamation about Jesus in the kerygma, a stress which of course carries important christological implications. Yet when all these subtle differences are assembled, the *distinction* between Bultmann and these followers is not all that significant, at least in terms of christological origins. Indeed, Bultmann always held firmly to the position that there is an implied Christology in Jesus' historic message, especially in his call to decision with respect to the kingdom:

> He [Jesus] gave no teaching about his own person, but he said
> that the fact of his work was the ultimate decisive fact for
> men. . . . What is decisive is not *what* he proclaims but *that* he is
> proclaiming it. . . . But his call to decision certainly implies a
> Christology—not as metaphysical speculation about a heavenly
> being nor as a characterization of his personality somehow
> endowed with a messianic consciousness, but a Christology which
> is proclamation, summons.[23]

Emphasizing the messianic character of Jesus' "activity" (Bornkamm),[24] or what Ernst Fuchs refers to as "language event,"[25] does not undo the fundamental agreement shared between these post-Bultmannians and Bultmann himself. This is by no means to minimize in any way the importance of the contributions made by the "new questers," but only to suggest that in christological terms that school continues to locate the fundamental beginnings of Christology within the post-Easter communi-ty of faith and not in the claims of the historical Jesus. That being the case, the impact of Bultmannian form-criticism remains a continuing and important factor in the context of contemporary christological discussion.

One christological study—which although in some ways falling within the Bultmannian framework has opened up some new directions —deserves more attention than it has generally received. We refer to Willi Marxsen's *The Beginnings of Christology: A Study in Its Prob-*

lems.[26] Though Marxsen, like Bultmann, assigns specific christological titles only to the post-Easter community, he takes up the interesting position that the pre-Easter/post-Easter distinction is in fact a misleading way of getting at the issue of christological origins. In one sense Marxsen is even more skeptical than Bultmann when he says of historical analysis in the Gospels, "I am not able to differentiate between historical and tendentious traditions. The historical element has been screened by the tendency."[27] This suggests that Marxsen is in fact challenging form-criticism's criterion of "dissimilarity" as a test of historical validity,[28] for in his view one simply cannot draw a clear line between the pre-Easter proclamation of Jesus and the explicit Christology that blossoms only in the postresurrection era. Rather, Christology appears "where the *relationship* between Jesus and the believer becomes visible for the first time."[29] That relationship, Marxsen maintains, is visible in both the pre-Easter community and the post-Easter community, and he uses that "relationship" as his primary criterion for examining christological data. To look at one example of how this operates, Marxsen points specifically to the Mark 8:38 passage: "For whoever is ashamed of me and of my words in this adulterous and sinful generation, of him will the Son of man also be ashamed, when he comes in the glory of his Father with the holy angels [RSV]." Surely, Marxsen insists, the early Christians understood this saying in a christological manner, even though in transmitting the words of Jesus they did not transpose the saying into an explicit messianic pronouncement. It is the uniquely defined relationship between Jesus and his listeners that establishes Christology—in this particular instance a relationship that is messianically qualified by the coming of the Son of man. Wherever that relationship appears, one confronts a Christology just as clearly as if the specific designation were made either by Jesus or by the community. In fact, Marxsen argues that a saying such as Mark 8:38 is sometimes more profoundly christological than those more explicit messianic claims where the person of Jesus tends to be isolated from the dynamic of that relationship to his followers, a dynamic which for Marxsen is the crucial test of Christology, whether in the pre- or postresurrection contexts.[30]

There are undoubtedly important questions to be addressed to Marxsen's suggestions, but there is here an intriguing alternative to the standard form-critical procedure of allowing explicit Christology to be determined essentially by the use of certain christological designations or titles. Marxsen is aware that there is a conceptual distinction to be drawn between less-direct christological identifications (e.g., Mark 8:38) and the more precise titular affirmations that occur with increased frequency in the later strata of the tradition. Yet working well within the form-critical procedures for isolating the earlier, more historic layers in the Gospels, Marxsen has posed a new and promising criterion that offers some means of escaping the pre- and post-Easter cul-de-sac that has so characterized both Bultmannian and post-Bultmannian analyses of christological origins.

In general, however, the fact remains that form-critical presuppositions and approaches have produced a prevailing tendency in which Christology is viewed as essentially a product of the community of faith, at best allowing only for implicit christological affirmations by Jesus himself. To be sure, the post-Bultmannians have stirred up interest in those less-direct messianic hints found in the words and activity of Jesus, and that is of course very much a part of christological perspectives among current New Testament critics. But even that more positive trend is at least partially offset by recent attempts among other form/redaction critics to eliminate *all* Son-of-man sayings from the earliest layers, thus ever further widening the gap between Jesus' proclamation and the christological claims of the later church. Though we are scrupulously avoiding any detailed discussion of the various titles used in New Testament christological discourse, this Son-of-man problem is so directly and crucially related to christological origins that it seems absolutely necessary to offer a few comments in this regard.

The way in which one understands these Son-of-man sayings is bound to have a profound effect on where one comes out with respect to the question of Jesus' messianic self-awareness. Even the casual reader of the New Testament will notice that this title (Son of man) has been handled in a very prescribed and limited manner. It is surprising that the title is the only presumed messianic designation that the synoptic writers have placed directly on the lips of Jesus, and, where it is so used, it is consistently set forth in the third person, so as to suggest at least the possibility that Jesus was referring to someone other than himself. In the one Markan incident where Jesus is described as having admitted to the *Christos* title (Mark 14:62), his words even there immediately shift to a third-person saying about the coming of this Son of man. Add to all this the oft-observed fact that the title in the Synoptics is never used by anyone other than Jesus, and that with one exception (Acts 7:56) the title disappears entirely in the New Testament literature outside the Gospels.

All this has aroused a great deal of curiosity among critics, and for the present context it is important to point out that even Bultmann included some Son-of-man sayings within the earliest tradition, insisting, of course, that Jesus used the Son-of-man title to designate the one who was to come at the end of the age, and that the church only later identified that apocalyptic figure with the resurrected Christ. Accordingly, Bultmann found the Son-of-man title simply an expression used by Jesus to state

11

his confidence that the kingdom of God was about to supplant the present age.[31] Of course, many non-Bultmannian critics have not only accepted the use of this title in the tradition, but have also characteristically understood its meaning in connection with Jesus' own messianic proclamation.[32] The point is simply that the Son-of-man sayings have had strong and widespread support as being in some sense authentic, and that such support has come even from those critics generally deemed to be the most negative in terms of what they accept as historical tradition and what they reject.

Now, however, a number of recent studies have picked up on a segment of a position defended long ago by H.B. Sharman to the effect that the Son-of-man sayings and the kingdom-of-God statements are not linked in the Gospels.[33] Philipp Vielhauer, for example, carrying through with that conclusion, understands all the Son-of-man sayings as secondary,[34] and that position has been essentially maintained by Hans Conzelmann.[35] Norman Perrin, pointing out that the Son-of-man title is virtually nonexistent in Jewish apocalyptic tradition, has likewise insisted that the Son-of-man sayings are absent from the genuine Jesus tradition in the Gospels.[36] The issue remains unsettled, and the debate will no doubt continue for some time to come. This development is mentioned here because of the obvious significance it has for the current state of christological discussion. After all, here is the one, clear title that has had wide recognition, even among form critics, as being in some way inherent in the proclamation of the historical Jesus, and now serious doubts have been raised concerning its very existence in the earliest tradition. The consequences for the discussion of christological origins are enormous, and again, all this must be seen as a part of the context of current christological debate.

In one way or another, the whole form-critical approach has provided some important stumbling blocks that cannot be avoided by any serious attempts to probe the origins of Christology. However, all this should not blind us to the fact that there remain a substantial number of New Testament scholars who have not bowed the knee to Bultmannian form-criticism and whose refusal to do so has provided us with a far more positive assessment of the christological character of Jesus' historic ministry. For example, some New Testament scholars have in one way or another simply rejected the underlying claims of form-criticism, thereby avoiding a most serious threat to the reliability of the Gospels. One of the more interesting examples of this within the modern critical stream is the case offered by certain Scandinavian scholars who have argued that the oral tradition was transmitted in a rabbinic-like manner and that material thus preserved contains a more or less reliable picture of the historical Jesus.[37] For them, oral tradition was preserved substantially intact and then later incorporated into written Gospels, a view that offers a strong challenge to the Bultmannian notion that the preliterary tradition was constantly changing. With similar results, certain British New Testament critics, while dealing positively with methods of form-critical analysis, have simply rejected the principle that whatever reflects the thinking of the early church must finally be considered inauthentic.[38] Well known among New Testament students are the conclusions of Joachim Jeremias to the effect that Jesus' unique sense of sonship (hence, christological self-awareness) is reflected in his use of the Aramaic as *Abba* when making references to God,[39] and Oscar Cullmann has valiantly defended the actual use of "Son" as a self-designation of Jesus.[40] Others, without resorting to any explicit claims on Jesus' part, argue that the messianic title is in some sense demanded by the very fact that Jesus was tried and convicted on that presumed claim.[41] All this, if accepted, makes more feasible a christological awareness in the person of Jesus.

C.F.D. Moule's *The Origin of Christology* is one recent example of such efforts specifically to locate christological origins well within the message of the historical Jesus.[42] Moule discusses the problem by focusing on the contrast between those who view Christology as the result of an *evolutionary* process and those who prefer to understand it in terms of *development*. Moule's overall analysis is clear, even though there is admittedly some overlapping between what can be described as development and what can be defined as evolution. The "evolutionist" sees a fundamental break between the historic claim *of* Jesus and the later claims *about* his person; in short, in Moule's terms the evolutionary understanding corresponds to the form-critical conclusion that Christology is at most implicit in the message of Jesus. The "developmentalist" sees christological patterns growing directly and materially out of the self-affirmations of Jesus; as such, this position, though recognizing that certain changes did take place in christological formulations, still insists that there is a material continuity between pre- and postresurrection patterns. It is this second pattern to which Moule adheres, insisting that the combination of both continuity and change suggests the notion of development rather than evolution in the formulation of New Testament Christology.[43] Indeed, Moule is aware of the many differences that exist among the various New Testament Christologies, and he knows too that the Gospel records do reflect a certain christological reshaping brought about by the later Christian communities. Yet his position is clear when he says, "My main point is not that all Christological expressions in the New Testament are adequate for modern statements of Christology, but that they are all more successfully accounted for as insights, of varying depth, into what was there in Jesus, than as a result of increasing distance from him."[44]

Moule then goes on to test his "development" hypothesis in relation to the four main christological titles: Son of man, Son of God, Christ, and *Kyrios*. In each instance, Moule finds the christological substance already present in the mind and thought of Jesus. And what is probably even more surprising in light of much modern christological discussion, Moule understands such christological designations in ontological, not merely functional, terms. Though he appears to do so with a certain hesitation, Moule suggests that preexistence itself falls within the framework of the "developmental," so that even that "high" christological dimension has a place within the self-awareness of Jesus.[45]

Moule's christological conclusions are extremely important, not only because they so clearly locate Christology within the self-affirmation of Jesus, but also because they are conclusions that come from one whose scholarly reputation is so widely established and recognized within the main fold of modern New Testament criticism. In another survey and assessment of current New Testament Christologies, I.H. Marshall draws christological conclusions that are quite parallel to those of Moule.[46] And though Marshall is an avowed evangelical in theological persuasion, the fact is that he too brings to his study an awareness and acceptance of mainstream critical methods. The Tübingen scholar Martin Hengel, known especially for his extensive work in the backgrounds of New Testament thought,[47] similarly supports the notion that Christology had explicit beginnings within the pre-Easter message of Jesus.[48] Though perhaps more cautious than Moule or Marshall, Hengel also emphatically locates the idea of divine sonship within the realm of the historic proclamation of Jesus. If Hengel is a bit hesitant to attribute the notion of preexistent sonship to Jesus himself, he nevertheless finds that idea present in the earliest layers of the synoptic tradition and thus at least in extremely close proximity to the historical Jesus. To be sure, Hengel recognizes the distinction between explicit titles, on the one hand, and more implicitly articulated christological claims, on the other. However, in line with the conclusions of both Moule and Marshall, Hengel does not finally see any material break between the claims of Jesus and the later, post-Easter proclamation.[49] Perhaps most significant of all, these three latter scholars are of the unanimous opinion that "ontological" perspectives on Christology do not depend on any direct interaction between the kerygma and the more remote Hellenistic world.

All this is said essentially to sharpen what surely remains the most fundamental issue in the contemporary debate with regard to christological origins. Though the Bultmannian position remains intact among an impressive number of New Testament critics, including those commonly designated as post-Bultmannians, there is at the same time a substantial wing of critical opinion that, from varying standpoints, supports the traditional notion that Christology began with Jesus. These issues are still very much alive, unresolved, and any responsible christological discussion, whether biblically or theologically pursued, must make its way through such a maze of conflicting opinion. On critical grounds, one may dismiss the notion of a pre-Easter Christology, or with the same critical tools, one may support the opposite conclusion that Christology did in fact begin with Jesus of Nazareth. But one cannot fail to recognize that these two modes of viewing christological origins can and do produce vastly differing results in one's understanding of the nature of God's self-disclosure in the historical Jesus. On the one hand, one can move with Bultmann along the form-critical existentializing pathway,[50] a pathway which has led some (not Bultmann) to question the New Testament's "once for all" claim for the person of Jesus.[51] Or by insisting that the New Testament's Christology in fact grew directly from the one for whom that claim was made, one can then proceed to the Johannine assumption that Jesus' transcendence comes ultimately from his own "I am." The point is that christological discussions must finally wrestle with this issue, even if the scourge of ambiguity remains to plague us to the very end.

A closely related problem, and one which has also played an important role in the understanding of christological origins, is the issue that centers on the formative environment of New Testament thought generally and in particular on the resulting christological formulations. The especially crucial christological issue in this regard concerns the notion of the divinity of Jesus, as expressed in the designations Son of God and *Kyrios*. Was that mode of christological affirmation appropriate to, compatible with, a Jewish monotheistic tradition? Or was Hellenistic religion the more likely vehicle behind the formulation and transmission of these concepts? Does Christology find its religious home in the Greek mysteries or in an incipient gnosticism already beginning to appear at the time of the rise of Christian affirmations about Jesus or in some self-styled combination of all these? To understand, first, the nature of these settings, and then, second, to relate christological origins to those various options is a discussion that continues to have a prominent role in modern New Testament investigation.

The monumental work of Wilhelm Bousset marked the beginnings of the contemporary phase of this discussion.[52] In that work Bousset made his now well-known case for the Hellenistic mysteries as the cradle of New Testament christological formulations, especially as these expressions became explicit in the work of the apostle Paul. That particular segment of the so-called history-of-religions school clearly held sway through a substantial portion of the critical discussion that was to ensue, and the substance of that position was, with some modifications, reaffirmed in more recent times in the work of Bultmann.[53] Bultmann was no doubt better informed than Bousset about the Palestinian thought-world in which the earliest phase of Christian expression took shape, but he nevertheless remained convinced that the primary locus of Christian soteriological and christological formulations was the Hellenistic, gentile world of thought and belief. Bultmann agreed with Bousset that Jewish messianic and apocalyptic interpretations soon were overshadowed by the Hellenistic *Sitz im Leben* and that a "divine nature" Christology finally supplanted the earlier apocalyptic setting in such a way that *Christos* itself lost that original eschatological function as a title.[54] Hence the earliest community's anticipated deliverer, the one who was expected to return on the clouds in judgment, soon was transformed, via gentile categories of thought and expression, into the *Theios Aner*. Given the strong affinities between these two scholars, it should constitute no great surprise to discover that the preface to the fifth German edition of Bousset's *Kyrios Christos* was written by none other than the same Rudolf Bultmann. In that preface, Bultmann's sympathies are clearly allied with the main lines of Bousset's interpretation, even though Bultmann's work incorporated the progress research had made in the meantime.[55]

This whole issue concerning the environment of christological origins has also met with much controversy, and the tendency today moves in a direction quite different from that of Bousset and Bultmann. Partly due to important textual discoveries (especially Qumran documents and the Gnostic materials from Nag Hammadi) resulting in new assessments of both Christianity and Judaism in this formative period, the need to reexamine old assumptions has become evident. Recent scholarship has turned its attention especially to the Jewish context out of which Christianity emerged. It is of course not simply a matter of turning *from* Hellenism *to* Judaism as the more legitimate context out of which to view early Christology, for there has emerged in recent studies a profound recognition of the variegated character of both Judaism and Hellenism, and of even further complications which confront us in the merging of these two traditions well before the rise of Christianity. More than thirty years ago now, W.D. Davies provided us with a powerful reminder that rabbinic thought itself was a reflection of such an involved process of the interweaving of these traditions.[56] For Davies even Paul's most ontologically phrased christological statement in Colossians 1:15 was to be understood in the context of rabbinic thought and expression, and he shunned the notion that it is necessary to link such passages directly to the philosophical and religious outlook of the gentile world.[57] Davies' insistence upon Jewish traditions as a (the?) primary context of Pauline thought has carried over in recent years to a far more generalized tendency to emphasize the Judaic or Hellenistic/Judaic side of New Testament backgrounds as a whole. In light of all this, some modern interpreters have raised searching questions about some fairly standard conclusions in New Testament scholarship. Some have questioned even the notion so cherished among Protestants that justification by faith in Christ is *the* glass through which Paul's thinking must finally be understood.[58] Martin Hengel's extensive study[59] has strongly argued that at the time of the Maccabean crisis Judaism had already undergone a significant transformation wrought by its encounter with Hellenism, and E.P. Sanders' recent study of the thought of Paul carries on with this fundamental conclusion that Palestinian Judaism in its Hellenized dress was the formative setting for Pauline thought.[60] Of course, the older notion of a clearer distinction between Palestinian Judaism (at least in its Judean form) and Hellenistic Judaism, together with the conclusion that Christian thought is better explained by the latter, continues to have some significant support.[61] But more pertinent to this essay is the fact that there *is* an increasing tendency among New Testament authorities to relate even such titles as Lord and Son of God to that rich and varied background of thought that marked both Palestinian and Diaspora Judaism, and that the existence of such titles does not necessarily depend on direct contacts with the gentile world.

These developments are surely apparent in the many ways in which recent christological analyses have proceeded. For example, Ferdinand Hahn suggests that between Palestinian (Jewish) Christianity and Hellenistic Christianity per se there existed a Hellenistic Jewish-Christianity whose *Sitz im Leben* is clearly located in that Hellenized Judaism found both in Palestine and in the Diaspora, and that it was precisely within this Hellenistic Jewish-Christianity that the title Lord (Kyrios) assumed its "divine" connotations.[62] While Hahn agrees that the earliest layer of Palestinian Christian tradition reserved the "Kyrios" title essentially for the one who was to return in glory,[63] he still insists that such affirmations about Jesus' divine authority *and* substance do not await ultimate contact with the Hellenistic/gentile world.

All this certainly does betray a change, sometimes subtle, still taking place within the perspective of New Testament scholarship, a change in which the locus of christological expression is being viewed increasingly in connection with its Judaic and Jewish-Christian setting. The Bousset/Bultmann history-of-religions tendency to locate ontologically defined Christologies exclusively within the nexus of gentile tradition (e.g., mysteries, Gnostic patterns) has surely had to face serious challenges in recent studies. Some whose form-critical methods are in substantial agreement with those used by Bultmann are nevertheless taking a significantly different view of the underlying character and substance of the *Sitz im Leben* out of which Christian traditions emerged. And, without any doubt, all this has a way of moving christological expressions into closer contact with the historical Jesus. After all, even Bultmann saw that the earliest Palestinian material was in all probability to be associated with the historical Jesus.[64] If those earliest layers encompass even the possibility of a "divine nature" Christology, then it is simply not possible to dismiss summarily those higher christological affirmations from the historical Jesus himself. The rediscovery of Jewish roots of New Testament thought is indeed of tremendous significance in the search for the origins of Christology.

Thus far, then, we have concentrated on the broad framework of christological discussions out of the perspective of New Testament critical scholarship. These comments have dealt essentially with the question of origins, and they are introduced not so much with an aim of debating the issues, or indeed in order to lay out our preferences on one side or another. There is one further matter that is pivotal to everything said about Christology, and that is the whole affirmation of the resurrection. Whether one argues that Christology began within the consciousness of Jesus, or later, somewhere within the life and faith of the early Christian community, the substance of Christology is always shaped by, created by, understood through the New Testament's resounding affirmation "He is risen!" That resurrection may be seen as mere confirmation of Jesus' own work and words, or it may be understood as the very atmosphere in which Christology itself was born. However that may be, the importance of the resurrection in the New Testament's story is such that some specific comments are necessary to round out this introductory discussion.

It was again the form-critical school that so fundamentally isolated the resurrection as the dividing line between the historical Jesus and the kerygma in the early church. For Bultmann, the implicit Christology in Jesus' call to decision in light of the inbreaking kingdom was made explicit by that resurrection faith. In that context, the crucified Jesus came to be viewed as the Christ, the exalted Son of man who would soon return to consummate the kingdom he had announced in his historic ministry. Yet even when Bultmann spoke thus of the resurrection as that great divide, he was not articulating the existence of an empty tomb or, for that matter, the presence of a *soma* that could in any way be defined in normal historical terms as an *event*. The "event," rather, was the proclamation of the risenness as it was aroused in the faith of the earliest Christian community. The resurrection, therefore, was for him not that which occurred in Jerusalem (Luke) or Galilee (Mark/Matthew) or both

18

(John), but in the affirmation itself: "The real Easter faith is faith in the word of preaching which brings illumination. If the event of Easter Day is in any sense an historical event additional to the event of the cross, it is nothing else than the rise of faith in the risen Lord."[65] All this means, of course, that the resurrection as the "raw material" of Christology is in the end inseparable from affirmations *about* the historical Jesus. As Bultmann understood this matter, the confirmation of the resurrection is to be isolated not in an empty tomb or in material manifestations but in the proclamation of the Word and the response of the believer to that same Word.

All this is so well known among contemporary New Testament students that further elaborations or assessments of this "existential" approach to the resurrection are unnecessary. Suffice it to say that a large number of modern discussions of the resurrection have followed the Bultmannian model, most intensively, of course, those interpreters who are more clearly identified with Bultmannian form-critical analysis. Conzelmann reflects essentially the same approach when he says, "History cannot establish the facticity of the resurrection."[66] Willi Marxsen, though attempting to answer certain objections raised with respect to the subjectivity of his own interpretations of the resurrection, still insists that the *extra nos* implied in the New Testament narratives of the resurrection is in fact nothing beyond that same "reality" attested to by the various symbols of exaltation. And thus, for Marxsen, that *extra nos* is not to be identified or confirmed in an empty-tomb/appearance tradition. What is "resurrected" is that reality (transcendent) which gave christological meaning and significance to the life and, especially, the death of Jesus, and by which also is affirmed his continuous reign and anticipated return in glory as the Son of man.[67] All this is in one way or another a repetition of the Bultmann dictum "The faith of Easter is just this—faith in the *Word* of preaching."[68]

In any event, there is a substantial wing of New Testament interpretation that has consistently and emphatically defined "resurrection" not in terms of its historical manifestations but in terms of revelation and response. For these, the "truth" of the resurrection is found not in what happened "on the third day" but in the proclamation of the ultimate significance of Jesus: Paul's "Word of the cross." It seems fair to say that while the Bultmann school has not reduced the resurrection to a mere psychic phenomenon,[69] it *has* defined that event more specifically in relation to its ongoing proclamation and reception, and certainly not to any event of past history. It was in that context that Bultmann understood the beginnings of Christology, a Christology which therefore turns out to be defined in functional, existential terms rather than in more objective, ontological formulations characteristic of more tradi-

19

tional Christian theology. It would seem fair to say not only that the resurrection *establishes* a Christology but also that, for Bultmann and his followers, the way in which that resurrection is understood and articulated determines the actual form which Christology assumes.

This existentialized, demythologized understanding of the resurrection has encountered criticism from many corners, especially from those whose theologies (Christologies) are more traditionally and evangelically defined. But in recent years there has emerged a renewed emphasis on the historical character of the resurrection, most notably set forth in the exegetical and theological reconstruction in the work of Wolfhart Pannenberg.[70] Pannenberg, who operates both as a critical exegete and systematic theologian, while not resorting to a traditional or orthodox historicism, has nevertheless restated in bold terms the objective, historical dimension he understands to be inherent in the resurrection. He does recognize that there are serious problems in so articulating the character of the resurrection. After all, the very claims that are made for this "event" place it in a category that is *sui generis*, and there can be no adequate analogies to articulate its character and meaning. The resurrection, Pannenberg argues, is an *eschatological* event that has revealed Jesus as history's own end. Sometimes Pannenberg's terminology actually seems reminiscent of Bultmannian language, especially when he thus characterizes Jesus as an "eschatological event." But the important distinction remains, and that is that Pannenberg will simply not allow an understanding of Jesus' resurrection which turns out to be *merely* a proclamation about the meaning of the past. Rather, that resurrection is itself an event, and contrary to that stream of modern thought described immediately above, Pannenberg articulates the objectivity of the resurrection by references both to the empty-tomb narratives and the witnesses to Jesus' appearance.[71] There is some overlapping here with traditional form-criticism, for Pannenberg agrees that Jesus' nonmessianic ministry was *transformed* into Christology only in light of the resurrection. But it is in the understanding of that very resurrection that Pannenberg's approach displays its distinctive character, for what in Pannenberg's view divides the nonmessianic historical Jesus from the Christ of faith is not an affirmation but an event.

These brief remarks about Pannenberg do justice neither to his thought nor to the broader scene in which those thoughts are set forth. Here is a uniquely creative christological study, one that has renewed for our day an emphasis on the resurrection in bluntly nonexistential terms. Where that will lead over the next several decades cannot be determined. However, Pannenberg's emphasis on the "event" character of the resurrection has significantly challenged form-critical "orthodoxy," and it provides an important new context in which christological questions can now be historically and theologically raised. Pannenberg's understanding of the resurrection has of course led to his own extensive analysis of Christology in the thought of the church, and surely this more historicized view of the resurrection event does appear to be making its way into the thinking both of New Testament exegetes and systematic theologians attempting to articulate Christian faith in the modern world. Hans Küng, for example, though still reflecting strong Bultmannian affinities, nevertheless insists that the resurrection event is "real" and not just "a way of expressing the significance of Jesus' death."[72] This stance is even more emphatically reflected when he says: "Easter there is not a happening *merely* for the disciples and their faith. Jesus does not live *through* their faith. The Easter event is not a function of the disciples' faith. . . . But Easter is an event primarily for Jesus himself. Jesus lives again *through God—for their faith*."[73] Our point is simply that reaffirming the resurrection as an event rather than as a myth has within it the potential to redefine the whole character of christological discussions. Of course, an existentialized, functionalized understanding of Christology "from below" continues to be a very prominent fact of the current debate, as is evident in a recent collection of essays edited by John Hick entitled *The Myth of God Incarnate*.[74] The preface of Hick's collection makes abundantly clear the stance of the book's contributors when it calls for a theology which recognizes that Jesus' identity as "God incarnate, the Second Person of the Holy Trinity living a human life, is a mythological or poetic way of expressing his significance for us."[75] Surely much of the liberal, critical stream of modern Christian thought remains thoroughly at home with Christologies in which the resurrection is thus mythologically rather than historically interpreted, and where divinity is existentially rather than ontologically understood. For some, this whole process has led more radically to a Christology void of any necessary connection with the historical Jesus,[76] while others alternatively have attempted to locate the authority of Jesus somewhere within the boundaries of his own historic person. But once the resurrection is offered up with full historical and ontological significance, the whole picture assumes an altogether different stance. Indeed, it would not be carrying the argument too far to say that the resurrection is a prism through which Christology comes into view, and the angle of that prism will surely determine the shape that such Christology will assume. Hence, the future of christological understanding will in no small measure be determined by the outcome of the historical and theological inquiry into the nature of the resurrection.

Where, then, *do* we stand in this last quarter of the twentieth century? What justifies a festschrift with Christology as its integrating theme? Surely, although contemporary views of Christology continue to display widely variant patterns, there is among New Testament critics and theologians a marked consensus affirming Christology in some form as the mainspring of that literature and of the community of faith out of which it emerged. If at the beginning of this century there was no clear consensus that the New Testament reflected this "once for all" significance of the person of Jesus, now the climate is radically changed. Unquestionably, the weight of scholarly opinion in recent decades has forced anyone seriously attempting to understand New Testament faith to do so with full weight given to christological affirmations. The Harnackian notion that the "essence" of the New Testament and of early Christianity is to be defined through a set of moral and spiritual values first enunciated by Jesus the teacher, though attractive to our rationalistic predilections, simply has not held up under critical scrutiny. To be sure, the claims about Jesus are not of "one substance" in the New Testament: At one and the same time, Jesus is set forth as the one who taught "with authority," the one "conceived by the Holy Spirit," as the one whom God made "Lord and Christ," as the "Son" through whom God has spoken in these latter days, as the one to come in "great power and glory," and perhaps the most cosmic of all, as the "Logos made flesh." With the rediscovery of that which we call kerygma along with the baffling problems surrounding the ability to isolate the "true" and "authentic" picture of that historical figure about which and around which the New Testament community centered its life and practice, a new stage has been set which could scarcely have been anticipated at the turn of the century when Harnack was attempting to isolate the "essence" of Christianity. In a sense, there is a *potential* Christology at the conclusion of even the historian's quest, a reaching out for the new, the distinct, the unprecedented, the original. Historical criticism at the beginning of this century seemed to offer the tools by which historians might eventually and even compulsively agree on just where the uniqueness was to be found in the person and message of Jesus. Harnack without any doubt reflected that kind of historical criticism at its very best, and every New Testament scholar and interpreter is indebted to the work of such pioneering investigations.

But work goes on and discoveries are made and new methods are employed, as surely proved to be the case in our century. In our view, that progression has had the clear effect of forcing us back to the christological drawing board, for frankly and bluntly the efforts to isolate that historically "proved" authenticity have always failed. Whether one follows the details of Bultmannian analysis or not, that very analysis made clear the impossibility of hanging theological affirmations on a historical consensus. That consensus never existed in the first place, and if it had, such a consensus would have yielded to ever-changing patterns, which biblical historians in this century have found to be a way of life. The form-critical method has of course contributed substantially to the atmosphere of historical uncertainty among New Testament historians, but that method is not the only means of qualifying historical perceptions of the past. For example, the science of archaeology along with dramatic discoveries thereby attained has made it at least theoretically possible that tomorrow's newspaper will reverse conclusions once held with virtual certainty. But Christology is a "once for all" claim, and that affirmation does not emerge finally from the results of historical investigation. Such a claim rests rather with the ultimate meaning ascribed to that figure in history—eschatologically, ontologically, soteriologically, ethically, existentially—and, in the end, christologically. It is that dimension of ultimate significance which in one way or another comes through in the New Testament, where it is finally affirmed: The Word became flesh and dwelt among us, full of grace and truth. Wrestling with an understanding of that claim functionally, existentially, mythologically, ontologically is what the "essence" of Christian thought is all about.

So we conclude this introduction with that as our *apologia*, if indeed such is needed. The christological discussions herein contained are of course offered by those who have known Harvey K. McArthur and who here honor him with the fruits of their own labors in the enterprise of articulating the history and meaning of the New Testament: its literature, its history, as well as its theological and existential significance. We are delighted and extremely grateful that so many distinguished students of the New Testament have willingly contributed of their time and effort to participate in this project (see Parts I and II; also George Johnston's essay in Part IV). But we are also gratified that some outside of the New Testament "club" have been willing to draw upon the tools and content of their respective disciplines to help articulate a fuller and broader understanding of New Testament Christology (see Parts III and IV). Perhaps some will find it a bit strange that we include an essay by the one whom the volume is intended to honor. But we are convinced that this has a significance of its own, and that far from being a desire on his part to "honor" himself, it is the means chosen intentionally by the editors to say what this whole volume is intended to express, namely, that the world of contemporary New Testament scholarship is fuller and richer because of the contributions of Harvey K. McArthur.

23

CHAPTER 2

Doing the New Testament Right: Synoptic Reflections of a Layperson

Kenneth Cragg

"Now you have done me right" is a Shakespearean response when one's health is drunk. So it seems a proper borrowing for a festschrift saluting a scholar and colleague of long devotion to the New Testament and its study. But the title here owes itself rather to an intriguing phrase in 2 Timothy 2:15. Timothy is there enjoined to give proof of his skill, "doing right by the word of truth (ὀρθοτομουντα τον λογον της ἀγηθειας)." The phrase has taxed translators and commentators. *Orthos*, of course, is "right," or "straight," while *tetoma* (middle-perfect of *temnō*) means "to cut." "Rightly dividing the word" is the seventeenth-century *Authorized Version*. *Recte tractantem*, runs the Vulgate: "to handle the claims of truth like a master."

A whole variety of metaphors cluster around the phrase. Some have hinted at the dissection of remains or the scrutiny of the entrails of sacrificial animals for cryptic secrets. There have, regrettably, been writers who handled the text like a corpse or made it one in the process. And obscure esotericism is by no means unknown. But dismissing these, one might draw closer to the academic vocation by understanding the "right handling" as the business of the steward, or labor officer, distributing to people what their tasks required. Or there is the idea for which the *New English Bible* opts, that of "driving a straight furrow" through the farmer's soil. Or again, is it the discernment of travelers picking their way through a forest or across a moor, reading the map of the landscape? Or again, the imagery may be that of a mason cutting stone or marble to fit the architect's plan for a building. Then, finally, there is the hint that right handling has to do with the hospitable skills

Kenneth Cragg was Professor of Islamic Studies at the Hartford Seminary Foundation, 1952–59. Formerly Anglican Bishop of North Africa, he is presently living in retirement in England.

that have discretion for the needs and appetites of family and guests around the table.

The compound word, it seems, is unknown in classical Greek and occurs in the New Testament here only. Uses in the Septuagint (Proverbs 3:6 and 11:5, e.g.) favor the "way" image, where the pilgrim's "righteousness" directs or rectifies his path. "Following the rules of the divine oracles" is another rendering, while J.B. Phillips leaves some ambiguity in suggesting: "who knows to use the word of truth to the best advantage."

Here, perhaps arbitrarily as to metaphors but not, it is claimed, as to the whole they describe, we propose to take the two clues of the way over the map and the art with hospitality. For arc not these the scholars in their task and the servants in their ministry? We must will not only to be right *about* the word of truth as perceptive students, but right *with* it as responsible providers. The *New English Bible* links these quaintly in "driving a straight furrow, in your proclamation." But the double obligation of all exegesis, to a text and for a situation, by scholarship in community is certainly the concern of this letter among the pastorals in the New Testament. All interior perception of meaning is for the outward mediation of it, and clearly the worth of either belongs with the other. Truth is not served if it is not brought home or if it has been lost on the way. "Doing the New Testament right" means having both a caring possession and a lively communication of its content. There are guests as well as quests to have in view. "That you also may have fellowship with us" was the heartbeat of the apostles. The quest of Jesus in their scriptures is never rightly only academic and historical. Our search for the comprehension others may come by will often be the major factor in our own.

An open intention of hospitality, through a patient literacy ourselves —these we take to be the twin elements of rightness with the word. Openness to the world, as shall be argued, was in fact the very quality that made the New Testament "new," in contrast to the studied privacy of the old order and its intense preservation, even within its own vision of a world congratulating itself in Abraham of its irreducible exceptionality. But this New Testament quality of belonging with humankind itself derived from its own reading of its generative events in Jesus as the Christ. The will to be universal is indeed the prime cause of the documentation, in Gospels and Epistles, of the faith itself. Yet its will for the world emerges squarely from its own content and character constituted by Jesus as the Christ. Our whole exploration of the interaction of these two convictions defines what we take to be the New Testament's understanding of itself.

25

These no doubt are large claims, and they deliberately simplify a vast field of issues, hypotheses, and conjectures surrounding them. It is a field that, in our chosen "map" metaphor, is strewn with daunting boulders and crisscrossed with confusing tracks and bypaths. We are likely to resemble Charles Darwin stepping into his shoreline forest in *The Voyage of the Beagle*, ardent for discovery and meaning and finding himself halted within a yard by the impeding abundance of the questions to ask. Bent on specimens, he could afford to gather them minutely, for the botanist is not an explorer. But such is not our case, nor are we examining items abstracted for laboratories and museums. Our duty is to see a whole, to identify and hold the central clues. Our task is synoptic, with respect not merely to three Gospels regularly so described but also to the panorama of New Testament event and faith and literature as a trinity of experience. From Galilee to Patmos there is endless and, in measure, appropriate scope for the meticulous mind. But if it yields only "mint and anise and cumin," which obscure the weight and import of the whole, then we thwart our quest and cheat our guests and in both senses the New Testament is wronged.

This does not mean that the panoramic concern—our business with the map and landscape—neglects the crucial problem as a whole, namely, the issue about Jesus the proclaimer and Christ the proclaimed, about the Gospel *of* Jesus in and from Capernaum and the Gospel *concerning* Jesus as the Christ. These have been seen by many to be fundamentally disparate, not to be integral as one kerygma. On that view, there are two broad choices: either to opt for a Jesus without the church, a Jesus who may be variously characterized as prophet, revolutionary, moralist, charismatic healer, visionary, mystic, or zealot, or to acknowledge a Christ of faith, developed or altogether detached from actual history as to Jesus. If we take the second, the essential fact of Christianity is the fact of belief, not the fact of history, except in the sense that beliefs *become* facts of history. The apostolic kerygma, or preaching, grounds itself in its own conviction, and other rootage is finally irrelevant if accessible, or inaccessible and, anyway, not relevant. Its authenticity is only, and adequately, existential.

These two broad alternatives, with the subtle graduations to which they are susceptible, do not do the New Testament right, for on either of them it would not exist. The gospel of Jesus the preacher-prophet survives only in the context of the church-community documenting him as such—but only in the larger terms of Christic suffering and, therein, of divine significance. Textually, then, the thesis to the contrary is a reductionism made in spite of its own source.

The second alternative is a reductionism in another sense, for it presumes to isolate a kerygmatic Christology from the Palestinian

26

matrix where the documents that warrant such convictions firmly place them. Seen as map to landscape, the Gospels, as we shall see with special reference to the fourth Gospel (where the christological is most developed), steadily relate the Christ figure to the Jesus history. They insistently tie back the mission of kerygma universality to the historical personality and his movement in Galilee. We cannot well possess a literature—albeit using it all the time—with interpretations that deny its ruling consensus and its very raison d'être.

This is not to say that the New Testament is to be accepted merely because it exists. Such an attitude would be quite disloyal to its own temper. Rather, the position for which we are pleading, in the double thrust of scholarship and communication, is one that grows precisely from the central issue where the two reductionisms have originated, for in their wrong way they have "rightly divided" the New Testament territory into its features, and both, in a commendable way, have been concerned for communicative responsibility vis-à-vis Jesus teaching and Christ saving.

What is meant by its temper and its territory? Simply that the New Testament is thoroughly participatory in nature. It embodies the experience it narrates. The truth it claims to speak finds expression in its word (to use the terms of 2 Timothy 2:15) by being lived. It is itself written within the implementation of what it presents. Its own history in sources and forms and missives stands within the history it documents.

The point is illuminated by contrast with the Qur'ān. There revelation is understood as divine mediation of speech received verbatim, in Arabic, by the chosen and single prophet, Muhammad. The text of the deliverances verbally transmitted to his mind and tongue is again orally recited to and by the faithful. Calligraphy is its utterly congenial art form, just as memorization is its due reception in piety and love, while education and law turn upon its categorical quality as guidance and reminder. To be sure, the content is involved in historical circumstance; like all revelation, it is situational in its incidence on earth. But the experience in its obedience is not taken up into its text. It does not wait three centuries to grow "canonical." It carries no epistles from prophet to people. Nor does it offer parallel portrayals of a personality. Its text is not required to be generated by communal possession of events. It addresses a future that it does not need for its final shape.

In all these ways it is fundamentally in contrast with the New Testament. That cluster of Epistles and Gospels reflects whence it came in what they are. If we see them as definitive, it is only because they are themselves the process of definition. Hence that dispersion in space which requires letters, that lapse in time which produces gospels.

27

Community is inseparable from the very fabric of the New Testament and is itself the setting in which its own meanings find shape.

Jesus was not a prophet who through twenty-three years steadily transmitted promptly inscribed heavenly sentences to attentive amanuenses. Scribes truly heard him, but they were not of that attentive vintage. So we do not have Galilean Qur'ān. On the contrary, Jesus taught and died undocumenting and undocumented. Perhaps we could find an imaginative symbol of the situation in that (inserted?) incident in John 8:3-11, when Jesus wrote on the ground. It could be that he was only doodling in the sand. But even were the script intelligible it was doubtless quickly erased by the exodus of feet. Nothing could be more eloquent of the unwrittenness of Jesus in the days of his ministry—and the church apart. His parables were only and always on the winds of Galilee or within the walls of synagogues. It was the memories of disciples that gave them, via the Gospels, to the wideness of the world. And the giving of them is a story of bewildering fascination across an interlude of years by virtue of an energy they had themselves produced. It is the nature of that energy that must be studied in order to understand both its source and its sequel, which, as we have said, are the twin features of the entire literature.

But first it might be well to reflect how this quality of the New Testament ought to determine the attitudes of its readership. How can we be infallibilist with a scripture which came to being only in this precarious and mind-engaging fashion? We cannot well absolutize that which does not come in absolute form. We live with the incarnational, not the verbal, understanding of the revelatory thing. If the significance of Jesus as the Christ came only on the condition and risk of apostolic apprehension, then we may not assert its authority in incongruous terms of a dictation not its own. Christian faith is "according to [its] scriptures" in this decisive sense that its mediation trusted and recruited minds it did not override or immobilize. We must consider it to be addressing a like-mindedness today. Its custodians, whether ecclesial or scholarly, whether historians or dogmatists, will overplay their hand if they neglect this vital character of a text that reaches them as this did.

But what are the source and the sequel of the energy that had the Christian literature as its expression, and how do the forms of that writing enshrine it? These are the open questions that, although never rightly closed, may be rightly resolved—sufficiently for an intelligent and no less open faith.

The source was the teaching ministry of Jesus of Nazareth. To this they come back as a needle to its north. (We will deal later with the alleged "disinterest" of the Epistles in that point of departure.) "Jesus came preaching" is the outset. The salient theme of that preaching was the concept and the presence of the kingdom of God. In some sense the presence of the kingdom was implicit in the consciousness within the preaching. It is here that many interrogatives arise. But what seems clear is that in the quality of liberation, of immediacy, of compassion, and of power, which lay within the affirmation of the kingdom, it could itself be understood as knocking at the doors. However we see the works of charismatic healing that accompanied the preaching, they certainly reinforced its meaning and gave token of its nature. Both word and deed were bound up with the personality that spoke and acted.

Two further points emerge. First, this "presence" of the kingdom happened, in the Jesus form, in a context of messianic anticipation. Such anticipation was endlessly varied in its particulars and quality, and there are continuing mysteries as to how we should read its implications within the consciousness of Jesus and whether the sense of its personal import grew in progression with the shaping of the context. Second, that context became increasingly one of hostility and rejection. The story of Jesus, if we can follow the consensus of the Gospels, is not one of increasing external following but one of inexorably deepening crisis, at least as far as authority and establishment were concerned. Though "common people heard him gladly," the immediacy of divine compassion and the reality of liberation stood in explicit conflict with tradition and official leadership. Whether over the sabbath, the law, self-righteousness, or the vested interests of covenant custodians, the message, and so the personality, of Jesus antagonized and alarmed the prevailing forms, and people, of Jewish society and history. Hence his ministry and meaning together headed into rejection.

It is that contour of impending tragedy which the Gospels unmistakably trace on, or rather as, their map of things. Their unison is a climax of suffering. They are also clear that Jesus faced this without being deflected. Though it may be possible for later hypothesis to read in this set-toward-crisis character of the course of Jesus' life either a complex apocalyptic kind of hope calculating to force the divine hand to rescue him in eschatological intervention, or some kind of zealotry risked and finally betrayed into failure, the evangelists do not see it so. They see the pattern of suffering as fulfilling a precedent of sacrifice, and they attribute to Jesus the creative vision, and action, which seize upon that pattern as truly the messianic secret and, seeing it, fulfill it in the living context of the actual hostility. We may attribute that insight to the subsequent church, making it the improbable architect of its own origins. But we cannot avoid observing that the New Testament itself is unanimous in deriving what may be called "the mind of the church about the Christ" from "the mind of the Christ." It leaves us in no doubt about where the great original belonged.

29

Belonging as it did to Jesus, it was no arbitrary thing, devised to fulfill a letter or to satisfy a scheme. Precedents there were, in Jeremiah and that strange figure "the suffering servant" in Second Isaiah. But the New Testament writers do not see them realized in Jesus for the simple reason that the prophets, or some of them, had glimpsed them. That would be to miss *why* they foreshadowed an abiding meaning. It is true there are some purely circumstantial "fulfillments" in the New Testament's citation from the Old. ("A bone of him shall not be broken," "He shall be called a Nazarene," and the like. The second of these has a puzzling ring.) But the testimonia that lie behind New Testament writing, collections of fulfilled scriptures in Acts for example, have to do with deep, not tedious, senses in which earlier sufferers for truth had disclosed what is seen as determining the mind of Jesus.

Here a vital clue would seem to be the crucial parable of the vineyard and the tenants, itself replete with Old Testament imagery. Present in all three synoptic Gospels, it is fair to see it as pivotal to the whole ministry (Matthew 21:33-46; Mark 12:1-12; Luke 20:9-19). It condenses an entire history of recalcitrance and obduracy in the human reception of the custody of nature and nationhood and of the law by which that custody was to be ordered. As the Qur'ān has it in reference to those servants the prophets, (Sura 2:87) "some they said were liars and some they put to death." Jesus in the parable sees himself in that long sequence of what the later evangelist described as "the sin of the world." His experience of ministry, inwardly read on the long road from Capernaum to Jerusalem, clearly set him in the same context.

Yet there is that mysterious "more than prophecy" somehow in the perspective. The words of the owner of the vineyard, "I will send to them my son," seem utterly incongruous against this background of rejection. Why risk the very heir to recoup a year's harvest? Plainly the things that can be comprehended within a cash nexus or a tenant custody, the law, subordination, fruits, and obligation, are being transcended in what becomes the ultimate appeal, no longer now to their duty but to their heart relationship. "Him they will reverence." The Creator's love is beyond and above the Creator's law, as its original and its ultimate secret. But the new level of relationship evokes a new level of rejection. "This is the heir; come let us kill him." No longer withholding fruits in default, the tenants are now defiantly rejecting authority.

Are we present here at the inner meaning of Jesus' awareness of dimension in his ministry? Clearly there is an obdurate humanity in its conscious officialdom for God's heritage. There has been the appeal of the kingdom of God made in its ultimate terms of compassion and intimacy, inviting the human into that immediacy of fellowship with

God that law proposes and mercy alone achieves. At the center of both the appeal and the obduracy, loyally obedient to divine will at the core of the danger, Jesus stands vulnerable and hopeful, in a quality of love he had always attributed to communion with his "Father."

This consideration has brought us to the heart of the New Testament's association of "the servant" and "the Son." Christology is first about action before it is about status, even as the Messiah is only known for *who* he is by *how* he is. When we have the pattern we can identify the person. It is this way in the New Testament, and here lies its claim to be a unity. Innumerable pages have been devoted to the discussion of how concepts of divinity were generated in the rise of Christianity—wisdom or Logos hypostases, Roman deification, Gnostic or docetic speculation, theosophic ideas, cross-cultural factors, or even a lack of discipline with an elastic term like Kyrios.

Whatever may be said about the presence of these factors, there seems to be a deep sequence in the prophetic to the messianic, to the Christic, to the worshipable, to the divine, in the concreteness of Jesus' ministry and the filiality in which it was achieved in its patterns of prayer, its core of teaching, its heart of compassion, and its climax of sorrow. Many have doubted that the "suffering servant" paradigm weighed with Jesus in the interpretation of his ministry and its end, though the vocabulary (of "ransom" and "being set at naught") is there in the record. If in the messianic we have the crucified, then in this Christhood according to Jesus we have the divine action. For in the ultimate sense the messianic constitutes that response which is worthy of God and adequate to answer the human situation. The New Testament confidence, therefore, is that "in Christ God was reconciling the world to himself [2 Cor. 5:19, RSV]" and "having the Father" we "have the Son also." All else in Christology derives from this confidence and must be held within it.

Such, it may be responsibly claimed, is the witness of the New Testament. The resurrection is its open warrant—not, however, as some fortuitous or arbitrary reversal of things, but as the inner quality of the love that suffers, the Easter that belongs in Gethsemane. "Designated Son of God in power . . . by his resurrection [Rom. 1:4, RSV]" means the manifest ultimacy of those criteria of God on which Jesus proceeded in his obedience to the crisis of vocation constituted for a love like God's in a world like ours. And for the New Testament this is history and event. But the faith that is born of it is needed to recognize it. The literature that enshrines both faith and event is the fruit of recognition.

Recognition being inherently communal, the literature is communally oriented. It holds together the source in Jesus and the sequel in the church. It consists of Gospels and Epistles—in the one the story whose theme we have tried to focus on, in the other the nurture in life of its meanings and demands. The first of these was openness to the world.

For if messiahship be according to Jesus, then its achievement is not national independence from Rome but human liberation from evil. Bringing law to its fulfillment in the order of grace, it may not be confined to the people of Torah. In this sense the drama of Saul's conversion epitomizes the logic of Jesus' messiahship. But the drama is within a wider development of realization that loosens the rigorous bonds of the old regime. When this happens it is the finest instincts of that old order which are fulfilled, with an enthusiasm and a finality it could never itself fully muster or long sustain. The vital new criterion lay in Jesus and the cross.

That source in Jesus and the sequel in apostolate are the making of the New Testament. The world of the Epistles writes the story of the Gospels. The story in the Gospels originates the world of the Epistles. These educate the community in the meaning of its faith and in the corollaries of that faith relating to worship, conduct, and creed. This education proceeds within the pastoral concept and from the *Sitz im Leben* of the faithful in a variety of locations, all of them—shall we say unfortunately?—west and north of Jerusalem and Antioch. Thus the definition of the Christian existence happens *in via* and in its epistolary form yields a range of precedents to order further times and places in the principles of liberty of conscience, attitudes to paganism, care of unity, decisions as to Judaic ritual law, and the rest. The point of central interest here is the temper in which Christians are to be what they are. Epistles exist because the church is one and churches are many. Dispersion means diversity, but diversity is tied into an intention after unity, and a pastoral nurture of it.

That same diversity stimulates the processes out of which the Gospels come. But their task is different. It is to possess church and churches with the Jesus-source from which their being comes, to bridge the distance of place and the lapse of years. The Palestinian history is taken by all of them to be vital. Their retrospect of what is assumed to be the sequel conditions their presentation of its source but is never other than involved with it. The conditioning leaves taxing problems for the student. There is no doubt that matters at issue within the churches —midrash legacies, the growth of liturgy, way-finding in the Jew/gentile tangle, local tensions, and current concerns engaging past history —deeply affected the Gospel narration. The vineyard-tenant parable, which we earlier assumed to be pivotal, may owe its prominence to the community's interest in the meaning of Jewish destiny now that the church had come to be. That accent need not be seen as disqualifying the Jesus relevance found in it. But the convergence of the two motifs

32

seems evident, and there must always be controversy about their relative emphasis in assessing the whole.

This situation recurs everywhere in the Gospels. They cannot be detached from a living, developing, and self-discovering community. Complex as the resulting textual problems are, and will no doubt remain, their very presence underlies the fundamental fact that church-defining within itself binds itself insistently to Christ-describing, and the sense it has of fulfilled Christhood is firmly linked with the Jesus story.

So linked, the Gospels, like all other writing of time past in time present, enjoy the advantage—or incur the liability—of hindsight. In all history written there is this selective relation to history occurred. What comes into historiography is what what happened meant—for historians. Their perspective is inevitably retrospect. The evangelists in this are no exception. We cannot anywhere ask for fact about the past that is not interpreted fact. The notion of so-called bare fact is illusory, for its very bareness merits—and gets—oblivion. What may and should be asked for is an interpreting communication of fact congenial to its significance—"doing it right" in other words. The concern here with the New Testament Gospels is not to deprive them of their *parti pris* but to learn whether it belongs authentically with its material.

To undergird the position here of alert but hopeful confidence, it will be right to study this hindsight situation where it is most crucial, namely, in the fourth Gospel. Some have found that Gospel altogether enigmatic. Recurrent vivid eyewitness details everywhere—Jesus wearied at the well, Jesus lingering in the place where Martha met him, Jesus repairing to the Mount of Olives when "each went to his own house"—yet all of them in a creative construct of authorship as literary as Shakespeare's *Hamlet*. We do not ask about Hamlet's *ipsissima verba* when he talks of "the native hue of resolution sicklied o'er with the pale cast of thought." There is no stenographer at hand. Its truth is that he lived it, and the writer has altogether captured what he lived.

This is the situation in John's Gospel. How else should we understand the great prayer of chapter 17? Does it not express the summation of Jesus' ministry as from within his own awareness of its nature and sequence but out of a long-range experience of its significance such as only discipleship could register? Consider its themes, prayed out of sonship, lived under fatherhood: ministry discharged, truth manifested, disciples treasured and kept, knowledge entrusted, a world to teach, a glory attained. These are all of the essence of the Jesus story, but they are set in the light from a future that has now become real with the writer.

The writer's present possesses the future of the past. It has to be so with all extensible things. To sow seed, if there is no miscarriage, is to sow a harvest. What takes time is nevertheless at a time. Modern aeronautics are in the notebooks of Leonardo da Vinci; the future gave them wings already in his mind. Do not the battlefield at Gettysburg and Lincoln's "appropriate remarks" belong together? Authorship is born of theme, and theme is alive in authorship. The direct speech of Hamlet's soliloquies is not disqualified because we know the pen is Shakespeare's, for it is the burden of Hamlet's tragedy that gave the pen its words.

In the Hebraic tradition, too, there is this instinct to understand the past in the perspective of its future. How else should we understand Hosea's sense of having been led into a marriage which in its unfolding involved him in the bitterness of marital betrayal, "Go marry a harlot," and so the prophethood of a broken heart. Readers need not have literal minds but literary minds. Their perspective is artless if it substitutes the letter for the life.

Does not this consideration help us in discernment with the alternative that literalists have sometimes proposed to us as readers of the fourth Gospel, namely, that Jesus was either true and divine or false and mad? Claims that would have to be attributed to insanity if only human then find credibility on a nonincarnational concept of the situation. It then seems to be supposed that Jesus is man in a masquerade that only fitfully hides a surreptitious divinity. This is to distort both the nature of the text and the meaning of "the Word made flesh." To say "I came to save the world" or "Come to me and drink" is not to claim a sort of deus ex machina facility operating bizarrely in the human scene. It is to have the whole significance of a ministry and personality distilled into an invitation so authentic as to come by such expression in a literature born of the response.

Take the point further. Is not the future of the faith present when John gives the feeding of the multitude the context of long eucharistic passages? "He that was" is there in "he that is." Again there is the same inspired anachronism where conscious interpretative skill joins the Galilean charisma with the perpetual celebration of the bread from heaven. One must not misread the highly metaphorical language or the insistent linkage with the concrete history.

What about the narrative in chapter 1 of how the two disciples followed Jesus by invitation to "behold the Lamb of God"? Could they *in situ* have begun their discipleship in such express and conscious terms? If so, how do we explain their pained and stumbling education into the cross and Jesus' reading of the messianic task? But like Hosea's marriage, that initial obedience held within its sequence the recognized secret of redemptive love. Indeed, they followed "the Lamb of God." That ultimate clue, in the writer's mind, is already implicit in their answer, for without embarking there could have been no voyage and no harbor.

Yet again, the sharpness of Jesus' confrontation with "the Jews" in the fourth Gospel, while reflecting the current encounter in what can be called "the Johannine circle," belongs with the point of departure in Jesus, and the continuum is seen to be significant. There is a kind of bifocality. The earlier is not just remote, and the near is not newly emerging. The connectedness illuminates both.

Examples abound, and in measure, although not so pointedly, the Synoptics share them. Scholarly points at issue abound also. An essay such as this sets out to be cannot suffice them. But they do not contravene, and should not be allowed to obscure, the central conviction as to a literature communally shaped from the Christhood of Jesus and from life in its saving meaning.

Does this understanding of the New Testament tally with the alleged unconcern of the Epistles about the ministry of Jesus? Many have used that supposition to bolster the thesis of a dicthotomy between Jesus as he was and the faith about the Christ. That thesis in turn serves to buttress the idea that Christhood is constituted solely by the kerygma that preaches it, independently of antecedent events. Were the silence of the Epistles to be proved it might facilitate the Bultmann-style notion that the actuality of Jesus as the Christ stands only in people's response to the idea of him as such. On that view the theology of the New Testament moves backward into a cul-de-sac.

That is an incongruous position in itself, whatever one may think of the motives that inspired it. But are the Epistles so silent after all? Certainly not 1 Peter, with its vivid sense of the Gethsemane scene. As for the Pauline letters, which supposedly for these critics are most in mind, the whole case rests mostly on an obtuse reading of a single passage, that in 2 Corinthians 5:16 (RSV), which speaks of no longer knowing Christ "from a human point of view." Far from being a disclaimer of interest in Jesus, the text disowns traditional concepts of the Messiah, of the way the Christ would be. Those notions looked for a nationalist, a zealot, a political messiah, or an apocalyptic figure riding on the clouds in response to expectations that meanwhile withdrew from the human world until its inevitable crisis supervened. Once the actual messiahship according to Jesus, the Christhood of the cross, had been understood, these old things passed away. Consequently, all human nature had become susceptible to new beginnings. Therefore "we estimate nobody by this-worldly ideas." Such knowing no one "from a human point of view" can scarcely refer to a misogynist repudiation of the human fellowship! The context has to do with the debt owed by the disciple to a crucified Lord in whom he died to the "old self." Such debt to the Christ of the cross can in no way exclude the dimensions—those already traced here—that led up to it. No, the early church did not overlook the story of how it all began.

The Epistles are a different genre of writing from the Gospels and, belonging to the same matrix, are not to be supposed to be doing the Gospels' task for them. Yet the instinct to preserve traditions of the words and character of Jesus that ripened into gospels was not an abandoned instinct when pastoral education of the church was the concern. Nor did the resurrection faith veil the past of Jesus, for it could only be interpreted out of things suffered, and things suffered were intelligible only out of things done and taught.

"I . . . am persuaded in the Lord Jesus" writes Paul in Romans 14:14 (RSV), "that nothing is unclean in itself." It can hardly be that he is not quoting or echoing Mark 7:14-19. Even the unusual word *koinos* for "unclean" is the same. "Why do you pass judgment on your brother?" Paul asks in the same chapter (14:10 [RSV]). Had not Jesus said the same? The warning in both Jesus and Paul about the *skandalon*, the stumbling block, is identical. "Repay no one evil for evil [Rom. 12:17]" is close indeed to Matthew 5:39. A catalog would be tedious. Nor is it in verbal citations only that Paul's debt to Jesus is evident. It has to do with the whole ethos of the gospel.

So, to conclude our "map" of the testament we measure the Logos Christ by the *Christus patiens*, and the Christ-suffering belongs (as the creed suggests in having only that verb for his whole life, "born . . . suffered") with the Jesus from Nazareth of Galilee. It is time to turn to that other hope of "doing the New Testament right," which we said involved us with guests for its meaning. They are potentially ours from every direction of culture and belief and discourse. Islam is a good example, for the way in which it requires Christians to be articulate in the trust of faith can be deeply rewarding for their own Christian comprehension. The themes proposed here keep us close to the ruling features of the Christian territory we have aimed to map and explore.

Traditional controversy between the two faiths of the New Testament and the Qur'ān tends to revolve around familiar issues, often doggedly pursued and left in irreconcilable impasse: incarnation, Jesus' divinity, his death as not occurring or being necessary to a divine forgiveness, the corruption of the Gospels, the puzzle of the Trinity.

Instead of persisting with these, it is wiser to take them on the flank by developing instead certain other themes which, while vital to Islam, are also uncannily close to the features of our New Testament map. These are (1) the reach of prophetic vocation, (2) the action of divine mercy in

36

forgiveness, and (3) the question of theodicy in theology. These three are interdependent.

In all the foregoing there is understood a sequence from Jesus to Christ to Lord, from teaching to suffering to glory, from being prophet to being rejected to being redemptive. That sequence in the story of Jesus warrants the Christian belief that there is more than prophethood in prophethood's own entail. To be spokesperson in any sense on behalf of the divine is to incur the rejectionism of the human. To serve truth is to experience the antagonism that refuses it. Jesus suffers in that he teaches and in that experience, with the precedents from earlier sufferers, he identifies the messianic vocation.

In his prophethood until the emigration to Medina, Muhammad suffered a similar experience of travail and danger. Indeed, he is warned that he may well die without seeing the fruit of his vocation. But, in the Quranic sequence, that jeopardy, real and heroic as it is down to the *Hijrah*, or emigration of A.D. 622, is exchanged for an active campaign of militancy in physical, armed form designed to ensure the survival both of the prophet-word and the prophet-person. It is assumed that these must survive together, for without the unique messenger what prospect is there for the message? It is further assumed that their mutual survival necessitates and justifies the force that achieves it. Moreover, the whole situation is set in a struggle for *haram* sanctuary, where worship and pilgrim access to it had for long been taken in power terms in Arabian society. Medina, Muhammad's new city, became a sanctuary base from which to strive for possession of his birth city, Mecca, where meanwhile the deities of Muhammad's adversaries were ensconced.

The New Testament situation is altogether in contrast. The deepest feature of the contrast, however, is the directly opposite sense of what should happen when prophetic ministry, through rejection, heads toward tragedy. Here the precedent of the greatest Old Testament prophets is vital. For them martial encounter would be a suffocating travesty of the word they preach. Defenselessness, in that physical sense, must be their posture. The evil in society that opposes them is an enmity to truth, which necessarily turns into a justified enmity to a cause if the prophethood becomes belligerent. People say, "He is our enemy and a menace to our status quo." He proves that is so if he fights them with their own weapons.

It is this necessary fidelity to truth as suffering that is the heart of Jesus' teaching. Prophet-teacher and sufferer-savior become one. So the teaching is itself confirmed and so too the evil—to which he has not succumbed either by silence or by imitation—is mastered. It is by the travail that outloves the transgressors that they themselves are healed.

37

Reflection on these dimensions of the prophetic, in the given setting of the perversely human, would seem to be at the core of New Testament hospitality of mind to the concerns of Islam. Nowhere is the phenomenon of prophethood more central than in Islam, whose Qur'ān —although it reads it differently—has a no less lively sense of a sinful society besetting the prophet's path. The whither and the how of the prophetic vocation are therefore issues of intimate unity and disparity between the faiths.

Allied to that issue is the New Testament sense of a need beyond the prophetic or the didactic. Prophecy must transcend its verbal self, for the word alone does not avail. People are not perfectible by exhortation or by wisdom. In the career of Muhammad the dimension that took over from and for the prophetic was rulership. With Jesus it was the cross. In either case there has to be "more than a prophet." Islam remains firmly committed to its belief that prophethood (the "word" of the Lord) is the ultimate form of the divine provision in the human crisis, namely, guidance and reminder. It is equally clear that statehood and power are the means to implement the prophetic mission when misguidedness resists. On both counts the New Testament is otherwise. Teaching culminates in—and power flows from—a love that suffers.

The second theme was to be the divine mercy in our forgiveness. It belongs close to the first. Islam sets the *Raḥmah* of God at the heart of its worship and invokes it constantly in the *Bismillāh*: "In the name of God the merciful Lord of mercy." It is among the most precious of its focuses of devotion and theology. This is common ground with the New Testament. Yet once again the contrasts are radical. Islam is unable to identify the mercy of God in the Passion of Christ. There is here, of course, the long controversy about the historicity of the death of Jesus arising from the denial in Sura 4:158: "They did not kill him, they did not crucify him: it was only in the realm of seeming." We will not stay here with the complex exegesis of this passage or with the echoes of the docetic issue with which it is involved. The question as to history—was he or was he not crucified?—is for Islam only part of a larger moral and theological resistance to New Testament faith about the cross. It is not simply that Jesus *did* not suffer, since God rescued him. It is also that he *should* not and *need* not.

He should not suffer, not merely because it is false to think that God would abandon his prophet-servant to the calumny of enemies bent on his destruction, but also because it is immoral to believe in suffering, on behalf of others, as a means to their being forgiven. The Qur'ān is resolutely individualist in its insistence that "no bearer has a burden that is not his own" and that "God does not exact of any one what he has not himself committed" (e.g., Sura 6:164, 17:15, 7:42). On this ground *all*

Christian concepts of redemption are excluded and denied, some no doubt legitimately so, when they have misstated the meaning of redemption as though it implied some arbitrary transference of guilt. The New Testament itself corrects such imperceptive theories of the cross.

But to disallow in its real form the meaning of sin-bearing is to miss the whole wonder of the love that bears and saves, and tragically to impoverish the human world. What love takes, in relationship, is not the guilt of the wrong as act or thought, but the entail of the wrong as pain and suffering. So taking it, in contrast to indifference, resentment, or retaliation, it takes it away. This is what Jesus did in the suffering of the cross. If we can see the evil which reared it as representative of our sinful selves—and repentance is so to see it—then we hear ourselves forgiven in the pardoning Christ. For the New Testament both suffering and pardoning are the disclosure in Christ of the nature of God, for in every evil situation restoration happens only this way. To believe it so, because of God, and in God, as Christ embodies it, is the ultimate assurance of a moral universe.

To see this covers also that other Quranic stance of misgiving about New Testament conviction. Islamically speaking it is not only that Jesus *should* not but also that he *need* not suffer. The cross is not only improper to him but unnecessary, something superfluous to a divine capacity to forgive effortlessly and by word alone. Why should the omnipotent mercy need to operate through a savior who "enables" the forgiveness? He merely says, "Be," and it is. A "means" whereby God makes our pardon ours is something redundant, to require which is to have—at best misunderstood, at worst distrusted—the divine mercy and its explicit power.

Again a situation patiently to disentangle. A forgiving power characteristic of God? Truly, the question is not whether but how. Forgiveness cannot be given arbitrarily; it has to be received. Were it divinely effortless we would not be the willful humans the Qur'ān knows us to be, or the sin would not exist in the first place. The *need* for the redeemer is within the divine forgiveness, given the creatures that we are and given the righteous will of the love that is God's. Omnipotence is not the effortless ability to do anything. It is rather the adequacy of a sovereignty that is undefeated.

This "need" of the cross within the divine purpose bringing all things into one relates intimately to our final concern for a hospitable handling of the New Testament. Where there is a will to mediate there is always a way to understanding.

Thus far in these pages we might seem to have been assuming that "the word of truth" in 2 Timothy 2:15 was the New Testament itself.

Had we in fact done so it would of course have been a mistake. Many questions of the canon still lie ahead. We can by no means be sure to what area of existing "Christian" documents, or in what sense, the writer in this pastoral letter to Timothy referred. Perhaps to none as such, but rather to the gathering consensus of the Christian faith, scriptuarized or not, at that point.

There is justice, however, in our apparent identification of the phrase with the scripture, for tentatively and hazardously these Epistles and Gospels did achieve a status that brought them into a lectionary of faith and set them eventually in a single Bible with the inherited writings of the old regime of Jewry. It is that ultimate fact of the canon which warrants placing in one context in this essay the essential content of the faith and its steady, if precarious, embodiment in scriptures, for in broad terms it is the interaction of these two that has generated the New Testament both as life and as literature.

The very core of both is "God in Christ." For the Christian the divine sovereignty is known to us humanly, in Christ, because in him what we may be bold to call the human liability of God is fulfilled in compassionate response. With exceptions, the theology of Islam allows no need for a theodicy, that is, for a faith that there is an "ought" at the heart of transcendence. Muslims are tuned to and by the thought that God in inscrutable power has no necessary relation to, need of, or responsibility about the human. God has no essential need of the world. The creation may reflect divine compassion but cannot rightly claim it. History may register divine providence but may well experience God's irreproachable indifference. God is not necessarily love, although mercy may characterize God's relationship as will may determine.

For the Christian, however, questions *to* God are inseparable from the question *of* God. A divine transcendence not essentially related to the meaning and the pathos of the human world is a contradiction in terms. A supreme being sublimely self-exonerated from the issues of time would be an eternal bystander, not "the Lord of the worlds." What some might see as the divine right to indifference, the Christian sees as divine abdication, an essential atheism in the strict sense of the term, a not-God-ness.

There is always an intellectual temptation to suppose that one is doing honor to God by thinking God inscrutably immune from human liability. The Qur'ān has given the Muslim centuries ground for that cast of mind. But by no means entirely so. The meaning of creation and the centrality of mercy point the other way. It is the faith of the New Testament which confidently centers its theology in theodicy, the justification of God in the justification of humankind, and both in the assurance that "God was in Christ." The suffering glory of the Messiah is the clue to the sovereign glory of God.

At the end of his celebrated study *The Quest of the Historical Jesus*, Albert Schweitzer expressed the view that the first disciples themselves reached no clear and "whole" conception of Jesus. Hence the moving and often quoted final conclusion of his book:

> He comes to us as one unknown, without a name, as of old by
> the lakeside He came to men who knew Him not. He speaks to
> us the same word: "Follow Thou Me" and sets us to tasks which
> He has for us to fulfill for our time. He commands, and for those
> who obey Him, whether they be wise or simple, He will reveal
> Himself in the toils, the conflicts, the sufferings which they shall
> pass through in His fellowship, and, as an ineffable mystery, they
> shall learn in their own experience Who He is.

Such, memorably said, is for us today the personal end of the quest of Jesus, where ours of him responds to his of us. But if it was no less so in the first days, may we not recognize in the New Testament, its Gospels and Epistles, the learning experience that stirs and guides and teaches all the rest?

CHAPTER 3

The Criterion of Dissimilarity:
The Wrong Tool?
Reginald H. Fuller

Quite independently of each other, the late Norman Perrin and the present writer formulated in a systematic way a number of criteria of authenticity that were being used especially in Germany to enable the critical reconstruction of the Jesus tradition in the Gospels.[1] One criterion in particular has proved to be highly controversial. This is what I originally called the criterion of distinctiveness. The definition of it was taken from Bultmann's discussion of the similitudes: "(1) the similitude is authentic where its content is opposed to Jewish morality and piety; (2) where it reflects the eschatological temper characteristic of Jesus' proclamation; (3) where such teaching exhibits no specifically Christian traits." And I drew from Bultmann the conclusion that "traditio-historical criticism eliminates from the authentic sayings of Jesus those which are paralleled in the Jewish tradition (apocalyptic and rabbinic) and those which reflect the faith, practice and situations of the Post-Easter Church as we know them outside the gospels."[2] Norman Perrin designated this criterion as the "criterion of dissimilarity" and took his formulation of it from Hans Conzelmann's celebrated essay "Jesus Christus." Conzelmann presented it this way: "So far as the reconstruction of the teaching is concerned the following methodological basis is valid: we may accept as authentic material which fits in with neither Jewish thinking nor the conceptions of the later [Christian] community."[3]

This criterion has been vigorously attacked, especially in Great Britain.[4] The most thorough critique has been offered by Morna Hooker, now Lady Margaret Professor of Divinity at the University of Cambridge, in the last of her three discussions of the subject.[5] There she

Reginald H. Fuller is Professor of New Testament at Virginia Theological Seminary in Alexandria, Virginia.

marshals no less than nine arguments against this criterion. To my knowledge, only one voice has been raised in Britain in defense of the criterion, and that is David Mealand's.[6]

The most important criticisms can be summarized as follows. The remainder of this essay will be devoted to answering each point in succession.

1. Our knowledge of first-century Judaism and of early Christianity is limited. Hence what we take to be dissimilar may not in fact have been so. Further knowledge may wipe out all that passes the criterion of dissimilarity and leave us nothing.[7]

2. Since Jesus was a first-century Jew, he must have agreed with first-century Judaism, and his followers must have agreed with him in many things.[8]

3. The criterion is circular. The same materials (viz., the Gospels) are used to establish both what the early church taught and what Jesus taught. There is no way of breaking out of the circle.[9]

4. The criterion does not give us what we want. We want to know what is *characteristic* of Jesus; the criterion instead gives us only what is *unique*.[10]

5. Several object to the skepticism involved in the use of the criterion. It leaves a distorted picture of Jesus because it may throw away much that is genuine.

6. The criterion is subjective in its application. This objection is expressed in different ways. Some contend that it is a faith assumption to presume that there was something unique about the historical Jesus. Hooker makes two points in this connection: (a) its decision on what is dissimilar is subjective and (b) its decision on Jesus' unique eschatological stance is subjective as is shown by the various interpretations scholars of Jesus' eschatology offered.[11]

7. Some critics of the criterion have argued that it is safe so long as it is used positively, that is, if used not to eliminate material as unauthentic but to establish it as authentic.[12]

As far as I know, Norman Perrin never published any reply (although he did have a vigorous argument with Hooker at the SNTS [Society of New Testament Studies] meeting in 1971). And the Germans who use the criterion tend to ignore any criticisms unless they are uttered in German. It therefore behooves me, as one who has been the object of attack, to reply. I will try to answer each point in turn.

1. It is true that our knowledge both of first-century Palestinian Judaism and Christianity is deficient, but in regard to Judaism the situation has considerably improved since the discovery of the Qumran materials. We now have some knowledge of the eschatological stance of certain groups who stood nearest to the origins of the Christian

movement, and so we are able to see the difference between them and the message of Jesus. It is theoretically possible that another discovery similar to the Qumran finds would turn up evidence for a community holding precisely the same eschatological stance Jesus did. But we need not fear this, for one would expect that such figures would have provoked so much opposition that they would have been crucified or otherwise disposed of, and perhaps have launched a movement marking a radical shift from Judaism, although in the case of Jesus the Easter event must also be factored in. Meanwhile we have to work with the evidence we have, remembering always that all historical reconstructions can never claim more than a high degree of probability, never absolute certainty. Users of the criterion of dissimilarity have sometimes been guilty of claiming such certainty. (Norman Perrin, who could be very dogmatic about his conclusions, was probably guilty of that at times.) Still, we have to work with what we have.

It is equally true that our knowledge of the early Christian community is limited. But the evidence that we do have is there, and where it is applied in the use of the criterion of dissimilarity its use is not likely to be undermined by the discovery of fresh data. We do know that the earliest community proclaimed that Jesus entered upon his messianic office at his exaltation (Romans 1:3; Acts 2:36) and that a development occurred in which his messianic office was dated backward first to his baptism (or possibly to his transfiguration and then to his baptism) and finally to the moment of conception/birth.[13] This justifies our suspicion that Jesus material in which messiahship is attributed to him in the post-Easter sense is either the creation or the adaptation of the post-Easter community.[14] Such material should be laid aside, at least provisionally, in any reconstruction of the Jesus tradition.

2. It is certainly true that Jesus agreed with Judaism on many points and that his followers would have agreed with him. I pointed this out in one of my discussions of the criterion of dissimilarity, and the critics have duly noted it, although they have usually complained that this was only a grudging concession.[15] And it is true that neither Norman Perrin nor the Germans have shown much awareness of this obvious fact. We have to define the sort of questions on which agreement is to be expected if Jesus was a first-century Palestinian Jew and the disciples followers of Jesus, and the sort of things on which there are differences for very good reason. On the Jewish side, Jesus obviously agreed with Judaism that God was Creator, that God was active in history, particularly in Israel's salvation-history, that God demanded righteous conduct through the law and spoke through the prophets, and so on. These matters are generally accepted truths of the Jewish religion, without which no one, including Jesus, would be a true member of the

44

Jewish community. Where Jesus can be shown to differ, and therefore where he exhibits himself as most characteristic, is the *way* (recognized by the application of the criterion of dissimilarity) in which he held these truths. Jesus offers in his word an immediate experience of God as creator. He enunciates the immediate demand of God. He confronts men and women with the immediate eschatological presence of God.[16] In all these issues, Jesus agrees with, and yet his stance is distinct from, Judaism, and it is in this distinctiveness that we see what is most characteristic of Jesus.

As for his agreement with the early church, we can for instance establish that he and they agreed that God could be addressed as Abba. This is sometimes taken by the objectors as a demonstration of the inconsistency with which the criterion of dissimilarity is applied. But there is a difference. Paul says that for the believer to call God "Abba" is something that can be done only in the Holy Spirit, through whom the believer has been adopted into a relationship with God. Jesus' use of Abba, on the contrary, does not depend on a relationship into which he has been brought by the hearing of the apostolic proclamation or by baptism into the name of Jesus. For him that relationship expressed in the use of Abba is primal and unmediated. And he does not teach as an abstract truth that men and women can call God "Father." He invites them through his word into the privilege of calling God "Abba," so that they are dependent upon him in doing so. Thus there is both similarity and dissimilarity between Jesus' use of Abba and Paul's use—similarity in that the same word is used, dissimilarity in that in Jesus' proclamation it is made possible for others by response to his eschatological message, while for Paul it is made possible by response to the apostolic kerygma and reception of the Holy Spirit. The criterion of dissimilarity here points not to absolute difference but to continuity amid discontinuity.

3. Circularity of argument is always a danger when sources are limited. What is needed is a *dos moi pou stō* outside the Gospel materials. The authentic Pauline letters, and especially the pre-Pauline materials within those letters, provide the best starting point.[17] The next best bet is the primitive christological material enshrined in the keryg-matic speeches in Acts.[18] The use of this material gives an entrée into the different levels of tradition within the Gospels and enables us (with other methods, such as the distinction between connecting links and the bodies of pericopes) to reconstruct painstakingly the three levels of the Gospel traditions: the Jesus level, the community level in oral tradition, and the redactional level of the evangelists. Unless we are prepared to take the risk of distinguishing between these three levels, we reduce the whole of the Gospels to one level. This is then assigned indiscriminately to the Jesus level,[19] or equally indiscriminately to the redaction level.

The first results in uncritical incredulity, the second in a skepticism far more thoroughgoing than that of which the critics of the criterion of dissimilarity complain.

4. There is a logical distinction between what is characteristic and what is unique, but I would argue that when applied to Jesus the two turn out to be largely identical. It might be objected that this is a faith assumption rather than an objective application of the dissimilarity test. But Jesus' crucifixion points to a radical difference between his stance and Judaism, and given the shift that took place between the early first-century Judaism and the earliest post-Easter community, it is surely reasonable to assume on purely historical grounds that the primary cause of this shift was the appearance of the earthly Jesus. Consequently, there must have been elements in his teaching and activity that distinguished him from the Judaism in which he was reared. This assumption is legitimately made in the case of all figures who altered the course of history, for example, Socrates. In the historical Jesus the major feature that satisfies our criterion in this regard is of course his eschatological stance.

5. Does the criterion of dissimilarity unduly narrow reconstruction of the earthly Jesus, his message and ministry? It all depends on what motivates the interest in the earthly Jesus. If one is an old-fashioned Ritschlian liberal Protestant like Harnack, or an equally old-fashioned orthodox conservative like H.P. Liddon, for both of whom the earthly Jesus was the direct object of faith, one will not be satisfied with the historical Jesus of Bultmann, or with that of Bornkamm and Conzelmann. But if the reason for inquiry into the historical Jesus is to provide a legitimate basis for the post-Easter kerygma, then I would submit with Leander E. Keck that "the thorough criticism [in which I would include the use of the dissimilarity test] of the Gospels does provide us with sufficient data about Jesus that the contour of his life as a whole can come into view, and that this can be the core of Christian preaching and the dominant datum with which theology works."[20] These data may be summarized under six headings: (a) Jesus' eschatological message, (b) his radical demand, (c) his teaching on God, (d) the authoritative call to follow him, (e) his voluntary self-exposure to rejection and martyrdom in his commitment to his message, and (f) the radical questioning of the Jesus cause by his followers as a result of his rejection and martyrdom and the reinstatement of their faith in him through the Easter event. These six data—and there are doubtless others—comprising as they do a critically assured minimum, provide an adequate basis for the kerygma of the post-Easter community, which interpreted Jesus' career, viewed in the light of Easter, as the eschatological act of God.

6. Is the criterion of dissimilarity subjective in its application? The

first form of this charge, namely, that it is a faith assumption to suppose that there was something unique about the historical Jesus, has been dealt with under objection four (above) in connection with the relation of what is unique to Jesus to what is characteristic of him. The second form of this charge deals specifically with the question of Jesus' eschatological stance. It is alleged that the disagreement among scholars as to what this stance was renders all decisions on that score subjective.[21] First I would contend that this should not impede us from endeavoring to reconstruct Jesus' eschatological proclamation to the best of our critical ability and from submitting our results on this subject to the judgment of our peers. Morna Hooker does the same when she accepts the parables as likely to go back to Jesus, despite the fact that their eschatological message is variously interpreted.[22] And Hooker exaggerates the degree of scholarly disagreement in Jesus' eschatological stance. If on Hegelian lines we regard Schweitzer's thoroughgoing (future) eschatology as the thesis, and Dodd's realized eschatology as the antithesis, we may discern the emergence of a synthetic consensus in such scholars as Jeremias, Cullmann, and Kümmel, all of whom in various ways combine present and future elements in their reconstruction of Jesus' eschatology. The Bultmannian existential interpretation should be seen precisely as a modern hermeneutical restatement of Jesus' eschatological message rather than as an exegesis of it. It is a statement of what that message may *mean* for today (in the German context, no doubt) rather than what it *meant*. Basically, it operates with the same synthesis of future and present eschatology.

7. It is attractive to restrict the criterion of dissimilarity to a positive function, that of discovering what can reasonably be attributed to the pre-Easter Jesus rather than to the post-Easter Kyrios. For our concern is precisely to find out what that Jesus did say and do. In practice, however, it generally tends to be used both positively and negatively. It is used positively when, for example, it is argued that Jesus' radical demand is authentic on the ground that it differs both from contemporary Judaism and from the post-Easter church. It is used negatively when it is decided that any saying which reflects the explicit Christology of the post-Easter community is not authentic to Jesus. Actually, the critics of the criterion of dissimilarity sometimes object that its users do not apply it radically enough—as when, for example, it is objected that passages adduced for an indirect or implicit Christology in the pre-Easter Jesus should be rejected. This objection seems quite unwarranted, for there is a real difference between implicit and explicit Christology,[23] and the implicit Christology can be eliminated only if it is interpreted in an explicit sense. There is a real difference between a Jesus who confronts men and women with the eschatological presence

47

(in word and deed) of the living God, and one who overtly adopts messianic titles as self-designations. The first challenges his hearers to a response, the other answers the questions before they are asked. We would agree that especially the negative use of its dissimilarity should be conducted with great caution and with a consciousness of the tentative character of its results. Its practitioners, myself included,[24] have tended to be too dogmatic about our eliminations from the authentic Jesus material.

In conclusion, it can be said that the criticisms of the criterion of dissimilarity were valuable insofar as they challenge its users to be more tentative about their results. But I still believe it to be the best tool we have if what we want is a critically assured minimum, rather than a maximum that appears excessively vulnerable to skepticism and doubt.

CHAPTER 4

Did Jesus Have a Distinctive Use of Scripture?

John A.T. Robinson

One of the most succinct summaries of the issues involved in the relation of the historical Jesus to the Christ of the church's faith is Harvey K. McArthur's "From the Historical Jesus to Christology,"[1] originally delivered as an address to C.F.D. Moule's New Testament seminar at Cambridge when I, alas, was away being Bishop of Woolwich. It states with great clarity the various positions one can take, although I would incline more to what McArthur calls "the historical risk school," while he would lean toward "the immune from historical risk school."

In this I am an unashamed follower of C.H. Dodd, who surprisingly gets no mention in the work, rather than of the German-American tradition that runs through Kähler and Bultmann to Tillich and Knox. Indeed, one of the moments that has seared itself upon my memory was when I was taken as a young teacher of the New Testament by my friend and host John Knox to the weekly faculty luncheon in the halcyon days of Union Theological Seminary. I had no idea that I was to be more than a guest sitting at the feet of the great. When suddenly at the end of lunch Knox turned to me with the indication that I was now "on" and was to address the assembled company, it was like a nightmare. I rapidly decided that attack was the best and indeed only form of defense and, greatly daring, took the initiative by continuing the friendly riposte I had been making to Knox about his position and Tillich's and why I found it untenable.

I now realize that this was but continuing a classic conversation held there between Tillich and Dodd some years earlier, in 1950, described

John A.T. Robinson, an Anglican bishop, is currently Dean of Chapel and Lecturer in Theology at Trinity College, Cambridge.

by Langdon Gilkey in the appendix to Dillistone's life of Dodd. In it Tillich is recorded as saying to Dodd:

> "Then there are *two* risks, a 'double risk,' involved for the Christian: one that the witness of the New Testament refers to an actual historical figure, and the second that the figure so described is the Christ." "Yes," said Dodd, "there are two risks, one historical and the other religious—and a historical faith cannot escape either one." Tillich said he could not tolerate such a double indemnity, so to speak, and stuck to his "single risk" theory. . . .
>
> Dodd then went on to maintain—and I don't think Tillich agreed with him—that the preliminary, historical risk was really not all that great. He clearly felt relatively comfortable with the "high level" of probability that was entailed in the assertions, via historical inquiry, that there was a historical Jesus and that the main characteristics of his life, relevant to his role as the Christ, could be known with great probability.[2]

For myself, I want to side with Dodd on each count. I do not believe it is possible to ensure immunity against historical risk. There comes a point, reached perhaps only after a thousand qualifications, when the credibility gap gets too great; other candidates come into view when the question "Lord, to whom else should we go?" is asked. But equally I believe, and the belief grows stronger rather than weaker the longer I spend on New Testament work, that the Gospels afford good confidence that we can reach down to bedrock tradition about the historical Jesus. This is increasingly so in relation to the fourth Gospel. But here I would like to fasten on one relatively small clue, to be found in all the Gospels, which I am not aware has been noticed by those who have worked on the criterion of "dissimilarity." Indeed, although Dodd himself in his highly suggestive contribution *According to the Scriptures* believed that the church's "most original and fruitful process of rethinking the Old Testament" must have originated in the creative mind of the Master himself,[3] he never raised the question whether Jesus' own use of scripture might at any point be so distinctive as to provide a test of authenticity. It is this that I would like to explore as a tribute to the stimulus that Harvey McArthur's unflagging zeal for "the quest" has afforded to one of its distant pursuers.

I start with a simple—and innocent—question: Why do people quote scripture? The reasons run into one another, but confining myself for the purposes of this essay simply to the evidence of the Gospels, I would discern four:

1. The *allusive use* is the most common use in all ages. Consciously or unconsciously people put their thoughts into the words of scripture because it seems to say what they want to say better than they themselves could, for the extra aura of authority that its words convey, or for overtones or echoes of meaning that its associations introduce. This is the most common reason for quotation of any kind, and in the Gospels it is found constantly on the lips of Jesus, of other speakers, and of the evangelists. Often in this allusive use it is difficult if not impossible to tell whether a quotation is actually intended at all (e.g., in the ransom saying of Mark 10:45), and for now I shall confine myself to sentences or phrases printed in boldface in Kurt Aland's United Bible Societies' Greek text.[4] But, especially in apocalyptic, half the art of the allusive use of scripture is precisely the release of images and associations that depend on *not* being tied down to precise or pedestrian quotation. It is well known that the book of Revelation, while soaked in the Old Testament (particularly Daniel and Ezekiel), never once quotes a specific text. And this is characteristic of other apocalyptic passages, for example 2 Thessalonians 2, Didache 16, and, within the Gospels, Mark 13:24-27, all of which contain a pastiche of allusive phrases.

It is not necessary to give detailed instances of the allusive use, but quick and obvious examples would be:

- The echo of Isaiah 5:1-7 in the parable of the wicked tenants (Mark 12:1-12 and pars.), whether this is made explicit, as in Mark and Matthew, or not, as in Luke and the Gospel of Thomas.
- The echo of Jeremiah 22:5 in Matthew 23:38 = Luke 13:35: "Your house shall be left to you," whether or not the quotation is completed by what is probably the scribal addition of "desolate."
- The use of Psalm 22:1, the cry of dereliction, by Jesus on the cross (Matthew 27:46 = Mark 15:34), or Psalm 22:7 by the evangelists to describe the passersby "wagging their heads" (Matthew 27:39 = Mark 15:29).
- The evident allusion to Isaiah 35 and 61 in Jesus' answer to the disciples of John the Baptist (Matthew 11:5 = Luke 7:22) or to Psalm 110:1 and Daniel 7:13 in his reply to the high priest (Mark 14:62 and pars.) or to Jacob's ladder (Genesis 28:12) in John 1:51.

This recourse to scripture is clearly no test of whether the words are dominical or reflect the theology of the church, for it occurs indiscriminately. For example, in John 1:23 the reference to Isaiah 40:3 is placed on the lips of John the Baptist, while in the Synoptics (Mark 1:3 and pars.) the same quotation forms part of the evangelists' comment. Echoes of scripture are found in many contexts: on the lips of the crowds

51

at the triumphal entry, "Blessed is he that comes in the name of the Lord [Ps. 118:26]" in Mark 11:10 and parallels and John 12:13; on the lips of Jesus' enemies at the cross, "He trusted in God; let him deliver him if he will have him [Ps. 22:8]" in Matthew 27:43; in hymns of the church (e.g., the Magnificat and Benedictus in Luke 1); and in the evangelists' descriptions, for instance, of the weighing out of the thirty pieces of silver (Zechariah 11:12) in Matthew 26:15 and of the division of Jesus' garments by lot (Psalm 22:18) in Mark 15:24 and pars.

2. The second use of scripture, into which the first soon flows, is what might be called the *confirmatory use*. It is to show how the events of the life of Jesus fulfill the Old Testament. It is often difficult to decide where allusion passes over into claims for fulfillment. Thus the partition of Jesus' clothes which in the Synoptics (Mark 15:24 and pars.) is described allusively is in John (19:24) seen as confirming the Old Testament. Or again, the citation of Isaiah 6:9-10 ("that seeing they may not see," etc.), which in Mark (4:12) and Luke (8:10) is a clear allusion, in Matthew (13:13) and John (9:39) is first introduced more indirectly (not in boldface type) and is later followed up by a fulfillment formula (Matthew 13:14-15; John 12:38-40). This second usage is especially characteristic of Matthew, with fourteen instances (although Matthew has more actual examples of the first usage). But it is surprisingly rare in Mark and Luke, where the allusive use is far more common, especially in Luke. Mark has only three examples of fulfillment quotations, and in each case they are introduced by "as is written": the double citation of Malachi 3:1 and Isaiah 40:3 with reference to John the Baptist in 1:2-3; the citation of Isaiah 29:13 ("This people honours me with their lips but their heart is far from me") in 7:6; and that of Zechariah 13:7 ("Strike the shepherd and the sheep shall be scattered") in 14:27. Of these, Luke retains only one, expanding the quotation from Isaiah 40 (3:4-6), but, like Matthew (11:10), reserving that from Malachi 3:1 for its use on Jesus' lips after the departure of John's disciples (7:27). Luke adds only three fulfillment quotations of his own: a double one (Exodus 13:2, 12; Leviticus 12:8) to show how the presentation of Jesus in the temple complied with the Levitical law (2:23-24); the citation of Isaiah 61:1-2 in Jesus' sermon at Nazareth (4:17-19); and the reference, again on Jesus' lips, to Isaiah 53:12 ("He shall be numbered with the wicked") in 22:37.

In John the fulfillment quotations outnumber all the other uses put together, but this merely indicates that when John actually quotes scripture it is more often than not for this purpose. Nonspecific echoes of Jewish ways of thinking and speaking are much more numerous. Most of the fulfillment quotations, as in Matthew, are comments of the evangelist: 2:17 (on the cleansing of the temple); 12:15 (on the triumphal entry); 12:38, 40 (on the unbelief of the Jews); and 19:24, 36-37 (on details of the crucifixion). But there are two, from the last discourses, on Jesus' lips: 13:18 ("He who eats bread with me has turned against me," from Psalm 41:9) and 15:25 ("They hated me without reason," from Psalm 69:4). And there is one, in 7:38, referring to an unidentifiable *graphē*, "Streams of living water shall flow out from within him," where whether one attributes it to Jesus (with the RSV) or, more probably, to the evangelist (with the NEB) depends on how one punctuates. In any case, this confirmatory use of scripture certainly provides no criterion for distinguishing the usage of Jesus from that of the early church, and the strong probability must be that the claim to fulfillment (e.g., especially of the "suffering servant" in Luke 22:37) is read back on to his lips rather than the other way around.

3. Third, there is what might be called the *argumentative use* of scripture—either contesting the meaning or interpretation of a passage or using it to prove one's point. The two naturally flow into each other, since the point usually depends on the interpretation. Sometimes both sides quote scripture to argue their case. Obvious examples are the devil and Jesus in the temptation narrative (Matthew 4:7-10 = Luke 4:4-12) or the Sadducees and Jesus in the dispute about resurrection (Mark 12:18-27 and pars.). In Matthew (22:37, 39) and Mark (12:29-31) it is Jesus who cites the summary of the law, and in Luke (10:27) it is the lawyer, while in the case of the rich young ruler it is Jesus who quotes the ten commandments in all three versions (Mark 10:19 and pars.). It is surprising that these four examples are the only clear instances of this usage of scripture in Luke. Mark (7:10; 10:4, 6-8) and Matthew (15:4; 19:4–5, 7) also record Jesus' arguments with the Jews over *korban* and divorce, which turn on the true interpretation and intention of scripture, while Matthew twice (9:13; 12:7) makes him refer his opponents to the real meaning of the text, "I desire mercy not sacrifice" (Hosea 6:6). Matthew also has the five antitheses of the Sermon on the Mount (5:21, 31, 33, 38, 43), where Jesus deepens and corrects what was said to them of old, and in the case of oaths (5:34-35) himself quotes scripture in his retort. There is only one specific example of this third use in John (7:42), where the crowds refer to the fact that according to the scriptures the Messiah is to be of the family of David and to come from his village Bethlehem (cf. 2 Samuel 7:12; Psalm 89:3-4; Micah 5:2). Yet in a real sense the whole central section of the fourth Gospel is one long argument with the Jews about the meaning of scripture, focusing on the comment "You study the scriptures diligently, supposing that in having them you have eternal life; yet, although their testimony points to me, you refuse to come to me for that life" (5:39-40). Yet it is figures like Abraham, Moses, and Isaiah who are adduced as witnesses, rather than

53

texts about them or from them. It is largely accidental, too, that appeals to principle, like the precedence of circumcision over the sabbath (7:22) or the requirement in law of at least two witnesses (8:17), are not grounded in actual quotations, as the latter is by Matthew (18:16) and Paul (2 Corinthians 13:1; cf. 1 Timothy 5:19) by allusion to Deuteronomy 19:15.

All the instances of this argumentative use of scripture occur within the Gospels in conversations rather than in the evangelists' own comments. This is what one would expect, though clearly it is no test of whether they go back to the original interlocutors. Argument over the interpretation of scripture is as old as scripture itself; "the Bible to prove" has ever been one of the church's most ready weapons. The interpretations of texts at Qumran and the argumentative use of scripture by Paul, to go no further, show that the appearance in the Gospels of this form of apologetic is nothing distinctive.

4. There is a rarer and subtly different use, which could be called the *challenging use* of scripture. It also occurs, by definition, in polemical contexts and is an extension of the last usage. But it is not so much contending about the interpretation of scripture or arguing one's case from scripture as delivering a challenge by asking a question, using the Bible to pose rather than to prove. It is set in the interrogative mood and throws down a gauntlet: "What do you make of the text or passage in which . . . ?" It is characteristically introduced by a formula such as "Have you not read?" (Mark 2:25; 12:10, 26; Matthew 12:3, 5; 19:4; 21:16, 42; 22:31; Luke 6:3) or by a question beginning with *pōs*, "how" (Mark 9:12; 12:35; Matthew 22:43; Luke 20:41), or "What do you think?" (Matthew 22:42). There is always an element of *paraprosdokia*, or turning the tables on opponents, of going over on to the initiative with them—not continuing the argument about agreed texts but tossing something at them to compel them to rethink their presuppositions.

A good example of the difference is in the debate with the Sadducees already mentioned (Mark 12:18-27 and pars.). They cite scripture to try to entangle Jesus in its interpretation. He, though saying they err in not knowing the scriptures or the power of God, answers their question, "Whose wife will she be?" not by citing a contrary scripture passage but on his own authority. But then he turns on them for their disbelief in the resurrection and throws at them a text from the book of Moses, "at the [passage about the] bush," which appears to have nothing to do with the case, challenging them to see that it implies that God is the God not of the dead but of the living. There is no further argument; they must either see or not see.

Mark has two other instances from the same chapter, all three being used also by Matthew and Luke. The first comes at the close of the parable of the wicked tenants (Mark 12:10-11 and pars.). When the story seems to be over, Jesus comes back at his opponents with the words "Or can it be that you have never read this text: 'The stone which the builders rejected has become the main corner-stone. This is the Lord's doing and it is wonderful in our eyes'?" (Psalm 118:22-23). There is, and is meant to be, no reply.

Later on (Mark 12:35-37 and pars.), Jesus once more takes the initiative when, according to Matthew (22:41), Jesus asked the assembled Pharisees, "What is your opinion about the Messiah? Whose son is he?" The Pharisees replied, "The son of David." The debate seems to be proceeding within familiar parameters. Then comes the unexpected use of scripture (Psalm 110:1) to challenge their accepted assumptions: " 'How then is it,' [Jesus] asked, 'That David by inspiration calls him "Lord"?' For he says, 'The Lord said to my Lord, "Sit at my right hand until I put your enemies under your feet." If David calls him "Lord," how can he be David's son?' " And again, "Not a man could say a word in reply."

Mark introduces this last incident with the words "How do the scribes say . . . ? [12:35]," which is similar to the puzzled question of the disciples in 9:11: "Why do the scribes say that Elijah must come first?" Jesus replies that not only must Elijah come but that he has come. Then in a confused passage, which Matthew smoothes out (17:12), Jesus turns on them with an apparently unrelated counter-question: "How is it that the scripture says of the Son of man that he is to endure great sufferings and be treated with contempt?" (9:12). Again we have the same posing use of scripture, although this time without reference to a specific text.

With this must be considered the appeal to scripture in an earlier polemical passage, Mark 2:24-28 and parallels. Here again there is no actual citation, but the form is the same. In answer to the Pharisees' objection to the plucking of grain on the sabbath, Jesus replies not with a text but with a story: "Have you never read what David did when he and his men were hungry and had nothing to eat? How he went into the house of God . . . ?" (see 1 Samuel 22:1-6). He is not arguing the interpretation of scripture, and it does not logically demonstrate that "the Son of man is sovereign even over the Sabbath." The biblical example is flung down as a challenge and a scandal.

There are no independent examples of this use of scripture in Luke, but Matthew has another that must be placed in this category. To the indignant question of the chief priests and scribes at the triumphal entry, "Do you hear what they are saying?" ("Hosanna to the son of David"), Jesus replied with a counter-question, citing Psalm 8:2: "I do; have you never read that text, 'Thou hast made children and babes at the breast sound aloud thy praises'? [21:15-16]." Such ripostes are not invitations to argue the meaning of a text or attempts to prove anything. They are intended to pose and to stump—and they do.

Finally, there is a further example from John (10:33-36). The Jews accuse Jesus of blasphemy: "You, a mere man, claim to be a god." He comes back at them with a question drawing on Psalm 82:6: "Is it not written in your own law, 'I said: You are gods'? Those are called gods to whom the word of God was delivered—and Scripture cannot be set aside. Then why do you charge me with blasphemy because I, consecrated and sent into the world by the Father, said, 'I am God's son'?" This comes near to the argumentative use of scripture, yet it is not primarily an argument about the interpretation of texts, countering or inviting other interpretations. As in the other cases, it stops the argument altogether, merely provoking one more attempt at arrest (10:39). Nor is it used to demonstrate Jesus's sonship: the consonance of his deeds with the Father's will can alone do that (10:37-38). It is a challenge to deeper discernment, to stop and think again.

The nearest parallel in the Gospel material to this is that of parables to pose a challenge: "What do you think about this Simon? From whom do earthly monarchs collect tax or toll? From their own citizens, or from aliens? [Matt. 17:25]"; "What do you think? Suppose a man has a hundred sheep . . . [Matt. 18:12-13]"; "But what do you think about this? A man had two sons . . . [Matt. 21:28-32]"; "Now, which will love him most? [Luke 7:42]"; "Which of these three do you think was neighbour to the man who fell into the hands of robbers? [Luke 10:36]."

It is widely agreed that in the parables and in the questions Jesus put, as distinct from the answers frequently supplied to these questions, there are some of the most characteristic and identifiable features of Jesus' teaching. In this fourth use of scripture, I suggest, there is a similar mark of distinctiveness. In one instance, that of the wicked tenants, it is intimately associated with a parable, and Matthew Black[5] has argued convincingly that the connection between the story and the scriptural quotation is original, depending on a pun lying behind the Greek of *ben* ("son") and *eben* ("stone"), which is attested elsewhere (e.g., in the saying of John the Baptist, "God can make children for Abraham out of these stones [Matt. 3:9 = Luke 3:8]"). In any case, this use of scripture, though the occurrences are insufficient for statistical confidence, has three marks that pass the same tests of authenticity as the phrase "the Son of man": (a) it alone of all the uses, or titles, occurs always on the lips of Jesus and of no others; (b) it has multiple attestation of synoptic and Johannine usage; and (c) it has no similarity, to my knowledge, to the usage either of Qumran and the rabbis or of subsequent Christian writers in the Epistles and Acts. The other three uses—to allude, to confirm, and to argue—are so common both before and after that one must at least ask if this is not a point to be added to those listed by Joachim Jeremias[6] at which we could be in touch with the *ipsissima vox*. That is not to say, any more than with the occurrences of the Son of man, that every one goes back to Jesus. The example peculiar to Matthew (21:16) must be suspect; and Matthew also seems to have added the introduction "Have you not read?" in 12:5 and 19:4. But the question presents itself whether this should not be included as one of the remembered forms of Jesus' teaching, like his distinctive use of *amēn*, which for his contemporaries marked off its originality and authority from that of their scribes.

CHAPTER 5

Jesus and Israel:
The Starting Point for
New Testament Christology

George B. Caird

The central problem for New Testament Christology, as it has been traditionally formulated, may be simply stated. What were the steps, what was the process, by which the church advanced, within a single generation, from memories of Jesus of Nazareth, whom his friends and followers had known as a person, outwardly at least like themselves, to a belief in a cosmic Christ, who might properly be worshiped alongside God the Creator without violence to an essential monotheism? Was the process a development, in which external influences were no more than a stimulus to the unfolding of that which was fully present in germ from the beginning? Or was it a mutation into a new species, a syncretism in which the external elements predominated over the meager contributions of historical memory?[1] In the history of scholarship from Wellhausen to the present day the initiative has lain with those who adopted the second view, the probability with those who, always somewhat defensively, adopted the first.

In this essay it will be argued, no doubt with the wisdom of hindsight, that this dichotomy need never have occurred, because it arose initially from a twofold error of method. First, it is an accepted principle of historical research that, in attempting to reconstruct a portion of the past out of fragmentary evidence, one should begin at the point where the evidence is least subject to doubt or conflicting interpretation. Thus, in the quest of the historical Baptist, one begins not with the Lukan nativity stories and speculations about John's relationship with Qumran, or with the evidence of the second and fourth Gospels, in which John appears merely as a forerunner of Jesus, but with the Q tradition of John's preaching. It must be admitted that, in the quest of the historical

George B. Caird is Professor of New Testament at the Queen's College, Oxford.

Jesus, the application of this principle has sometimes led to dubious conclusions. P.W. Schmiedel, for example, was attempting to follow this rule with his "foundation-pillars," texts to which he ascribed "absolute certainty," although his nine texts included several that subsequent research came to regard with more than common suspicion.[2] So too were the exponents of the "criterion of dissimilarity," which Morna D. Hooker has shown to be critically ill-conceived.[3] But such false starts do not invalidate the principle they were meant to exemplify.

The vast majority of books on New Testament Christology have started with a treatment of the titles by which Jesus came to be addressed or described. It is clear today, as it was apparently not clear to the great scholars of earlier generations, that each one of these titles is an area of maximum ambiguity.[4] To use these as a foundation is to build on sand. One must look for another starting point, which will make it possible either to reduce the range of ambiguity or otherwise to come to terms with it.

The second error in method has been pointed out recently by C.F.D. Moule: The formulation of the christological problem with which this essay began is only half the question, and the second half of it at that.[5] It treats Christology as though it were exclusively a question about Christ's relationship to God, that is, in traditional terms a question about his divinity. Moule has called our attention to the equally pressing and more fundamental question of Christ's relationship to humankind. In the first instance he regards this as a distinctively Pauline theme, on the ground that Paul alone explicitly formulates the concept of the corporate Christ in whose representative person all humankind has died and risen. But he goes on to argue that the same concept is implicitly present elsewhere in the belief that Christ's death is of universal significance. The notion that one person may die for another, that the death of one may atone for the sin of the other, is no Christian innovation or monopoly. But what must Jesus have been to justify the enormous confidence that his death had universal validity? What understanding of his own mission and person must we attribute to him if that confidence is to be anchored in historical reality?

It is inherent in Moule's case that the answer to the more familiar question about Christ's relationship to God was not sought by the early church independently of the answer to this other question about his relationship to humankind, and that the modern scholar will be wrong to look elsewhere for the origins of Christology.[6] A problem with Moule's thesis is that, like so many theologians of all schools and traditions who have accepted the humanity of Jesus as a dogma without firmly grasping it as a historical fact, he seems to be in too much of a hurry to progress from the particular to the universal.[7] This may be unfair to him, for when he finally comes to discuss in what senses Jesus may be said to fulfill the scriptures, he briefly hints at what seems to be the indispensable middle term between the two.

> Jesus, in an extraordinary way, turned out to be occupying the position that, according to the Scriptures, had always been intended for Israel, and, through Israel, for all mankind. . . . A widely shared and recognized experience had found in Christ that corporate sonship, that true Israel, indeed that Adam or renewed mankind, by belonging to which Christians found a right relation both to God and to one another as fellow-members of the People of God.[8]

It is this hint, already adumbrated in the work of Manson, Dodd, Munck, and Jeremias,[9] that will be pursued here. The belief in the solidarity of Jesus with all humanity is historically grounded in his solidarity with the Jewish people. The conviction that Jesus has taken away the sin of the world, enshrined as it is in scripture, hymn, and creed, is prima facie a concept so difficult that it is hardly surprising if millions of our contemporaries find it incredible. The hypothesis that Jesus, being a Jew, felt himself to be so implicated in the history and destiny of his people, so identified even with those from whose attitudes he profoundly dissented, that he could not but suffer for their sins—this is at least historically manageable. Could it be, then, that here is the secure starting point from which all christological deliberations ought to proceed?

Before the evidence is examined, let it be noted that this proposal has two advantages to commend it. The first is, as I have tried to show elsewhere,[10] that it makes the career of Jesus psychologically credible. This point may be illustrated by the problems raised in the history of doctrine about his baptism. Already in the first century, Christians were asking why, if Jesus was the sinless Son of God, he needed to undergo a baptism of repentance (Matthew 3:14-15). The solution offered by traditional orthodoxy is that Jesus, knowing himself to be without sin, identified himself with sinful humankind, thus establishing a solidarity where none existed before. But that is a docetic view of Jesus that severs his links with the particularities of history. Jesus had no need to create a new solidarity, but only to accept one which already existed in his membership of Israel. Provided that one starts from the evidence of Q, one may affirm that John's baptism was not a summons to all humankind to repent under threat of that final judgment which would bring the world to an end. It was a manifesto to Israel, calling the Israelites to repent of their national sins in face of a coming judgment that might well be the the end of Israel, for it would decide who was and who was not a true child of Abraham, with the grim possibility that, for lack of true native sons and daughters, God might be compelled by the nation's intransigence to raise up children to Abraham from the stones of the wilderness. How could faithful Israelites like Jesus do other than identify themselves with a national movement of renewal?

The second advantage of this approach is that it enables one to start where in any case Jesus' own contemporaries must have started. He did come into an environment in which there was already much debate about what it meant for Israel to be God's holy people. His distinctive contribution to this debate was the proclamation that the kingdom of God had arrived (or was imminent). Now amid all the uncertainties that adhere to that phrase one thing is certain: to a Jew the sovereignty of God was inconceivable apart from its corollary, Israel. It was bound to be understood either as God's sovereignty over Israel or as God's sovereignty exercised through Israel over the world—or, most probably, as both.[11] Whatever modifications Jesus may have introduced into the traditional Jewish ideas about God's sovereign rule, there is not a shadow of reason to suppose that he departed from them at this one cardinal point. Indeed, there are strong indications to the contrary.

Some of the evidence lies in plain view on the surface. Matthew, whose Gospel reaches its climax in the apostolic commission to make all nations disciples of Jesus, nevertheless retains and even emphasizes the tradition that during his earthly ministry Jesus sent his disciples, and believed himself to be sent, only to the lost sheep of the house of Israel (Matthew 10:5-6; 15:24).[12] Luke, the one contributor to the New Testament whom we know to have been a gentile, in spite of his obvious interest in the gentile mission, begins his Gospel with a group of pious Jews "looking for the consolation of Israel [2:25, RSV]," "looking for the redemption of Jerusalem [2:38, RSV]," and ends it with Jesus reassuring Cleopas and his companion that they had not been mistaken in hoping "that he was the one to liberate Israel [24:21, RSV]," and his second volume opens with a question from the disciples about the restoration of sovereignty to Israel, which elicits from Jesus a gentle rebuke to their impatience, but not to the assumptions underlying their question (Acts 1:6-8). The first letter of Peter, directed to predominantly if not wholly gentile congregations (1:14, 18), is addressed to "the exiles of the Dispersion [1:1, RSV]."[13] John the seer has a vision of "a great multitude, from every nation, from all tribes and peoples, and tongues [RSV]," but he hears them enumerated in the heavenly roll call as twelve thousand from each of the tribes of Israel (Revelation 7:1-9). Paul, the apostle to the gentiles, who devoted much of his ministry to the cause of gentile equality with Jews, and ultimately sacrificed both liberty and life to this very cause, is nevertheless quite clear that the gospel is "for the Jew first, but also for the Gentile [Rom. 1:16]," and that gentile converts are like branches from a wild olive grafted on to a Jewish stock (Romans 11:16-18). And the letter to the Ephesians, which, be it by Paul or by another, is the most explicitly universalist book in the New Testament, assures gentile Christians that they, who were once "separated from Christ, alienated from the commonwealth of Israel, and strangers to the covenants of promise," have now become "fellow citizens with the saints" (Ephesians 2:12, 19, RSV).

But behind all this there is more striking, and at the same time more directly christological, evidence to be found in what the New Testament writers betray, quite incidentally to the exposition of their theme, about their underlying traditions or assumptions. Dodd has brilliantly demonstrated how, by isolating the theological preoccupations of the evangelist, it is possible to identify within the fourth Gospel a pre-Johannine tradition about Jesus that is markedly more political in tone than anything that can be detected in the synoptic Gospels.[14] The same technique may be adapted to reveal other characteristics of the pre-Johannine tradition. One of the most obvious characteristics of Johannine theology is that the mission of Jesus is from start to finish directed at the world: It is the world, created by God, yet resistant to God's purpose, that is the object of God's redemptive love, and Jesus is presented throughout as the Savior of the world, and his death as at one and the same time the world's judgment and salvation. The evangelist is of course aware that in the historical drama being presented the part of the world was played by Jewish actors, but the severity with which he depicts them has in it no anti-Semitism, since they are to him only the local embodiment of that dark world which could not be saved except by the death of God's son. But beneath his universalism he allows us access to an earlier stratum of belief in which the universal was as yet implicit in the particular; it was the divine purpose, of which Caiaphas in virtue of his office became the unwitting prophet, that Jesus should die for the Jewish people rather than allow the whole nation to be destroyed. And if subsequently his death should be seen to have a wider validity, it was because in the first instance he had surrendered his life for his own people (John 11:50-51).

The Pauline letters contain overt statements about Jewish priority, but there are also more subtle hints that this priority lay at the roots of Paul's christological thinking. When Paul sets out to prove to the Galatians that gentiles can enjoy parity with Jews "in Christ," it is not enough for him to prove that "in Christ Jesus you are all sons of God [Gal. 3:26, RSV]"; he must first prove that they are sons of Abraham (3:7). Moreover, when the argument has reached its climax in the

62

declaration that in Christ "there is neither Jew nor Greek [3:28, RSV]," Paul says that "when the time had fully come, God sent forth his Son, born of woman, born under the law, to redeem those who were under the law, so that people might receive adoption as sons [4:4, RSV]." This apparent limitation of the scope of redemption is the more remarkable in that those to whom the letter is addressed were gentiles who had previously been "in bondage to beings that by nature are no gods [4:8, RSV]." It is evident that in Paul's thinking the theological affirmation of Christ's solidarity with all humankind rests on the historical fact of his solidarity with his Jewish compatriots.

The same point emerges in quite a different fashion when Paul comes to restate this argument in his letter to Rome. The central part of this letter is a comparison and contrast between Adam and Christ. Superficially it might appear that the possibility of Christ's solidarity with all humankind in a new humanity is being established directly and solely on the ground of the empirical fact of solidarity of all humankind in Adam. Adam is not merely the first man; he is also Everyman and he is the whole human race. To be in Adam is indeed to inherit the effects of the "first disobedience," but it is also to do as Adam did,[15] and it is to be implicated in the corporate life of that worldwide entity, the human race, of which the first Adam was the eponymous founder.[16] Thus Adam is "a type of the one who was to come [5:14, RSV]" in that he provides a full pattern of relationship between the one and the many. Yet when one looks below the surface, Paul's history of humankind turns out to be a Jewish history. Whether he looks at it as the history of "our old self [Rom. 6:6]," in which the one significant event between Adam and Christ is the giving of the law, or as the history of grace and salvation, in which the emphasis is shifted from the law to the call of Abraham, he takes his outline from the Old Testament, and it never occurs to him that the gentile nations should be allowed to have any independent history of their own. This fact is all the more impressive because in Romans 5—7 it is no part of Paul's purpose to argue that possession of the law puts the Jew in a different category from the gentile. In a sinful world the only effect the law could have was to multiply the original transgression of Adam and make it universal wherever law held sway (5:20). The law was intended to control and restrain, but not to alter the sinful status of its adherents; and in the practical experience of those adherents, it had actually been used by sin to foment the very offenses it forbade (7:7-12). Only when the Old Testament was read as a book of grace and promise, as "the oracles of God," was there any advantage in being a Jew (3:2). Thus by a different route one arrives at the same conclusion that Christ's qualification for being the head of a new humanity lay in his total identification with not merely Adam but also a very Jewish Adam.

The qualifications that entitled Jesus to be the pioneer of salvation for all humankind are discussed also in the opening section of the letter to the Hebrews. Jesus,[17] the son in whom God has at last spoken, was appointed by God to be heir to the whole universe (1:1-2), and into this inheritance he has now entered in consequence of his atoning death and subsequent exaltation (1:4). His appointment is adumbrated in the Old Testament in a series of passages that assign to him a dignity beyond that of any angel (1:5-13), including the angels through whom the law was given (2:2), since those angels were no more than "ministering spirits sent forth to serve, for the sake of those who are to obtain salvation [1:14, RSV]." The true significance of Christ's appointment can, however, best be seen through the study of Psalm 8, according to which, as Paul expounds it on the basis of the Septuagint text, humankind was destined by God to live "for a little while" lower than (subject to) the angels of the old order, but subsequently to be crowned with glory and honor, with all things under human authority (2:5-8). But it was in keeping with God's eternal plan that this human destiny should be fulfilled in the first instance by Jesus, and that only in association with him should the many sons and daughters be brought to the glory spoken of in the psalm (2:9).

In this brief summary of the argument, it has been assumed, along with the great majority of commentators and translators, that the author took Psalm 8, as any modern reader would, to be a psalm about humanity. Recently, under the influence of C. Spicq, a new school of thought has arisen, according to which the author took the psalm to be "messianic" and therefore a direct prophecy of Christ. This view can be maintained only at the cost of some violence to the syntax. But even if it were correct, it would not greatly modify the sense, for nothing can alter the fact that the person referred to in the psalm is in it designated "man." But to say that the psalm is a psalm about Christ qua human being is not very different from saying that it is a psalm about human destiny, now fulfilled by Christ.

It is interesting to note in passing that exactly the same point may be made about each of the uses of this psalm by Paul. In 1 Corinthians 15:25-27, for example, it would be correct to say that the psalm is applied directly and messianically to Christ: "He must reign until he has put all his enemies under his feet. The last enemy to be destroyed is death. 'For God has put all things in subjection under his feet [RSV].' " But this passage is part of a continuous argument in which Adam and Christ are contrasted, and it follows hard on the statement that "for as by a man came death, by a man has come also the resurrection of the dead [15:21, RSV]." In other words, Paul can properly apply the psalm to Christ because he sees Christ as "the last Adam" (15:45). "The first man was from the earth, a man of dust; the second man is from heaven. As was the man of dust, so are those who are of the dust; and as is the man of heaven, so are those who are of heaven. Just as we have borne the image of the man of dust, we shall also bear the image of the man of heaven [15:47-49, RSV]."

On either theory of the exegesis of Hebrews 2:9-10, therefore, Christ is seen as a representative figure, and the unique place that he holds in the eternal purpose of God is seen in relation to the destiny of all humankind. "For he who sanctifies and those who are sanctified have all one origin. That is why he is not ashamed to call them brethren [2:11, RSV]." Thus up to this point in this letter one is clearly dealing with the same problem of the one and the many that has already been confronted in the letters of Paul. Nor is there even the slightest doubt that the author is thinking in universal terms. The initial statement that Jesus was appointed heir to the whole universe (*panton*) is picked up in the "all things" (*panta*) of the psalm and in the author's somewhat pedantic footnote that "everything" means exactly what it says, neither more nor less (2:8). In pursuance of his goal, Jesus tasted death "for everyone." It comes, therefore, as a surprise when a few verses later the author introduces between Jesus and all people, between the one and the many, an intermediate term: "It is not with angels that he is concerned but with the descendants of Abraham [2:16, RSV]." Nowhere in the letter is this theme further developed. It appears to be almost as much of an aside as the reference to the devil in the previous sentence. Certainly the author gives no sign of being aware of the Pauline thesis that Christ is "the offspring of Abraham" mentioned in God's promise (Galatians 3:16; cf. Genesis 12:7). He appears instead to be quoting from a different source: "But you, Israel, my servant, Jacob, whom I have chosen, the offspring of Abraham, my friend; you whom I took from the ends of the earth, and called from its farthest corners [Isa. 1:8-9, RSV]." He is assuming that the appointment of Jesus to be pioneer (*archegos*) of a universal salvation is entailed in and deducible from his relationship with Israel.

This assumption, then, is shared by Paul, John, and the author of Hebrews, and in the light of what has been called the surface evidence it is vastly improbable that in this respect the two later authors were dependent on the earlier. This line of christological thought must have been pre-Pauline. At first glance this inference may not seem very startling, for it might be supposed that anyone who read the book of Genesis as a unity would naturally understand the call of Abraham to be God's way of dealing with the predicament of humankind illustrated in the previous chapters and therefore to be for the benefit of all humankind. But this is not the way Jewish readers were accustomed to

65

interpret the scriptures. The author of 2 Esdras, for example, who starts like Paul from Adam and the evil seed sown in his heart (4:30), draws from the sequence of events in the Old Testament conclusions that are particularist and exclusive:

> From every forest of the earth and from all its trees thou hast chosen one vine, and from all the lands of the world thou hast chosen for thyself one region, and from all the flowers of the world thou hast chosen for thyself one lily, and from all the depths of the sea thou hast filled for thyself one river, and from all the cities that have been built thou hast consecrated Zion for thyself, and from all the birds that have been created thou hast named for thyself one dove, and from all the flocks that have been made thou hast provided for thyself one sheep [5:23-26, RSV].

Against deep-rooted convictions of this sort, the point that our three New Testament theologians take for granted must have required a Copernican revolution in belief about Israel's place in the purposes of God. And it is this revolution that provides the appropriate context for the study of the ambiguities in the christological titles.

If approached in this way, one element in the ambiguity of the titles becomes apparent: of the six titles (Messiah, King of Israel, Son of David, Son of God, Son of man, and Lord), the first five either express or are capable of expressing precisely that identification with Israel which is assumed by Paul, John, and the author of Hebrews as the basis of their Christology. The first three are synonyms, each of which may be regarded as placing the holder of the title over against Israel as a ruler in whom divine authority is vested; and it is this aspect of their meaning which is relevant to questions about the relation of Jesus to God. But it is characteristic of ancient ideas of kingship that from a different point of view the king *is* the nation, since its national identity is summed up in his representative person. Nation and king are to this extent interchangeable, that the functions of the one may be fulfilled by the other and texts applicable to the one may be transferred to the other. Thus in Daniel 7 the four beasts are symbols alternately of empires and of kings, and it is hardly surprising if the "one like a son of man" should have been given just such a dual interpretation. In Isaiah 55:3-5 the prophet takes it for granted that the royal covenant with David can be transferred to the nation at large. Son of God is a title that can be applied to the king (2 Samuel 7:14; Psalm 2:7), but also to the nation (Exodus 4:22; Hosea 11:1). And the three possible theories about the term "Son of man" are that it was a periphrastic self-reference used by Jesus, that it meant "man" as in Psalm 8, and that it was derived from Daniel 7, where it stood for Israel.

The New Testament provides ample evidence that these ambiguities were thoroughly explored within the early church. The theme of the one son and the many sons appears not only in Paul, John, and Hebrews, but in the synoptic tradition. The Synoptists all understand Son of man as a self-reference, but they also associate it with Daniel 7 (e.g., Mark 14:62), as do John (5:27) and the author of Revelation (1:13). Paul and the author of Hebrews both, as has been seen, interpret it as a reference to Psalm 8. But if one grants that it was feasible for the early church to advance its theological thinking by exploring the fruitful possibilities of ambiguity, there can be no a priori reason to deny that Jesus could have done the same.

The whole case of those who have argued for a discontinuity between the teaching of Jesus and the theology of the early church is based on the premise that the christological titles must have had a single clearly defined sense, so that if they meant one thing they could not at the same time mean another. But in face of the irrefutable evidence that the early church explored in a creative fashion the ambiguities of these terms, this premise looks extraordinarily thin. Why could not Jesus have used "son of man" as a periphrastic self-reference and have chosen this form of self-designation precisely because of its associative links with Daniel 7 and Psalm 8?

Because we have been so long accustomed to the notion that if Jesus did indeed have anything to say about his own person it must have been couched in the form of a dogmatic claim to a status of well-defined authority, it is difficult to adjust to any other view of him. Yet a great deal of his teaching is presented in the form of a question. It has been said of the episode of Caesarea Philippi that the question is more significant than the answers, since Jesus is not only aware that he poses a problem to his contemporaries, but considers it right that he should do so. However, it may equally be said that the episode exemplifies Jesus' most characteristic method of instruction by the posing of a question. Even the pronouncements of the so-called pronouncement stories notoriously leave questions still to be asked ("Pay Caesar what is Caesar's and God what is God's"). There is in particular one passage in the Gospels which portrays Jesus engaging in exactly the kind of exploration of amibiguity that has here been suggested might be attributed to him. "How can the scribes say that the Christ is the son of David? . . . David himself calls him Lord; so how is he his son? [Mark 12:35-37, RSV]." The unanimous attestation of the New Testament that Jesus was the promised Messiah of David's line does not allow one to conclude that Jesus was denying (or that Mark thought he was denying) the equation; he did not need to be told that the scribes had ample scriptural authority for the teaching he ascribed to them. What he was suggesting is that Messiah is an equivocal term and that the traditional equation did not exhaust its significance. It is, moreover, of importance that here, as so frequently elsewhere, the teaching of Jesus is couched in the form of a question.

All this points strongly to the hypothesis that the earliest christological thinking of the church had its origin in the ways in which Jesus thought and spoke about himself and that, however deeply he may have pondered the further implications of his mission, his starting point was his own relationship to the people of which he was born a member. It was precisely as the person appointed by God to be the fulfillment of Israel's destiny that he came also to be recognized, first as the fulfiller of the destiny of humankind, and in consequence as the bearer of a more than human authority and the embodiment of a more than human wisdom.

PART II
Christological Perspectives in the New Testament

CHAPTER 6

The Christological Foundation
of Early Christian Parenesis

Ferdinand Hahn
(Translated by Harvey K. McArthur)

In a number of works, Martin Dibelius has demonstrated the distinctive character of the early Christian parenesis. Above all, his *Die Formgeschichte des Evangeliums* and his commentary on the letter of James marked out the right directions.[1] Even before Dibelius the significance of the structured catechetical tradition had been proved by Alfred Seeberg.[2] Later, further meaningful insights were achieved by C.H. Dodd,[3] E.G. Selwyn,[4] and others. In addition there have been numerous special studies of the parenetic patterns in the household codes,[5] the lists of virtues and vices,[6] and the teaching on the two ways,[7] and also studies of individual injunctions within the parenetic materials.[8]

Parenesis was intended for the instruction of the Christian community rather than for its missionary activity. As the letter of James makes clear, the responsibility for maintaining and transmitting this material was entrusted to the early Christian teachers.[9] Parenesis was intended to help Christians lead a life consistent with their faith. It was everywhere taken for granted that this parenesis was directed to people who already belonged to the Christian community.[10]

The development of parenesis took place in two ways. On the one hand, sayings attributed to Jesus were adapted for the instruction of Christians,[11] as is illustrated by the Sermon on the Mount in Matthew's Gospel.[12] On the other hand, parenetic materials from numerous other traditions were brought together, arranged under various headings, and then transmitted for the use and guidance of Christian communities. This is clearly indicated by the hortatory sections of the New Testament letters.[13] This study concerns itself exclusively with the parenetic materials in the letters of early Christianity.

Ferdinand Hahn is Professor of New Testament at The University of Munich.

The most obvious characteristic of this parenesis is that it was derived from a wide variety of sources.[14] Pagan, Jewish, and Christian items were brought together and transformed into a new unity.

A second characteristic of this material is that in the process of revision and transformation a specifically Christian element played a decisive role, namely, the love commandment as it had been proclaimed and interpreted in the message of Jesus.[15]

A third characteristic may be added. The parenetic tradition was structured somewhat loosely but nevertheless according to certain regular topics that form a relatively constant pattern.[16] It was addressed to baptized persons, it was intended for the preservation of faith and love in the concrete affairs of daily life, and it contained a reminder of the coming eschatological fulfillment. This pattern appeared in widely varied forms.[17]

A fourth hallmark of the parenetic tradition is its general character. To use the formulation of Martin Dibelius, it is *"usuelle" parenesis*. This means that the teaching was not normally directed toward specific issues in the life of a given congregation but was intended to provide guidance and orientation more generally for the appropriate behavior of Christians. However, parenetic teaching directed toward a specific situation (*"aktuelle" parenesis*) is presented in Paul's first letter to the Corinthians and in Philemon.[18]

Finally, it is appropriate to point out that this parenesis is completely without legalistic character. If we use typical New Testament language instead of literary classifications, this parenesis is exhortation (*paraclēsis*) in the sense of encouragement and admonition. And it is admonition that is tied firmly to the gospel message while at the same time expressing the freedom of responsible Christian behavior.[19]

What has just been said provides an indication of the site of tradition, where this parenesis was used and from which it came. It did not come from the Jewish-Christian sector, where Torah continued to play a decisive role and the words of Jesus were understood as an interpretation of Old Testament law.[20] Rather, this type of parenetic instruction came from a sector of early Christianity characterized by the freedom from the law that was expressed in the Antiochian mission to non-Jews and especially by the agreement reached by Paul at the apostolic council of Galatians 2 and Acts 15.[21] This created the need for a distinctive starting-point for the patterning of Christian life. In view of the commitment to proclaim the gospel to all people, it was only natural that regulations from pagan traditions would be added to those from the Old Testament and contemporary Jewish life.[22]

It is in connection with the general (*usuelle*) parenesis that it is often said the Christianization of the borrowed materials can be recognized at the most in the introductions, while only in the later writings were Christian elements worked more thoroughly into the materials.[23] That is undoubtedly correct, especially when one observes the extensive penetration of the later materials with Christian theological motifs. This is most clearly visible in the deutero-Pauline letter to the Ephesians. Yet it cannot be doubted that from the very beginning Christian presuppositions dominated when non-Christian materials were appropriated. This is particularly evident where the christological foundation of the parenesis is at issue.[24]

Already the framework and basic pattern of the early Christian parenesis makes this point clear. Thus, where there is reference to baptism,[25] it is always baptism "in Jesus' name," with stress on the participation in the salvation effected by Jesus. This is true, however the work of Jesus—or the effect of baptism—is understood in detail. Correspondingly, not only is the central position of the love commandment of a remembrance and reception of Jesus' own message, but also the behavior of believers is seen in the closest connection with the actual person and career of Jesus and its manifestation of the loving activity of God.[26] Furthermore, the eschatological conclusions include the expectation of the end fulfillment, and especially the return of the Lord. This is understood even when it is not explicitly stated.[27] Even the letter of James, which is so limited in its christological references, has remarkable stress on this motif.[28]

It is interesting to note that originally the primitive Christian parenesis was closely linked with Jesus' proclamation of the kingdom. This is apparent from the relatively widespread motif of inheriting the kingdom of God as in Galatians 5:21 and 1 Corinthians 6:9-10, as well as in James 2:5. In Ephesians 5:5 this motif is expanded to include an explicit christological reference, "inheritance in the kingdom of Christ and of God." Furthermore, the use of the kingdom of God concept in Romans 14:17 and 1 Corinthians 4:20 points toward this connection, though Paul seldom uses this language.[29] In those two passages, unlike Galatians 5:21 and 1 Corinthians 6:9-10, the present aspect of the kingdom is stressed.

In this connection the question must be raised about the relevance of the words of Jesus in parenesis. The love commandment, used in the interpretation and application of Jesus' teaching, is firmly rooted in his announcement of the breaking in of God's reign.[30] The love commandment is the sole basis for the individual instructions of the early

Christian parenesis. All specific statements function as expressions of this commandment. This is true even where commands from the decalogue are introduced.[31] It is equally true, however, in passages in which other sayings of the Lord are presented. The latter, as is well known, are not introduced or emphasized. Instead, they stand alongside other instructions, whether those come from Old Testament, contemporary Jewish, or pagan sources. No special quality is attributed to them, since the traditional parenetic material as a whole is placed under the authority of Jesus, his proclamation of the kingdom, and the love commandment. However, it is only natural that occasionally the words of Jesus give the parenesis a distinctive profile.[32] Naturally, alongside these are regulations that are typically Christian.[33] Since some of the materials were derived from pre-Christian tradition, there was good reason for the call to test these materials to determine which were truly appropriate in the context of believers' lifestyle (1 Thessalonians 5:21; Philippians 4:8-9; Romans 12:2b). Furthermore, they were urged to keep in mind specifically Christian instructions (1 Thessalonians 4:1-2; 1 Corinthians 4:16-17; Philippians 4:9). Special attention was called to the contrast between Christian and other—especially pagan—lifestyles (1 Thessalonians 4:5).[34]

As already noted, the parenetic instructions lacked any legalistic character, so both in Paul and in the letter of James there is reference to freedom.[35] While the individual injunctions do not attempt a casuistic regulation of life, it is equally true that they do not leave the decision over behavior simply free. Alongside the basic love commandment are indicated outside boundaries and points for general orientation that are to be observed.[36] But these do not take away from the individual believer, or the local congregation, responsibility for specific decisions; rather, they are intended to assist them in coming to the appropriate decision. In this context there appears the admonition to seek unanimity (Romans 12:16; Philippians 2:2; 4:2), but above all there is an appeal to the work of the Holy Spirit. The reference in James 4:5 to "the Spirit which he has made to dwell in us" is just as significant as the mention of the Spirit in 1 Peter 4:14, or in the numerous Pauline texts (1 Thessalonians 4:8; 5:19; Galatians 5:16, 17, 22-23, 25; Romans 12:11) or in Ephesians 4:3-4, 23, 30; 5:18. "Walking in the Spirit" is precisely the motif that binds together baptism and parenesis (Galatians 5:16; Romans 6:4; 7:6; 8:4-11).

The references to the words of the Lord and to the proclamation of the kingdom do not of themselves develop an explicit christological position. And in the majority of cases the appeal to the Spirit is an appeal to the Spirit of God, although in early Christianity it was assumed that this was mediated through Christ (Acts 2:33).[37] The christological basis is more clearly indicated when the parenesis is set in a framework involving the return of the Lord.[38] In such cases it is assumed that Christ appears as the judge or, at the very least, that he has a decisive function in connection with God's judgment.

However, in this christological basis for the parenesis the reference is not exclusively to the future; instead, the returning Christ is the present Lord to whom the addressed members of the congregation belong and in whose fellowship they live. Therefore it is no accident that in parenetic texts there occurs frequently the expression "in the Lord"[39] or "in Christ." The close juxtaposition of this formula with the statement "the Lord is near" in Philippians 4:4, 5 is as striking as the phrase "my ways in Christ" in 1 Corinthians 4:17 for the Pauline parenesis.

In the household code of Colossians 3:18—4:1 the phrase "in the Lord" appears in a highly significant fashion with a double reference.[40] On the one hand, the traditional "as is fitting" or "as is acceptable" —borrowed from Hellenistic ethic—is linked with "in the Lord" (Colossians 3:18, 20). This identifies a way of life that can be followed only in fellowship with Christ and with other Christians. This is true even when the behavior involved can scarcely be distinguished from similar behavior in Jewish or pagan circles. On the other hand, this demand is connected with the summons to serve the Lord Christ (3:24),[41] while at the same time there is emphasis on the role of Christ as Judge in the phrase "knowing that you also have a Master in heaven [4:1, RSV]." Thus, in this relatively early household code[42] there is provided a basic model for the christological foundation of parenesis in early Christianity.

Such passages as 1 Thessalonians 4:1-2 or 1 Corinthians 4:16-17 demonstrate that for Paul the christological foundation for all parenesis is a self-evident presupposition. The same is true, though in a different way, for the Epistle of James.[43] Still, it was not until the deutero-Paulines and 1 Peter that the christological motif in the parenesis was more fully developed. Passages such as Ephesians 5:1-2, 8, 14, and 1 Peter 2:22-25; 3:18-22 make this tendency entirely clear.

Special reference needs to be made to the passages that form a transition to the parenetic sections of New Testament letters. Admittedly, these transitions were created by the authors of the letters, but they contain so many motifs in common that they must have been borrowing from an already established complex of motifs. The major parenetic section in 1 Peter is found in 2:11—4:11. The author prepared the way for this parenesis with an introductory passage consisting of 1:13—2:10. In this introduction, 1:18-21 provides an extended christological base, while 2:4-10 provides the ecclesiological base.[44] The remaining sections of the introduction, 1:13-17 and 1:22—2:3, deal with the contrast between the old and the new, the theme of holiness and rebirth through baptism which enables and demands a renewed life.[45] One discovers

75

precisely the same basic motives when one compares with 1 Peter not only 1 Thessalonians 4:3-7 and Romans 12:1-2, but also Hebrews 10:19-25 and 12:12-17.[46] The same situation is discovered when one examines also Colossians 3:5-9, 10-15, and Ephesians 5:21-33. This cannot be developed in detail here, but a few observations may be made about Ephesians 5:21, 22-33, since nowhere is the christological foundation of early Christian parenesis so extensively and forcefully displayed as in this passage.

The author of the letter to the Ephesians has provided the parenetic section of his letter, which consists of the last three chapters, with a clear theological framework. He exhorts his readers to walk in a manner worthy of their calling and to live in unity (4:1-6), and he combines this with references to the gifts of the Spirit and an appeal to build up the body of Christ (4:7-16).[47] Then follows what is more strictly the introduction to the parenetic section, in which the pagan and Christian lifestyles are contrasted in terms of the old and the new humanity (4:17-24).[48] The exhortation concludes with an appeal to put on the "spiritual armor" that is the prerequisite for the Christian life (6:10-20).[49] The core of the extended parenesis is shot through with specifically Christian motivations, which are evident especially in 4:32, 5:1-2, 5:(8b-)14, and 6:5-8.[50] But nowhere in all the parenetic traditions of the early Christians is the explicitly theological argumentation so much in the foreground as in 5:21, 22-33, where the household code from Colossians 3:18—4:1 has been taken over and reworked.[51]

The first section of the three-part household code (5:22-33; 6:1-4; 6:5-9) was built up by the author in connection with the christological-ecclesiological motif of the first major section of the letter.[52] Here he argues in two different ways: the argument from analogy, and the argument from the role of Christ as founder of the church. The two arguments are intertwined, but in substance they are distinct. The position of the husband as "head" of the wife parallels the position of Christ as "head" of the church (v. 23a, 23b),[53] and in similar fashion the subordination of the wife parallels the subordination of the church (v. 24a, 24b). The same may be said for the love of the husband for his wife and the love of Christ for his church (v. 25a, 25b).[54] But another dimension is introduced into these parallels when it is said that Christ is himself the Savior of the body (v. 23)[55] and that he "gave himself up for her, that he might sanctify her . . ." (v. 25-27).[56] Here is expressed the presupposition on the basis of which the parallel is at all possible, namely, Christ's saving function and act; here also is identified the sphere within which the exhortations to the individual believers are to be realized. This is possible only in the church as the sphere of salvation within the still existing world. Therefore Christ is referred to already in verse 23 as the Savior of "the body," and verse 25 says he gave himself up "for her," that is, for the church.

The statement in verse 28, "Even so husbands should love their wives as their own bodies," refers back over verses 25b-27 to verse 25a: "as Christ loved the church" (cf. v. 29). But the author is not content with the reference to the soteriological function of Christ and the relation of the marriage partners to the church. He is concerned with the unity in the marriage and in the salvific sphere of Christ's body. Again he proceeds from a parallel. As the baptized (v. 26) are members of Christ's body (v. 30), so the wife belongs to her husband and in this sense is his "own body" (v. 28).[57] Thus, in employing the commandment to love the other "as oneself," it is appropriate to speak of the love for the wife as love for "himself" and "his own body" or "his own flesh" (v. 28-29).[58]

From this perspective it is understandable that for the author the traditional motif of the social subordination of the wife to her husband is no longer valid in the sphere of the body of Christ.[59] Thus it is that in the preliminary statement before the beginning of the household code it commands, "Be subject to one another out of reverence for Christ [v. 21, RSV].[60] And in substance the same emphasis occurs again at the end of the passage (v. 33). For the "respect" or "reverence" of the wife for her husband is, just like the "respect" or "reverence" for Christ, nothing other than the expression of a relation of reciprocal love.[61]

Yet the chain of thought is still not complete. Once the code word "flesh" has been utilized as a synonym for "body" (v. 28, 29),[62] the author is in a position to use the quotation from Genesis 2:24. That the partners in a marriage "become one flesh" has a meaning not solely for nature and creaturehood. It is not simply an anthropological statement. Rather, this text about human marriage finds its completion first in connection with the unity of the head and the body of the church —therefore the reference to its character as a "mystery" (v. 32).[63] The unity experienced in human marriage in the sphere of Christian faith becomes the expression for the unity within the church as the sphere of salvation made available through Christ. Thus it becomes a visible witness to the reality of the new humanity through identification with Christ as Savior and in the participation in the company of those who believe in him.[64]

The far-reaching interpretation in this specific text of Ephesians 5:22-33 in comparison with the oldest parenetic tradition is astonishing. Nevertheless, it cannot be regarded as anything exceptional. It simply develops what from the beginning was implicit, and at least sometimes partly explicit, in Christian parenesis as exhortation for a life in faith and responsibility. There never existed in early Christianity a parenesis that was not linked with the message of the gospel and with a christological foundation.

Christological Perspectives in the Predicates of the Johannine *Egō Eimi* Sayings

Harvey K. McArthur

A distinctive feature of the Gospel of John is the repeated occurrence of *egō eimi* ("I am") phrases. This phenomenon is more striking in Greek than in English, since in classical and Koine Greek the first-person singular is indicated by the form of the verb, and the *egō* is unnecessary unless some special emphasis is intended. Admittedly there are occurrences of *egō* in Greek literature where only the most doctrinaire interpreter could insist that some special emphasis is intended. But even when allowance has been made for these deviations from the rule, the frequency of the *egō eimi* combination in John as over against Greek literature in general and the other Gospels in particular constitutes a notable phenomenon.[1] The distinctiveness of the Johannine usage is clearly demonstrated by the statistics. Passages where the word order is reversed or words intervene between the *egō* and the *eimi* are not included in the following figures:[2]

Total N.T.	4th Gospel	Apocalypse	Joh. Ep.	Matthew
47	24	4	0	5

Mark	Luke	Acts	Rest of N.T.
3	4	7	0

The truly significant occurrences of *egō eimi* phrases fall into two categories:[3] (a) Those without any expressed predicates: 6:20; 8:24, 28, 58; 13:19; 18:5, 6, 8; and (b) those with expressed predicates: 6:35, 41, 48, 51; 8:12; 10:7, 9, 11, 14; 11:25; 14:6; 15:1, 5.

There are three major theories concerning the occurrences of *egō eimi* without expressed predicates. (1) Some scholars hold that they reflect a colloquial Greek idiom in which *egō eimi* is the equivalent of "It is I" or "I am he" or the like. Clearly this is an appropriate interpretation in

John 9:9, where the man formerly blind insists that he is indeed that person, saying *egō eimi*, "I am he." Some of the occurrences of this same phrase on the lips of the Johannine Jesus are obvious parallels to this usage, for example, 6:20 and 18:5, 6, 8. But those who take this position affirm that all occurrences of *egō eimi* without expressed predicates fall into this category and that in every case a predicate is implied by either the immediate context or general context.[4] (2) Many modern scholars are not satisfied with this solution and, while conceding that some passages without expressed predicates are correctly interpreted as involving implied predicates, insist that in at least some instances these passages follow a pattern derived from the Hebrew scriptures, their translation into Greek, and the continuing Jewish usage. According to this view, some of these passages—most frequently at least John 8:58 and 13:19—constitute a divine self-revelation on the part of Jesus. (There continues to be a dispute as to which passages in the Hebrew scriptures gave rise to this theophanic usage.)[5] (3) A third position is that some of these passages may intend to reflect a divine self-revelation on the part of Jesus but that this usage is derived not specifically from Hebrew-Jewish models but rather from a more widespread Eastern and Hellenistic style.[6]

I am personally persuaded by the arguments advanced in support of the theory that some of the *egō eimi* passages without predicates do indeed reflect Hebrew-Jewish usage, and that in these passages the evangelist understands the statements to imply a self-revelation of deity on the part of Jesus. Certainly some of the passages may reflect the colloquial usage and equal "I am he" or the like, for example, 6:20 and 18:5, 6, 8. The situation is complicated by the possibility that the Johannine author, with his demonstrated love for double meanings, may sometimes be deliberately ambiguous.[7] Thus, in chapter 18, when the soldiers come asking for Jesus of Nazareth, he says to them *egō eimi*. In the context the initial meaning must be simply "I am he." But when the evangelist reports that the soldiers then fell to the ground before him it is legitimate to ask whether the phrase does not carry some more impressive force. For me the decisive considerations supporting the thesis that some of the absolute *egō eimi* passages are theophanic following a Hebrew-Jewish pattern are: the absence of plausible implied predicates (especially in 8:58 and 13:19); the absence of clear examples of the absolute *egō eimi* in Hellenistic or Gnostic literature (although these literatures include *egō eimi* sayings with predicates); the evidence of the Hebrew scriptures, the Septuagint, and later rabbinic literature that Yahweh was identified in this code language.[8]

A decision concerning the background of the absolute *egō eimi* in John does not automatically resolve the more complex issue of the provenance of the phrases with *egō eimi* plus predicate. This latter question involves the larger problem of the provenance of the Johannine discourses. This issue and others connected with the *egō eimi* plus predicate phrases will be considered in the subsequent sections as follows:

1. Provenance: The background of the Johannine discourses and the *egō eimi* phrases with predicates.
2. Historicity: Are the *egō eimi* sayings with predicates actual sayings of Jesus?
3. The actual texts: What observations may be made about the seven (thirteen) texts taken as a group?
4. Contemporary appropriation: What is the continuing significance of these passages for the contemporary Christian community?

1. Provenance

In 1925 Rudolf Bultmann published an epochal article in which he argued that John's Gospel is fully intelligible only when it is recognized that behind its thought-world and terminology stands the mythology of gnosticism, more specifically the Mandaean form of gnosticism.[9] He was building on the research and translations of earlier scholars, but his article was the boldest and most massive argument for the Mandaean hypothesis,[10] and critics referred to what developed as the "Mandaean fever." Bultmann cited twenty-eight points at which there is an apparent parallel between Johannine and Mandaean passages. In each of these twenty-eight cases, he cited first verses from John's Gospel and then a series of statements from the Mandaean literature. In most cases these parallels were accompanied by still further parallels from the Odes of Solomon, the Acts of Thomas, or the Acts of John, and occasionally passages from other literature out of the early Christian period. The extant Mandaean literature is centuries later than John's Gospel, but Bultmann insisted that the Gospel had been dependent on an earlier form of that literature. He argued that the Johannine thought-world presupposed a mythological background but that the evangelist had moved out of and away from that mythology. In other words, the evangelist—or his community?—demythologized the myth and so must come after the myth. The eleventh of Bultmann's twenty-eight points dealt specifically with the *egō eimi* phrases with predicates, and there are Mandaean parallels such as "I am a shepherd," "I am a fisherman," "I am the ambassador of light," "I am the word of the first life," "I am the son of God whom the father has sent here." It should be added that while Bultmann stressed the Mandaean background of the fourth

81

Gospel he was quite aware that the evangelist utilized the terminology of that conceptual world for purposes in conflict with Mandaean thought.[11]

Almost anyone reading carefully through Bultmann's article will agree that there are numerous and striking parallels between John's Gospel and the Mandaean and related literature that Bultmann quotes. (However, if one reads the Mandaean literature itself, the overall impression is that its thought-world is strange and bizarre to one nurtured on the language of the fourth Gospel.) It is much more complicated to attempt an explanation of the observed similarities. The most obvious problem in the theory of Bultmann is that of chronology. The extant documents of the Mandaeans are from the sixteenth century, and while they clearly originated at some earlier period, they cannot have reached roughly their present form until the seventh or eighth century. This is demonstrated by the various allusions to the emergence and dominance of Islam. At that time the movement was concentrated in the Mesopotamian valley, where it continues to the present day as a small sect south of Baghdad. Yet the existence of the group may be traced back to the third and fourth centuries A.D. by coins and tablets. Furthermore, linguistic and other evidence indicates that while the group spent most of its time in the Mesopotamian valley, its origin was west of there in Syria, Palestine, and Transjordan. And Rudolph, in his major study of the Mandaeans (1960-61) concluded that Mandaeanism had its origin in the pre-Christian Syrian gnosis of West Aramaic culture.[12]

Unfortunately there is as yet no consensus on the origins of Mandaeanism or for that matter of gnosticism in general. Developed Gnostic systems emerged in the second century A.D. and were sharply attacked by such Christian leaders as Irenaeus, Tertullian, and Hippolytus. The movements were so diversified and widespread geographically in the second century that it is natural to assume they existed in some form in the preceding century or two. Irenaeus, indeed, appears to have regarded the Simon Magus of Acts 8 as the founder of the entire movement and as the leader of what is known later as the Simonian group, but it is possible that Christian apologists have confused the Simon of Acts 8 with a later figure by the same name. While recent discussions have not solved the problem of the origins of gnosticism, some terminological clarity has been achieved. Since the colloquium on gnosticism held at Messina, Italy, in 1966, there has been a growing tendency to restrict the term gnosticism to the full-fledged systems which may be documented from the second century, while "gnosis" is used more loosely to describe a wider variety of religious movements in which salvation is dependent upon "knowledge." Still more helpful terminologically is the distinction between "pre-Gnostic" and "proto-Gnostic." The former term is used to describe motifs or movements before the second century by those who insist that before that century there was no fully developed Gnostic system but only isolated motifs that were later organized into a system. But the latter term ("proto-Gnostic") is used by those who hold that even before the second century these motifs existed as part of developed systems. Those who follow in Bultmann's train use the term proto-Gnostic, since this makes more plausible the theory of Johannine dependence on a specifically Gnostic system. Unfortunately these distinctions do not of themselves solve any problems, but they do allow a more rational classification of various current views (although the line between pre-Gnostic and proto-Gnostic may be thin, and likewise the line between proto-Gnostic and gnosticism).

Over more recent decades substantial attacks have been launched against the position represented by Bultmann. In 1939 Ernst Percy published *Untersuchungen über den Ursprung der Johanneischen Theologie*,[13] in which he argued that the fourth Gospel was not dependent on Mandaean or Gnostic concepts, since the Johannine views on dualism, the Redeemer, and redemption are significantly different from those in Mandaeanism and gnosticism. He argued further that gnosticism developed out of early Christianity and that Mandaeanism was a late form of gnosticism. Subsequent discoveries and research have made it more difficult to argue that gnosticism developed out of Christianity. Furthermore, while there are clear differences between Johannine and Gnostic emphases, scholars are divided as to whether to stress the differences or the similarities. It is well known that a half-filled glass of water may be described either as half full or half empty.

C.H. Dodd's magisterial study *The Interpretation of the Fourth Gospel* (1953) discussed Mandaeanism, concluding that "alleged parallels drawn from this medieval body of literature have no value for the study of the fourth Gospel unless they can be supported by earlier evidence."[14] Dodd specifically rejected Bultmann's argument that the developed mythology evident in Mandaean literature must have preceded the simpler allusions in the fourth Gospel, though this did not entirely dispose of Bultmann's contention that some references in the fourth Gospel are not fully intelligible unless one presupposes an unexpressed mythology similar to that in Mandaean literature. Dodd was not so explicit in the rejection of gnosticism as a possible background for the Gospel, but it is clear that he preferred to interpret the fourth Gospel out of the Hebrew scriptures, the Septuagint, Plato, and the Hermetic literature rather than out of the Gnostic world of thought.

In 1961, C. Colpe published *Die Religionsgeschichtliche Schule*, which was in effect an attack on the attempt to interpret John out of Mandaean or Gnostic categories. He argued that one cannot retroject back into the first century of the Common Era, or still earlier, the full-fledged systems known to us from the second century. Single motifs from the later systems *can* be found in the earlier period, but the presence of the isolated motifs does not justify the assumption that the developed systems existed. More specifically, he argued against the existence of the *Urmensch-Erlöser* myth in the earlier period, contending that it did not develop until the Manichaean movement. In terms of the later refinement of definitions, he was insisting that the first century reflects the existence of pre-Gnostic but not proto-Gnostic movements[15]

Of particular interest was the second edition of Eduard Schweizer's *Egō Eimi* (1965).[16] In the 1939 original edition, he had accepted in general the position of Bultmann concerning Johannine dependence on Mandaeanism (though skeptical about the possibility of identifying a written *Vorlage* used by the evangelist). However, in the 1965 edition the introduction stated that while he still believed in a pre-Christian origin for Mandaeanism in the vicinity of Palestine, he was no longer prepared to argue for direct dependence by the evangelist on that Mandaean tradition. In fact, somewhat earlier he had indicated that the discussion by C.H. Dodd had convinced him more stress should be laid on the Old Testament background of Johannine thought, that is, as over against a Mandaean or Gnostic background.[17]

Jan-A. Bühner's *Der Gesandte und Sein Weg im 4. Evangelium*, (1977)[18] is the most recent and substantial attempt to demonstrate that the Johannine motif of the Messiah as one sent from God was based on the Old Testament and rabbinic concept of the *schaliach*. Bühner recognizes that throughout the eastern Mediterranean world there was a common pattern of the legal messenger and his responsibilities, but he contends that the precise form that this takes in the fourth Gospel reflects the nuances of Judaism rather than those of gnosticism. There is need for much further discussion of Bühner's contentions, but it is not clear that they will be universally persuasive. For example, he cites a number of *egō eimi* sayings with predicates from later Jewish and rabbinic materials.[19] But a comparison of the dozen or so passages with the Johannine materials underlines two points: (1) the comparative paucity of these occurrences alongside their concentration in the fourth Gospel and (2) the contrast in form between the Jewish passages listed and the Johannine. Those from Jewish literature simply follow the pattern already found in the Hebrew scriptures, for example, "I am Raphael," "I am Michael," "I am Metathron," "I am the angel of death." But it is immediately clear that these differ from the Johannine "I am the bread of life," "I am the light of the world," "I am the true vine," and so on, which are closer to the Mandaean parallels than to the Jewish (though this does not settle the issue of dependence).

In addition to these efforts to assuage the "Mandaean fever," mention needs to be made of the major recent commentaries by C.K. Barrett, R.E. Brown, and R. Schnackenburg. All reject or at least minimize the dependence of the Gospel on Mandaean or Gnostic thought.[20]

Since the experts have not yet achieved unanimity in their views about the origins of gnosticism or Mandaeanism, other New Testament scholars are compelled to make their own decisions on the basis of their "feel" for the course of the debate. My own tentative conclusions, which are somewhat against the stream of current criticism, are as follows:

First, in view of the widespread and diversified forms of gnosticism which existed in the second century, it is probable that there were movements in the first century that must be called proto-Gnostic rather than merely pre-Gnostic. So far as Mandaeanism is concerned, I accept the conclusions of Rudolph[21] that Mandaeanism began apart from Christianity and was present in some form during the first century.

Second, assuming the existence of proto-Gnostic and proto-Mandaean movements in the first century, it is probable that the evangelist and his community borrowed some of their concepts and terminology from such movements. This general probability applies specifically to the *ego eimi* sayings with predicates in John's Gospel. But pending the discovery of additional first-century documents, it is not possible to say much more about the details of this dependence.

I am nudged toward the hypothesis of Johannine dependence on proto-Gnostic thought by the sharp above-below contrast that runs throughout the Gospel. Certainly the evangelist would not have supported an ultimate dualism, but the radical contrast that is expressed exceeds what might have been expected from the Jewish tradition or popular Platonism (see 3:3, 7, 13, 31ff.; 6:35, 38, 41-42, 50-51, 58, 62; 7:29; 8:23, 42). I am influenced also by the claim of Bultmann that the Johannine Jesus reveals chiefly that he is the Revealer-Redeemer; in fact, the content of the revelation is remarkably limited.[22]

2. Historicity

Are the *ego eimi* sayings with predicates the actual sayings of Jesus, or are they more naturally understood as sayings produced by some segment of the later Christian community? The informed reader of the previous section will have recognized that my acceptance of a proto-Gnostic background for the Johannine discourses leads almost inevitably to a negative verdict with respect to the historicity of these sayings. But the fundamental objections to the historicity of these sayings are not dependent on theories about Gnostic motifs in the Johannine material.

The real difficulty in regarding the *egō eimi* sayings as the actual sayings of Jesus is created by the contrast between the teachings of Jesus as described in the Synoptics and the presentation in the fourth Gospel. The difference is one both of content and of style. Certainly it has been argued that Jesus may have had more than one teaching style and content, and these may have varied depending on the audience. Thus it has been suggested that the Synoptics reflect his public teaching, while the fourth Gospel reflects his more intimate conversations with his disciples.[23] But there are difficulties in this hypothesis. For one thing, John 18:20 reports Jesus as saying to the high priest that the latter should have no difficulty in determining his teaching, since he had taught nothing privately that he had not also said openly. At the very least this must express the understanding of the evangelist, who assumes the identity of Jesus' public and private teaching. More decisive for the present purpose is the fact that the elements in the Johannine account of Jesus' teaching that contrast with synoptic portrayal appear in his public addresses as well as in his private conversations with his disciples.

As far as content is concerned, the central contrast is in the open and high Christology of the fourth Gospel. The authority with which the Jesus of the Synoptics spoke and acted did give rise to such questions as "Who then is this, that even wind and sea obey him? [Mark 4:41, RSV, and pars.]" and "Why does this man speak thus? It is blasphemy! Who can forgive sins but God alone? [Mark 2:7, RSV]." But the disciples are reported not to have recognized his christological role until Caesarea Philippi, and even then there is no suggestion of his preexistence or his oneness with God. Certainly the synoptic Jesus did not use such language about himself. In John's Gospel the high Christology is explicit from the very beginning in the language of the evangelist (the prologue) and in the statements by his earliest followers. In chapter 4 he explicitly identifies himself to the Samaritan woman as the Messiah, and high christological claims are made by Jesus both in public pronouncements and in statements to his disciples. The *egō eimi* sayings with predicates are simply a continuation of this open proclamation of his own person. Those in chapters 6, 8, 10, and 11 are addressed to a general public, while those in chapters 14 and 15 are addressed to the inner circle. The contrast is not absolute, since the Synoptics contain the so-called "bolt from the Johannine blue" in Matthew 11:25-27 (Luke 10:21-22), and there are *egō* sayings attributed to Jesus in these Gospels.[24] But the contrast is unmistakable, and it is underlined by the nature of the controversies reported respectively in the Synoptics and in John. In the latter the controversies center around the claims made by Jesus for himself, as would certainly have happened had he made such claims.

If the content of the *egō eimi* passages indicates an openly declared high Christology in John that contrasts with the teaching recorded in the Synoptics, it is equally true that the style of the proclamation is a contrast. While there are a limited number of *egō eimi* passages in the Synoptics without predicates, there are no occurrences of *egō eimi* with predicates like those in John. The contrast remains clear whether one regards the *egō eimi* sayings with predicates as developments out of proto-gnosticism or a reflection of Jewish or rabbinic terminology. In either case, few would regard these Johannine sayings as historical.

If these sayings originated in the language of the Johannine community and not on the lips of Jesus, how are we to understand the thought-process by which this modification of the tradition took place? A partial answer begins with the recognition that the evangelist was not a Ph.D. candidate working in a seminar on historiography. This is not to belittle his achievement, since it may be an almost unmixed blessing that he was not a modern researcher of that type. He was a believer who had heard and appropriated the Christian message. As he appropriated it, his own conceptual world was transformed by the new faith, but the new faith also underwent change as it worked like leaven in the conceptual world of this new believer. To some extent the new faith had to be expressed in the categories the evangelist was already using. This type of change is easily demonstrated from Christian history. Presumably the earliest Palestinian Christians found the title Messiah or Christ entirely adequate to express their concept of Jesus. But when the message moved into the outside gentile world, the affirmation that Jesus was the Christ would have been intelligible to listeners only after a preliminary lecture on Jewish messianic expectations. Even then the title might not have been religiously satisfying to them. Thus the title Messiah soon lost its special significance and was replaced by terms that were religiously more satisfying, for example, Lord, Son of God, and Savior. William Barclay, with his gift for putting positively what might appear to some to be negative, observes concerning the Johannine discourses:

> We can be fairly certain that Jesus did not make these claims for
> himself, at least not in the way in which the discourses make
> them. What we have here is not the precise words which Jesus
> spoke, but that which the Christian church discovered and knew
> him, under the guidance of the Spirit, to be.[25]

Only the most resolutely conservative scholars would insist that Johannine *egō eimi* sayings are the literal words of Jesus. Most others would agree broadly with the quotation from Barclay, but some might seek a further clarification of the language. Does it assume that the Johannine language identified Jesus as he was objectively and permanently, or does it express instead what he was for a given group in a given cultural situation?[26]

3. The Actual Seven (Thirteen) Texts

It is not feasible to discuss each of the seven (thirteen) predicates that appear in the *egō eimi* passages, but a few observations may be made about the group as a whole. Perhaps the most important observation is that each of the predicates is a way of identifying Jesus as the bearer of "life." This is immediately clear in four of the seven statements (RSV):

I am the bread of *life* [6:35, 48].
I am the light of the world; he who follows me will not walk in darkness, but will have the light of *life* [8:12].
I am the resurrection and the *life* [11:25].[27]
I am the way, and the truth, and the *life* [14:6].

Furthermore, in the remaining three passages the motif of life is present explicitly or implicitly in the immediate context. Thus 10:7 ("I am the door of the sheep [RSV]") is followed in 10:10 by the statement "I came that they may have life, and have it abundantly [RSV]." In the good shepherd passage (10:11, 14) it is affirmed that the good shepherd lays down his life for his sheep, and though it is not explicitly stated, the point is that he lays down his life so they may have life. Finally, in the "I am the true vine" passage (15:1-10) the thrust of the argument is that believers have fruit-bearing life only insofar as they remain in vital connection with the "true vine." So it is no exaggeration to affirm that all occurrences of *egō eimi* with predicates are affirmations that Jesus is the life-bearer and life-giver.[28]

The identification of Jesus as the life-giver is scarcely surprising, since the focus of the proclamation in the fourth Gospel is on (eternal) life. The term life (*zoē*) occurs thirty-six times in this Gospel, and in seventeen of these occurrences it is further defined as "eternal life." A comparison of the passages with and without the adjective eternal makes it clear that the two forms are used interchangeably, that is, the same concept is intended even if "eternal" is not included. Eternal life is not a standard Greek term; it appears to have emerged in Jewish Greek with the literal meaning of "life of the age," that is, "life of the age to come." In the Synoptics, with or without "eternal," it appears to refer to existence beyond death, though in John's Gospel it is an experience entered into at the moment of positive response to Jesus (cf. 3:36; 5:24, et al.). It is correct to say that "eternal life" is what the Gospel is all about, and for the evangelist Jesus is the bearer of that eternal life.

A second observation about the *egō eimi* passages with predicates is best expressed in the form of a question: Is it accidental or deliberate that there are precisely seven different images used in these passages?[29] Unfortunately this tantalizing question does not have a clear-cut answer. For much of the eastern Mediterranean world seven was a mysterious and significant number. Furthermore, the Apocalypse of John, which belongs somehow to the Johannine literature even though not written by the evangelist, used patterns of seven so extensively that some believe it is the key to the overall structure of that book. But one cannot interpret the Gospel of John in the light of the Apocalypse, and the term seven never actually occurs in the Gospel. However, many have speculated that the Gospel deliberately cited seven miracles in the ministry of Jesus, specifically identifying the turning of water into wine as the "first of his signs" and the healing of the nobleman's son as the "second sign" (2:11 and 4:54). It is somewhat curious that the count is not continued beyond this point, and the reader is left to wonder whether the evangelist had precisely seven miracles in mind. Some have noted that the Gospel has no "I am the water of life," which might have been anticipated along with "I am the bread of life," "I am the light of the world," and so on. Such an *egō eimi* saying would have been particularly appropriate in 4:1-42 (the Samaritan woman) or 7:37-39 (Jesus' words on the last day of the feast). It could be argued that the tradition already contained seven such sayings and that there was no room for an "I am the water of life" saying. Such speculation is only speculation and cannot provide a basis for insisting that the evangelist deliberately reported seven and only seven *egō eimi* plus predicate sayings. If one believes that the evangelist was concerned with a sevenfold pattern in this connection, one must probably argue that the Gospel was an "in house" document, that is, a document to which the original readers brought information no longer available to others. This is a genuine possibility, but it cannot be demonstrated on the basis of present evidence.

Another observation concerns the relation of these passages to the cluster of terms referring to "truth" or "true" (*alētheia, alēthēs, alēthinos*). The statistics indicate the prominence of these terms in comparison with the rest of the New Testament:

	Total N.T.	Fourth Gospel	Three Epistles	The Apocalypse	Rest of N.T.
alētheia	109	25	20	0	64
alēthēs	26	14	3	0	9
alēthinos	28	9	4	10	5
Totals	163	48	27	10	78

Three of the seven passages use one or the other of these terms, either in the passage itself or in the immediate context:

6:32-35 (rsv) Truly, truly, I say to you, it was not Moses who gave you the bread from heaven; my Father gives you the true (*ton alētheinon*) bread from heaven. For the bread of God is that which comes down from heaven, and gives life to the world. . . . I am the bread of life; he who comes to me shall not hunger, and he who believes in me shall never thirst.

14:6 (rsv) I am the way, and the truth (*he alētheia*), and the life; no one comes to the Father, but by me.

15:1 (rsv) I am the true (*hē alēthinē*) vine, and my Father is the vinedresser.

A fourth passage could probably be added to these three. In 8:12 ("I am the light of the world") there is no "true" or "truth" in the immediate context. But one remembers that the prologue refers to Jesus as "the true light (*to alēthinon*) that enlightens every man . . . [1:9, rsv]."

There has been much discussion about the precise nuance given by the evangelist to these terms.[30] But for the present topic there is one central question: Is Jesus identified as the true life-bearer over against false earthly claimants, or, alternatively, is the language the expression of a heavenly versus earthly dualism—either the dualism of a popular Platonism or that of pre-gnosticism or proto-gnosticism? Perhaps no one answer can cover all the passages. Thus in 10:7, 9 ("I am the door") there appears to be a contrast between Jesus and other historical persons who claim the same role (cf. 10:8 [rsv]: "All who came before me are thieves and robbers"). Scholars differ as to the identity of these "thieves and robbers," but presumably they were historical people. The same thrust is apparent in 10:11, 14 ("I am the good shepherd"), where other would-be shepherds are identified as "hirelings." In these passages there is no hint of the heavenly-earthly contrast. In the bread discourse of chapter 6, however, there is an explicit contrast between the heavenly bread which gives life and ordinary earthly bread. At the same time, the apparent "put-down" of Moses (6:32) suggests that Jesus is here contrasted with Moses and the manna of the exodus. So the evangelist may have had in mind both the heavenly-earthly contrast and the conflict between Jesus and other religious figures.

If the "light of the world" passage (8:12; cf. 9:5) is read against the background of other sayings about light in the Gospel, especially in the prologue, then it seems likely that the evangelist thought of Jesus as the light from heaven over against mere earthly light. Yet once again there is the hint of a contrast between Jesus as the light and others who might make a similar claim (cf. 1:8, with its reference to John the Baptist). In 11:25 ("I am the resurrection and the life") the only contrast—if any is intended—is that between resurrection at the end of history and resurrection present in the encounter with Jesus. In 14:6 ("I am the way, and the truth, and the life") there is no heavenly-earthly contrast, although it is possible that there lies in the background a contrast between Jesus as the way and other religious leaders who made a similar claim (see the use of "the way" at Qumran). In John 15:1, 5 ("I am the true [alēthinē] vine") there is no explicit reference to the earthly-heavenly contrast, but it is likely that implied in the alēthinē is the sense that Jesus is the heavenly vine as over against mere earthly vines. At the same time, the widespread use of "vine" for Israel may well mean that the evangelist had also in mind the contrast between Judaism and Christianity.[31] Thus in some of the passages the heavenly-earthly contrast is in the foreground; in others the contrast is between Jesus and rival historical figures; in some both contrasts may be involved.

4. Contemporary Appropriation

Before dealing directly with the possibilities of contemporary appropriation, there are—at least in the minds of some—two obstacles which must be removed. These issues were touched on in Section 2, "Historicity," but they require more direct confrontation. The first obstacle is essentially theological and is hinted at by the phrase "contemporary appropriation." The phrase itself suggests that there is, or may be, some difference in the way the first-century Christian community "appropriated" the Johannine language and the way that same language should be appropriated today. This suggestion is understandably resisted by any who hold that theological language not only points toward a truth or reality but actually articulates that truth or reality in an absolute and permanent form. This issue affects not just Johannine language but all theological language, whether that of the Bible itself or of subsequent generations. I would argue that theological language is essentially "pointing language," that is, it points toward a perceived truth or reality. The language of the pointer is substantially conditioned by the particular time and place in which the pointing occurs. Thus the cultural context in which the pointer lives will affect the language of the pointing. It would be my contention that it is impossible for a modern Western person to think and feel in the categories of the first century, whether those of the Palestine world or the larger Hellenistic world. Individuals may claim to repeat the first-century words and to believe them in precisely the same sense as did the evangelist behind the Fourth Gospel. In actual fact the words may be the same, but the tune is not! No matter how faithfully first-century Greek sentences are translated into English, they do not convey the same undertones and overtones for the modern reader that they did for the reader of the first century. (And this is true whether one regards the first-century world-view as superior or inferior to that of the present.) This issue could be discussed at greater length, but it is adequate here simply to underline the presupposition behind this section, namely, that the conceptual world of the Johannine community was radically different from ours and that it is therefore necessary to find other language to convey the truth and reality to which it sought to point. The difference between the language of the Synoptics and John is itself evidence of the appropriateness of a language change when a given truth is transferred from one cultural context to another. In the same fashion, we are called upon to seek, or at least to consider, new language in view of our cultural differences with the world of the Johannine community.

A second obstacle is of a different kind and will be an obstacle to a quite different group of people. It is an obstacle created for some by the argument that the "I am" sayings are not necessarily the actual words of Jesus. It was suggested earlier that the evangelist attributed to Jesus words which he, and presumably his community, found most adequate to express the significance Jesus had for them and their religious experience. They could have written a theological treatise, as was done in the case of 1 John, and then the reader conditioned by nineteenth-century historiography would not have been disturbed by the attribution to Jesus of words which he probably did not speak. In all likelihood the Johannine community was not disturbed by this process, if it was even conscious of it. To use an old illustration, those early Christians were working out for themselves the meaning of the words that the earlier tradition had brought them in the same way that the Platonic dialogues worked out the meaning of Socrates' teaching as seen from the perspective of the subsequent years. Some of the words of Jesus, or words assumed to be his actual words, undoubtedly initiated this process, and they carried it further in the ongoing life of the community. In the fourth Gospel there is a trivial illustration of how this development of the words of Jesus may have begun. All readers of the Synoptics will have noted the frequent occurrence of Jesus *logia* beginning with the formula "Truly, I say to you." This introductory formula occurs some fifty times in the Synoptics. And the same formula occurs some twenty-five times in John's formulation of the words of Jesus. But in the Johannine formula the "truly" is always doubled, for example, John 1:51 (RSV), "Truly, truly, I say to you, you will see heaven opened, and the angels of God ascending and descending upon the Son of man." Surely only the most resolute literalist would insist that Jesus sometimes used one "truly" and sometimes two, and that the synoptists selected only the one group of sayings while John selected only those with two occurrences of "truly"![32] While in this instance the evangelist made only a minor stylistic variation from the earlier tradition, it demonstrates that he did not feel obliged to retain precisely the words received in the tradition, but was prepared to amplify them so as to bring out more clearly their intent as he understood it. The rewriting in the Johannine discourses may have gone far beyond this innocuous stylistic change, but in principle the procedure was simply an extension of the same process. The significant question for the modern reader should not be Are these the literal words of Jesus? but rather How can we express in today's terminology the meaning that the Johannine community found in Jesus and conveyed through the words they attributed to him?

It was pointed out that all the *egō eimi* sayings with predicates were ways of identifying Jesus as the bearer and giver of life. But the "life" referred to was not ordinary physical life, nor was it primarily "life after death" (though the evangelist undoubtedly anticipated some form of existence after death). Rather, the evangelist was speaking of a particular kind or quality of life, more specifically a life in which this earthly existence is linked with the eternal source of all life. In fact, this is the central thrust of the Gospel as a whole, as is expressed in the concluding statement of chapter 20 ("and that believing you may have life in his name"). No doubt there are many ways this central affirmation might be reexpressed in different terminology, but one of the simplest reformulations would be to affirm that Jesus in his ministry emerged as the bearer of and witness to the meaning of human existence.

It will be remembered that Paul Tillich in *The Courage to Be* (1952) classified human anxiety in three forms and suggested that one or the other of these predominated in various ages of history. Thus the Hellenistic world displayed anxiety in the face of fate and death; at the end of the Middle Ages the dominant anxiety was that created by a sense of guilt and condemnation, while in the modern world emptiness and meaninglessness predominate as the source of anxiety. Whatever quarrels some may have with Tillich's schematization, it does seem true that in the Western world the dominant anxiety is that induced by emptiness and meaninglessness. The average modern-day person is not obsessed by the question of what happens after death and does not seem to experience Luther's "pangs of an awakened conscience." But modern-day people are haunted by emptiness and meaninglessness, and much of their lives are frenetic efforts to fill the void. This malaise cannot be made to disappear simply by stating that the drama of Jesus' career witnesses to the meaning of human existence! But this kind of language may serve as a bridge to the questions which stir people deeply and the answers proclaimed in the Christian tradition.

Certainly it is not being suggested that the classic "I am" sayings in John should be replaced for liturgical or devotional purposes by such phrases as "I am the meaning of human existence"! This would be to replace powerful symbolic language with a prosaic phrase. But some such understanding of the symbols may help to refill them with the vitality and significance they once carried.

CHAPTER 8

Logos Ecclesiology in John's Gospel

Paul S. Minear

In a volume devoted to christological perspectives, it may seem strange to introduce an essay on ecclesiology, and especially on logos ecclesiology, inasmuch as scholars are conditioned to associate the term logos almost exclusively with christological formulas. This unusual association of the term with ecclesiology must then be justified in what follows. Moreover, to explain the essay's inclusion in this volume, it must be shown that in this regard John's ecclesiology conditions his thinking about the Messiah.

Several convictions that have tended to dominate recent research must therefore be challenged. One is the conviction that this evangelist was relatively unconcerned with ecclesiological matters.[1] In my view this attitude is quite mistaken. A second is the conviction that in origin the prologue was separate from the rest of the document and that it exhibited radically different literary and conceptual patterns, of which the idea of the logos is typical.[2] Successive rereadings of the Gospel have convinced me that the logos symbol actually links the prologue closely to the thought of the later chapters. A third conviction is reflected in the almost universal tendency of English translators to capitalize the noun *word* in the prologue but never in the later chapters. The basis for this tendency is the assurance that only in the prologue did the evangelist use logos as a technical and personal title for Jesus. This practice of capitalization distorts the Johannine way of thinking about Christ and the church.[3] In his vocabulary the logos symbol disclosed rather the interdependence of ecclesiology and christology. In what follows I shall try to make good on this challenge of prevailing convictions.

This essay represents an effort to recapture certain thought-patterns of the evangelist in all their baffling subtlety. Honest interpreters recognize

Paul S. Minear is Winkley Professor of Biblical Theology, Emeritus, at Yale University.

the audacity and the difficulty of such an effort. It is no simple matter to adapt one's own linguistic habits to John's elusive vocabulary or to restructure one's mental processes into some degree of conformity with his. Virtually every term in his lexicon of symbols carried a range of connotations foreign to us; ears must be sensitized to catch those reverberations. Distortions of his thought-processes are inevitable, yet one can still seek to reduce the degree of such distortion.

For one thing, the tendency to import the technical jargon of the theological seminar into the nontechnical language of the evangelist can be resisted. He would probably have found the term ecclesiology meaningless; at least he never used the basic word *ekklēsia*. More significant for the present purposes, in his use logos conveyed a broad spectrum of meanings, many of which were quite untechnical in any theological sense. It could refer to vague rumors or popular gossip (21:23); to a familiar proverb or brief adage (4:37; 15:20); to a person's passing remark (2:22; 4:39; 7:36); to the citation of a specific verse of scripture (12:38); or to a more general appeal to scripture as a whole (10:35; 15:25; 18:9). In passages like these, one should take care not to inflate the theological significance of the term, though of course in other passages that significance should not be reduced to such trivial dimensions as these.

A second precaution: Words other than logos which John used to convey similar meanings should not be excluded from consideration. On various occasions the plural *logoi* carried the same weight as the singular (e.g., 7:40). On other occasions the evangelist, without perceptible shifts in meaning, employed other nouns: *phonē, hrēma, entolē, lalia* (5:25; 8:43; 12:50). Often he relied on verbs rather than nouns. In interpreting his language, we must try to become as flexible as he; linguistic paralysis can only frustrate efforts to retrace his thoughts. Reliance on dictionaries can produce such paralysis if it leads us to assume that words are separate boxes, each containing a fixed quantity of meaning. For John the unit of thought was often an entire sentence, indeed often an entire paragraph. For him each idea evoked many synonyms and antonyms. The affiliations of one idiom with its neighbors provide better clues to the movement of his mind than do fixed definitions of successive words.[4] Each cluster of concepts must be expounded as a whole; no single concept can be grasped apart from the cluster.

This principle applies not to a single paragraph or chapter but to the Gospel as a whole. In an important sense, the entire document comes as a single unit.[5] Should one segment seem inexplicable, the first recourse must be to search the other segments on the assumption that the Gospel is self-explanatory, that the evangelist himself represents the best judge of what he was trying to say. In their treatment of the prologue, scholars have often ignored this principle. Confronted by the mysteries of the logos in 1:1, and assuming that the later chapters help little in dispelling those mysteries, they proceed to ransack the literature of pre-Johannine centuries for potential sources of the logos idea. A premium has often been placed on the ingenuity of scholars in finding parallels to the prologue and on their deftness in persuading other scholars of the cogency of those parallels. And there is no dearth of parallels to be located and sifted, no limits to scholarly ingenuity. Although much can be gained, and in fact has been gained in this process, one result must be regretted. The cleavage between the prologue and the rest of the Gospel has been so accentuated that it becomes difficult to explain why and how any author could have combined them. And this has meant that the potential contributions of the later chapters to an understanding of the prologue have disappeared.

A further result is this: New Testament hermeneutics as applied to the fourth Gospel has become all too glaring an example of the sins specified by Susan Sontag in her essay "Against Interpretation."[6] Those sins need not be detailed here, though every biblical exegete should be urged to examine them carefully. They are implicit in our assumption that our task is to replace an ancient text with "a duplicate world," with "a shadow world of meanings." Our way of understanding that text is to reduce it to words within our own control. By distinguishing form from content, we can substitute our definition of content for the author's own thought. This enables us to dig beneath the text for a subtext that seems more intelligible and more acceptable. Our success in finding a modern equivalent for the ancient phenomenon then hides from ourselves the fact that we have carried out an impious and cowardly attack on the text. Sontag says that this process poisons our own sensibilities "like the fumes of autos." Our interpretation becomes "the compliment mediocrity pays to genius."

Perhaps these caustic comments will induce us, in seeking to interpret John's thinking about the logos, to move out of the habitat of our own familiar ideas in order to enter the habitat of his unfamiliar thinking. In any case, our first requirement is to listen acutely to seven passages in which the logos concept is affiliated with other concepts in illuminating clusters.

Cluster One:
JOHN 5:19-29

Logos[7] appears in this passage only once, yet in such a way as to be typical of the entire Gospel: "I tell you truly, whoever hears my logos and believes in the one who sent me has eternal life; that person does not come under judgment but has passed from death to life." The sentence appears to establish a close correlation between hearing Jesus' word and hearing Jesus. The two are so nearly equivalent that the reader wonders what the term logos adds to the thought. A further correlation is established between hearing Jesus' word and believing in God as the one who had sent him. The act of hearing creates an axis connecting three persons: the sender, the one sent, and the believer. The context warns the reader not to be content with a simple equation between logos and Jesus' teaching, for nothing short of eternal life is communicated.[8] The logos operates in such a way as to free its hearer from final judgment, to enable him or her to pass from death to life. To use the idiom of the prologue (1:13) or the dialogue with Nicodemus (3:7), we can say that the logos has demonstrated its power to engender a new birth. This can be true, of course, only when we attribute a very strong sense to the action of hearing this logos; akouein here connotes nothing short of full obedience or complete identification with the speaker. There is no appreciable distance between hearing the logos and having eternal life. This correlation certainly gives a distinctive resonance to the term logos.

Later verses in the same chapter (5:25ff.) corroborate these inferences. In those verses voice (phonē) appears as a surrogate for logos, and it becomes clear that wherever Jesus' voice is heard he is himself present (much more than a truism in John). And this voice, because it is heard by the dead, by those in the tombs, consists of much more than audible sounds; it exerts authority to convey to the dead the life which the Father has in himself and which the Son also has received from the Father (v. 21). Here the logos is assigned power to penetrate the tombs, to strike the hour of final judgment, to serve as the place and time of resurrection.[9] If capitalization is used to call attention to distinctive and significant uses of a term, word in verse 24 deserves to be capitalized.

Still other nuances in the Johannine vocabulary come to the surface in the preceding verses (5:19ff.). Here the audible component is fused together with the visual; what the Son says is what he sees. Furthermore, the actions of saying and seeing merge into the action of doing. The Father is at work; the Son sees and does the same things, things described in terms of love, of honor, and of giving life to the dead. All these continuities become coordinates of the idea of logos. So when Jesus says "my logos," he points not only to himself but to a reality beyond himself, a reality that is coextensive with God's works, God's judgment, God's life. Because the Son does "only what he sees the Father doing [v. 19]," his logos becomes no less primal than the day of creation and no less final than doomsday. His logos serves to situate the life of the community within these boundaries.

Cluster Two:
5:30-47

In this paragraph John continues his report of the debate between Jesus and the Jews, and this debate makes clear the juridical orientation of Johannine thinking. A vast trial is proceeding, and the mission of Jesus introduces the readers into the very course of a cosmic judgment scene.[10] The Jews accuse Jesus of defying the law, and Jesus reverses the charge. In John's report of attack and counterattack, the character of the supporting testimonies becomes decisive.

> The testimony which I have is greater than that of John; for the works which the Father has granted me to accomplish, these very works which I am doing, bear me witness that the Father has sent me. And the Father who sent me has himself borne witness to me. His voice you have never heard, his form you have never seen; and you do not have his [logos] abiding in you, for you do not believe him whom he has sent [5:36-38, RSV].

Several new correlations of the idea of the logos appear within this thought-complex. The logos constitutes God's own testimony, presented within this very courtroom. The testimony of God corroborates the testimony of other witnesses in this trial: the witness of John the Baptist, of Moses, and of the scriptures. Most decisive of all is the witness provided by the works God has granted Jesus to accomplish. What Jesus has said he has first heard (v. 30); what he has revealed he has first seen. The witness he has given is nothing but the witness given to him; his authority is not his own but God's. In his trial by the Jews, this is his line of defense.

In their trial by Jesus, his accusers disclose a composite guilt. They have rejected the testimony of the Baptist, the testimony of Moses, and the testimony of the scriptures. Most damning of all, they have rejected the testimony of God, and that rejection receives a triple definition in John's text. Unlike Jesus, they have never heard God's voice, have never seen the form of God, have never had God's logos abiding in them. In this triple definition we encounter the repetition of two corollaries of the logos idea: hearing God's voice and seeing God's form. But the third corollary is new: God's logos is described as something residing within or dwelling among a community (the *you* of v.38 is plural). This context assumes that the logos has a communal habitat. The covenantal people of God is to be located wherever this logos abides (the present participle *menonta* and the preposition *en* carry important ecclesiological implications); in fact, the abiding of the word becomes one way of discerning the boundary between the community that is faithful to the Mosaic testimony and its counterfeit. This passage shows further that in the community where the logos of God abides are found such gifts as salvation, life, glory, and love. And where those gifts are present, it becomes difficult to distinguish the ecclesiological from the christological or the theological dimensions of the one logos.

Cluster Three:
6:52-71

This text appears to establish a correlation between the actions of hearing and seeing, on the one hand, and on the other hand, the action of eating the flesh of the Son of man. Although, of course, the immediate dialogue partners do not understand this correlation, John expected the readers of the Gospel to comprehend the mystery.[11]

Chapter 6 represents one of the basic pivots in the movement of the narrative, for it brings to a conclusion a conflict between Jesus and his adversaries, the leaders of Israel. This debate centered in the identification of the life-giving bread, given to Israel by God from heaven. John's readers have been prepared for the negative outcome of this debate in the Capernaum synagogue, at least so far as "the Jews" had been concerned. They would have fully expected the Jews to misconstrue the issue "How can this man give us his flesh to eat? [v. 52]."

It was the reaction of the disciples that was more surprising, both to John and his readers, and perhaps even to Jesus. The *Revised Standard Version* translates that reaction "This is a hard saying [logos]; who can listen (*akouein*) to it?" But we must ask what that logos referred to; what made it so hard to understand that the disciples were impelled to "draw back"? To them the "offense" was so great as to cause them to fall away (cf. 16:1-3), to cease to be disciples. Only two things can explain this "apostasy." The reference to Jesus' flesh and blood is intended to remind readers of Jesus' death "for the life of the world." Furthermore, those who abide in him by eating his flesh are those who join him in that sacrificial dying. It is the conjunction of those two things that makes this logos so offensive, so difficult to obey that many disciples fall away; yet it is that same double truth that makes Jesus' words the medium of "spirit and life (v. 63)." In this case, Jesus logos or words (*hrēmata*) are simultaneously death-dealing and life-giving and quite inseparable, in fact, from the bread of heaven that became flesh and blood in the martyr who called others to join him in that "kamikaze" conspiracy. No passage in the Gospel makes clearer the rigor of discipleship. In fact, the very rigor demonstrated the truth of Jesus'

100

saying, "No one can come to me unless it is granted him by the Father [v. 65]." John's readers were by no means surprised at Judas' betrayal, for they would have readily grasped the force of the question "Who can obey such a logos? [v. 60]."

Here, then, is another mysterious cluster of associations. John's thought passes very smoothly from the single *word* (logos) to the plural *words* (*hrēmata*), and as smoothly from hearing to seeing, from dying to ascending, from death to life, from obeying the logos to eating flesh and drinking blood, from the act of eating the bread to that of maintaining a relationship to Christ in which the disciple "abides in me and I in him." Logos as both word and bread connotes that complex relationship of mutual abiding.[12] This cluster of metaphors and symbols appears to be the native habitat of John's thought. Each metaphor retains its own distinctive affiliations, yet the meaning of each figure becomes directly contingent on those affiliations. The total stream of consciousness is much greater than the sum of its parts. This is surely due in part to the fact that the entire stream is dominated by Christian memories of the passion story and by a corresponding awareness of all that is involved in the eucharistic prayer "Lord, give us this bread always [6:34]." What makes the logos in verse 60 so hard is the fact that it was so much more than a saying. It was nothing less than the life that is given through death.

Cluster Four:
8:31-47

At first sight this text adds little to the fabric of ideas in chapter 6. The debate between Jesus and the Jews continues, with even greater emotional intensity. In the former debate, however, the issue appears to focus on the response by *individuals* to the logos of life. In this new round of argument, the issue centers in the division of the Jews into two *communities*, believers and unbelievers. Which of these two communities constitutes the true family of Abraham? The presence or the absence of the logos provides the answer:

If you abide in my logos you are truly my disciples [v. 31].

You seek to kill me, because my logos finds no place [to abide] in you [v. 37; cf. 5:38].

In both cases the pronoun *you* is plural, giving to the preposition *in* a communitarian dimension. In which community does this logos find a home? Whatever the answer, John understands the logos as much more than a verbal message or the body of teaching as a whole. To be sure, the logos confers knowledge of the Father, for Jesus speaks of what he has seen of the Father. But this logos creates a relationship between parent and family; it generates a community of children who are simultaneously children of Abraham and of God. It liberates these children from slavery, makes them immune to death, sets them to doing the Father's works and to continuing the Son's mission. The symbol of an indwelling logos includes this whole panoply of implications, though of course John recognizes that Jesus' hearers would not experience these effects of the logos until "you have lifted up (raised on the cross) the Son of man [v. 28]."

Conversely, there is nothing bland about the dereliction that falls on that community in which the logos finds no home. They are slaves deluded into believing in their own freedom, fornicators who rely upon their own purity. They have become sons not of Abraham but of the devil, who is the archetypal progenitor of their lies and murder. Because they are committed to the belief that it is Jesus who has a demon, it is impossible for his logos to find a place in them. The polemic is fierce indeed.

To sum up, the term logos here connotes a veritable chain of being. Its presence or absence determines Israel's origin and paternity, its identity and freedom, its unity and destiny. A further affiliation appears in this text: There is a virtual equivalence between the thought of keeping (*terein*) the logos (vv. 51, 52, 55) and the thought of the logos abiding in the house (v. 35) of God. The thought of keeping connotes much more than the idea of obeying specific commands. Not only does this "house" retain and hold fast the logos life committed to it, but it also guards, protects, and fulfills that life (14:15, 21, 24; 15:10, 20; 17:6, 15). The way in which Jesus had kept God's logos (8:55) has become the effective standard by which the true family of Abraham keeps Jesus' logos. In fact, life itself is truly defined by this action (v. 51). Still other passages in the Gospel identify this keeping of the logos with the love of Christ (14:23, 24). The chain of logoi (the Father's logos, "my logos") is none other than the chain of life and the chain of love. These associations are central to the patterns of thought in this Gospel.

Cluster Five:
12:44-50

At the close of chapter 12 John relayed the final appeal Jesus had made to the authorities. This location gave to these words the impact of a manifesto that made clear the results of faith or of rejection.

I have come as light into the world, that whoever believes in me may not remain in darkness . . . [whoever] does not receive my sayings has a judge; the word that I have spoken will be his judge on the last day . . . The Father who sent me has himself given me commandment what to say . . . and I know that his commandment is eternal life [12:46-50, RSV].

Although the idiom in this paragraph is typically Johannine, familiarity with that idiom does not in itself enable us to follow easily the movement of John's thought. One notes first the recurrence of several affiliations to which we have already called attention. For instance, as equivalents to the noun logos, John uses a variety of expressions: sayings, commandment, what I say. There is also a familiar alternation between hearing, keeping, seeing, and believing. Furthermore, there is an explicit identification of eternal life with the chain of being and the chain of sending.

Of greater significance for the present discussion are three correlations that receive fresh accent. First, the logos of Jesus ("what I say") is explicitly identified here with God's commandment (*entolē*). To keep the word is to obey that commandment. Commentators are divided on whether these two expressions are entirely synonymous or whether John preserved a distinction between them.[13] But no one is willing to deny a close affiliation between the two. Much depends on how one thinks of this commandment. Is the primary reference to God's commands as embodied in the Torah? Or is it to Jesus' command of love, with all its implications? The best answer in this context is to give full weight to the identification of this command with eternal life, and with the appearance of this command in the form of light.

This correlation of logos and light is the second new feature to be observed in this paragraph. What are we to make of it? "I have come as light into the world, that whoever believes in me may not remain in darkness [v. 46, RSV]." Logos and life are here associated with light. All three come into the world as a commandment from God. It is virtually certain that this is the same cluster of ideas that we find in the prologue: God, word, life, light, darkness (1:1-5). It is almost as certain that both these Johannine passages echo the Genesis account of creation: There, too, God speaks and God's word is a command: "Let there be light." There, too, the command was heard and obeyed, with the accompanying separation of light from darkness. It was that command which John identifies with eternal life. Jesus had come as a response to that command, as life and light, so that no one need any longer walk in darkness.[14] In short, John understood logos as a link between the believer in Christ and that primal action of God in creation.

The third new feature is an even clearer definition of an eschatological function of logos that corresponds to this protological function: The logos will serve in the last day as the judge of everyone who rejects Jesus. It could hardly be otherwise if what Jesus said was identical with what God had commanded him to say. This kind of thinking situated the action of believing (or of rejection) within the widest conceivable horizons, the first day of the creation and the last day of judgment. At the same time, those horizons lost their distance insofar as the encounter with Jesus' logos brought hearers within immediate contact with eternal life. The conception of logos in the prologue was in no way more distinctive or more decisive than this conception as found in Jesus' manifesto to the Jews in chapter 12.

Cluster Six:
JOHN 17:6-19

Here there is a sharp contrast to the picture in chapter 12 of the logos that serves as the Judge of all who rejected Jesus. There are two assurances in Jesus' prayer: "I have given them your logos . . . they have kept your logos." The context of these two statements provides several alternative ways of describing the relationships between Jesus and these men. That context emphasizes the fact that those relationships are bound up with the giving and the keeping of *God's* logos. The act by which Jesus gives God's logos corresponds to the act by which God gives those same men to Jesus. It also corresponds to Jesus' act of disclosing God's name to those men. Further, it corresponds to the act of calling and commissioning: "As you sent me into the world, so I have sent them into the world [v. 18]." Consequently the gift of God's logos is inseparable from the gift of that alienation from "the world" which draws upon them that world's hatred (v. 14).[15] Finally, this gift of God's logos marks the establishment of an unbreakable bond: "they are yours, mine are yours, yours are mine." To speak of the gift of the logos is a Johannine way of epitomizing the total self-giving to this community of both the Father and the Son.

A similar cluster of affiliations accompanies the idea of the *keeping* of God's logos by these men. For them to keep that word is to know that everything that Jesus has done originates from God and expresses loyalty to his assignment from God. To keep that word is to maintain unity among themselves, a communal unity that matches the oneness of Father and Son (v. 11). To keep that word is to accept with joy their mission in the world, in which they themselves will be guarded from the attacks of the devil. Finally, and this is the culminating petition of Jesus for these accredited representatives, to keep God's logos means that they will be sanctified (consecrated, glorified) in the truth. God's logos is explicitly identified with this truth in which they complete their assignment. So the whole conception of this logos derives from this sanctification. To what does John refer here? Clearly the norm of sanctification is provided by the action of Jesus himself. His own path to the glorification of God becomes the path for them too. For them to keep God's logos means that Jesus will be glorified in them (v. 10) as God is glorified in Jesus (v. 1). The presence of God's logos in them will thus mark the decisive frontier between the world which is ruled by the devil and the community that in possessing God's name abides in this truth.[16] In this connection John equates God's logos not with truth in general or with any abstraction of the mind, but with a very specific instance of glorification, for which another word would be crucifixion.

Cluster Seven:
17:20-26

The closing petition in Jesus' prayer is introduced by a very explicit identification: "I do not pray for these only [the apostles other than Judas who were present in the Upper Room] but also for those who believe in me through their [logos] [RSV]." John had in mind here his own readers, Christians of the second generation who no longer had available to them the leadership of the apostles who had known Jesus before his death (cf. 21:23, 24). They form a second-generation link in the chain of life of the church.

It is significant that their story is epitomized in a way similar to that of their predecessors. In one sense, of course, their story began with the logos of the apostles. But in a deeper sense it began with the earlier logos of Christ (vv. 8, 13, 18) and with the logos of God (vv. 6, 14, 16). The chain of life is described as a chain of glory (v. 22), which had its ultimate origins "before the foundation of the world [v. 24]."

The end of the story, also, is clearly expressed: "that they also, whom thou hast given me, may be with me where I am, to behold my glory [v. 24, RSV]." In the phrase "where I am" John was thinking simultaneously of the realm to which the Lord had ascended and of the fellowship with him of all who keep God's logos.[17]

The prayer also indicates the most significant features in the period intervening between the primal and the final glory for this second generation. They will become one by being "in us." They will enable the world to believe that God has sent Christ. They will be "inhabited" by God's love or, rather, will become the native habitat of both the Father and the Son (vv. 22, 23, 26). That love will eliminate any distance that might separate the members of such a community from the realm of glory.[18] Along with its other coordinates—glory, the name, life, knowledge of the truth, acceptance of the role of being sent—that love will enable them to orient every successive situation toward one beginning and one end. In other words, where this logos is, there Christ is.

Having now completed the first task, that of exploring the logos ecclesiology in the later chapters, we may undertake the second objective: to explore the possible connections in Johannine thought-patterns between that ecclesiology and the christology of the prologue.

We begin with the three assertions of the first verse: "In the beginning was the logos. The logos was with God. The logos was God." It would appear that these assertions answered three questions of high importance to John: *When* did this logos originate? *Where? Whose* was it?

Frequent references to the first of these answers have already been noted. It was necessary that the logos the evangelist discovered at work in the church of his day be traced to the glory of God before the foundation of the world. The sending of the Son by God belonged among the primal origins. The phrase "in the beginning" reflects the fact that here the evangelist was linking together the inner life of his own community and the Genesis story of creation. The story of the second-generation church, the story of the apostolic mission, the story of Jesus' work—all these were united in the keeping of God's logos. There was no measurable distance between the origins of that logos and the successive acceptances of it.

The answer to the question *where* is, in Johannine thought, equally relevant to the locus of the churches' contact with the logos: "with God" (*pros theon*). Throughout the Gospel, Jesus is reported as testifying that the logos belongs to God. It is God who sends Jesus and commands what he is to say and do. It is God whom Jesus sees and reveals. The logos is God's (5:38; 8:55; 10:35; 17:6, 17). Accordingly, Jesus must constantly remind his followers, "The [logos] which you hear is not mine but the Father's who sent me [14:24, RSV]." All who, in response to the Father's love, believe in the logos will join Jesus "where I am" (17:24), and John leaves no doubt where that is: *pros theon*. Logos as a metaphor has this spatial component.

The prologue's answer to the questions *whose* and *who* ("the logos was God") is also entirely consistent with the perspective of the later chapters. Not only does the logos belong to God, it also conveys to humanity God's name, authority, light, glory, truth, life, and love. As with all these coordinates, one can say that where God's logos is, there God is. A decisive expression is the assurance that the eternal life received by the "dead" is nothing less than the life that "the Father has in himself [5:25, 26]." Even more decisive are those passages in which the sending of the logos, followed by its acceptance, creates a situation that can be described in terms of oneness between Father and Son ("You, Father, are in me and I in you") and in terms of a comparable oneness between God and all who receive the same logos ("I in them and you in me . . . and they . . . in us" [17:21-23]). Logos designates a single reality that may be referred to either as God or as God's logos. This alternation is precisely what one finds in the opening verses of the Gospel; John's ultimate reference is to a logos *theo*logy.

In the next few verses in the prologue we read of the role of the logos in creation: "All things were made through the logos, and without the logos was not anything made." The positive declaration is reinforced by the negative. *All* means all! But the following assertion indicates the type of creative work the evangelist had in mind: "In the logos was life; and the life was the light of humankind." Here biblical scholars are likely to complain of the liberty I have taken in translating the Greek text. In three verses I have written "the logos" where most English translations give "he" or "him." Why this disparity? Because the Greek is ambiguous; it is capable of supporting either translation. The Greek uses demonstrative and relative pronouns in the masculine gender, and because logos is a masculine noun, the pronouns can be rendered in English either by *it* (the logos) or by *he* (Christ as the logos of God). Thus an important question is raised: Did John *at this point* intend to use logos as a personal title for Christ?

I say *no*, despite the fact that recent English translations say *yes*, inasmuch as they use *he* and *him* in these verses. There is one exception: The *New English Bible* recognizes that a problem exists. It translates the first clause of verse 2 *"The Word*, then, was with God at the beginning, and through him all things came to be."* Does the logos ecclesiology of later chapters shed any light on this issue?

There is no doubt, of course, that those later chapters explicitly speak of Christ as the light of the world and the life of humankind. Yet it is also characteristic of those chapters that they speak more frequently of God's logos as conveying to humanity light and life. In the sending of Jesus into the world, God's life has been made accessible. Where people receive this life, they are "born not of blood nor of the will of the flesh nor of the will of man, but of God [1:13, RSV]." Ultimately it is God's logos that creates the community of God's children and abides within that community. It is God's command "Let there be light" that creates light among humankind; John, in fact, says that this "commandment is eternal life [12:50]." It is in his obedience to that command that Jesus came "as light into the world." The ultimate reference in Johannine thought is to God's logos; and it is that reference which is expressed in 1:2-5. In such a reference, John's experience of the life received in the church converges with his reflections on the Genesis story of creation.

In this argument I do not deny that John identified the logos with Christ or that he attributed to Christ a role in the creation of all things. I simply urge that in the first paragraph of the prologue, consistently with the orientation of his thought in later chapters, John wished to stress the role in creation of *God's* logos. The more specific advent of Jesus comes into view only with verse 9, his world-creating activity being mentioned in verse 10. The thought of the opening paragraph (vv. 1-5) provides an ontological horizon for that historic mission of Jesus, defining the first link in the chain of life and the chain of love. This reading of the prologue's opening paragraph brings it into close conformity to our analysis of Cluster Five, in which Jesus himself distinguishes between his own authority and God's and in so doing distinguishes between himself and the logos that he has spoken (12:47-49).

The prologue refers for the final time to the logos in verse 14, with the famous clause "the logos became flesh and dwelt among us." How is this clause best interpreted? Do later chapters aid in such an interpretation?

The customary answer is this: By logos John had in mind here simply the human person Jesus. *Flesh* refers to his humanity: He became a human being, composed of flesh and blood, born of a human mother, dying a human death. By *us* John referred to Jesus' contemporaries, those living in Palestine at the same time, who heard and saw that human person. He could not have meant the later community of believers to whom John was writing. By *among* (the usual translation of the Greek ἐν), John could not have meant *in* or *within* us, nor could he have been speaking of Jesus' presence with those with whom he made his home after his ascension. In other words, verses 14 and 16-18 present christological and not ecclesiological assertions.

Our study of the seven clusters should cast serious doubts on the adequacy of this customary answer, for it distorts Johannine thought-patterns. The time-perspective of those patterns gave a larger place to the retrospect of faith after the glorification of Jesus. The perspective for all thinking about the life-giving work of Christ has been determined by the communal existence of those who have been "born of God" (v. 13), by those who have beheld the glory of Father and Son, who have received grace upon grace, and who can testify concerning the indwelling of the Father and the Son. As I approach the prologue not as a preface to, but as a summary of, the entire Gospel, I find in the opening paragraph a characteristic Johannine emphasis on a logos *theo*logy, in the second paragraph (vv. 6-11) a characteristic emphasis on a logos *christ*ology, and in the third paragraph in verses 12-18 a characteristic emphasis on a logos *ecclesi*ology. More significantly, in the succession of these emphases, the prologue distinguishes as well as unites the three links in the chain of being that characterizes Johannine ontology.

In all this, I have been lifting up the continuities between prologue and Gospel. Are there no discontinuities, contrasts, contradictions? Must we not agree with an often observed and theologically important contrast, which we can define in these terms: In the prologue logos is personalized, *the Word* becomes *he*; in the rest of the Gospel that never happens? E.C. Hoskyns writes that the prologue refers "to a clearly defined person rather than to a circumlocution for God, or as a poetic personification of an abstract idea."[19] C.K. Barrett writes more cautiously, "The word logos is indeed not used as a Christological title after the opening verses; but it is consonant with the Christological teaching of the later parts of the Gospel."[20]

I wish to contest this majority opinion, though I can do no more here than sketch the outlines of an alternative thesis. I would agree that in later chapters distinctions are drawn between Jesus and his logos (5:24; 6:60; 8:31, 37, 43, 51-52; 12:48; 14:23; 15:3, 20). In these contexts the logos is not made identical with Jesus' person or used as a christological title. Jesus does not say, "I am the logos." Yet I would also argue that similar distinctions are drawn in the prologue—between Jesus and the logos of verse 1, between Jesus' glory and the glory of the Father, between Jesus and the grace and truth that have come through him. What is said of the logos in chapter 15 can be said of the logos in chapter 1. "The Word of the Father is the word of Jesus, the word of Jesus becomes that of the disciples if his words remain in them (15:7, 8), for this is what makes disciples of them and allows them to bear fruit."[21]

But let us look at the other side of the dialectic. I agree that in the prologue the Word becomes identified with the person and work of Jesus; it is no longer an abstract idea; it is not a circumlocution for God, but it stands as a "christological title" like other "titles" in the Gospel, although the term *title* may itself be quite un-Johannine. But I would argue that the same identification appears also in the later chapters. And I would present as evidence those clusters in which hearing and seeing Jesus are identified with hearing and seeing God and also those clusters in which the action of believing, of accepting, or of keeping the logos of Christ produces a situation in which Christ himself abides in the believers, making his home with them, so that they abide in him. In these passages the idioms of speaking and hearing are subtly transmuted into idioms of compresence. The logos of Father and the logos of the Son become through the Spirit the personal presence of Father and Son in ways wholly consonant with the thought of the prologue. We will not be able to recognize this consonance, of course, without modifying our usual reactions to the prologue and to the later chapters, or without allowing our thought symbols to become as fluid as John's, or without suffering the kind of cleansing of thought-processes that Jesus' logos accomplished among his first disciples (15:3). Where the cutting-cleansing by that logos proceeds in God's children, there Jesus himself, the person whose story John takes as a supreme paradigm, abides in them (15:3-4). Such an allegory as that of the vine suggests how John could simultaneously distinguish between Jesus and his logos and yet identify that logos with the personal presence of Jesus himself. Within the Johannine perspective, the doctrine concerning incarnation is a doctrine concerning the church; to understand the life of the church is required before an interpreter can grasp many nuances in John's thinking about Christ.

It is hoped that, quite apart from the specific issues that are involved in the exegesis of the prologue, this study will enrich the understanding of the logos-idiom as a significant type of social symbolism. I conclude by summarizing certain dynamic features in this symbolism.[22]

1. The logos-metaphor was "group-binding" in that it indicated not only the cohesive element in the existing community, but also the fabric that connected that community to its ancestors and its descendants.

2. The same metaphor was "time-binding" in the sense of establishing invisible linkages between the present experience of that church and the primal origins of life and light "before the foundation of the world." The logos served as an imaginative definition of cosmic creativity.

3. The logos symbolism bound each immediate situation to the realm of the Transcendent; it was by and through the logos that the Father and the Son made themselves present within the church during the time intervening between the origin and the end of the church's story.

4. The same symbolism bound the ontological to the ethical by identifying quite specifically the character of the logos which would administer final judgment upon all God's people "in the last day."

5. This symbolism enabled the community to hold on to the covenantal, legal, and prophetic traditions of Israel; it made those traditions a supporting reality to the radically new lineage of Abraham (Cluster Four), to the community that relied on Christ to provide manna in the wilderness (Cluster Three).

6. The logos-ideology enabled people caught up in the bitter battles with the synagogue and its leaders to perceive an ultimate significance in the causes and consequences of those battles.

7. The logos idiom did justice to the strategic importance of conceptual thought, to the permanent uniqueness of Jesus' teaching, and to the rhetorical efficacy of the church's preaching, while at the same time it

inhibited tendencies to "freeze" the basic message into verbal, legal, and doctrinal formulations. It combined various kinds of seeing with various kinds of hearing and so, in fact, covered all the various ways by which people respond to the manifest will of God.

8. It is difficult to perceive how Jesus both *speaks* God's logos and *is* God's logos, but that difficulty comes from the fact that the logos fused the cognitive and the emotional, the doctrinal and the mystical, the liturgical and the missiological, the historical and the ontological dimensions of the church's experience of God's gift in Christ.

9. The symbolism of hearing, accepting, and keeping the logos was equally cogent in articulating the experience of both the faithful individual and the faithful congregation. It fused individual and communal memories, duties and hopes. It strengthened the will of a martyr church to accept violent persecution as the essential mode of glorifying God and of being sanctified in the truth (Cluster Six).

10. If the logos Christology was a major Johannine contribution to Christian thought, another contribution, equally significant, was the insistence on the part of the Johannine Christ that his logos was not his own but the Father's, and that, when his followers "kept" this logos, both the Father and the Son took up their dwelling among those followers. The logos symbol was able to express this compresence, this mutuality in consecration, this interdependence in mission.

Unless I am mistaken, it is the very richness of this logos pattern of thought that prompted Harvey McArthur, in summarizing his own quest for the Jesus of history, to adopt this pattern as highly relevant to the situation faced by the modern historian:

> In saying "yes" to this living Word, I am also saying "yes" to the witness of the community that this Word was not plucked capriciously or cleverly out of the air but that it was the Word lived and proclaimed in Jesus of Nazareth—that the Word became flesh before it became kerygma.[23]

CHAPTER 9

Attempts at Understanding the Purpose of Luke-Acts:
Christology and the Salvation of the Gentiles

Karl Paul Donfried

In the scholarly discussion today there are primarily two conflicting theses with regard to the intention of the book of Acts: (1) The Roman apologetic thesis and (2) the Pauline/gentile mission apologetic thesis.

The position of the Roman apologetic thesis was outlined as long ago as 1721 by C.D. Heumann, who argued that Luke-Acts was written "as an apology for the Christian religion" to the pagan magistrate Theophilus.[1] Typical of this position is the conclusion of Overbeck: "In this presentation one cannot deny the specific intention of rejecting political slander against Christianity, and it cannot, as it is developed in Acts, be addressed to any other audience than to the gentiles standing outside the church."[2] P.W. Schmiedel, building on the observations of Overbeck, also sees a political *Tendenz* in Luke's "desire to say as little as possible unfavorable to the Roman civil power."[3] This understanding of Acts is continued by Johannes Weiss,[4] C.H. Turner,[5] H.J. Cadbury[6] (very cautiously as one of several motives), and B.S. Easton[7] and continues into the present in the work of Hans Conzelmann,[8] Ernst Haenchen,[9] Horst R. Moehring,[10] and Werner Georg Kümmel.[11] Representative of this position is Kümmel's assertion that "the aim of defending the Christians against the charge of enmity toward the state is unmistakable."[12]

The Pauline/gentile mission apologetic thesis recognizes that there are apologetic elements in Acts (note, e.g., the terms ἀπολογεῖσθαι and ἀπολογία in 22:1; 24:10; 25:16; 26:1, 2, 24). Their intention, however,

Karl Paul Donfried is a Professor of New Testament in the Department of Religion, Smith College, Northampton, Massachusetts. He and Harvey K. McArthur were colleagues at the University of Heidelberg during a sabbatical, and both have participated in the Columbia New Testament Seminar.

112

is not political, but rather to defend Paul as an orthodox teacher of Israel and to defend the legitimacy of the gentile mission. Basic to this thesis, represented by Jacob Jervell,[13] are two presuppositions: (a) that Luke is addressing Christian readers and (b) that he is trying to solve actual problems these readers have. With regard to the first presupposition, both C.K. Barrett[14] and F.F. Bruce[15] have suggested a similar understanding of Luke's audience, since it appears most improbable that Roman political authorities would be willing to read through all this highly technical, if not unintelligible, theological argumentation, with its frequent reference to Israel and the Old Testament. In support of his second presupposition, Jervell writes that only "in a milieu with a Jewish-Christian stamp could such a lengthy explanation of the justification of the circumcision-free Gentile mission be required"[16] as is found in Acts. It is precisely in such a context that Paul must be defended from charges of disloyalty to the Jewish traditions.

Before reviewing further Jervell's understanding of Paul's "apologetic speeches," we need to come to terms with his overall understanding of Luke-Acts. The basic question that Luke is attempting to answer in Acts is "Why does the church carry on the gentile mission, and how has it come about?"[17] Jervell regards as in error the understanding that claims that the gentile mission is inaugurated only after Israel has rejected the gospel. Rather, before the mission to the gentiles can proceed, the promises of scripture must be fulfilled with regard to Israel. This has, however, occurred in the conversion of the repentant Jews. Thus, the Christian proclamation has divided empirical Israel into two groups: the repentant and the unrepentant. "In Acts, Israel continues to refer to the Jewish people, characterized as a people of repentant (i.e., Christian) and obdurate Jews."[18] And so Jervell can add that the "addition of Gentiles is a part of the restoration of Israel."[19] Only because at least some Jews have repented can the mission proceed to the gentiles. While throughout Acts the gospel is proclaimed to both Jews and gentiles, at the end the concern for the obdurate part of Israel finally ceases, since they have had ample opportunity to repent. A future mission to the Jews by the gentiles is not envisioned by Luke as it was by Paul in Romans 9—11.

Since it is important for Luke that the gentile mission be understood as part of the restoration of Israel, his peculiar problem is how to deal with those obdurate Jews and conservative Jewish-Christians who were charging that Paul was a "radical" intent on destroying the heritage of Israel. Luke denies the validity of this accusation and proceeds to develop a vigorous defense of Paul particularly in Acts 21—28, but also elsewhere in Acts.[20]

Jervell summarizes the first eight chapters in Acts as involving the

113

activity of the twelve apostles among the Jews with reports of "Jewish mass conversions. . . . Salvation belongs to the restored Israel, while the obdurate Jews are to be excluded from the people, salvation and history."[21] It is in such a context that Luke must now defend Paul's attitude toward Israel and the law as orthodox. For this purpose the speeches of Paul, dramatized in terms of political trial scenes, were primarily created. They are not political apologies. The Romans are backdrops and stagehands that permit Luke to develop a major defense of Paul to the conservative Jewish-Christian element of his community. That defense consists of one major theme: "Paul's preaching of Christ really consists only in what the law and the prophets say about the Messiah."[22] All the speeches in this section are constructed to elaborate this theme. The verdict is clear: Paul is not a false teacher of Israel. Jervell's conclusion is in direct opposition to the Roman apologetic thesis: "The issue is not legal protection on the basis of *religio licita*. Viewed from the perspective of Luke's ecclesiology, the issue is the justification of the church's existence, and indirectly a concern for the Gentile mission."[23]

There is, however, one other factor that might be added to Jervell's critique of the Roman apologetic thesis, Acts 23:11 (RSV): "The following night the Lord stood by him and said, 'Take courage, for as you have testified about me at Jerusalem, so you must bear witness also at Rome.'" The necessity for Paul to go to Rome is reiterated and dominates the remaining chapters in Acts. It is "the Lord" who now informs Paul, as previously in 21:11 it was the Holy Spirit: "Thus says the Holy Spirit, 'So shall the Jews at Jerusalem bind the man who owns this girdle and deliver him into the hands of the Gentiles.'" [RSV]. One should also pay attention to Luke 12:11-12, where it is explicitly stated that when one is brought before rulers and authorities, the "Holy Spirit will teach you in that very hour what you ought to say [RSV]." The point is that throughout Luke-Acts it is God through the Holy Spirit who is moving and carefully directing the church from Jerusalem to Rome. This movement, while guided by the Spirit, uses a variety of instruments, including miracles and human agencies, to foster its goal. Do the Roman authorities in Acts 21—28 serve this divinely ordained goal of getting Paul to Rome safely? Why is it that the authorities, often hostile to Jesus and to Paul, are now, almost artificially (how, for example, do we understand the role of the Asiarchs), rescuing Paul from the hands of the Jews? Is it possible that with Acts 23:11 the final segment of Heilsgeschichte is initiated? What function do the Roman authorities have in Luke's literary creation? Perhaps they serve both as a backdrop for the defense of Paul's orthodoxy and as protection for Paul from the

Jews, so that the goal of Heilsgeschichte—namely, Rome—can finally be achieved.

The broad strokes of Jervell's interpretation may be correct. If this interpretation of Luke-Acts is substantiated by the texts, then there is little plausible reason to continue the suggestion that Acts, in particular, reveals a political apologetic *Tendenz*. To argue for such a *Tendenz* is possible only when certain texts are taken out of their specific setting in Luke-Acts.

The question is how one tests whether the proposal just made is a valid interpretation of Luke-Acts. In view of the fact that there has been a strong tendency in Lukan research simply to repeat certain propositions without the requisite detailed exegesis always necessary, we begin with a partial listing of those texts that deal with the problem of Judaism, on the one hand, and those with possible Roman/gentile implications on the other. It will be of particular importance to determine whether the Roman/gentile texts can continue to support the political apologetic thesis.

Judaism/Israel		*Roman/Gentile*	
Luke	1:5f.		
	1:54		
	1:68f.		
	1:77		
	2:22	Luke	2:1
	2:25		2:32
	2:32		
	2:34		
	2:38		
	2:46		
	3:8		3:1
			3:6
			3:14
			3:19
	4:29		4:26
			4:27
			7:5
			8:13

Judaism/Israel (cont.)	Roman/Gentile (cont.)
9:32	9:7
	12:11
13:34ff.	13:1
	13:29
	13:31
14:24	
16:31	
	18:32
19:47	
20:20,26	
	21:12
	22:25
	22:38
23:2,5,18ff.,23,25	23:4,14,20,22
	23:47
24:53ff.	24:47

	Acts	1:8
Acts	2:36	2:8ff.
	2:39	2:39
	3:1ff.	
	3:12–13,14–17	
	3:26	
	4:3	4:27
	5:17ff.	
	5:31	
	5:39	
	6:11ff.	

Judaism/Israel (cont.)	*Roman/Gentile* (cont.)
7:39	
7:51ff.	
7:58	
8:1	8:4ff.
	8:26ff.
	8:40
	9:15
10:39	10:1ff.
	10:28
	10:35
	10:45
	12:1
	12:20ff.
13:30	13:12
	13:28
	13:46ff.
14:19	14:5
	14:27
	15:7
	15:23
	16:19ff.
	16:35
	17:8
18:6	18:2
	18:12
	19:31
	19:37ff.
21:20	21:28
21:28	21:32ff.

Judaism/Israel (cont.)	*Roman/Gentile* (cont.)
22:18	22:15
	22:21
	22:25,29
23:20ff.	23:10
	23:26ff.
24:5ff.	24:25
25:8	25:8
	25:9
	25:13ff.
26:6	26:24ff.
26:16ff.	26:31-32
	27:42
28:17ff.	28:29

The overall point of the texts in the left-hand column is that salvation has been offered to Israel in God's revelation in Christ, but many in Israel have repeatedly rejected this opportunity. Luke 2:32 clearly shows that God intends this offer of salvation both for gentiles and for Israel. Because of the Jewish rejection of Jesus and his word, often with violence, the focus of salvation increasingly shifts away from Israel (Jerusalem) and toward the gentiles (Rome) as Luke-Acts progresses. The increasing forsakenness of Israel is made clear in Luke 13:34ff. and 14:24, just to cite two texts. The guilt and violence of the Jews is evident throughout Luke's interpretation of the passion narrative and continues throughout Acts—the Jews are always out to get the Christian missionaries. This rejection of Israel then reaches its consummation in Acts 28:17ff. Simultaneously, the strong movement toward the gentiles becomes clear through a steady repetition and actualization of Luke 2:32, as is evident in Luke 21:24; Acts 10:45ff.; 13:46ff.; and 28:29.

That Luke is attempting to explain the validity of the gentile mission for his predominantly Jewish-Christian congregation in light of possible reservations, if not sharp criticisms, appears to be likely from a review of these texts in the left-hand column.

We now turn to the texts in the right-hand column. Special attention will be focused, on the one hand, on those texts that speak against the political apologetic thesis outlined above and, on the other hand, on those texts that have been understood as self-evidently speaking in favor of such a thesis.

A matter that should be discussed is the political sympathies of those ruling in Palestine during the period under study. Judea was a client kingdom under Herod the Great, and it became an imperial province in A.D. 6, being ruled by an equestrian procurator until A.D. 66, except for the period from A.D. 41 to 44, when Claudius allowed Herod Agrippa I to rule Judea as client king. To whom were the Herodian rulers, including Herod Agrippa II, loyal? Can one assume that the answer is Rome? Can one agree with Samuel Sandmel's evaluation: "It is a fair summary to say that Agrippa (II) was undeviatingly on the side of the Romans"?[24] Did Luke assume this? These matters have an important bearing on the exegesis of certain texts in Acts, such as Acts 12:1ff. and the entire trial cycle beginning with Acts 21.

Let us now examine selected texts from column two:

Luke 3:19; 9:7; 13:31; Acts 12:1 and 20ff. These texts contain certain negative evaluations of Herodian rulers.

Luke 23:4. This and other related texts in the passion narrative are intended primarily to demonstrate not Roman innocence but Jewish responsibility for the death of Jesus. To argue that the political apology theme is primary is to wrench these texts from their context in the entirety of Luke-Acts.

Acts 13:4ff. The story of the conversion of the proconsul of Paphos, Sergius Paulus, is to demonstrate the conversion of a gentile despite the opposition of the Jew, Elymas. Paul and Barnabas make reference to precisely such conversions in 14:27 and 15:3.

Acts 14:5ff. This passage, in which both gentiles and Jews, together with their respective rulers, were molesting and stoning the Christians, causes great difficulties for the apologetic thesis of Conzelmann and others. My question to the Conzelmann/Haenchen thesis is Why are gentiles explicitly included in this description? Would it not have been easier simply to omit them?

Acts 15:3. What we have here is analogous to the positive reference to the centurion in Luke 7:5. There is nothing in either place that supports a pro-Roman political apology.

Acts 16:19ff. This pericope is one of the stronger in support of the apologetic thesis, and Conzelmann[25] explicitly interprets it in such a way. This may be. Two questions should be raised: (1) What is the rationale for outlining the severity of the magistrates' action in 16:22-23? Simply to repeal it at the end of the story? Why the reversal? (2) Could this entire passage be interpreted in the sense that Roman authorities show more respect (v. 29) to Paul than the Jewish authorities

119

and are even willing to reverse themselves when necessary (vv. 38-39), a step the Jews are unwilling to take throughout Luke-Acts because of their obstinacy? Or is it one of the main purposes of this pericope to introduce the "Roman appeal" theme (vv. 35ff.)? This theme, which is developed in Acts 21—28, becomes the major factor that allows Paul to get to Rome safely. Of these three options, the last is the most likely. If this is so, we have no direct support for the political apologetic thesis in these verses.

Acts 18:2ff. If Claudius' expulsion of the Jews from Rome included Jewish Christians, as is likely, this would be an awkward text in support of the Conzelmann position.[26]

Acts 18:12ff. The purpose of this scene is to illustrate the basic charge many Jews and Jewish Christians had against Paul: He persuades people to worship God "contrary to the law." At best, Gallio's attitude is one of "Leave me out of your disputes—I don't care." But if Sosthenes is to be identified with the Sosthenes of 1 Corinthians 1:1, then Gallio's attitude becomes one that is considerably less than neutral toward Christians.

Acts 19:23ff. Does verse 38 support thesis one (Haenchen, et al.)? Before this can be answered, one must pay careful attention to the verses that precede this "riot in Ephesus" pericope, namely, verses 21-22 (RSV): "Now after these events Paul resolved in the Spirit to pass through Macedonia and Achaia and to go to Jerusalem saying, 'After I have been there, I must also see Rome.' "

It appears as if Acts 19:23-41 is a frame that connects 19:22 to 20:1. It points the finger to the *Jewish* conflict, which is the critical problem in the exercise of Paul's ministry. Thus, it is stressed that the Asiarchs (v. 31) ("men elected for the promotion of the imperial cult")[27] are open to Paul, and the town clerk states that Paul and his associates are not "blasphemers of our goddess [v. 37]." Unrelentingly Luke demonstrates that Paul's primary conflict is with only one group: those of the *Jewish* tradition.

Acts 21:32ff. In the midst of harsh Jewish criticism the Roman soldiers come to the defense of Paul. This now becomes a prominent motif throughout the remainder of Acts. Roman authorities become an instrument of the Holy Spirit in rescuing Paul for the goal of preaching to the gentile world from the capital of the empire, Rome, and this, according to the final words of Acts 28, he does "unhindered."

Acts 22:22ff. Despite accusations and attack by the Jews, and initially by the Roman authorities, the Roman citizenship motif safeguards Paul.

Acts 23:10ff. The tribune rescues Paul from a hostile Jewish audience. This event points not only to the hostility of the Jews, but also to the divine intervention of God in preserving Paul for his journey to Rome.

This is precisely the point of verse 11 (RSV): "The following night the Lord stood by him and said, 'Take courage, for as you have testified about me at Jerusalem, so you must bear witness also at Rome.'"

Acts 23:26ff. A concise repetition of the "Jewish hostility/divine protection because of the Roman citizenship" motif.

Acts 24:24ff. Felix is open to Paul but is not persuaded about the truth claims of Christianity. Felix leaves Paul in prison "to do the Jews a favor [v. 27]."

Acts 25:8ff. Festus, too, is interested in "doing the Jews a favor" (v. 9). What is the point of this emphasis—to point out the guilt of the Jews? If anything Festus, as Felix, appears coolly neutral, but with a slight bias in favor of the Jews, not recognizing that they, as Roman officials, are furthering God's intention with regard to Paul—namely, Rome and the unhindered advance of the gentile mission.

Acts 25:8ff. Again, with reference to the Jewish hostility/appeal to Caesar theme, Paul claims that he is not guilty not only with regard to the law of the Jews but also with regard to Caesar. This latter point should be stressed, because it is for this reason that Paul will be able to preach and teach "about the Lord Jesus Christ quite openly and unhindered [28:31, RSV]" in Rome.

Acts 25:23ff. Festus has found "nothing deserving death" in him (v. 25). The point of Festus' address is to reiterate unambiguously the negative Jewish attitude toward Paul.

Acts 26:1ff. Although addressed to Herod Agrippa II, the speech of Paul has only one intention: to vindicate himself before the charge of Jews and Jewish Christians, which is that he stands in conflict with "the promise made by God to our fathers [v. 6, RSV]." This entire chapter contains many factors that lend credence to Jervell's overall hypothesis.[28]

Acts 26:24ff. Both Festus and Agrippa agree that Paul is not guilty of the Jewish charges. Does Luke use these people as a jury that delivers the final verdict of "not guilty" with regard to the supposed conflict between Paul and Judaism? Probably. Now that the issue has been solved, Paul can proceed to Rome via the "appeal to Caesar" motif of Luke.

Acts 27:42. Is this Roman centurion another of God's vehicles in making certain that Paul arrives in Rome safely so as to fulfill God's plan? This is likely.

Acts 28:28-30. The culmination of God's plan in history, as described by Luke in his two-volume work, has been reached. Paul is in Rome, able to preach God's message of salvation to the gentiles in an open and unhindered fashion. "They will listen [v. 29]." The final rejection of the obstinate segment of Israel takes place in Acts 28:25-27, which is also a strong vindication of Paul. It is not Paul who stands in conflict with the promises of God to Israel, but that part of Israel which has rejected Jesus.

This cursory examination of selected texts would suggest the overall plausibility of Jervell's interpretation of Luke-Acts and the necessity for subsequent critics to modify and correct the "Roman apologetic" thesis in light of it.

CHAPTER 10

Christological *Tendenz* in Colossians 1:15-20: A *Theologia Crucis*

Wayne G. Rollins

This study proposes that from the standpoint of the author of Colossians, the *theologia crucis* found in the second strophe[1] of the Christ hymn in Colossians 1:15-20 constitutes the *crux interpretum,* not only for the hymn, but also for the theology and Christology of the letter as a whole.

Since Friedrich Schleiermacher first noted the hymnic structure of Colossians 1:15-20,[2] this passage has been the center of attention in Colossians studies. Earlier exegetes found it the key to the Christology of Colossians, which they characterized as "cosmological."[3] They saw in it "the highest point attained by Christology in the New Testament."[4] The prime objective of the author was seen as the proclamation of Christ as preexistent Lord of the universe.[5] Eduard Lohse summarizes this point of view:

> Col[ossians] develops its Christology on the basis of the Christ-hymn: Christ is the first-born of all creatures, in whom all things have been created and have their existence; and he is the first-born of the dead, whose blood on the cross has brought about cosmic reconciliation (1:15-20). Nothing is said about Christ's victory over the constraining power of sin, law, and death. The stress is on Christ's triumph over the cosmic principalities. . . . The exalted Christ is head over all powers and principalities (2:10) and is preached among the Nations as Lord over everything (1:27). The believers have already been placed in the domain of his rule (1:13). These verses delineate the world-wide significance of the Christ-event.[6]

Wayne G. Rollins was Professor of New Testament at the Hartford Seminary Foundation. He is presently Professor of Religious Studies and Coordinator of the Graduate Program in Religious Studies at Assumption College, Worcester, Massachusetts.

123

Turning from summaries to the exegesis of specific passages, however, one finds that the generalized theories concerning the cosmological character and "height" of Christology in Colossians cannot stand unqualified. Lohse himself points this out on four separate counts.

First, Lohse notes the complex provenance of 1:15-20; it consists of two elements, a pre-Pauline hymn and editorial interpolations. He notes further that the interpolations are critical for understanding how the author wishes the pre-Pauline hymn to be understood. Citing the interpolation of two phrases, "the church" in 1:18 and "by the blood of his cross" in 1:20, Lohse comments, "The author of the letter gives this cosmological train of thought a *new direction* by designating *the church* as a place where in the present Christ exercises his rule over the cosmos."[7] He adds, "By means of these two glosses the hymn's statements receive solid *historical* reference. The reconciliation which relates to the whole world originated in the vicarious death of Christ; the rule of Christ, however, is a present reality in his body, the church."[8]

Second, Lohse indicates that the Christology of the first strophe (1:15-18a) and that of the second (1:18b-20) are not identical, and that the second is intended as commentary on the first: "The right understanding of the cosmological statements of the first part of the hymn is disclosed only by the soteriological statements of the second strophe."[9] Citing specifically the reference to "blood of the cross" and "reconciliation" in strophe two, Lohse concludes, "A 'theology of glory,' which might view the consummation as already achieved, is corrected by the 'theology of the cross' (cf. 2:14-15)."[10]

Third, Lohse points out that (a) *the materials directly preceding the hymn,* namely, the petitionary and thanksgiving introit in 1:9-14, and (b) *the materials directly following the hymn,* namely, the epexegetical commentary on strophe two in 1:21-24, constitute a context, created by the author, indicating "how the Christ hymn ought to be understood."[11] Commenting on the materials preceding the hymn, Lohse cites the phrase "forgiveness of sins" inserted as an appositive to the word redemption in 1:14, and notes that "by defining 'redemption' as 'forgiveness of sins' " the author "*indicates in what sense the following hymn is to be understood.* All speculations about knowledge of higher worlds are confronted by the assertion that nothing can surpass nor supplement the forgiveness of sins."[12] Commenting on the theme of "reconciliation" developed in the materials immediately following the hymn, Lohse comments, "The reconciliation is thereby *no longer understood in a cosmic context;* rather it is related to the community which is addressed by the word of reconciliation."[13]

Fourth, Lohse insists that the author's intention in deploying the

Christ hymn is to be understood in the context of the theological conflict with the "philosophy" being advocated by the Jewish-Gnostic group in Colossae. The author is answering the Errorists. But, as Lohse carefully notes, "the answer . . . is *not stated in terms of a Christian metaphysic.* Rather, the author of Col[ossians] confronts the 'philosophy' with an antithesis that is *historically grounded.*"[14] To this we might add Ernst Percy's observation, "It is now apparent that Paul used the Christology of the hymn in Col. 1 with clear reserve in the interest of resisting the false-teachers. . . . Paul was responding as a Jew and thinking as a Christian about the crucified and resurrected one. So he was never hesitant to place the cross and the parousia in the center of things, nor to subordinate all else to the historical Kerygma."[15]

In view of the above hints and suggestions that in Colossians 1:15-20 the author may be attempting to shift the audience's concern from cosmology to history and from a *theologia gloriae* to a *theologia crucis,* we propose to reopen the question of the function of the two-strophe Christ hymn in Colossians 1:15-20, examining its role from the perspective of three contexts: (1) the *historical* context of the controversy with the Colossians Errorists; (2) the broader *literary* context of Colossians 1:9-24 in which the hymn is set; and (3) the broader *theological* context of the letter's purpose as a whole.

COLOSSIANS 1:15-20 in the Context of the Religious Conflict at Colossae

In Colossians we detect three distinct points of view at work in the religious controversy at Colossae: (a) the point of view of the author, (b) that of the Colossian Christians, and (c) that of the Errorists. Since the Christ hymn appears in the text as part of the author's attempt to negotiate his own position with respect to the other two, it is necessary to examine the positions of all three to see if it is possible to achieve a clearer understanding of the hymn's function in the historical context.

A. The author of Colossians is presumably not know personally by the Colossian Christians (2:1, 5), but has been recently apprised of the conflict at Colossae by Epaphras, newly arrived at the author's site, the presumed founder of the church at Colossae (1:7) as well as at nearby Laodicea and Hierapolis (4:13), two sister churches in the Lycus valley. He has some acquaintance with two Colossian Christians, Nympha (4:15) and Archippus (4:17), and sends them greetings from three Jewish Christians in his company, Aristarchus, Mark (the cousin of Barnabas), and Jesus Justus (4:10-11), as well as from two gentile Christians, Luke and Demas (4:14). Tychicus and Onesimus, gentile assistants, will deliver the letter (4:7-9).

To make his case effective, the author must develop his position not only with respect to the Errorists, who stand opposed to the author on most issues, but also with respect to the peculiar brand of Christology and theology that has developed in the Colossian church, which, it can be assumed, will be close to but not necessarily identical with the author's point of view. His objective will be not only to discredit the Errorists, but also to realign the position of the Colossian Christians with the "first truths" of the Pauline Christian kerygma if necessary.

B. *The Colossian Christians,* to whom the letter is addressed, are gentiles, the "uncircumcised" (2:13). Many are married (3:18-21); there are slaves as well as free among them (3:22—4:1). Prior to conversion,[16] their lives were marked by immorality, impurity, covetousness (3:5), hostility, and evil deeds (1:21). The gospel they first received (1:5), presumably from Epaphras, included the familiar Pauline emphasis on faith, hope, and love (1:4-5), as well as joy (1:11), the forgiveness of sins (1:14, 2:13), and teaching on the spirit (1:8). They have been baptized, and their baptism has been interpreted by their Christian teachers as a dying and rising with Christ (2:11-12), which in turn implies a dying to their interest in "elemental spirits of the universe [2:20]." One of their hymns, adapted by the author in Colossians 1:15-20,[17] expresses a cosmological Christology emphasizing the priority of Christ over these elemental spirits. The crisis they currently face involves a newly arrived group of Christian Judaizers, condemning their "gentile" understanding of the Christian life as inadequate for achieving fulfillment (2:10) and perfection (1:28, 3:14).

C. The third faction, the *Errorists,* are a Jewish-Gnostic sect.[18] The description of their beliefs and practices in 2:8-23 is one of the fullest we have of any of the Pauline "opponents." A primary feature of the sect, according to the author, is its religious *legalism.* They have elaborated a set of cultic ordinances (2:14, 20) that include circumcision (2:11-12), dietary rules (2:16), ascetic practices ("Do not handle, do not taste, do not touch [2:21]," "self-abasement," and "severity to the body" (2:18, 23). An element of *mysticism* is also evident in the reference to the visions (2:18), in which they take such pride, and to "angel worship," which is to be taken not as the practice of worshiping angels but as the cultic conviction that in worship they share in a mystical sense with the angelic host in praising God.[19] Their legalism and mysticism are rooted in a metaphysical world-view that regards the *stoicheia* (2:8, 20), or "elemental spirits of the universe," as determinative of heavenly and earthly destinies but also as prescriptive of the rules of piety and the moral life. They understand their cultic-religious system as the elaboration of a "mystery" hidden for ages but now come to light in their teaching (1:26, 2:2).[20] Finally, the Errorists are effective propagandists,

126

aggressive in their teaching (2:8) and captiously persuasive in their arguments (2:4, 8), condemning (2:18) those who reject their teachings and who refuse their hard-line distinction between Greek and Jew, circumcised and uncircumcised (3:11).

Who were the Errorists? J.B. Lightfoot long ago suggested they were "Christians in some sense."[21] though if so, clearly of a Judaizing strain comparable to the Galatians' opponents who are described as Judaizers (Galatians 2:14), insisting on observance of the law (passim), on circumcision (5:2-12), on the observance of days, months, seasons, and years (4:10), on distinctions between Jew and Greek (3:28), and on subservience to the *stoicheia* (4:3, 9). If Christian, their Christology might have resembled that of the Jewish-Christian opponents in Hebrews who identified Jesus as one of the angelic host (Hebrews 1:4ff.).

Is it possible to identify them more precisely? Again, J.B. Lightfoot's proposal that they are a Jewish-Gnostic sect of the Essene or Therapeutae type is still attractive,[22] all the more since the discovery of the Qumran texts. The similarities are sufficient to suggest that the Qumran covenanters provide a viable model for understanding the mentality and practice of the Colossian Errorists. First, the references in Colossians to "feasts, new moon, or sabbath [2:16] ," and to the "dogmatizing" that is rooted in a *stoicheia* philosophy (2:20), echo a key motif at Qumran. One has only to read the Manual of Discipline and the Thanksgiving Psalms to realize that at the center of Qumran piety was the belief in a cosmic order of "dominions" of light and darkness that establish not only the times and seasons of prayer but also the course of history. They do not operate autonomously; they are ordained in all their courses by God, marking out the seasons of God's judgments and mercies, which are to be observed with scrupulous care. The Manual of Discipline reads:

> He shall bless Him [with the offering] of the lips at the times
> ordained by Him: at the beginning of the dominion of light, and
> at its end when it retires to its appointed place . . . at the entry
> of the [monthly] seasons on the days of new moon . . . a sign for
> the unlocking of everlasting mercies at the beginning of seasons
> in all times to come. At the beginning of the months of the
> [yearly] seasons and on the holy days appointed for remem-
> brance, in their seasons I will bless Him . . . according to the
> Precept engraved forever, at the beginning of the years and at
> the end of their seasons when their appointed law is fulfilled, on
> the day decreed by Him.[23]

As Vermes observes, the Rule of Qumran "required them to worship God in the correct manner at set times, these set times conforming to the eternal and unchanging laws affecting the rhythm of time itself."[24]

Second, when the author of Colossians identifies his gospel and Christ as God's "mystery" (1:26; 2:2; 4:3), he is most likely meeting the Errorists' claim that they are the divinely appointed guardians of God's "mystery." The evidence from Qumran supports this hypothesis. "Mystery" language abounds in the Qumran scrolls.[25] The covenanters held that God had revealed to them the "hidden things" "concerning which Israel in general had gone astray—even His holy sabbaths and His glorious festivals, His righteous ordinances, the ways of His truth and the purposes of His will, 'the which, if a man do, he shall live.' "[26] Such "mysteries," they held, were hidden from ordinary people, revealed only to the elect,[27] whom God endows with "the perfect way of understanding" creating a "house of perfection" among them.[28]

Third, numerous linguistic parallels exist between the vocabulary of Qumran and that of the Errorists.[29] They long for "perfection"[30]; they describe themselves as "sons of light" opposed to the kingdom of darkness[31]; they practice the discipline of poverty, purity, mortification of the flesh, and self-abnegation[32]; and they insist on circumcision.[33] In addition, the covenanters at Qumran rely on visions as a source of authentic religious knowledge[34] and speak in mystical terms of their participation in angelic worship, as indicated in one of the liturgical fragments at Qumran: "May you be as an Angel of the Presence in the Abode of Holiness to the glory of the God of [hosts]. . . . May you attend upon the service in the Temple of the Kingdom and decree destiny in company with the Angels of the Presence."[35]

In summary, the Colossian Errorist cultus and that of Qumran appear to share the following qualities: They are *ascetic,* engaging in practices that will mortify the flesh; they are *legalistic,* insisting on strict observance of calendric, dietary, liturgical, and moral rules; they are *ritualistic,* engaged in a diurnal regimen of religious offices; and they are *exclusivistic,* "hating" or "disqualifying" outsiders, priding themselves on their community of the elect.[36]

With this general sketch in mind, one might ask what appeal such a cultus might have for the Colossian Christians. Eduard Lohse offers such an analysis. In his judgment their appeal resides in a number of factors: (a) the offer of a secret revelation concerning the divine plan of history; (b) the offer of a way of coming to terms with the astral forces and of being delivered from the "mysteries of evil" and the dominions of darkness; (c) the offer of divine fulfillment and perfection; (d) the offer of moral and religious absolutes; (e) the charge that a gospel without law is inadequate.[37] To Lohse's list one might add (f) the appeal of ascetic discipline as a means of freeing oneself from the passions of the flesh, and (g) the appeal of a well-structured and rationalized "philosophy" with a detailed metaphysical base.

What objections would the author have to the teachings and claims of the Errorist cultus? Although it must be acknowledged that many of the spiritual goals advocated by the Errorists would be shared by the author (e.g., the goals of wisdom, knowledge, fulfillment, deliverance from the powers of darkness, maturity, insight into the divine mystery), the author would at the same time have fundamental objections to the Errorist understanding of the content, source, and means of attaining these goals, and of the type of community such goals would naturally engender. In Colossians, as in the key Pauline letters, one can detect the firm recognition of a fundamental theological, spiritual, and psychological dichotomy between a religion of law and a religion of gospel,[38] between an attitude of boasting and thanksgiving,[39] between a religious discipline focused on visions, angels, and ascetic practices, and a discipline focused on love, peace, and the "word of Christ,"[40] between a socially divisive and a socially unifying religious community,[41] between a wisdom of metaphysical and cosmological "philosophy" and the wisdom and knowledge of the crucified Christ.[42] It is with such a sense of dichotomy in mind that the author begins the apologia to the Colossian Christians against the Errorists in Colossians 1:9-23.

Colossians 1:15-20 in the Immediate Literary Context of 1:9-23

To meet the threat of the Jewish-Gnostic "philosophy" and to introduce his own understanding of "the mystery of Christ [4:3]," the author opens his letter with a line of argument that will lead progressively from presuppositions held in common by the author, the Errorists, and the Colossian Christians, to a statement of the central principle that divides them. This opening apologia in 1:9-23 provides the point of departure for the entire letter and consists of four distinct literary units:

1:9-14   A Petitionary/Thanksgiving Introit
1:15-18a A Hymn on Christ and Creation (Strophe A)
1:18b-20 A Hymn on Christ and Reconciliation (Strophe B)
1:21-23   Epexegetical Commentary on Strophe B

Each of these units will be discussed briefly, with respect to the role each plays in the broader argument of the whole.

1:9-14: A Petitionary/Thanksgiving Introit. This section consists of a series of petitions for the spiritual well-being of the Colossians (1:9-11), blending into a confessional statement of thanksgiving in 1:12-13. The section constitutes a virtual glossary of key theological terms and phrases which in all likelihood are significant not only for the author, but for the Colossian Christians and Errorists as well, constituting key issues in the three-way debate. These phrases and terms include the references to "fulfillment," "knowledge," "wisdom," and "spiritual understanding" in 1:9; the reference to "walking," "good works," "bearing fruit and growing," and "knowledge of God" in 1:10; the allusion to "power," "glory," "patience," and "long-suffering" in 1:11; and the references to "thanksgiving," to "a lot in the inheritance of the saints in light," to "deliverance from the authorities of darkness" and "transferring into the kingdom," and "redemption" in 1:12-14.

Lohse notes the unusually high number of parallels to Qumran vocabulary in this section,[43] indicating that they are probably key theologoumena also among the Errorists. But he also notes with Käsemann and others that there are "traditional phrases" here, probably drawn from the baptismal liturgical context of the Colossian Christians.[44]

In constructing this mosaic of traditional Christian and Jewish (Errorist) terms and phrases the author seems to have three purposes in mind. First, he is reminding the Colossians that many of the spiritual goals proffered by the Errorists already are and always have been part of the Christian spiritual panoply. Second, he is pointing out that some of these goals, understood by the Errorists as yet to be realized in the future (e.g., deliverance from the "dominion of darkness," "transfer to the kingdom," and sharing in the "inheritance of the saints in light"), are already realized and "confessed" in Christian practice. Third, through the highlighting of certain distinctive Christian phrases in interpolative fashion in this sequence of "traditional terms," the author underlines key differences between the Errorist way and the Pauline way. These phrases include "with joy [1:11]," "the son of his love [1:13]," and the appositive phrase "forgiveness of sins [1:14]," all three of which serve to remind the reader of the profound contrasts in religious ideals and beliefs between the two groups.

1:15-18a: A Hymn on Christ and Creation (Strophe A). Many critical attempts have been made to retrieve two poetically balanced strophes of equal length from the entire Christ hymn in 1:15-20.[45] However, as Lohse suggests, these proposed reconstructions "meddle too much with the given text" without sufficient warrant.[46] Far more satisfactory is Lohse's own strophic rendition of the hymn, requiring no deletions and transpositions and recommending only two phrases (in brackets below) as editorial interpolations:

130

Strophe A :15   *He is* the image of the invisible God,
                The first-born before all creation,
          :16   *For in him* all things were created
                      In the heavens and on earth,
                      The visible and the invisible,
                      Whether thrones or dominions, principalities
                          or powers;
                      All things are created *through* him and *for* him
          :17   *And he* is before all things
                      And *in him* all things are established
          :18   *And he* is the head of the body, [the church],
Strophe B   *He is* the beginning,
                The first-born from the dead,
                      In order that he might be the first in all things,
          :19   *For in him* all the fullness was pleased to dwell
          :20   *And through him* to reconcile all things *toward
                    him,*
                      Making peace [through the blood of his cross]
                          through him
                      Whether on earth or in the heavens.[47]

Strophe A, or perhaps the whole of the hymn, is regarded by most commentators as a piece borrowed from the active worship life of the Colossian Christians and possibly employed by the churches in the Lycus valley and throughout Asia.[48] It appears to be a Christian adaptation of Hellenistic Jewish wisdom speculation, which spoke in hymnic form of wisdom as the first of God's creation and as the mediator of God's creative and reconciling power.[49]

Why does the author introduce this cosmologically framed Wisdom-Christ hymn in 1:15-18a? The answer seems to lie in the controversy with the Jewish-Gnostic Errorists. Martin Dibelius makes this telling observation: "The situation has caused Paul to speak of things which otherwise . . . he only touches upon with allusions."[50] The implication of this observation is that the cosmological motif is introduced at this point in the letter not because it is a central motif or controlling concern in the author's theology but rather because it has become a central issue in the critique leveled by the Errorists against the Colossian Christians.

The author's purpose in employing Strophe A at this point is to remind the Colossian Christians that in their cosmological hymn they have effectively repudiated the Errorist advocacy of a *stoicheia*-oriented cultus. He reminds them they have already subscribed to the confessional statement that Christ, not the *stoicheia,* is the revelation of the "unseen God" and the purveyor of God's will, and that the meaning of the created universe is to be found not in the stars but in Christ, whom they have fitly called the "head" or originative and governing principle of the *corpus creationis* (σῶμα).[51]

By incorporating this borrowed strophe in his *apologia*, the author indicates he is not averse to the use of cosmological imagery to express the universal theological implications of his Christology, especially in combatting the mythic-cosmic claims of the Errorists. He will employ a similar mythic-cosmic metaphor in 2:15, where he portrays Christ as victor in the aftermath of a battle with the principalities and powers. But in the strophe to follow, and in much of what follows, the author will attempt to move his audience to consider further who the Christ of Strophe A is from the standpoint of the controlling motifs in his own theology, and how and where it is that this Christ reveals the will and "mystery" of the "unseen God."

1:18b-20: A Hymn on Christ and Reconciliation (Strophe B). Critical scholarship has proposed two hypotheses with respect to the provenance of Strophe B. The first is that Strophe B is the second half of a two-part hymn, borrowed from the Colossian Christians in unaltered form. The second is that Strophe B is an edited version of the above, rearranged and interpolated by the author. Neither of these hypotheses, however, has proved satisfactory.

The first hypothesis is unsatisfactory because it fails to explain the marked differences between Strophe B and Strophe A. Strophe B lacks the ordered chiastic structure of A. It seems to be studded with unpoetic, interpolated phrases that bear closer affinity to the cross-centered theology of 1:21—2:3 than to the cosmic-oriented theology of Strophe A. Strophe B also lacks the refined symmetry of form and content with Strophe A that one might expect in paired strophes.[52] The second hypothesis is unsatisfactory because every attempt to reconstruct the original, uninterpolated hymn ends in what appears to be an arbitrary and procrustean effort.[53]

In view of the above, we would like to propose a third hypothesis regarding Strophe B that requires no deletions or rearrangements and that accounts for the lack of symmetry and balance with Strophe A. According to this hypothesis, the original hymn borrowed from the Colossian Christians is the present Strophe A (1:15-18a). Strophe B, however, is not part of the original hymn of the Colossian Christian community, but is rather the creation of the author, constructed from key kerygmatic phrases in the Pauline tradition along with theological commentary by the author. Designed as a transparently awkward match for the elegant poetry of Strophe A, Strophe B nevertheless has the serious theological purpose of stating unmistakably to the Colossian

Christians as well as to the Errorists that the cosmological *theologia gloriae* of their hymnody (Strophe A) has to be balanced with a soteriological *theologia crucis* to be faithful to the gospel (1:5). The author's intention is not to displace the cosmological Christology of the "hymn," but rather to amplify it with a *pesher*-like addendum of a second, extemporaneous strophe, aimed at forcing a shift in the current theological debate from the cosmological sphere, where the Errorists have chosen to draw the line of battle, to the historical sphere, where the Pauline kerygma of cross, gospel, church, and mission elects to draw the line.

A brief verse-by-verse commentary on Strophe B will reveal the extent to which the *theologia crucis* of B is offered as a corrective to A, and at the same time will set the tone for the soteriological thrust of the remainder of the epistle.

1. Strophe B, as an editorial creation of the author, actually begins with the addendum of the word ἐκκλησία ("church") to the term σῶμα ("body") in 1:18a. The effect is to transpose the concept of Christ's body from a cosmic to a historical phenomenon,[54] a theological direction maintained through the rest of the letter, where Christ's σῶμα is explicitly identified with the fleshly (1:22), with the historical mission church (1:24), and with reconciled human community (3:15).

2. The relative pronoun ὅς at the beginning of Strophe B functions as an exegetical amplification of the ὅς in 1:15, informing the reader that the one "who is the image of the unseen God" is not an angel or one of the *stoicheia,* but the one whose blood was shed on a cross (1:20).[55]

3. The description of Christ as the "beginning, the first-born of the dead" in 1:18b, with its subsequent note of reconciliation in verses 20 and 22, echoes the Pauline discourses on the Second Adam and new creation in 2 Corinthians 5:16ff. and 1 Corinthians 15:45ff. With these phrases the author provides tacit elaboration of the εἰς αὐτὸν ἔκτισται in 1:16 of Strophe A, indicating that the purpose "for which" the first creation took place was in fact the second creation of reconciliation inaugurated by the one who died on the cross.[56]

4. The ἵνα clause in 1:18c, "that he might be preeminent in all things," is the most explicit statement of the author's intention in Strophe B. For the Errorists, the phrase "all things" (τά πάντα) represented a fundamentally metaphysical concept. It referred to all created things, both on heaven and on earth, but fundamentally understood the created "all" in terms of a creative drama that was essentially cosmological and metahistorical in character.[57] We see the author's resistance to this fundamentally metahistorical understanding of the "all" in two ways.

First he resists this metahistorical understanding of the "all" from a

133

cosmological perspective. For the Errorists the most important events were happening in the upper spheres, with the *stoicheia*. But in 1:23 the author introduces an unusual phrase. He states that the mission of the present church is to preach the gospel "to every creature under heaven" (ἐν πάσῃ κτίσει τῇ ὑπὸ τὸν οὐρανόν) or "to the whole creation under heaven." This phrase is significant for two reasons. First, the expression "every creature" is "whole creation" or borrowed from the first line of the cosmologically oriented Strophe A, where we read in 1:15 that Christ is the "first-born of all creation" (πάσης κτίσεως). By repeating the phrase in verse 23 with the addition of "under heaven," the author is contending that this "whole creation" includes the earthly and the historical and is not limited to the heavenly. Second, the author is going beyond this affirmation to the radical proposal that *the "under heavenly" realm is the locus of God's present activity.* The "under heavenly" rather than the "heavenly" is the place where God's new eschatological creation is taking place, and in this sense preempts preoccupation with the "things above."[58]

The second level at which he resists the metahistorical understanding of "the all" is at the *social* level. Two passages in particular make this plain. The first is 1:27-28. In verse 28 the expression "every man" (or "every person," πάντα ἄνθρωπον) occurs three times! In the preceding verse the author makes the point that God has called him to manifest God's "mystery" *"among the Gentiles."* He elaborates the point in verse 28 with the phrases, "warning every man," "teaching every man," "presenting every man perfect in Christ." The point is clearly aimed at the social exclusivism of the Errorists. This social exclusivism is spelled out by implication in the second passage, 3:11, where we encounter the classical christological formulation "Christ is all and in all." Read out of context, this passage can easily be construed as having primarily a metahistorical or cosmological thrust: "Christ is all, including the whole created universe." But in context the point is quite different. In this passage, the author is addressing people who already have this metahistorical or cosmological perspective. In directing their attention to the "allness" of Christ, he is contending that Christ is more than metahistorical, he is also in history; he is more than cosmological, he also reigns in his church "under the heavens." The author's point is quite apparent when one notes the first half of the verse, which offers the classical christological statement that in Christ it is not possible to say, "One is a Greek and another a Jew, one is circumcised the other is not, one is barbarian or Scythian, slave or free, for Christ is all and in all." For the author, the style of the Errorists is to divide communities, to "disqualify" (καταβραβευέτω, 2:18) along lines of class, race, or orthopraxis; but the style of the "body of Christ" is to unite and "govern" (βραβευέτω,

3:15) with "peace" into which all have been called in one body (3:14-15).

5. The ὅτι clause in 1:19-20 ("all the *plēroma* was pleased to take up residence [in Christ] and through him to reconcile all things to him, making peace through the blood of his cross") parallels the ὅτι clause in verse 16 of Strophe A, contrasting God's first act of creating all things with the second act of reconciling all things and making peace.

To emphasize the fact that God's peacemaking takes place in the concrete events of history, the author uses an expression that would have been unacceptable to any Gnostic tradition, stating that "all the *plēroma*" (an intentional redundancy) chose to dwell in the Christ who died on the cross (1:19). He adds insult to theological injury by radicalizing this expression further in 2:9, where he states even more explicitly that "*all* the *plēroma* of the *Godhead* dwells in him [Christ] bodily (σωματικῶς)." Though we cannot explore the various interpretations of these passages, it is clear that the author shares the radically distinctive incarnational theology of the early church, which held that the "heavenly" had manifested itself decisively in the "earthly" and that the "unseen God" was made visible in the "son of his love" (1:13) in the "body of his flesh" (1:22), and now in the fulfilling (2:9) and reconciling life of the church in the world.[59]

With this second strophe and its theology of "reconciliation,"[60] the author is turning the reader's attention from the contemplation of the primordial past, when all creation was set into motion with its eternal laws and its hierarchy of celestial and terrestrial powers, to a discernment of the historical present, to the "now" (νῦν, 1:22) of God's activity, visible in the cross, in the growing and fruit-bearing of the gospel from Jerusalem to Rome, and in the burgeoning of communities in which the estrangement and hostility (1:21) that had so long characterized the family of humanity is being overcome.[61]

6. The author's concern to pinpoint the cross as the locus of God's present activity is highlighted by the repetition for emphasis of the prepositional phrase δι᾽ αὐτοῦ in verse 20. The phrase occurs twice in verse 20, once at the beginning, where it refers to Christ as the medium of God's reconciliation, and once at the end, where its meaning is more problematic, though its function is clearly to emphasize a point.

In this second position the phrase can refer either to the δι᾽ αὐτοῦ at the beginning of verse 20, thus emphasizing God's reconciling act in Christ, or it can refer to the expression halfway through the verse, αἵματος τοῦ σταυροῦ αὐτοῦ, in which case it emphasizes the "blood of the cross" as the specific locus for God's peacemaking. It is most likely that the author is playing on the ambiguity of the antecedents in order to capture the meaning of both, in which case he is telling his readers,

135

"through him, the crucified one!"[62] in order to make the point once again that the Christian kerygma has its focus in history, not in cosmology.

7. The final pair of phrases, εἴτε τὰ ἐπὶ τῆς δῆς εἴτε τὰ ἐν τοῖς οὐρανοῖς ("whether the things on earth or those in the heavens") is of interest because it mirrors the reference to "heaven and earth" in verse 16 of Strophe A (ἐν τοῖς οὐρανοῖς καὶ ἐπὶ τῆς γῆς), but in reverse order. It may be that in reversing the order of "heaven and earth" to "earth and heaven," the author is simply responding to a desire for literary chiasmus. It may also be, however, that he is making a theological point with his chiasmus, reminiscent of the Matthean version of the Lord's prayer (Matthew 6:11), which suggests that for *all* God's will to be done it must not be done only in heaven, but on earth as well.

1:21-23: Epexegetical Commentary on Strophe B. The function of this section is to extend the theological meaning of Strophe B. It is clear in the opening verse of this epexegetical section that the author has shifted attention from creation to fall, from concern with the primordial unity of the created universe in verses 15ff. to concern with the estrangement and enmity in mind (διανοία) and action (τοῖς ἔρροις τοῖς πονηροῖς) that have since developed. For the author the central theological, christological, and anthropological issue is not creation (Strophe A) but reconciliation (Strophe B).

In many respects the theological intention of this section is self-evident. We have already commented on the phrase "every creature *under heaven*,"[63] but there are two additional phrases worthy of special comment with respect to our theme. The first is the phrase "in his body of flesh by his death" in verse 22. With this statement, clearly amplifying the reference to the "blood of his cross" in verse 20, the author is leaving no doubt as to the point he is making, namely, that to understand the heart of the Christian kerygma one must return to the most shockingly concrete of places, to the blood, flesh, and death of the cross.

The second passage is the personal note the author adds at the close of this passage with the words "of which I, Paul, became a minister [1:23]." Moving from the Errorist concern with cosmology, asceticism, visions, and angels, the author comes down on the role and occupation of the Christian, namely, *ministry* in service of the gospel. Unlike the Errorist discipline designed to isolate the self from the world, ministry for the author involves engagement with the world, replete with suffering and struggle (1:21—2:3). Though the author does have a vision of final glory (1:12; 3:3-4), he sees in the present an overriding demand for sharing in a *vita crucis* for the sake of the upbuilding of the "body of Christ," "the church" (1:18, 24) as part of God's continuing reconciling and peacemaking action (1:24; 3:11, 15).

Colossians 1:15-20 in the Context of the Epistle as a Whole

As in the other Pauline letters, the *theologia crucis* in Colossians remains the controlling christological motif. Though the Pauline correspondents frequently frame the primary theological issues in cosmological or metahistorical terms, the Pauline response invariably brings the focus back to a *theologia crucis* that finally locates God's creative and redemptive activity and the church's ministry in the midst of human community.

In Colossians, as we have seen, cosmology and metahistorical interests provide the point of departure from which the argument of the letter proceeds, but the *telos* of the argument, developed through the bulk of the letter, is soteriological. This soteriological emphasis dominates the remaining five sections of the letter.

a. The material in 1:24—2:6 emphasizes *Christ as God's mystery.* Though the topic might be cosmological in scope, it is clearly soteriological in intention, discoursing on the suffering the minister of God's mystery may have to undertake (1:24, 29; 2:1) in making manifest the "treasures of wisdom and knowledge" hidden in Christ. The author's emphasis on suffering has the effect not only of drawing the reader's attention to the need for real "fleshly [v. 24]" involvement in history with "every man" (three times; 1:27-29), even gentiles (1:27), but also of contrasting the Pauline theology of suffering-for-the-sake-of-others (2:1) with the Errorist theology of self-imposed suffering for the sake of their own honor (2:23; cf. 2:18).

b. In the next section, 2:6-23, on *the Errorist philosophy,* the author describes in detail the propaganda technique, the cultic ritualism, the exclusivism, and ascetic legalism of the Errorists, closing with the ironic observation that their attempts to repudiate the flesh (2:23) and achieve humility (2:18) result in just the opposite, cultivating instead a flesh-consciousness (2:23) and fleshly pride (2:18). Thus the salvation from the dominance of the flesh is to be found not in an Errorist escape from the world, but through participation in the historical, witnessing, growing community of the "body of Christ [2:19]" through baptism (2:11).

c. Chapter 3:1-17 consists of a long *parenesis.* The author opens with an ironic challenge: "If [you claim] to be risen with Christ, seek the things above where Christ is. . . . Set your minds on things that are above, not on things that are on earth [3:1-2]." The point of the irony is that the

Errorists (and some of their Colossian sympathizers?) who claim to be heavenly minded are in the end given to some very "earthly" vices, for example, preoccupation with the flesh (2:23) and pride (2:18). If they truly seek the "things above," the author suggests, they will do well to consider the "new nature" revealed in the "second Adam," Christ (3:9ff.). At the heart of the parenesis is the proclamation that the "higher way" is revealed in the down-to-earth creation of a new reconciling community in which the social distinctions, advocated by the so-called heavenly minded Errorists, are transcended, and in which the qualities of the "new nature" are allowed to rule in the everyday human relations among husbands and wives, parents and children, slaves and masters (cf. 3:18—4:6). These qualities are not the so-called heavenly virtues of self-abasement, rigorous devotion, and severity to the body (2:23), but the down-to-earth qualities of compassion, kindness, humility, meekness, long-suffering, forgiveness, love, maturity, peace, wisdom, and thanksgiving (3:12-17).

d. The *Haustafeln* in 3:18—4:1 simply extend the parenesis above, for example, reminding masters that their commitment to a "heavenly Lord" (4:1) involves them with earthly responsibilities to one another to act in justice and equality (4:1).

e. The *closing admonitions and salutations* in 4:2-6 and 4:7-17, respectively, continue to speak of Christian responsibility in history, praying that doors might open for the "mystery of Christ" (4:3) and urging the Colossians to make the best use of their time (4:5) and to practice effective and gracious speech with one another (4:6).

Nowhere in the Epistles is the historo-centric consciousness of the Pauline kerygma more evident than in the closing greetings with their characteristic list of names (4:7-17), tacitly but clearly demonstrating that the "body of Christ" involves concrete individuals with names, confronting problems of many shades and hues (cf. 4:10, 12, 17).

The letter terminates on a fitting note, which expresses as poignantly as any statement in the letter that although a *theologia gloriae* is an essential part of the Christian kerygma, the *theologia crucis,* as part of the "master plan of God [1:25]" is its continuing point of departure. The author closes with the words: "Remember my chains. Grace be with you [4:18]."

138

Chapter 11

Christological Perspectives in the Book of Revelation

Sarah Alexander Edwards

Nowhere in the New Testament are christological perspectives more decisive than in the book of Revelation. As this essay will show, they provide an effective exegetical tool for reconstructing the authentic literary and theological character of the book.

Because of its stylistic homogeneity, the diversity of the book of Revelation is not generally recognized.[1] The skill of an editor in imprinting an idiom upon the materials should not blind us to their intrinsic incongruity. Consider the fourth Gospel, for example. Although the final redaction has smoothed away many rough edges and produced a surface uniformity, contemporary Johannine scholarship discerns a complexity of underlying traditions as striking as the recognized sources behind the synoptic Gospels. So astute a critic as Raymond E. Brown detects at least four levels of composition and revision beneath the finished product.[2]

This essay is based on the premise that the book of Revelation, in its canonical form, is an amalgam of two originally separate works: (1) a Jewish apocalypse (4:1—22:7) and (2) a Christian document (1:1—3:22; 22:8-21).[3] John F. Whealon convincingly displays the literary and religious evidence for this hypothesis.[4] His critical analysis is so well done that there is no need to go over the same ground again. It is sufficient to note here that he finds the most important criterion to be the use of Christian concepts, values, and terminology in the Christian document and their striking absence (except in occasional glosses) from the Jewish apocalyptic core.

The christological perspectives of the book of Revelation provide further support for this hypothesis. In this essay "christological" is used

Sarah Alexander Edwards received her Ph.D. from the Hartford Seminary Foundation in 1974 with Harvey K. McArthur as *ordinarius*. She is currently Professor of Biblical Studies at Hartford Seminary.

in the broadest sense. The traditional distinction between messianism and Christology tends to blur their organic unity. Consequently, in my usage, christological refers both to the Christ-Messiah of Jewish expectation and to Jesus, the Christ of the church's faith.

The apocalyptic core of the book of Revelation seems to have been written during the decade following the destruction of Jerusalem in A.D. 70.[5] Its christological perspectives are quintessentially Jewish (see Table 1). The Christian document stems from a time of persecution, perhaps during the reign of Domitian, around A.D. 96.[6] Its christological perspectives are those of Palestinian—and Hellenistic—Jewish Christianity.[7]

Whether the Christian document was written to frame the apocalypse, or whether two independent compositions were joined together by a subsequent redactor, it is impossible to say. In either case, the purpose of the juncture was to make the complete work acceptable in church circles. Was the Jewish section originally written in Greek, or was it translated from Hebrew or Aramaic? Again, there is no evidence on which to base a responsible decision. Somewhere in the editorial process a few interpolations into the apocalyptic text were made. Their different christological perspectives make them easy to detect. Although they will be discussed later, for convenience they are noted here (RSV):

7:17: "the Lamb in the midst of the throne"
11:8 : where "their Lord was crucified"
12:17: those who "bear testimony to Jesus"
14:12: those who "keep . . . the faith of Jesus"
17:6 : "the blood of the martyrs of Jesus"
18:20: "and apostles"
19:10: "the testimony of Jesus"
20:4 : "testimony to Jesus"
21:14: "the twelve apostles"
22:3 : the throne of God "and of the Lamb"
22:7 : "and behold I am coming soon"

On the basis of this analysis, Jesus as the Christ is not the theme of the whole book. Some sensitive hermeneutics are involved here. To interpret the Jewish apocalypse as a witness to Jesus is like reading the ninth chapter of Isaiah as part of the Christmas story. Although to Christian ears the passage seems to foretell the coming of the Bethlehem Babe, in its original context the prophecy spoke only of the imminent birth of a royal child.[8] In the Easter liturgy we may also choose to read the Jewish scriptures by the light of the Paschal candle. This is our privilege as Christians. In so doing we affirm that the divine promises to Israel are

TABLE 1.

CHRISTOLOGICAL TITLES IN THE NEW TESTAMENT

Title	In the Sayings of Jesus	In the Book of Revelation	Stage of Development
Τό Ἀρνίον, the Lamb		yes	Davidic Messianism
Χριστός, Christ	yes	yes	Palestinian-Jewish Christianity
Υἱός Δαυίδ, Son	yes	(ῥίζα David)	do
Υἱός τοῦ Ἀνθρώπου, Son of man	yes	yes	do
Παῖς (ebedh YHWH), Servant	yes	no	do
Προφήτης, Prophet	yes	no	do
Ραββί, Rabbi	no	no	do
Υἱός τοῦ Θεοῦ, Son of God	Call God ábbá, Father	yes	Palestinian-Gentile Christianity
Κύριος, Lord	yes	yes	do
Ἄνθρωπος δεύτερος or ἔσχατος, second/last man	no	no	do
Λόγος, Word	no	yes	Hellenistic-Jewish and Hellenistic-Gentile Christianity
Σωτήρ, Savior	no	no	Hellenistic-Gentile Christianity
Θεός, God	no	no	

NOTE: This table is based on Reginald H. Fuller, *The Foundations of New Testament Christology* (New York: Charles Scribner's Sons, 1965), ad loc. Similar (but not identical) schema have been outlined by Ferdinand Hahn, *The Titles of Jesus in Christology* (New York: World, 1969), pp. 12–13, 347–50; Werner Georg Kümmel, *The Theology of the New Testament* (Nashville: Abingdon Press, 1973), pp. 8–9; C.F.D. Moule, *The Origin of Christology* (Cambridge: Cambridge University Press, 1977), pp. 2–3; and V. Taylor, *The Names of Jesus* (New York: St. Martin's Press, 1953), pp. 169–70.

fulfilled in the miracle of the resurrection. We should also acknowledge that the Hebrew people anticipated—and still anticipate—a very different fulfillment.

Christological Perspectives in the Jewish Apocalypse: REVELATION 4:1—22:7

In contemporary studies of the book of Revelation there is growing recognition of the essential Jewishness of the imagery in 4:1—22:7. For example, the woman in chapter 12 is now primarily understood as a symbol of "the people of God which brings forth the Messiah and the messianic times."[9] The two witnesses who receive "power to prophesy" for 1260 days (11:3, RSV) signify Moses and Elijah, the law and the prophets.[10] The 144,000 sealed individuals from the twelve tribes (7:4) represent the faithful remnant of Israel.[11] As in the Old Testament, earthquakes herald the coming of Yahweh in judgment; they also suggest the theophany at Sinai.[12]

The christological perspectives in the apocalypse are as Jewish as these symbols. Only after they have been understood in their own setting in Hebrew thought can they responsibly be read in the light of the Paschal candle.

The Word of God. For a Christian with ears attuned to the magnificent prologue of the fourth Gospel, it is difficult not to see in Revelation 19:13 "the Word [that] became flesh and dwelt among us [John 1:14, RSV]."[13] Nevertheless, except for the statement that "the name by which he is called is The Word of God [Rev. 19:13, RSV]," this apocalyptic figure on the white horse is totally alien to the gospel Lord. With blazing eyes and issuing from his mouth "a sharp sword with which to smite the nations [v. 15, RSV],"[14] this is the invincible agent of divine vengeance. This is the militant Messiah leading the army of heaven to victory in the great battle of the end-time. This is the eschatological embodiment of the wrath of Yahweh—what the French call *la colère blanche de Dieu,* the white anger of God[15]—come down to execute God's awful justice upon the wicked of the world. In Wisdom of Solomon 18:15-16 (RSV) it is written, "Thy all-powerful word leaped from heaven . . . a stern warrior carrying the sharp sword of thy authentic command." This apocalyptic warrior of the white anger of God is far removed from the Christ who prayed, "Father, forgive!" Thus the christological perspective of this title here is totally Jewish.

The Lamb. "The Lamb" is the pivotal title in the apocalypse. The way in which we understand its christological perspective will color our

142

reading of the other messianic terms. Because the name seems to echo the affirmation of John the Baptist when, as the fourth Gospel tells it, he first saw Jesus and said, "Behold, the Lamb of God! [John 1:29, RSV]," most scholars assume that in the book of Revelation the Lamb is Jesus.[16]

On the basis of christological perspectives, there are three reasons for rejecting this identification (except in the case of two Christian glosses): First, the Lamb is the most frequent messianic designation in the book of Revelation. It occurs twenty-eight times, or 43 percent of all christological titles. Yet it is found only in the Jewish apocalypse (see Table 2).[17] If it referred to Jesus as the Christ, it seems strange that the redactor did not use it at least once in the Christian document, thus binding the two parts of the book more closely together. Its absence is striking. Clearly the editor considered its christological perspective

TABLE 2.

LOCATION OF CHRISTOLOGICAL TITLES
IN THE BOOK OF REVELATION

Title	In Apocalyptic Core (4:1—22:7)	In Christian Framework (1:1—3:22; 22:8-21)	Total
Χριστός, Christ	4x	3x (all with Ἰησοῦς)	7x
Υἱός τοῦ Θεοῦ, Son of God	none (+2 Father/Son references)	1x (+4 Father references)	1x
Υἱός τοῦ Ἀνθρωπου, Son of man	1x	1x	2x
Lord ὁ Κύριος	20x: 4x christological 13x referring to God 3x sociological	3x: 2x christological 1x referring to God 0 sociological	23x: 6x christological 14x referring to God 3x sociological
Ἀρνίον, Lamb	28x	none	25x
Λόγος, Word	1x	none	1x

NOTE: This table is based on W.F. Moulton and A.S. Geden, eds., *A Greek Concordance to the New Testament*, 4th ed. (Edinburgh: T. & T. Clark, 1963), ad loc.

Jewish rather than Christian, and therefore unsuitable for his work.

Second, the Lamb of Revelation is not as close to the Lamb of the gospel as the English text would have one think. The usual New Testament word for Jesus as the Lamb is ὁ ἀμνός.[18] It is used as his title in John 1:29; 1:36; Acts 8:32, and 1 Peter 1:19. In these passages it opens up an important christological perspective, linking Jesus with the suffering servant of Isaiah 53:

κύριος παρέδωκεν αὐτὸν τοῖς ἁμαρτίαις ἡμῶν . . . καὶ ὡς ἀμνός ἐναντίον τοῦ κείροντος αὐτόν ἄφωνος. . . .

The Lord has laid on him the iniquity of us all . . . and as a lamb before its shearers is dumb . . . [Isa. 53:6-7].

Although there is no linguistic basis for linking the ἀμνὸς with the Passover lamb (τὸ πρόβατον in the Septuagint) by whose blood we are saved, the church soon made the connection.[19]

In the book of Revelation, the Lamb is not ὁ ἀμνός but τὸ ἀρνίον. The only other occurrence of this word in the New Testament is at John 21:15, where it is not used christologically. In the Johannine pericope the risen Lord walks with Peter on the beach and charges him, βοσκέ τὰ ἀρνία μου, "Feed my lambs!"[20] Thus the Master commissions his disciple to care for the young Christian community.

The Lamb of Revelation frequently carries a comparable communal connotation. In the opening scene of the apocalypse at the court of heaven, it is as the representative of the people of Israel, slain in the devastation of Jerusalem, that he is found worthy to open the scroll. When "the wrath of God is ended," those who had conquered the beast sing to Yahweh: "Great and wonderful are thy deeds, O Lord God the Almighty! . . . For thou alone art holy [15:3-4, RSV]." This is a conscious echo of the first song to Yahweh after passing safely through the Red Sea and seeing the pursuing Egyptians destroyed: "Who is like thee, O Lord, . . . majestic in holiness, terrible in glorious deeds, doing wonders [Exod. 15:11, RSV]?" The psalm of Exodus 15 was sung by "Moses, the servant of God, and the people of Israel [Exod. 14:31; 15:1, RSV]." The hymn of Revelation 15 was "the song of Moses, the servant of God, and the song of the Lamb [15:3, RSV]."

Third, the Lamb of the apocalypse not only represents the people of Israel but also symbolizes the Messiah of Jewish eschatological expectation. Raymond E. Brown suggests that by the first century τὸ ἀρνίον had become a standard apocalyptic term.[21] Perhaps that is why the New Testament never uses it as a title for Jesus.

At his first appearance in the book of Revelation, the Jewish messianic character of the Lamb is announced by his association with Davidic symbols, for the expected Messiah will be a scion of the house of David.[22] In the Hebrew scriptures David is described as the Lion of Judah (Genesis 49:9)[23]; modern Jerusalem identifies itself as his city by placing a lion on its coat of arms.[24] The root, or shoot, of David—the terms are interchangeable—is a messianic title older than "Son of David," though its meaning is the same.[25]

ἰδοὺ ἐνίκησεν ὁ λέων ὁ ἐκ τῆς φυλῆς Ἰούδα, ἡ ῥίζα Δαυίδ, ἀνοῖξαι τὸ βιβλίον . . . καὶ εἶδον . . . ἀρνίον ἑστηκός ὡς ἐσφαγμένον . . . καὶ ἔλαβεν τὸ βιβλίον. . . .

Lo, the Lion of the tribe of Judah, the Root of David, has conquered, so that he can open the scroll. . . . And I saw a Lamb standing as though it had been slain . . . and he took the scroll . . . [Rev. 5:5-7, RSV].[26]

The messianic meaning of this symbol is underlined again in Revelation 14:1 (RSV): "Then I looked, and lo, on Mount Zion stood the Lamb." Charles notes that in the Hebrew mind this mountain was associated with divine deliverance.[27] To see the Messiah standing in eschatological triumph upon its summit would signify that Yahweh had at last fulfilled his promise to the people of Israel and the house of David: "I have set my king on Zion, my holy hill [Ps. 2:6, RSV]."

Several passages link the Lamb with the throne of God. To see in them Christ exalted and seated on the divine throne[28] is to superimpose an inappropriate christological perspective upon this Jewish document. One verse that seems to suggest this is almost certainly the result of a grammatical error in translation. Revelation 22:1 (RSV) reads:

Ἔδειξεν μοι ποταμὸν ὕδατος ζωῆς . . . ἐκπορευόμενον ἐκ τοῦ θρόνου τοῦ θεοῦ καὶ τοῦ ἀρνίου.

He showed me the river of the water of life . . . flowing from the throne of God and of the Lamb.

The idea of separation is indicated so strongly by the double use of ἐκ, both as a participial prefix and as a preposition, that its partitive force must carry over to the Lamb as well. Thus the verse should be translated "flowing from the throne of God and from the Lamb." There are, however, two glosses which reveal that, reading the apocalypse in the light of the Paschal candle, the Christian editor does see the Lamb as the exalted Christ upon God's throne. In 7:17 (RSV) he intimates that "the Lamb in the midst of the throne will be their shepherd." Again, in 22:3 (RSV) the redactor notes that "the throne of God and of the Lamb shall be in" the new Jerusalem. Both these glosses are consistent with his Christology. He sees Jesus so highly glorified by resurrection that he himself "sat down with [his] Father on his throne [3:21, RSV]."

This statement and the two glosses are totally contrary to the theological reticence of scripture. Nowhere else in the entire Bible does anyone sit down with God upon the chair of majesty.[29] This reticence is normative for the rest of the book of Revelation. As Massynberde Ford observes, the Lamb is usually "near the throne but it is not explicitly stated that he shares it."[30] In a typical verse the host of heaven sings, "To him who sits upon the throne and to the Lamb be blessing and honor and glory and might for ever and ever [e.g., Rev. 5:13, RSV]!" Clearly God alone is on the throne, although the Lamb is near enough to receive adoration.

Thus, with the exception of two glosses, in the apocalypse the Lamb is not Jesus. Sometimes he represents the true Israel. Most frequently he symbolizes the Davidic Messiah of Jewish eschatological expectation.

The Son of God. Although the title Son of God is not used in this section of the book of Revelation, the relationship to which it points is indicated in 14:1. Standing in triumph on Mount Zion, the Lamb is accompanied by the 144,000 "who had his name and his Father's name written on their foreheads [RSV]." This is neither the intimate Abba-Father reality of the Gospels (e.g., Mark 14:36)[31] nor the Pauline affirmation that Jesus was "designated Son of God in power . . . by his resurrection from the dead [Rom.1:4, RSV]."[32] In accordance with this promise, every anointed king of Israel would become at his enthronement an adopted son of Yahweh.[33] So in this apocalypse "the title and the concept Son of God are . . . familiar to the author, but . . . only within the limits of what is possible for the Jew."[34]

The Son of man. Like every Judeo-Christian apocalypse, Revelation is to some extent dependent on the book of Daniel.[35] Chapter 14 is particularly close to Daniel 7. Both portray the court of heaven, the judgment upon the evil beast, the book, and the climactic arrival of "one like a son of man."[36] This is the only use of the title in this apocalypse. Although it may have referred to an anointed bringer of salvation, there is a general consensus that both in Daniel and here the "son of man" is a collective entity.[37] Like the Lamb, he represents the true Israel. Thus once again we encounter a characteristically Jewish christological perspective.

The Lord. The primary significance of the title Lord is always clear. Grammatically related to the verb κυριεύω, "have power over," it never fails to convey a sense of authority.[38] In actual usage several important shades of meaning have developed.

Sociologically, κύριος was the polite Greek word for a subject to use in speaking to the king, a slave to the master, even a woman to her husband. As a courtesy title it was devoid of any religious implications.[39] C.F.D. Moule comments, "κύριε is so common as a respectful address . . . that it would be as truthful . . . to reckon a school-boy's 'O Sir' as evidence that the school master had been knighted" as to read theological content into a biblical salutation.[40] Mary Magdalene is merely being polite to the man she mistakes for the gardener when she says, "κύριε, sir . . . tell me where you have laid him [John 20:15, RSV]." When one of the heavenly elders asks the seer of Revelation, "Who are these, clothed in white robes?" he answers, with no overtones of worship, "Sir, you know" (Revelation 7:13-14, RSV).[41]

Religiously, κύριος becomes the appropriate word for God. Before the exile, the Israelites rejoiced in knowing and using the divine name (e.g., Exodus 3:1-15), but after their return they considered it too sacred to be pronounced. Adonai, Lord, soon replaces Yahweh in the sacred texts. Thus the Shema becomes "Hear, O Israel, Adonai, our God is one Adonai [Deut. 6:4]." In the Septuagint, Adonai is translated κύριος.[42] It continues over into the New Testament as an appropriate title for God the Father. This is its usual meaning in the apocalyptic core of Revelation.

Ἅγιος ἅγιος ἅγιος
κύριος ὁ θεὸς ὁ παντοκράτωρ.

Holy, holy, holy, is the Lord God Almighty [Rev. 4:8, RSV].[43]

Κύριος may also be used as a title for the Messiah. So in Revelation it is written, Μακάριοι οἱ νεκροὶ οἱ ἐν κυρίῳ ἀποθνήσκοντες, "Blessed are the dead who die in the Lord [Rev. 14:13, RSV]." Countless Christian funerals notwithstanding, this beatitude almost certainly speaks of the great multitude of the martyrs of Israel whose robes have been washed in the blood of the Davidic Lamb-Messiah. Thus it falls within the christological perspective of this Jewish apocalypse.

The Christ. Originally Χριστός was an adjective meaning anointed. It referred to the Hellenistic habit of bathing daily and anointing the

147

body.[44] One of the best-preserved statues at Olympia commemorates a benefactor who presented the gymnasium with several large jars of perfumed olive-oil so that the athletes preparing for the games could top off their training sessions with elegant rubdowns.[45]

In the Septuagint the ancient Hebrew term *mašiaḥ* is rendered in Greek as Χριστός.[46] While this is in one sense an accurate translation, it unfortunately obscures the special significance of Jewish usage. Throughout the Old Testament it refers to the act of anointing a king to consecrate him for his office. The earliest instance goes back to the beginning of the monarchy: "Then Samuel took a vial of oil and poured it on [Saul's] head and kissed him and said: 'Has not the Lord anointed you to be prince over his people Israel? And you shall reign over the people of the Lord' [1 Sam. 10:1, RSV]." In subsequent Hebrew usage "anointed" turns into a proper noun, "the anointed one." Thus it becomes a title, first for the current king[47] and later in the "Davidic strand of Jewish messianic tradition" for the king who was to come.[48]

When ὁ Χριστός is used in the apocalyptic core of the book of Revelation it should be understood as " 'the Messiah' or 'the Anointed' or 'the Elect One' " in a purely Jewish sense,[49] and always in the context of eschatological triumph (see Revelation 12:10; 20:4; 20:6; for "Christ" read "Messiah"). The most interesting of the verses in which the title occurs is the heavenly shout after the seventh trumpet has sounded: Ἐγένετο ἡ βασιλεία τοῦ κοσμοῦ τοῦ κυρίου ἡμῶν καί τοῦ Χριστοῦ αὐτοῦ, "the kingdom of the world has become the kingdom of our Lord and of his Christ," that is to say, the kingdom of our Yahweh and of his Anointed One (Revelation 11:15, RSV). Of special interest is the phrase Χριστός αὐτοῦ. Although unique in the New Testament, it is a standard eschatological term in Hebrew scripture. Its use in this affirmation underlines the Jewishness of its christological perspective.[50]

On the basis of this analysis it may be concluded that in Revelation 4:1—22:7 the titles Word of God, Lamb, Son of man, Lord, and Christ, the mention of the Root of David, and the reference to the Son-of-God relationship do not point to Jesus as the Christ. Rather, in this apocalypse they consistently express a Jewish christological perspective.

Two glosses have already been discussed. Nine other interpolations have been added to this text. Perhaps they come from the hand of a scribe, perhaps they are the work of the redactor who framed the apocalypse with a Christian document. In either case, they seem to have been part of the book before it was admitted into the canon of the New Testament.[51] Indeed, they may have facilitated its acceptance by the church. Although none of these glosses involves a christological title, they are important in terms of the changing christological perspectives of the book as a whole. Their presence shows how early the church began to read the apocalypse in the light of the Paschal candle.

Five glosses involve the addition of the name Jesus to the text in the phrases "testimony to Jesus" or "faith of Jesus." Perhaps these were stock expressions in the preaching and catechesis of the early church. (In the Christian framework the phrase "the testimony of Jesus" appears as an integral part of the text.) In each example below the interpolation is italicized:

- The offspring of the woman with the twelve stars in her crown are identified as "those who keep the commandments of God and *bear testimony to Jesus* [Rev. 12:17, RSV]."[52]
- The angel tells the seer that he is a "fellow servant with you and your brethren *who hold the testimony of Jesus. . . . The testimony of Jesus* is the spirit of prophecy [Rev. 19:10, RSV]."[53]
- In the new Jerusalem the author of the apocalypse saw "the souls of those who had been beheaded *for their testimony to Jesus and* for the Word of God [Rev. 20:4, RSV]."[54]
- "Here is a call for the endurance of the saints, those who keep the commandments of God *and the faith of Jesus* [Rev. 14:12, RSV]." This interpolation is almost a doublet for the addition in 12:17, noted above.[55]
- The harlot of Babylon was drunk with "the blood of the saints *and the blood of the martyrs of Jesus* [Rev. 17:6, RSV]."[56] In an earlier period the martyrs would have been those bearing testimony to Jesus. During the widespread persecutions under Domitian, so many Christians paid for their witness with their lives that the word assumed its present meaning.[57] Charles notes, "This verse gives a Christian character to the originally Jewish source."[58]

In two glosses the apostles have been added to the apocalyptic text:

- At the fall of Babylon the call goes out to "rejoice . . . O heaven, O saints *and apostles* and prophets [Rev. 18:20, RSV]."[59] Without the apostles this verse would simply speak of Israel's elation at its eschatological release from the tyranny of Rome. With the apostles, the saints and prophets also seem Christian.
- In the new Jerusalem "the wall of the city had twelve foundations, and on them the twelve names of the twelve *apostles* of the Lamb [Rev. 21:14, RSV]." As Whealon points out, the twelve apostles are "a Christian substitute for the twelve tribes of Israel."[60]

149

There is also a gloss referring to the place where *"their Lord was crucified* [Rev. 11:8, RSV]." This is the only time in the apocalyptic core of Revelation when Jesus is called ὁ Κύριος. Since the Romans crucified many Jewish guerrillas as part of their effort to maintain control over the rebellious Palestinian province, the verse could be part of the original text—and the Lord would be the leader of a revolutionary band. However, the New Testament setting makes it more likely that it is a Christian interpolation.[61]

Finally, at the end of the Jewish apocalypse there has been inserted the promise "And behold, I am coming soon [Rev. 22:7, RSV]." As we have seen, this section is suffused with a fervent expectation of the imminent coming of the Davidic Messiah. "On Mount Zion stood the Lamb!" In the early church this eschatological hope was transformed into an eager longing for the second coming of Jesus as the Christ. This passionate awaiting of the Parousia becomes one of the major themes of the Christian portion of the book.[62] By inserting the motif here, the redactor provides a skillful transition to his own conclusion. Like the other interpolations, this also helps to unify the completed work.

Christological Perspectives in the Christian Framework: REVELATION 1:1—3:22; 22:8-21

The theological climate of these chapters is entirely different from that of the Jewish apocalypse. Hebrew eschatology has given way to Christian conviction. Instead of the saga of the Davidic Messiah, here is "the revelation of Jesus Christ [1:1]."

The Christian character of this revelation is clear. Throughout these chapters there are striking references to the Pauline letters. The salutation could have been adapted from Galatians: "John to the . . . churches in Asia: Grace to you and peace [Rev. 1:4, RSV]" (cf. Gal. 1:1-3). The benediction is close to that of Romans: "The grace of the Lord Jesus be with all the saints. Amen [Rev. 22:21, RSV]."[63] Like the great apostle, this author also sends seven letters to seven churches.[64] In addition to these Pauline references, there are striking echoes of the Gospels. The admonition to the church at Sardis, "Remember then what you . . . heard; keep that, and repent [Rev. 3:3, RSV]," reminds the reader that our Lord came preaching, "Repent, for the kingdom of heaven is at hand [Matt. 4:17; Mark 1:14, RSV]." Like Jesus' parable of the sower (Matthew 13:9; Mark 4:9, Luke 8:8),[65] each of the seven letters closes with the words, "He who has an ear, let him hear [Rev. 2:7, 11, 17, 29; 3:6, 13, 22, RSV]." Finally, there are allusions to the Lord's promises, as recorded in Luke and John, in the beautiful saying so dear to Christian devotion, "Behold, I stand at the door and knock; if anyone hears my voice and opens the door, I will come in to him and eat with him, and he with me [Rev. 3:20, RSV]" (cf. John 14:18, 23; Luke 11:5-10; 12:35-40).

In this new theological climate the Jewish christological perspectives of the apocalyptic core have been replaced by those appropriate to Palestinian- and Hellenistic-Jewish Christianity. Two christological titles that were used in the earlier section have not been continued here: (1) ὁ Λόγος, which does not function as a title for Jesus in the New Testament, outside of the prologue to the fourth Gospel; and τὸ ἀρνιόν, the strong Jewish messianic connotation of which makes it an unsuitable title for Jesus as the Christ.

It is worth noting that the author has not introduced any new christological titles in this section, although Rabbi, Servant, Prophet, and the second or last man were all used at the Palestinian- and Hellenistic-Jewish stages of Christianity to which his writing belongs (see Table 1). Perhaps he did not find Rabbi sufficiently Christian for his purpose. Its use in the New Testament is infrequent outside synoptic conversations.[66] When the evangelist uses it in the fourth Gospel, he finds it necessary to explain to his Greek readers that it means teacher (John 1:38). Neither Prophet nor second/last man seems to have been congruent with this writer's apocalyptic longing for the Parousia. Servant must have seemed too humble for his emphasis on the risen and glorified Lord.

Four other titles were used in the core section with Jewish christological perspectives: Son of God, Son of man, Lord, and Christ. Since the church also used them with Palestinian- and Hellenistic-Jewish christological perspectives, they have been brought over into the Christian portion of the book of Revelation. In this setting each has

suffer[ed] a sea-change
into something new and strange.[67]

Like the apostle Paul, this author has little interest in the historical Jesus. His attention is entirely focused on the Christ of faith. As the discussion following will show, each christological title he uses has been transformed in the light of the resurrection.

The Son of God. In the apocalypse, like every anointed Jewish king, the Lamb stood in a generalized filial relationship to God. In the Christian framework this relationship has been transfigured. When Jesus speaks here of God as Father it is with the same intimacy of exaltation out of which the glorified Lord utters his high-priestly prayer in John 17: "He who . . . keeps my works until the end, I will give him

151

power . . . even as I myself have received power from my Father [Rev. 2:26-27, RSV]" (cf. John 17:1-2; Revelation 3:5). One can almost hear the trumpets of heaven sounding behind the single use of the title: "To the angel [at] Thyatira write: 'The words of the Son of God, who has eyes like a flame of fire . . .' [Rev. 2:18, RSV]."[68] Surely it is this overwhelming sense of Jesus' glorification that leads this author to break the reticence of scripture and envision the risen Lord seated with his Father on his throne (Revelation 3:21). Finally, this resurrection perspective infuses the ascription "To him who loves us and has freed us from our sins by his blood and made us . . . priests to his God and Father, to him be glory and dominion for ever and ever. Amen [Rev. 1:5-6, RSV]."

The Son of man. In the light of the resurrection, Son of man is no longer an apocalyptic designation of the people of Israel but an honorific title for the exalted Lord.[69] Although Jesus frequently referred to himself as the Son of man in the Aramaic sense of "a person" or "me,"[70] it is clear that the earliest Palestinian church, amazed by Easter and anxious for the second coming, interpreted the term christologically.[71] That is how the author of these Christian chapters of the book of Revelation understands it: "Then . . . I saw . . . one like a son of man . . . his head and his hair were white as white wool, white as snow; his eyes were like a flame of fire, his feet were like burnished bronze [Rev. 1:12-15, RSV]." The flaming eyes and bronze-burnished limbs are taken from the picture of "one like a son of man" in Daniel 10:16. Lest there be any mistaken identification, this writer later endows Jesus, the Son of God, with the same attributes (Revelation 2:18). In Daniel 7:9 (RSV) the Ancient of Days (a circumlocution for Yahweh) was said to have "raiment . . . white as snow and . . . hair . . . like pure wool." When this description is applied to Jesus as the Son of man, he is thereby elevated to divinity.

The Lord. Like the other christological titles, in this Christian context ὁ κύριος has been transformed. Here it is no longer used sociologically or as a polite form of address. It functions only once as a name for God, in the stock phrase "the Lord God . . . the Almighty [Rev. 1:8]."[72] Mostly it belongs to Jesus. When it is used christologically it refers not to the Davidic Messiah but to Jesus as risen and glorified Lord. This is also the case in the Christian glosses that have been added to the apocalyptic core.

The book of Revelation closes with the petition Ἀμὴν ἔρχου κύριε Ἰησοῦ, "Amen. Come, Lord Jesus [Rev. 22:20]." The opening word underlines the seriousness of this request by echoing Jesus' idiomatic way of beginning an important pronouncement, Ἀμὴν λέγω ὑμῖν, "truly I say to you [e.g., Matt. 6:3]."[73] The rest of the petition translates the ancient Aramaic prayer Μαρανα Θα.[74] It is the primitive Christian response to the eucharistic injunction to "proclaim the Lord's death until he comes [1 Cor. 11:26, RSV]."[75] Thus the early church gave voice to its longing for the real presence of the glorified Lord both in the sacrament and at the end of the age.

The Christ. Except for a few clearly Christian interpolations, the title Christ was never used with a proper name in the apocalyptic section of the book of Revelation. In the Christian framework the situation is exactly the opposite: here Χριστός never occurs without the proper name Jesus.[76] This affirms that for the church the Messiah is always and only the man from Nazareth, exalted now and filled with the power of God. Of special interest are the four verses in which the name Jesus is used without Χριστός. This phenomenon suggests that at this stage of christological development Christ had not yet become a proper name.[77] In Revelation 22:16 (RSV) the Davidic implications of this title are conveyed by other attributes: "I Jesus have sent my angel to you with this testimony for the churches. I am the root and the offspring of David, the bright morning star." As we have seen, the root (ῥίζα) of David is a very ancient term for the Messiah as coming from the lineage of David. The Septuagintal version of Zechariah 3:8 adds Ἀνατολήν, the bright morning star, as a synonym for this inheritance.[78] In the Lukan infancy narrative this is a symbol of the Christ whose light will soon shine upon "the people who sit in darkness" (Luke 1:78-79, RSV). In Revelation 22:20, "Come, Lord Jesus," the absence of Χριστός seems to have been fixed in the primitive liturgy. In the *Revised Standard Version,* Jesus also stands alone in Revelation 1:9 and 22:21. Since Codex Vaticanus adds Χριστοῦ after Ἰησοῦ in both instances,[79] this raises the question of which text is to be preferred here. In any case, it is clear that in these chapters both Jesus and Jesus Christ denote the risen and glorified Lord of the church.

Conclusion

The christological perspectives of the book of Revelation support the thesis that this is an amalgam of two distinctive works: a Jewish apocalypse and a Christian framework. With the exception of eleven interpolations, the christological perspectives of the apocalyptic core are quintessentially Jewish and messianic; those of the later document reflect the Palestinian- and Hellenistic-Jewish stages of Christian thought. This thesis and these perspectives help us to understand better "the diverse and somewhat startling Christology of the book."[80]

Beneath this diversity the completed work finds theological unity in the theme of eschatological expectancy. Decisive divine intervention will soon bring an end to the suffering of the present age. The Davidic Messiah and the exalted Jesus are alike the "instruments of his peace." Behind every christological perspective stands the power of the living God.

PART III
Christological Perspectives in the Hebrew Scriptures and Other Faiths

The Messiah as Son of God: Peter's Confession in Traditio-historical Perspective

Bernhard W. Anderson

The synoptic Gospels agree in their reports that at a crucial point in his career Jesus put a question to the disciples about how people perceived his identity and that Peter, when pressed, responded, "You are the Messiah" (*christos,* the Greek equivalent of Hebrew *mashiaḥ,* the anointed one). The simple confession found in Mark's report (8:27-30) is varied in the other Gospels. According to Luke, Peter said, "You are the Messiah of God" (Luke 9:18-22), but the Gospel of Matthew gives a fuller confession: "You are the Messiah, the Son of the living God" (Matthew 16:13-20).[1]

In the New Testament the messianic epithet Son of God has various nuances, depending on the context in which it functions linguistically. Mark's Gospel reaches a climax with the Roman centurion's exclamation at the foot of the cross, "Truly this man was the Son of God! [Mark 15:39, RSV]"—a confession that forms an *inclusio* with the heavenly announcement made at the first in connection with Jesus' baptism (Mark 1:11; see the introduction to Mark's Gospel, 1:1). In a traditional formulation Paul proclaims the gospel concerning God's Son (Romans 1:3, 9; cf. Galatians 2:20), who "was descended from David according to the flesh and designated Son of God in power according to the Spirit of holiness [Rom. 1:3-4, RSV]." And the fourth Gospel presents a picture of the Messiah as the only-begotten and preexistent Son of God (e.g., John 1:14; 3:16). In the various New Testament usages it is not always clear whether the sonship metaphor expresses a filial ontology (being in relationship to God) or a metaphysical view of identity

Bernhard W. Anderson is Professor of Old Testament at Princeton Theological Seminary.

between God's being and human being. In the Gospel of Matthew, however, the usage of the term seems to pick up overtones from Israel's traditions, a phenomenon that is not surprising when one considers that this Gospel, above all, attempts to understand Jesus' messianic status and role as the fulfillment of God's purpose disclosed in the Old Testament.

A hint of a traditio-historical connection with the Old Testament is given in Matthew's expansion of Peter's confession to include the expression the Son of the living God. The theological cliche "the living God," is found numerous times in the New Testament (e.g., Acts 14:15; 2 Corinthians 3:3; 6:16; 1 Timothy 4:10; Hebrews 10:31; Revelation 7:2). The ancestry of the expression, however, reaches back into the Old Testament, where at various stages in the history of Israelite traditions Yahweh was known and confessed as "the living God" par excellence: *'El Ḥai* or, in the majestic plural, *'Elohim Ḥayyim* (e.g., Deuteronomy 5:26; Joshua 3:10; 1 Samuel 17:26; 2 Kings 19:4, 16; Psalms 42:2; 84:2; Jeremiah 10:10; 23:36; cf. Daniel 6:20, 26).[2]

It is not the purpose of this essay to discuss Matthew's Christology or to understand how his use of the title Son of God bears on emerging Trinitarian theology of the Christian church (cf. Matthew 28:19).[3] Nor is it claimed that exploration of the Old Testament provides an interpretive key for understanding a Gospel which is distinctively Christian, even when it seeks to trace the continuity of God's purpose through Israel's traditions to Jesus Christ. Rather, this study is informed by the modest interest in whether an exploration of the traditio-historical lineage of the view of Messiah as Son of God may have a heuristic value in helping to perceive nuances of meaning that otherwise might be overlooked and, in this perspective, cast light on Peter's confession according to Matthew.

In the Mosaic tradition, "son of God" is a metaphor for God's people, Israel. The first occurrence of the epithet in this sense is found in the Old Epic tradition of the exodus. Moses, the messenger of Yahweh, is to deliver this message to Pharaoh: "Thus says the Lord, 'Israel is my first-born son, and I say to you: "Let my son go that he may serve me"; if you refuse to let him go, behold, I will slay your first-born son' [Exod. 4:22-24, RSV]." Not too much should be made theologically of this passage; notice that in the execution of the commission the message from Yahweh is merely "Let my people go . . . [Exod. 5:1]." Here the metaphor son of God functions in a dramatic narrative that leads through the contest with Pharaoh to the climax of the plagues. In this narrative context the intention is to draw a parallel between

Pharaoh's firstborn and Yahweh's people who stand first in rank as offspring and heirs (contrast the reinterpretation in Matthew 2:15).

The metaphor, however, has important theological significance in the message of prophets who stand in the tradition of the Mosaic covenant, Hosea and Jeremiah. In a magnificent poem found in Hosea 11:1-11, Israel is portrayed as Yahweh's "son" whom Yahweh called out of Egypt. With loving care the divine Parent brought up the child, taught the child to walk, lifted the child tenderly; but the child proved to be rebellious, and further discipline was in store, though not a punishment unto death as could be legally expected in the case of recalcitrant children (cf. Deuteronomy 21:18-21). To be sure, "prodigal children" must suffer the consequences of covenant infidelity to the point of no longer being God's people ("not my people [Hos. 1:9]"), but in the end restoration will occur and "not my people" will receive the approving word, "sons of the living God [Hos. 1:10, RSV]."[4] Similarly, Jeremiah portrayed Israel as Yahweh's rebellious sons (Jeremiah 3:11-14), whose hope for the future rests solely in Yahweh's surprising freedom (grace). According to a passage in the Book of Consolation, Israel's consolation is based on Yahweh's special parental relationship with the children: "For I am a father to Israel, and Ephraim is my first-born [Jer. 31:9, RSV]."

In these instances sonship is understood in familial terms of status in the family, parental nurture and discipline, and rebellion against and restoration to parental love. Hence the metaphor applies to the people who stand in a special covenant relationship and therefore are called to behave as "sons of God" (cf. Deuteronomy 14:1-2). This usage is found at the very beginning of the collection of Isaiah's prophecies, where the introductory oracle puts "sons" ("children") in the emphatic position:

> Sons have I reared and brought up,
>   but they have rebelled against me.
> The ox knows its owner,
>   and the ass its master's crib;
> but Israel does not know,
>   my people does not understand.
> —Isaiah 1:2b-3, RSV

Unlike Hosea and Jeremiah, two prophets who stand in the tradition of Mosaic covenant theology, Isaiah of Jerusalem makes hardly any reference to the exodus and the Mosaic covenant in the wilderness. Therefore his message provides a transition to another covenant tradition in which the metaphor son of God applies not to the people but to the king, who in a special sense is the representative of God on the throne of Judah. The king, to be sure, rises from the midst of the people, but at his coronation he is exalted to a special status and given a distinctive role in God's cosmic administration. This view is reflected in the well-known passage Isaiah 9:2-7, which originally was composed by a prophetic poet laureate on the occasion of the birth of the crown prince: "For unto us a child is born, unto us a son is given. . . ." Since Isaiah speaks in the context of a new theology associated preeminently with Yahweh's election of David and his successors for a special parent-child relationship, the poet's language regarding the child reverberates with extraordinary meaning, as evidenced by the exalted throne-names that will be given to this "son" when he ascends the throne of David (9:6b). It is the Davidic king, the anointed one (*mašiaḥ*), who is the son of God.

This metaphor, when applied to the Davidic king, should not be regarded as a literary usage that can be isolated and studied by itself, for in this case "son of God" belongs to a larger symbolic whole—to "a characteristic linguistic world," as O.H. Steck puts it—at the center of which is the celebration of Yahweh's rule in Zion. This conceptual design—or perhaps it would be better to say symbolic design —manifested itself as a "stream of tradition" that maintained itself with remarkable constancy through the changes and fortunes of the centuries until the time of the early Christian community.[5] If Peter's confession, according to the Matthean formulation, has been influenced by this Old Testament tradition, it is important to understand the symbolic gestalt, or configuration, which is often designated as the Zion tradition or Davidic covenant theology.

Let us begin inductively with texts that are definitely Israelite in their formulation and that belong essentially to the Zion "stream of tradition" which persisted into the New Testament period. Two texts that deserve preliminary consideration are found in Psalms 2 and 110. Both these psalms, which had an important place in synagogue and church, have influenced Christian understanding of Jesus' status and role as God's Messiah.

That the royal title son of God belongs to a larger symbolic whole is evident from Psalm 2, which along with the Torah Psalm 1 has a leading position in the Psalter. (The first "Davidic collection" of psalms begins with Psalm 3.) Although the psalm came to be regarded "eschatologically," which may account for its present position in the Psalter, it was apparently composed at first for the occasion of the coronation of an Israelite (Judean) king. Gerhard von Rad maintains that the coronation ritual reflected in the psalm is similar to a ceremony observed in ancient

Egypt, including such elements as coronation in the temple, the submission of a divine decree which legitimates the king's rule, the king's ascension to the throne, and his ultimatum to surrounding nations.[6] Against this background, the structure of the psalm is understandable:

a. 1-3: The rebellion of the nations: a throne change was an occasion for revolution.
b. 4-6: The announcement of the king's installation in the sanctuary.
c. 7-9: The divine decree that legitimates the king as the representative of God's rule on earth.
d. 10-11: The king's proclamation: insurgent rulers in surrounding territories are warned to submit.

For the present purpose the decisive element of the coronation ceremony is found in the divine decree (c), which announces that the king on the day of his coronation is drawn into a filial relationship with the deity. In oracular language Yahweh announces to the king: "You are my son, today I have begotten you [Ps. 2:7, RSV]." In consequence of Yahweh's election of the king to the status and authority of son, he becomes the heir: "Ask of me, and I will make the nations your heritage, and the ends of the earth your possession [Ps. 2:8, RSV]."

The designation of the crowned king as Yahweh's son belongs to a larger symbolic design. The fundamental features of the "linguistic world" of Psalm 2 are, first, the portrayal of Yahweh as cosmic King, enthroned in the heavens (v. 4) and sovereign over the furious raging of earthly kingdoms (vv. 1-3; cf. the same picture in Psalm 46:6, 8-10). Second, the king of Israel is called Yahweh's "messiah" (anointed one, v. 2c); he is Yahweh's representative, through whom the divine order is realized on earth despite the vain military plots of the nations. Third, "Yahweh's king" is installed in the temple of Zion, Yahweh's "holy hill" (v. 4). Zion is an impregnable fortress, for it is the place where Yahweh dwells in the midst of the chosen people (cf. Psalm 46:1-3, 4-7).

Psalm 110, which also seems to reflect a coronation ceremony, does not use the metaphor son of God explicitly, but it too pictures the role and status of the king in a cosmic framework. The Hebrew text is difficult, and many of the details are obscure, but the following sequence emerges:

a. v. 1: In an oracle the king (*'adoni,* "my lord") is invited to ascend the throne and is given the position of highest honor: seated at Yahweh's right hand.
b. vv. 2-3: The king's rule, powerful against threatening foes, is

161

centered in Zion, from which Yahweh sends forth the mighty royal scepter.

    c. v. 4: With the authority of a divine oath, the king is granted priestly standing in Zion, on the analogy of Melchizedek, the Canaanite priest-king, who ruled in pre-Israelite Jerusalem (Genesis 14:18).

    d. vv. 5-7: Here much is obscure, but apparently there is presented a picture of Yahweh giving victory to the king and acting to put down international disorder.

Once again there is the "linguistic world" of the Zion tradition, in which the order of the cosmos is related to human history. The main features of the symbolic design are, first, Yahweh is the cosmic King whose kingdom is manifest in the tumults and disorders of the earth. Second, the earthly king is part of Yahweh's rule; indeed, he is given a position of authority on Yahweh's throne, seated at the right hand. Third, the temple is also part of the cosmic design, as evidenced by the emphasis on Zion and the priestly status of the enthroned king. Nations who storm against the holy hill, where Yahweh is present in the temple and where the king rules as Yahweh's representative, will be dashed to pieces.

Other psalms could be considered at this point, for instance, the psalms that celebrate Yahweh's ascension to the throne as cosmic King and Ruler of the nations (Psalms 47, 93, 95-99). But the two psalms selected provide a good place to start a study of the symbolic context to which the metaphor son of God belongs. Both psalms are quoted in various New Testament passages, and it is significant that Matthew quotes Psalm 110:1 in connection with Jesus' question about the identity of the Messiah: "Whose son is he?" David's son? Or, as the text seems to imply, the Son of God (Matthew 22:41-46)?

The Israelite notion of the king as son of God is related in some degree to mythical views that prevailed in the Ancient Near East. Eric Voegelin, one of the leading political philosophers of our time, has dealt with this subject in an illuminating way in his *Israel and Revelation* (1956), the first volume of his comprehensive study of order and history which has reached completion. Building on the works of Frankfort, Jacobsen, Eliade, and others, he seeks to understand the emergence of ancient Israel in the perspective of an ontology or philosophy of being. Israel, he maintains, emerged in a civilization in which the prevailing "cosmological symbolism" expressed "the mythical participation of society in the divine being that orders the cosmos." In Mesopotamia the empire in its spatial organization was regarded as the archetype of the order of the cosmos, on the principle of the correspondence between

162

macrocosm and microcosm. At the *omphalos* (navel), or sacral center, where heaven and earth meet and divine being flows into society, the social order was periodically regenerated. During the New Year celebration, the king, as the analog of the deity, took part in the annual victory over the powers of chaos. Egyptian culture too, according to Voegelin's philosophical analysis, was grounded in the "consubstantiality" of the divine order with the pharaonic order, Pharaoh being the mediator through whom the divine Maat (order, justice, truth) emanated into society. Pharaonic order was "a continuous renewal and reenactment of cosmic order from eternity." Through Pharaoh, in whom the presence of God was manifest, the humblest subject participated in the majesty of cosmic order. The Egyptian style of attunement of society with divine being created a static and stable civilization which survived without essential change for more than two thousand years.

Voegelin maintains that humanity's participation in the drama of being is illumined (or the meaning of the whole is "revealed") when one aspect of the total experience of reality is lifted out or sharpened up in human consciousness. This happened above all in the case of Moses, though there may have been some anticipation during the patriarchal period. It was Moses who led "an exodus from cosmological civilization" into a new historical awareness of human society over against the kingdom of God, not merely absorbed into the cosmos. Hence the exodus was not just an event of pragmatic history but, as the Old Testament portrays it, an event of divine liberation. In Voegelin's interpretation, this redemptive event was "an irruption of the spirit" which "transfigured the pragmatic event into a divine drama of the soul and the acts of the drama into symbols of divine liberation." The "inrush of divine reality," as he puts it, "created a new order of the soul and, through the agency of Moses, a new type of society living in immediacy under the Kingdom of God."[7]

Voegelin's analysis may be open to criticism because of his painting of the ancient mythical view of society in broad strokes.[8] Nevertheless, his study is extremely valuable in that it helps us to understand the linguistic world of so-called cosmological symbolism. Two features of the symbolic design deserve special attention: temple and king. The temple, regarded as a microcosmic replica of the heavenly temple (palace), is situated at the *axis mundi,* the point at which divine being and power are manifest.[9] The king is regarded as the representative or analog of God, the sacral person who mediates the blessings and peace of the cosmic realm to human society. In fact, texts from ancient Mesopotamia and Egypt speak of the king as "the image of God" in the sense that in his royal office he is the representative of the god on earth. It is striking, however, that in Israel the king, though regarded as Yahweh's son who

163

is installed on the holy hill of Zion, is never explicitly considered to be God's "image."[10]

In his illuminating exposition of Israel's exodus from cosmological civilization, Voegelin observes that Israel was repeatedly tempted to defect from the Mosaic covenant and to reenter the Sheol (realm of the dead) of mythical symbolism. The "great derailment" occurred, he says, when the people, under the duress of political necessity, demanded a monarchy like the surrounding nations. It is true that the prophet Samuel, a conservative voice for the old tribal confederacy, regarded the request as apostasy from Yahweh, the King (1 Samuel 8). David and his theologians, however, took a different view. Under Davidic leadership the two institutions that were alien to Israel's Mosaic tradition, namely, kingship and temple, were accommodated to the Yahweh faith.[11] The result of this new theology can be seen in the book of Psalms. Dedicated to David and perhaps containing some Davidic psalms, this collection includes a number of royal psalms besides the ones treated above (e.g., Psalms 18, 45, 72, 101) and a number of "songs of Zion," which deal with the centrality of the temple (e.g., Psalms 46, 48, 76, 84).

In the Davidic theology the king is regarded as son of God, as indicated in Nathan's oracle found in 2 Samuel 7. This text, which has apparently undergone an *Ueberlieferungsgeschichte* of its own, reflects the situation in which David planned to build a "house" (temple) for Yahweh. The heart of Nathan's oracle (2 Samuel 7:11-17) was the announcement that Yahweh intended to build a "house" (dynasty) for David. Yahweh pledged covenant loyalty (*ḥesed*) to the Davidic king in perpetuity,[12] thereby guaranteeing the stability and security of the throne during changes of administration or threat from outside forces (cf. Isaiah 7:1-9). For the present purpose the crucial sentence in the oracle is found in verse 14 (RSV): "I will be his father, and he shall be my son." Yahweh's promises of grace to David are elaborated further in Psalm 89, where it is said:

> He shall cry to me, "Thou art my Father,
>   My God, and the Rock of my salvation."
> And I will make him the first-born,
>   the highest of the kings of the earth.
> My [*ḥesed*] I will keep for him for ever,
>   and my covenant will stand firm for him.
>
> —Psalm 89:26-28, RSV

In other texts that set forth Davidic covenant theology it is clear that kingship and temple belong essentially to the cosmological symbolism.

In Psalm 78, for instance, the psalmist views the pre-Davidic history of Israel as a history of failure which, in the grace of Yahweh, led to the selection of Judah and to the election of the Davidic king and the Jerusalem temple.

> He rejected the tent of Joseph,
>   he did not choose the tribe of Ephraim;
> but he chose the tribe of Judah,
>   Mount Zion, which he loves.
> He built his sanctuary like the high heavens,
>   like the earth which he has founded for ever.
> He chose David his servant,
>   and took him from the sheepfolds.
> —Psalm 78:67-70, RSV

In this passage notice how the temple is described in cosmic perspective: "like the [cosmic] heights" in scale, "like the stability of the created earth" in its foundation (v. 69).

Another significant text in this regard is Psalm 132, a liturgy that celebrates Yahweh's choice of Zion as the place of Yahweh's tabernacling presence (*miškānōt,* v. 6).[13] The first part of the psalm (vv. 1-5, 6-10) recalls the traditions of David's resolve to build Yahweh a sanctuary (2 Samuel 7:1-2) and of how he discovered the ark in Philistine territory and brought it to Jerusalem in triumph (2 Samuel 6:2-15). The second part of the psalm (vv. 11-12, 13-18) highlights the twin convictions of the Davidic (or Zion) tradition: (1) Yahweh has made a special "covenant" with David, promising an unbroken succession on his throne; and (2) Yahweh has chosen Zion for a "resting place" in perpetuity, with the result that Yahweh's presence will bring well-being to the Davidic kingdom and the discomfiture of enemies who assault Yahweh's holy hill.

In these and other texts Davidic theologians portrayed the "messiah" or anointed king in the framework of a rich poetic symbolism. In cosmic perspective Yahweh is hailed as the King, enthroned in the heavens, who has chosen the Davidic king to be the representative of Yahweh's rule on earth and has chosen Zion as the place where Yahweh becomes present in the midst of the chosen people. Hence, both king and temple could be spoken of in the most glowing terms. With regard to the king, Israel's poets could use the extravagant language of ancient "court style." The king is the son of God (Psalm 2:7) and hence "the fairest of the sons of men [Ps. 45:2, RSV]." He is exalted to Yahweh's throne, where he sits at God's right hand (Psalm 110:5). As God's vicegerent, he is victorious over the powers of chaos ("sea" and "rivers," Psalm

89:25) and is the source of blessing that overflows beyond the boundaries of his kingdom (Psalm 72:7). To him is given the highest throne names: Wonderful Counselor, Divine Hero, Father perpetually, Prince of Peace (Isaiah 9:6). He is the source of the people's vitality, "the breath of [their] nostrils [Lam. 4:20, RSV]." He is endowed with the supreme gifts of Yahweh's Spirit (Isaiah 11:2), and hence his reign will be characterized by righteousness and peace.

The Davidic-Zion tradition clearly has many affinities with the cosmological symbolism of the Ancient Near East. But there are major differences that should not be underestimated. For one thing, in Davidic tradition the key salvific institutions of monarchy and temple are historically conditioned. The institution of kingship does not have primordial status, as in the "antediluvian" preamble to the Sumerian King List, which begins remotely "When kingship was lowered from heaven."[14] Rather, in Israel kingship had a humble historical origin in the time when Yahweh raised David from the sheepfolds and elevated him to be the shepherd of the chosen people (Psalm 78:70-73). Also, the temple of Zion was not a sacred place from time immemorial; rather, it became sacred for Israel at a particular historical time when Yahweh chose it as a place to dwell in the midst of the people.

Therefore, in spite of court hyperbole the king was not regarded as divine by nature or begotten as God's son from birth. On the surface, Psalm 45:6 seems to provide an exception, especially if we take the more difficult reading of the Masoretic text (also the Septuagint, quoted in Hebrews 1:8, 9) and translate: "Your throne, O God ('*Elohim*), is for ever and ever."[15] But just as a single swallow does not make a summer, so this isolated text does not mean that the Israelite court poet has taken over the Oriental deification of kings. As Psalm 2:7 puts it, the king is "begotten" of Yahweh on "this day," the day of his coronation; that is, he is elected to office by Yahweh, and hence his status, authority, and role as son of God are ex officio.

Finally, the Davidic "everlasting covenant" provided the basis for social stability, but it also allowed for social change, even historical catastrophe. Within this linguistic world the purpose of the cult is not to produce a static, changeless society—a pharaonic structure that is integrated into the order of the cosmos; rather, the purpose is to reshape social life according to the will of the cosmic King who, as announced in psalms of Yahweh's kingship, "comes to judge the world with righteousness, and the people with his truth" (cf. Psalms 96:13; 98:9). It was Isaiah of Jerusalem, the prophet who stood deeply in the Davidic tradition, who brought out most forcefully this eschatological dimension. He proclaimed the message that Yahweh is the Holy One who comes to judge and that nothing could parade as absolute before

166

Yahweh, no cultural values could be cherished as secure.[16] Hence Isaiah could portray the purification of the old city of Jerusalem in the consuming fire of divine judgment and the emergence from the flames of the faithful city, the new Jerusalem of Yahweh's intention (Isaiah 1:21-26). And he could draw a sharp contrast between the faithless reigning king in the Davidic line and the king of the future, whose reign would be the sign of God's presence in the midst of God's people, Immanuel (Isaiah 7:10-17). In prophetic expectation "the One who was to come" would be not just the son of David but, through divine election, the son of God. He would ascend the throne of David and inaugurate a government of endless peace and justice (cf. Isaiah 9:2-7).

This vision of the ideal king, the Son of God, did not square with the harsh and tragic realities of history. Isaiah's call for faith in Yahweh's covenant promises to David was hard enough to accept in the days of the Syro-Ephraimitic crisis (735-733 B.C.) when an alliance of small nations, Syria and Ephraim, attempted to force the Davidic state of Judah into a military movement to stop Assyrian aggression into the West (Isaiah 7). But the Davidic theological convictions were even more unbelievable in later historical crises when the Davidic state was threatened with disaster and when it finally fell under Babylonian assault in 587 B.C. Psalm 89, which has been alluded to previously, provides poignant evidence of the crisis of faith. The psalm begins on a hymnic upbeat, in which the psalmist praises Yahweh for promises of grace to David. Since Yahweh's "*ḥesed* was established for ever," his "faithfulness is firm as the heavens" (v. 2, RSV), hymnic praise soars into the cosmic realm where Yahweh is enthroned as king in the heavenly assembly and Yahweh's kingship is demonstrated by the triumphant rule of the Creator over all the insurgent powers of chaos (vv. 5-18).

O Lord God of hosts,
    who is mighty as thou art, O Lord,
    with thy faithfulness round about thee?
Thou dost rule the raging of the sea;
    when its waves rise, thou stillest them.
Thou didst crush Rahab like a carcass,
    thou didst scatter thy enemies with thy mighty arm.
                                        —Psalm 89:8-10, RSV

The announcement that "our king belongs to the Holy One of Israel [v. 18, RSV]" provides a transition from the cosmic realm to the earthly kingdom, where the Davidic king is elevated to the covenant relationship of son of God (vv. 19-37). But the psalm ends on the downbeat of

167

lament (vv. 38-51) in which the Anointed One (Messiah) suffers humiliation. The promises of grace to David are in question, for apparently the history of the throne succession is a history of failure. The suppliant raises the typical question "How long?" which resounds in laments found in the Psalter (e.g., Psalm 13) and elsewhere (e.g., Habakkuk 1:2-4).

> How long, O Lord? Wilt thou hide thyself for ever?
> How long will thy wrath burn like fire?
>
> . . . .
>
> Lord, where is thy [*ḥesed*] of old,
> which by thy faithfulness thou didst swear to David?
>
> —Psalm 89:46, 49, RSV

From this point on, the "stream of tradition" associated with the Davidic king and the temple of Zion follows a tortuous course. A significant point along the way was the prophetic proclamation of so-called Second Isaiah, the unknown prophet of the exile. A disciple of Isaiah of Jerusalem who stood firmly in the Zion tradition and scarcely mentioned the exodus, this prophet attempted a bold, new synthesis of Israel's traditions. First of all, he gave prominence to the exodus tradition in order to proclaim "the new exodus of salvation" that Yahweh held in store for the chosen people. Second, he democratized the "everlasting covenant" (*berît ōlām*) with David by applying it to the people (Isaiah 55:3-5) who, according to his message, have a future solely by virtue of Yahweh's unconditional grace and forgiveness.[17]

Another significant development in the history of the Davidic tradition was the reuse of the royal symbolism in worship of the second temple, long after the Davidic state had come to an end. Israel's poets had prepared for this cultic usage by using court language that was extravagant and hyperbolic, transcending the historical realities of the Davidic kings, even David himself. Gerhard von Rad concludes his treatment of the royal psalms found in the Psalter, psalms which originally referred to the reigning king, by saying that Israel's poets laid "a very magnificent purple robe . . . on the shoulders of the young successors of David at their accession." He goes on to say: "We do not know whether those who did homage to them were filled with real confidence, or whether they already had their doubts and were asking, 'Art thou he who is to come, or are we to wait for another?' "[18] Similarly, the symbolic significance of the temple of Zion did not wane, even though the second temple may have lacked the luster of the Davidic-Solomonic original (Haggai 2:3) or was superseded for all practical purposes by the synagogue. The Chronicler's history, written in the very late Old Testament period, shows that the older views of Davidic kingship and the temple of Zion were very much alive in some circles.

Despite all political changes and internal developments within the history of Israelite traditions, the tradition-stream associated with David and Zion persisted with fundamental continuity and recognizable identity into the period of the early Christian community, when the various Gospels of Jesus, the Christ (Messiah), were composed. It would be wrong to suppose that there was a straight-line continuity from the Old to the New. There was a decisive break in the history of traditions, owing to the distinctive claims of the Christian proclamation and to the new situation (Hellenistic-Roman) in which the gospel was interpreted. Nevertheless, it can scarcely be denied that the stream of tradition associated with David and Zion survived intact and provided a major resource, if not hermeneutical guide, for understanding the messianic identity of Jesus. This seems to be the case at least in the Gospel of Matthew, which attempts to understand Jesus' identity and role in the context of the promises of the Old Testament and which highlights the two epithets "son of David" and "Son of God" from the initial genealogy throughout the work.[19] Given this background of tradition, it is possible to understand in a new light Peter's typically Matthean confession, "You are the Messiah, the Son of the living God."
In a traditio-historical perspective, the confession embraces the features of a symbolic whole that we have considered: (a) God's cosmic kingship in heaven and on earth; (b) the elected king (the Anointed One) as the Son of God and therefore God's viceroy on earth; and (c) the exaltation of the "messiah" on Zion, the "holy hill," against which the assaulting hosts of chaos and evil cannot prevail.[20]

CHAPTER 13

Christology, Judaism, and Jews

Samuel Sandmel

Christology is intimately connected with a quasi-philosophical under-standing of the nature of God. The greater the measure of that philosophical understanding, the more complex and profound is the Christology; the less the measure of it, the less there is of Christology.

In this essay Christology is taken to mean what Christians *thought* Jesus was, as distinct from who he actually was. Such a separation is admittedly unrealistic. Nevertheless, to labor the distinction can serve a certain usefulness. Who was Jesus? He was a man, a Jew of Nazareth, who after a public career in Galilee went to Jerusalem where he was crucified and, his followers believed, vouchsafed a special resurrection. What was Jesus? He was the Son of God, the Christ, the Son of man, the Logos. These latter terms are familiar and precious to Christians, for quite apart from their meaning and substance they have provided the nexus, natural and necessary, between the *who* and the *what*.

It is well known that Jews of his time regarded as incredible the claim of the special resurrection of Jesus. In the polemics of that early period, they not only abstained from adulation of Jesus in terms of who he was, but, in the bitterness of controversy they denigrated him as a magician in the service of Satan. The Jewish documents (scattered passages in the rabbinic literature) deal exclusively with who Jesus was and disclose almost no knowledge of Christian assertions as to what Jesus was.

For the purpose of this essay, suppose that the bitter quarrels had not taken place and that the separation of Christianity from Judaism had not occurred. If that had been the case, what might have been the

Samuel Sandmel, Distinguished Service Professor of Bible and Hellenistic Literature, Emeritus, at Hebrew Union College, died in November 1979. The editors wish to express their gratitude to Frances Sandmel for editing the handwritten manuscript which he had already drafted for this volume.

relationship of Judaism to those religious ideas that came to be expressed in Christology? Can modern Jews and Christians expel from their minds all awareness of claims and counterclaims, arguments and controversies, and recollections of animosities and persecutions and now seek to address the theological and intellectual concerns that the supposition implies? That may not be possible, but again, suppose one tries to make the effort. Paradoxically, the effort itself entails hearkening back to those disputes, since the theological and intellectual issues are historically bound up in them. One may need to modify the hypothetical conditions. We shall not forget the disputes, but we shall avoid the disputatiousness; we shall not forget the basic differences, but we shall try to forget the heritage of bitter polemics.

In earliest times the basic issue as to who Jesus was involves an equally basic issue about the resurrection that seems to be often overlooked. That the Sadducees, who denied resurrection as a credible doctrine, should not have believed in the resurrection of Jesus seems natural. The Gospel passage that relates that the Sadducees confronted Jesus may or may not be historical; the event is allocated by the evangelists to the lifetime of Jesus and is a debate over resurrection in general. But the debates over resurrection with the Pharisees, who accepted the doctrine of resurrection, are allocated by the New Testament to the time after the earthly career of Jesus, and their issue is not the credibility of resurrection as such, but that of the particular resurrection of Jesus. That is, the Pharisees and the disciples of Jesus, having in common the belief in resurrection, still quarreled about the genuineness of the resurrection of Jesus himself.

The Gospels present aspects of these quarrels. For example, one can infer that to question or deny a particular resurrection on the grounds that a person had not really died was fairly broad. In John, Lazarus, to whom Jesus did not come in time to avert his death, had been in the grave four days before Jesus summoned him forth. The passing of those four days rules out the charge that Lazarus was only sleeping. The material is presented so that it refutes the allegation that death had not truly taken place. In Matthew, however, the quarrel concerns not death but the emptiness of the tomb—this borrowed from Mark. To the disciples' contention that the emptiness of the tomb proves that Jesus had been resurrected, the opponents charge that the tomb was empty because the body was stolen by the disciples. When I have presented this Gospel material to my Jewish students, they have had not the slightest difficulty in understanding it. So too, when I have reflected for them the general tone of the passages in rabbinic literature, they have grasped readily the kind of material found there.

As to what Jesus was, at least the phrase son of David is understandable, since in the ongoing Jewish thought the future Messiah is identified as the son of David. It is, however, when one moves to other christological terms that incomprehension on the part of Jews arises. The relevancy of my alluding to my students can now be indicated. There is every reason to believe that the Jews of the period of early Christianity failed to understand these christological terms in exactly the same way as ordinary modern Jews do.

That the word Christ translates into Greek the Hebrew word *mashiah* increases rather than diminishes the confusion and incomprehension. Jews at the time of Jesus had developed expectations that the Messiah would accomplish, or spur to accomplishment, a series of related eventualities: the destruction of the colonial power of Rome, the inauguration of a proper Jewish royal dynasty, the ingathering of the exiles from the lands of the dispersion, and the imminent arrival of the great judgment day. In the view of these Jews, Jesus accomplished none of the prescribed goals; therefore Jesus could not be the Messiah. Besides, the transformation of a single, climactic event—the coming of the Messiah as the Jews expected it—into two parts, first the advent and then the future second coming, was to Jews either farfetched or unauthorized. It needs to be clearly stated that some echoes of the Jewish expectations concerning the Messiah are dimly present in scattered passages in the New Testament.

Also, the association of the Christ with sin and atonement, and with his ending humankind's alienation from God, implies a definition of the Messiah different from that prevalent in Judaism. The difficulty is increased by the circumstance that the clearest expression of the relationship of the Christ to sin and atonement came from Paul, who was a Jew. How shall we explain that Jews have fallen far short of wishing to attempt to refute Paul simply because they do not get as far as understanding him, a necessary prologue to accepting or rejecting? If only the transformation from the "nationalistic" Messiah to the "cosmic Christ" had come from a gentile, the mystification would be reduced at least to the point of declaring that the cosmic redeemer was a gentile idea, not a Jewish one. But Paul was a Jew.

The way out is to delineate Paul as someone who, though Jewish, was culturally a Greek, not a Judean, and to ascribe his doctrine to his having absorbed the pagan environment of the Greek diaspora. Resistance to such a delineation is twofold. First, the Acts of the Apostles ascribes Judean connections to Paul: he studied under the great Pharisee Gamaliel, he could deliver an address in Hebrew, he had a nephew who was a resident of Jerusalem. While these details (none of which appear in Paul's letters) would suggest that he was at home in Judean Judaism, they are all reflective, in varying degrees, of Luke's special aims and do not merit the historian's reliance in any effort to define Paul's anteced-ents. Second, there exists in current New Testament scholarship the erroneous contention that there was no difference of any consequence between Judean Judaism and that of the Diaspora, or between Palestini-an Jewish-Christianity and that of the Diaspora gentiles.

The distinction between the national Messiah of the Jews and the cosmic atoning Christ of Christianity is more than a separation in conception. It is almost inevitably a barrier to elementary communica-tion.

What about the other christological nomenclature: Son of man (as a messianic title), Son of God, Lord, Logos? Do any rabbinic sources of the period of early Christianity reflect a knowledge of these and of their meaning, or offer any polemic using them? Not a one! What the rabbinic materials say, in disparaging Jesus, reflects no knowledge of any of the actual materials found in the New Testament, such as could or would have come from reading them. Rather, the adverse statements seem to come only from eavesdropping or from rumor. The ancient rabbis did not, as it were, reject the christological titles or the Christologies; they seem simply to have known nothing about them.

What these christological titles have in common is that they seek to answer the question "In what sense was Jesus divine?" Son of man, about which a huge amount has been written, would appear to be the least christological, in the sense that it does not define the relationship of the Christ to God. My own published view is that in Mark (where the word Christ is used only in 1:1 and may there be an added beginning) Son of man is meant to mystify rather than to reveal. The repeated motif in Mark that the Jews, including the disciples, were blinded as to who Jesus was could not be persuasive if such titles as King or Christ had been used. While Jews inherited the book of Daniel, which is the source for the use of Son of man as the equivalent of Messiah, the phrase Son of man in a christological sense is exclusively Christian.

As to the Son of God, it might be useful to try to keep this phrase quite separate from the virgin birth. One is justified in such separation in that the two narratives in Matthew and Luke ascribe the paternity of Jesus not to God but to the Holy Spirit. I have consistently taught that the virgin birth in no way meant something so specific as that the deity or the Holy Spirit instigated sex relations with the mother of Jesus. Rather, the virgin birth belongs rightfully in the general array of many, many tales of wondrous births that circulated throughout the ancient world.

Since Son of God, then, is not meant to imply some literal paternity, what did it mean? There seems no doubt that the import of the term is

173

that which would otherwise be expressed in such words as agent, deputy, or surrogate. The title stems from an idea, or rather a related set of ideas, derived from the views of God as transcendent. God is so majestic as to appear to be outside and beyond this world and not to enter into it directly. It is God's agent, deputy, or surrogate that does so.

A view of this kind emerges from people daring to analyze the nature of God and thereby distinguishing transcendence from immanence, even when these two words chance to fail to be used. While Old Testament and rabbinic literature reflect an awareness of transcendence and immanence, they exhibit no real philosophical analysis. Thus, angels in the Old Testament, or the *bat qol* ("heavenly voice") or *shekina* ("divine presence") in rabbinic thought, reflect simply intuition; they do not stand for analytical, and certainly not philosophical, insights.

True, the ancient rabbis derived from scripture what they regarded as attributes of God, that is, adjectives that described God. For example, Exodus 34:6-7 reads, "Yahve is a compassionate and pitying God, long-suffering and abundant in goodness and truth." Also, it is well known that the very name Yahve (which Jews came to pronounce "Adonai") was interpreted as signifying God in the attribute of mercy, as distinct from the name Elohim, which signified God in his capacity of administering strict justice. But attributes are scarcely a philosophical analysis. Indeed, to the extent that awareness of anything remotely resembling the philosophical was known, it was, in this literature, rejected. The ancient rabbinic literature scorned *minim*, who, so it is asserted, believed in two authorities. We do not know whether these two authorities were reflections of Persian deities of light and darkness or whether they are Grecian, balancing God with some subordinate deity or demiurge. Why do the sources tell us so little that one cannot define the particular "heresy" of the *minim*? Probably because the idea of two authorities was viewed as contradicting the unity of God. The original meaning of the verse "Hear, O Israel, the Lord our God, the Lord is One," according to my teacher Julian Morgenstern, is a quite literal proclamation of the unity of God. In a context of apparently many Yahves—for example, the Yahve of Shiloh, the Yahve of Bethel —it is saying, "Hear, O Israel, Yahve our God is a single Yahve." The reason that the verse (Deuteronomy 6:4) ". . . the Lord is one" came to be "the watchword of the Jewish faith" is that it appeared to be a biblical sanction for rejecting such antithetical views as those of the *minim*.

It is when we turn to Philo of Alexandria (20 B.C.-A.D. 40) that we encounter philosophical analysis. So transcendent is the deity for Philo that God is in effect outside the world. Indeed, God is beyond human knowledge, especially in divine essence and fullness. Humankind can come to know only *aspects* of God, not the divine self. The ancient rabbinic literature uses a variety of terms in replacement of "God," which word was too holy for ordinary use. The terms include The Holy One, The Place, and The Power. The latter two terms appear also in Philo, but no direct connection need be theorized. Philo's word for aspects is "powers," for which a synonym, as it were, could be "activities." The world was created, and that activity or power of God which did the creating by no means exhausts the fullness (*pléroma*) of God. So too is the universe ruled, but God's activity in ruling the universe by no means exhausts God's fullness.

Theos, so frequent in scripture, is not God but God's creative power. *Kyrios,* also frequent in scripture, is not God but God's ruling power. God, the transcendent, unknowable God, is *To On,* "the truly Existent."

Human beings of even the lowest capacities can know about *Theos,* for they can see that creation has taken place. Human beings of somewhat better capacities, viewing the regularity of the seasons and of sunrise and sunset, can know about the ruling power, *Kyrios.* Both these categories of humankind have come to this limited knowledge out of the perceptions of their senses.

A loftier category of humanity can proceed beyond the yield of the senses, this through reason and the proper use of the dialectic. But even such people, however great their gifts and faultless their reasoning, fall short of knowing God. What they can know is God's Logos.

The divine Logos is that attainable facet of God which is otherwise quite beyond the upward reach of understanding of the most gifted people and disciplined thinkers. Downward too, as God reaches to humankind, God goes no farther than the Logos (for otherwise God's transcendence would be contradicted). Stated in another way, Logos is that aspect of God, available to human reason, which functions for God. Through the gifts of reason, and the lesser gifts of their senses, humankind is enabled to know much *about* God, but never the divine self.

Philo, curiously, never defines Logos, though he speaks about it frequently. He also uses a variety of figures of speech. For example, the Logos is the firstborn of God. In Philo's allegory, the high priest is the Logos; "law" also is deemed a product of divine reason.

It is not surprising that the legend arose that Philo had become a Christian. It rests on the affinity between Philo's teachings and facets of developing Christology. Henry Chadwick has stated this admirably, that the student who wishes to learn Christian theology must begin with Philo.

A considerable amount of literature points to the doctrinal affinities of Philo on the one hand and Paul, the Johannine writings, and Hebrews on the other. One can conclude at this stage that there is *in theological substance* little in Christology that would have been alien to Philo or that would have repelled him. Had Paul used Logos rather than Christ, Philo could well have found himself in broad congruency with Paul's major views of God. As to other facets of Paul's thought, such as justification by faith, Philo would have been in no greater disagreement than some Christians such as the author of the letter of James (where "works" are rehabilitated). That is to say, in theological substance a Philo could well have found himself in the company of congenial minds. He himself could have written the passage in Colossians 1:15-20, at least as far as verses 15-17.

Where Philo would have stopped, to demur or to object, is the point at which the Christ and Jesus are identified. A Philo might have said, "The view of you Christians about the nature of God and the Logos is congenial to me; what I cannot go along with is your telling me that Jesus and the Logos were one and the same. I cannot accept this. Your identification of Jesus with the Logos rests on contentions about who Jesus was that I do not believe."

God's essence is unknowable, but the facets of God's essence came to be related to the need to solve the problem of transcendence and immanence. Hence, as Judaism went on to develop, there arose a system, enigmatic in its origin but crystal-clear in its manifestations, the flowering of Hellenistic Neoplatonism, exemplified in Plotinus and then in medieval cabalism. Not that the medieval cabalists knew Plotinus or knew of him, but the development from Philo to the gentile Plotinus entailed the emergence of a philosophic order more systematic than that of Philo's Logos and the powers. This took the form of a theory of "spheres," ten in number, descending from God, traversing the *cosmos noëtos* and reaching down into our sensible world. Though the route by which such Neoplatonism reached the cabala is not traceable, that it arrived is universally admitted.

This is not the place for a rounded exposition of cabalism. If one bypasses precision in terms, one might say that God's essence (what Philo meant by *To On*) is in cabalism the *en sof* (the unlimited one). From the *en sof* there emerges the *atzilut* (the divine emanation) into ten descending *sefirot* (spheres). These are the "divine powers": (1) *Keter,* the crown; (2) *Hochma,* wisdom; (3) *Bina,* understanding; (4) *Gedula,* greatness; (5) *Gevura,* strength; (6) *Tiferet,* beauty; (7) *Netzah,* eternity;

(8) *Hod,* majesty; (9) *Yesod,* foundation; (10) *Malchut,* kingship. In other systems of cabala, the order and the precise names of the spheres are different but similar.

Their complex of divine powers operates in the four worlds; *atzilut,* already mentioned, the emanation from God; *bria,* creation; *yezira,* fashioning; and *asuja,* the making. This fourth world is ours, the domain of human beings. (Of the developed angelology and demonology and other topics, there is no need to speak here.)

Relevant to our topic is a facet of the controversy that cabalism spurred: Were its doctrines consistent with the "pure" monotheism associated with the *sh'ma?* The accusation arose that it was not. Cabalists replied that it was.

Thus Christology and cabalism have in common that the effort to analyze the nature of the Godhead seems to those outside their efforts to compromise the purity of monotheism. Hence the christological disputes, for example, Arianism, arose out of the anxiety that the sole uniqueness of God was being trespassed against. The reply of both "christologers" (to coin a word) and cabalists was that of denial.

In the Middle Ages, Christians such as Pico della Mirandola were attracted to cabala. They clearly found it the reverse of alien. It fit congruently with Christology, or at least it seemed to.

The presence of Jesus in Christology has resulted in a curious bifurcation. On the one hand, there could be a Christology without Jesus. This indeed became the way of the Gnostics. The "radical" New Testament scholarship that came to despair of recovering the "Jesus of history" apparently needed the balance of a renewal of Christology. Hence the neoorthodoxy of two decades ago. Less radical theologians, unwilling to concede that the Jesus of history was not to be recovered, engaged in occasional name-calling. I recall a half dozen essays in which Rudolf Bultmann is denounced as a Gnostic, since theologically he was not interested in the man Jesus and historically came to his reluctant conclusion that Jesus is not to be found. Jewish scholars, especially those who never were confronted by the details of gospel scholarship, have ordinarily not shared in the skepticism of a Bultmann.

However, the constant reinterpretation of Christology by free, modern theologians, with this or that reservation, or the infusion of a brand-new meaning into a traditional term, has created new problems. (One of these is the capacity of some Christian theologians to ignore the consensus judgments of gospel scholars.) Certain terms have come to be altered almost into slogans, for example, eschatology and Heilsgeschichte. Is it not true that recurrently modern Christian theology is centered in a Jesus whom New Testament scholars have not confirmed?

177

For someone like me, if I may be personal, modern Christian theology defies my efforts to grasp it and to grapple with it. I believe I understand New Testament scholarship; I believe I understand ancient theological views. Is it my Jewish heritage that closes me off from modern theology, as was the case with the ancient rabbis? Perhaps. Or perhaps the difficulty lies elsewhere, in the omnipresence in modern theology of more quandaries than clarifications.

To what extent is the figure of Jesus an ongoing impediment to a Jew's understanding of Christology? Here one encounters a genuine perplexity. I think it is not exaggeration to state that since 1800 many more Jewish essays—historical, theological—have been written on Jesus than on Moses. Virtually all these writings have been affirmative and appreciative. Some even have had the objective of "reclaiming" Jesus for Judaism. In the view of this abundance of Jewish writings about Jesus, the incapacity of Jews to grasp the content, let alone the nuances of Christology, is puzzling. Is it that Jewish writers are uniformly "empiricist" and rigidly "historical" and averse to theology, even Jewish theology? One does not know. Perhaps the way in which cabalism came virtually to be winnowed out of the minds of Western Jews contributes to the situation. If cabalism is alien to the minds of Western Jews, how much more so Christology!

CHAPTER 14

The *Testimonium Flavianum:*
The State of the Question

Louis H. Feldman

One of the key questions concerning Jesus is whether we can find sources outside the Gospels and dating from the first century that corroborate or contradict details that are found there. The most complete (even if brief) and most important such passage is the so-called *Testimonium Flavianum* in Josephus' *Antiquities,* dating from A.D. 93/94. Ever since the sixteenth century, however, the question has been fiercely debated as to whether this passage is really by Josephus or whether it is in its entirety or in part the work of a forger.

The text of the *Testamonium Flavianum* reads:

Γίνεται δὲ κατὰ τοῦτον τὸν χρόνον Ἰησοῦς σοφὸς ἀνήρ, εἴγε ἄνδρα αὐτὸν λέγειν Χρή. ἦν γὰρ παραδόξων ἔργων ποιητής, διδάσκαλος ἀνθρώπων τῶν ἡδονῇ τἀληθῆ δεχομένων, καὶ πολλοὺς μὲν Ἰουδαίους, πολλοὺς δὲ καὶ τοῦ Ἑλληνικοῦ ἐπηγάγετο· ὁ χριστὸς οὗτος ἦν. καὶ αὐτὸν ἐνδείξει τῶν πρώτων ἀνδρῶν παρ᾽ ἡμῖν σταυρῷ ἐπιτετιμηκότος Πιλάτου οὐκ ἐπαύσαντο οἱ τὸ πρῶτου ἀγαπήσαντες· ἐφάνη γὰρ αὐτοῖς τρίτην ἔχων ἡμέραν πάλιν ζῶν τῶν Θείων προφητῶν ταῦτά τε καὶ ἄλλα μυρία περὶ αὐτοῦ Θαυμάσια εἰρηκότων. εἰς ἔτι τε νῦν τῶν Χριστιανῶν ἀπὸ τοῦδε ὠνομασμένον οὐκ ἐπέλιπε τὸ φῦλον.

About this time there lived Jesus, a wise man, if indeed one ought to call him a man. For he was one who wrought surprising feats and was a teacher of such people as accept the truth gladly. He won over many Jews and many of the Greeks. He was the

Louis H. Feldman, a native of Hartford, Connecticut, is a professor at Yeshiva University, New York City.

Messiah. When Pilate, upon hearing him accused by men of the highest standing amongst us, had condemned him to be crucified, those who had in the first place come to love him did not give up their affection for him. On the third day he appeared to them restored to life, for the prophets of God had prophesied these and countless other marvellous things about him. And the tribe of the Christians, so called after him, has still to this day not disappeared.

Introduction

The literature on the so-called *Testimonium Flavianum* concerning Jesus (Josephus, *Antiquities* 18.63-64) continues to grow, though the pace has somewhat slackened since the ferment of the late 1920s and early 1930s occasioned by the publication of the German version of the Slavonic version of the *Jewish War*[1] and by Robert Eisler's controversial volume.[2] With the lapse of half a century since the appearance of Eisler's work, it may be useful to examine the state of the question and to note what progress, if any, has been made toward its solution.

Bibliography

There is no ancient author for whom we possess more exhaustive bibliographies than Josephus. Heinz Schreckenberg's bibliography presents a year-by-year listing, starting with 1470, the year of the *editio princeps,* to 1968, with systematic coverage through 1965.[3] For most items Schreckenberg gives brief, though almost never critical, summaries. He classifies the items according to a scheme of twenty-five categories, one of which, number 17, deals with references to Jesus and early Christianity. A large percentage of the entries, particularly before the middle of the nineteenth century, are concerned with the *Testimonium.* The reader will, however, find numerous question marks, especially for the older entries, indicating that the author was unable to verify the entries. While it is true (as the greatest of Jewish bibliographers, Moritz Steinschneider, once remarked) that such works are terminated only by the binder, it is disappointing to note that there are numerous errors in the entries, as well as in the otherwise useful indexes of names and passages, and many hundreds of omissions. Most of these have been corrected in Schreckenberg's supplement, which brings the bibliography up to 1977;[4] the many that remain will be corrected in a forthcoming publication by the present author in collaboration with David A. Barish.

There are three significant bibliographies for the *Testimonium* proper: (1) Robert Eisler's *Iēsous Basileus ou Basileusas* (1929), translated into

English by Alexander H. Krappe, *The Messiah Jesus and John the Baptist According to Flavius Josephus' Recently Rediscovered 'Capture of Jerusalem' and the Other Jewish and Christian Sources;*[5] (2) my "Selected Literature on the Testimonium Flavianum (Ant. xviii.63-64"[6]; and (3) Paul Winter's "Bibliography to Josephus, Antiquitates Judaicae, XVIII, 63, 64."[7] Of these the most useful is that of Winter, who has a select bibliography, classified in three groups (with occasional quotations), defending authenticity, against authenticity, and maintaining the theory of interpolation. There are no systematic critical bibliographies. Dubarle comments critically on six recent publications.[8] My own systematic critical bibliography of Josephus in all his aspects, covering the period 1937 to the present, includes a section on the *Testimonium Flavianum.*

The Manuscript Tradition

Just as in a court of law under our system one must start with the assumption that the defendant is innocent until proven guilty, so one must start with the assumption that the text of the *Testimonium* is authentic, unless we can supply convincing evidence to the contrary. The passage appears in all the extant manuscripts. Unfortunately, the earliest of these, the Ambrosianus 370 (F 128), containing books 11-20 of the *Antiquities,* dates from only the eleventh century.[9] Another manuscript, the Vaticanus Graecus 148, dating from either the tenth or the eleventh century, contains the *War* and only the *Testimonium* itself. Schreckenberg's investigations have located only two manuscripts of any note containing this portion of Josephus: Yale 275, dating from the fourteenth century[10] but derived from a text type akin to Ambrosianus 370, and Bononiensis Graecus 3568, dating from the fourteenth or fifteenth century, which is closely related to the Codex Palatinus, dating from the beginning of the fourteenth century.[11] The *Testimonium,* moreover, appears in all the numerous manuscripts of the Latin translation that was made under the direction of Cassiodorus in the sixth century.[12]

Citations in Church Fathers

A point that has not been appreciated thus far is that despite the value that such a passage would have had in establishing the credentials of Jesus in the church's missionary activities, it is not cited until Eusebius does so in the fourth century. This is admittedly the *argumentum ex silentio,* but in this case it is a fairly strong argument against the authenticity of the passage as we have it, especially since we know that Justin Martyr in the middle of the second century (*Dialogue with Trypho* 8) attempted to answer the charge that Jesus had never lived and was a mere figment of Christian imagination. Nothing could have been a stronger argument to disprove such a charge than a citation from Josephus, a Jew, who was born only a few years after Jesus' death.

Yet an examination of Christian writers who mention Josephus shows a complete absence of references to the *Testimonium* before Eusebius.[13] To be sure, Pseudo-Justin, who died about 165, mentions (*Cohortatio ad Graecos* 9 and 13; Migne, *Patrologia Graeca* 6.257, 261, 268) only the name of Josephus as a historian who was most wise and worthy. Theophilus of Antioch, who died after 181-182, refers only to Josephus' *Against Apion* in his *Ad Autolycum* 3.20-23, sometimes quoting from the work, sometimes freely paraphrasing it. Minucius Felix, who wrote toward the end of the second century, again does not quote any passage from Josephus but does mention Josephus as a source for Jewish history (*Octavian* 33.4).

Irenaeus, who died about 202, mentions in passing Josephus' version (*Ant.* 2.238-53) of Moses' campaign in Ethiopia (frag. 33; Migne, *Patrologia Graeca* 7.1245). Clement of Alexandria, who died some time before 215 or 216, cites chronological data in Josephus (*Stromata* 1.21.147.2-3). Julius Africanus, writing in the first part of the third century, composed a world chronicle, of which only fragments are extant, in which he shows clear knowledge of and use of Josephus, and yet never alludes to the *Testimonium*. Tertullian, who died about 222, mentions Josephus (*Apologeticus* 19.6) as *antiquitatum Judaicarum vernaculus vindex* ("native defender of Jewish Antiquities"), clearly an allusion to the title of the work where the *Testimonium* appears, but does not allude to the *Testimonium*.

Hippolytus, who died about 235, has numerous parallels (*Refutatio omnium haeresium* [*Elenchos*] 9.18.2-9.29.3) with the passage about the Essenes in Josephus' *Jewish War* (2.119-66), though there is some question as to whether he was directly dependent upon Josephus or whether both drew upon a common source. That Hippolytus was acquainted with Josephus' *Antiquities* is indicated by the influence of Josephus' *Antiquities* 1.122ff. on *Elenchos* 10.31 and of *Antiquities* 20.224ff. on his *Chronicle* 740-41.

The case of Origen, who died in 253-54 and who appears next chronologically, is of special importance and has been dealt with often. Of the Christian writers mentioned previously, none cites from book 18 of the *Antiquities,* where the *Testimonium* occurs. Origen, however, cites no less than five passages from this book (*Ant.* 18.4ff. and 18.55ff. in his *Commentary on Matthew* 17.25; *Ant.* 18.110 and 18.130 in his

Commentary on Matthew 10.21; and *Ant.* 18.116ff. in his *Contra Celsum* 1.47). Moreover, he explicitly states (*Commentary on Matthew* 10.17) that "the wonder is that though he did not admit (καταδεξάμενος) our Jesus to be Christ, he nonetheless gave witness to so much righteousness in James" and "He [i.e., Josephus] disbelieved in Jesus as Christ" (*Contra Celsum* 1.47).

Horváth quite properly remarks that it makes no sense for Origen to express wonder that Josephus did not admit Jesus to be the Messiah if he did not even mention him.[14] Préchac suggests that Origen is citing from memory,[15] but inasmuch as he cites accurately some other passages from book 18 in this context, this seems unlikely. To be sure, Origen does say (*Contra Celsum* 1.47) that Josephus declares Jerusalem and the temple were destroyed in retribution for the execution of James, and there is no such passage in our text of the *Antiquities*. Origen may be thinking of Josephus' statement about the divine vengeance for the murder of John the Baptist by Herod the Tetrarch (*Ant.* 18.116). Alternatively, we may follow Baras, who suggests that the juxtaposition of James's martyrdom and the siege of Jerusalem in Hegesippus, as well as Josephus' own statement (*Ant.* 20.258) connecting these preliminary events with the suffering in the war that followed, may be the source of Origen's conclusion: *post hoc, ergo propter hoc.*[16]

That Josephus in Origen's text of him did mention Jesus seems probable from the fact that he on three occasions quotes from *Antiquities* 20.200, the reference being to James, τὸν ἀδελφὸν Ἰησοῦ τοῦ λεγομένου Χριστοῦ, "the brother of Jesus, who was called the Christ." Few have doubted the genuineness of the passage on James, and if it had been a Christian interpolation it would in all probability have been more laudatory of James. If the *Testimonium* had appeared in Origen's text of Josephus in anything like the form in which it appears in our manuscripts, it hardly seems likely that he would have complained, in effect, that James was accorded greater importance than Jesus himself. In answering Celsus' very effective charges against Jesus and Christianity, particularly as to the miracles of Jesus, Origen should most naturally have cited Josephus' *Testimonium,* which so explicitly refers to these miracles. It seems unlikely that Origen's text of the *Testimonium* was depreciatory, because in that case he would most probably have reacted more strongly against the passage and not merely have expressed wonder that Josephus did not admit Jesus to be the Christ. The most likely assumption is, then, that the *Testimonium* as read by Origen contained historical data in a neutral form.

In the fourth century, prior to Eusebius, Methodius, who died in 311, cites the *War* 6.435-37 verbatim but does not refer to the *Testimonium*. Contemporary with Eusebius, who died in 339-40, Pseudo-Eustathius, who died before 337, in his *Commentary on the Hexaemeron* (Migne, *Patrologia Latina* 18.707ff.), cites or refers to four passages in the *War,* book 4; thirty-five passages in the *Antiquities,* book 1; and fourteen passages in the *Antiquities,* book 2. Yet nowhere does he refer to the *Testimonium.*

Even after Eusebius it is a full century before we have another reference to the *Testimonium.* Basil, who died in 379, cites Josephus, *War* 6.201-13, as a source but says nothing of the *Testimonium.* Ambrose, who died in 397, cites Josephus twenty-five times, including one passage from *Antiquities* 16.22-31 and one from *Antiquities* 19.17-21 (the twenty books of the *Antiquities* were divided into two halves for textual purposes at an early point), but again there is no reference to the *Testimonium.* Josippos, who lived in the fourth or fifth century, knew Josephus in at least four places, including one passage from *Antiquities* (18.34) and two from book 20.179 and 20.196, but does not cite the *Testimonium.* Panodorus, a chronographer who flourished 395-408 and who is known through excerptors, often used Josephus but has no reference to the *Testimonium.* John Chrysostom, who died in 407, refers to no other ancient author, except Plato, as often as to Josephus.[17] He cites book 18, including the passage about John the Baptist (18.116-19), on four occasions but not the *Testimonium.* There is hardly a church father who is more vehement in his attacks on the Jews (see, e.g., *Homily* 1.4, 1.6); if Josephus had indeed had a negative portrayal of Jesus, it seems likely that he would have cited this to strengthen his tirade against the Jews. Conversely, if the *Testimonium* had been positive, he might well have cited it to show that the Jews were guilty of the crime of deicide. Again, Rufinus, who died in 410, and Sulpicius Severus, who died around 420, refer to Josephus but not to the *Testimonium.*

It is not until Jerome, almost a century after Eusebius, that we once again have a reference to the *Testimonium.* It is significant that despite the value of such a passage and despite the fact that he knows Josephus so well (he cites him no less than ninety times) he refers to the *Testimonium* only once. An examination of this citation (*De Viris Illustribus* 13.14; *Patrologia Latina* 23.662-63) shows that though he is clearly quoting, Jerome says that Jesus *credebatur esse Christus.* Hence his text said not that Jesus was the Messiah but that he was *believed* to be a Messiah. This would fit the statement, noted above of Origen, to whom Jerome was so indebted, that Josephus did not admit Jesus to be the Christ.

Orosius (at the beginning of the fifth century), Philostorgius (who died after 424), and Theodore of Mopsuestia (who died in 428), all knew Josephus' works but do not cite the *Testimonium.* Most significant of all,

Augustine cites Josephus seven times in his voluminous works, once from *Antiquities* 18.110; but despite the obvious value of such a passage for his polemics and for his attacks on the Jews, he does not cite it. It is not until Isidore of Pelusium (*Epistles* 4.252; *Patrologia Graeca* 78.1320), who died about 435, a full century after Eusebius, and Sozomenus, in his *History of the Church* 1.1.5-6 and 7.18.7, written between 443 and 450, that there are clear-cut citations of the *Testimonium* as in our text.

The *argumentum ex silentio* may be weak, but when it is so highly cumulative as here, it does seem to carry weight. One might object that Philo is similarly unmentioned by Christian writers before the third century, despite the usefulness of the Logos theory for Christian theologians. This can be explained, however, by suggesting that serious Christian theology does not start until the third century.

The Context

One objection to the authenticity of the passage as it stands is that it breaks the continuity of the narrative, which tells of a series of riots. Section 65 of book 18 seems to belong directly after section 62. Prior to the *Testimonium*, as Norden,[18] Thackeray,[19] and Moreau[20] have noted, we have a description of two riots; and after the *Testimonium* we have two others, all of them termed θόρυβοι, whereas in sections 63 and 64 the Christian movement is not called a θόρυβος but a φῦλον. Thackeray has ingeniously noted, moreover, that the phrase γίνεται δέ, which introduces the *Testimonium*, invariably introduces a calamity in Josephus and that perhaps the phrase that followed was "the beginning of new disturbances."

Pharr,[21] in a theory recently revived by Horváth[22] and Bell,[23] thus suggests that the original *Testimonium* contained a derogatory account of the manner of Jesus' birth, inasmuch as in the Paulina-Mundus story (*Ant.* 18.65-80) that follows there is a similar motif of a woman being tricked into having relations with a man posing as a god.[24] Such a story of how Mary became pregnant by a soldier Panthera is alluded to in Celsus (*ap.* Origen, *Contra Celsum* 1.32) and in the Medieval Jewish *Toledoth Yeshu*. Bell adds that the episode (*Ant.* 18.81-84) of the Jewish teacher who diverted to his own use Fulvia's donation to the temple may be a satire on Paul, whose converts included large numbers of women, though there is no indication or even accusation anywhere that Paul did anything of this sort.

Bammel notes the parallel with the episode (*Ant.* 18.85-87) that follows and that speaks of a leader who promised the Samaritans he would lead them to a place where Moses had deposited some sacred vessels.[25] The Samaritans looked upon Moses restored to life, or one of his descendants, as the final Redeemer; and the Samaritan Book of Asatir, entirely devoted to divulging the so-called secrets of Moses, ends with a triumphant messianic oracle. Hence the juxtaposition of such an incident with the *Testimonium* may indicate that the latter was similarly messianic in its bent. Indeed, one might note that the Slavonic version of Josephus' *Jewish War,* between 2.174 and 175, similarly associates Moses with the Messiah, since it is said that some remarked about Jesus, "Our first lawgiver is risen from the dead."

As already noted, however, if the original passage were derogatory one might have expected some of the numerous early church fathers who had read Josephus to comment on it and to object to it. They not only do not do so, but also they praise Josephus, as did Pseudo-Justin in the second century (*Cohortatio ad Graecos* 9.13; *Patrologia Graeca* 6.257, 261, 268), as most wise and worthy.

If there was a passage about Jesus in the *Antiquities,* this may help to explain the Talmud's silence about Josephus. The Talmud, to be sure, is not a history book. Still, it does occasionally mention such historical figures as Herod and Titus; and if Josephus was of such distinguished ancestry, learning, and achievements as he claims to be, one might expect that the Talmudic sages would have mentioned him at least casually. Moreover, from a political point of view, Josephus' opposition to the revolutionaries and his aim of seeking an accommodation with the Romans is consonant with the attitude of the great Pharisaic leader Johanan ben Zakkai (cf. Talmud, *Giṭṭin* 56 a-b and pars.). Similarly, Josephus' blackening of Herod in the *Antiquities* should have found a responsive chord among Talmudic leaders, who were bitter about his slaying of scholars (*Baba Batra* 3a-4a; *Ta'anit* 23a).[26]

Some have asked how, if one assumes that the *Testimonium* is totally interpolated, Josephus could have passed over in total silence an event and personality of such significance. But even if one regards the passage as genuine, it is remarkable that Josephus passed over the incident totally in the *Jewish War* and that he devoted a mere two paragraphs and a single cross-reference to it in the *Antiquities.* In paying so little attention to Jesus and to early Christianity, he was not alone, however. One would have expected a writer such as Velleius Paterculus, for example, who dealt particularly with the reign of his much-beloved emperor Tiberius and whose work definitely reached the year 29 (the date of Jesus' crucifixion, since he mentions the death of the empress in that year [2.130.5]), to have mentioned Jesus if he really seemed important. Even Tacitus, who has such an extensive account of Tiberius' reign, mentions nothing about Jesus in connection with that period; his only mention of him comes when he discusses the fire in Rome during the reign of Nero, when Christians were accused of arson (*Annals* 15.44).

Trilling concludes that the *Testimonium* is a Christian interpolation and that Josephus maintained silence about Jesus not because of his animosity toward the Christians but the contrary, since an enemy of the Christians would have drawn attention to them and protected the Jews from reproach.[27] It is hard to believe that one favorably disposed toward the Christians would have passed over in utter silence what to the Christian is the key event in human history, the life of Jesus.

It is significant, but seldom noted, that none of the passages relevant to early Christianity—about Jesus, John, and James—is to be found in the parallel passages in the *Jewish War*. This may be explained by noting that the *Antiquities* covers this period often at considerably greater length, though the events in Pilate's procuratorship that are narrated in *Antiquities* 18.55-62 (37 lines in Niese's Greek text) are told at almost the same length (35 lines in Niese's Greek text) in *War* 2.169-77. Alternatively it may be concluded that the Christians had become more important during the interval between the time of the composition of the *War* and that of the *Antiquities*. Another possibility is that the passages are inserted for a specific purpose, to show the power of the Pharisees in getting Jesus condemned and of the Sanhedrin in condemning James.[28] However, Josephus refrains from specifying that the people "of the highest standing" who accused Jesus (*Ant.* 18.64) were Pharisees and he puts the chief blame for the condemnation of James upon Ananus, the high priest, who he specifically notes was a Sadducee (*Ant.* 20.199). As for the condemnation of John, it is neither the Pharisees nor the Sadducees who are held responsible, but Herod the Tetrarch (*Ant.* 18.116).

The Language: General

William Dulière, noting that there are forty-one people bearing the name of Jesus in the Septuagint, the New Testament, and Josephus (twenty-one in the last), to which one should add the passages referring to Jesus in the Talmudic corpus and those bearing the name of Joshua in Hebrew texts, raises the question of which Jesus is referred to in any given passage.[29] But despite the frequency of the name, there are too many details in our *Testimonium*—particularly the messianic claim, the connection with Pilate, the reference to the crucifixion, the alleged resurrection on the third day, and the reference to the Christians named after him—to allow for any doubt that it is the Jesus of Nazareth and of the Gospels that is meant.

As indicated by the rash of articles contesting it, a great stir was created by Eisler's extraordinarily detailed and extremely learned, though erratic, attempt to show that our text represents the result of tampering by Christian censors who inserted their own interpolations.[30] Despite his erudition, Eisler had an ability to tear passages out of their context and to twist the meanings of words to suit his theory. Eisler's work, however, won the support of one really important student of Josephus, Henry St. John Thackeray, who had originally believed the whole to be a Christian interpolation but who, under Eisler's hypnotic influence, came to regard it as partly interpolated. While Eisler's attempted restoration of the original text of the *Testimonium* appears arbitrary, his notion that the text as we have it has a substratum of authentic material seems increasingly confirmed by stylistic studies of it.

In particular, Thackeray, the prince of Josephan scholars, who went so far in his study of Josephus' language as to compose a lexicon to Josephus for his own use so as to see how precisely each word is used in Josephus and whether there is evidence of shifts of style in various parts of his works due to the help of "assistants" or to other reasons, noted that the phrase "such people as accept the truth gladly" ($\dot{\eta}\delta o\nu\dot{\eta}$) is characteristic of the scribe in this part of the *Antiquities,* since the phrase appears eight times in books 17-19 (supposedly the work of the Thucydidean assistant) and nowhere else in Josephus.[31] Christian interpolation is unlikely, since the word in the New Testament and in early Christian writings had a pejorative connotation. George C. Richards, another careful student of Josephus' language, notes several other stylistic peculiarities indicating that the passage is authentic.[32]

Felix Scheidweiler, however, dates the reworking of the passage to the second half of the third century and to the circle of the followers of the Christology of Paul of Samosata on the basis of the phrase $\sigma o\phi\grave{o}s$ $\dot{\alpha}\nu\acute{\eta}\rho$.[33] Franz Dornseiff replies that when Josephus called Jesus $\sigma o\phi\acute{o}s$ he meant merely that he was important,[34] but it is hard to support such a neutral meaning for this word during this period. One must not impute too much significance to the choice of individual words in a passage which is too short to be definitive in any stylistic study.

Thinking it unlikely that Josephus would have written that Jesus was a teacher of such people as accept the truth gladly, Thackeray suggests that "truth" ($\tau'\dot{\alpha}\lambda\eta\theta\acute{\eta}$) should be emended to "the unusual" ($\tau\dot{\alpha}\dot{\eta}\theta\eta$),[35] which indeed is palaeographically very close to the manuscripts; but the word $\dot{\alpha}\acute{\eta}\theta\eta s$ is not characteristic of the writer (or assistant) of this part of the *Antiquities,* occurring nowhere after book 13.

Other emendations have been proposed by Ernst Bammel, notably reading $\dot{\alpha}\pi\alpha\tau\acute{\eta}\sigma\alpha\nu\tau\epsilon s$ for $\dot{\alpha}\gamma\alpha\pi\acute{\eta}\sigma\alpha\nu\tau\epsilon s$, deleting the $\mathring{\eta}\nu$ in $\dot{o}$ $X\rho\iota\sigma\tau\acute{o}s$ $o\mathring{v}\tau os$ $\mathring{\eta}\nu$, and reading $\dot{\alpha}\pi\eta\gamma\acute{\alpha}\gamma\epsilon\tau o$ for $\dot{\epsilon}\pi\eta\gamma\acute{\alpha}\gamma\epsilon\tau o$.[36] These are palaeographically very close to our text, but the question remains whether the Christian editor would have been so much concerned with palaeographical probability. To omit the $\overset{?}{\eta\nu}$ in the key passage concerning the recognition of Jesus as the Messiah is to indicate that Jesus *is* the Messiah; and this would raise the question of why Origen, who knew this book, would explicitly declare that Josephus did not recognize Jesus as the Messiah.

Again the phrase that Jesus "won over many Jews and many of the Greeks" would have been impossible for a Christian who knew that Jesus had insisted that he had been sent only to the lost sheep of the house of Israel (Matthew 10:6; 15:24). But we may reply that by the time Josephus wrote the *Antiquities* the Gospels had come to include such a passage as that in which the risen Jesus tells his followers to make disciples of all nations (Matthew 28:19). By this time, moreover, the course of Christianity had been set by Paul to include primarily non-Jews, and attempts were made to depict Jesus' friendliness to Samaritans and to others.

A number of scholars have pointed to phrases in the *Testimonium* that are characteristic not of Josephus but of Eusebius. Jacques Moreau, for example, notes that the phrase εἰς ἔτι τε νῦν (*Ant.* 18.64) is such and concludes that the passage is a total interpolation.[37] Zeitlin goes so far as to argue that the passage was written by Eusebius, pointing to the phrase "the tribe (φῦλον) of Christians," which is found here (*Ant.* 18.64) and again, for the first time thereafter among the church fathers, in Eusebius.[38] Ch. Martin presents the hypothesis—it is hardly a definitive solution as implied by the title of his article—that originally Josephus merely reported the beginnings and early progress of the Christians, and that Eusebius, on the basis of Origen's marginal comments "correcting" Josephus, wrote the passage as we have it.[39] To J. Spencer Kennard, however, the fact that Eusebius, who is the first to cite the *Testimonium,* quotes it differently in his three works is evidence that he is not the forger.[40] Solomon Zeitlin replies that the variants are due to later scribes and do not prove that Eusebius was not the author.[41] Furthermore, Clement of Alexandria, for example, when he quotes, constantly varies the text. Kennard suggests that even though Eusebius is partial to the use of the word φῦλον, at most its use in his citations of the *Testimonium* may indicate only that the text bears the imprint of Eusebius' editing.

André Pelletier,[42] following Théodore Reinach,[43] says that the *Testimonium* is basically authentic, that Josephus may have had access to an early Christian confession and recorded some of its phrases, and that Josephus' remark about the attachment of the Christians to their master fits in with Josephus' statement about his attachment to Bannus in the wilderness (*Life* 11-12), and gives an air of authenticity to the piece. However, he says, the phrases "if it is fitting to call him a man" and "he was the Messiah" seem to have originated as a marginal gloss, perhaps from an early fourth-century polemicist (one is tempted to think of Eusebius). The statement about the attachment of the Christians to their leader is very differently worded from that about Josephus' relationship to Bannus.

Haim Cohn asserts that the passage cannot be authentic,[44] though it is demonstrably not feasible to differentiate clearly between what stemmed from Josephus and what did not. Resorting to pure conjecture, he suggests that the passage originally was anti-Christian, showing how the Jews, in their loyalty to the Romans, did all they could to nip the new movement in the bud and praising the wise statesmanship of Pilate. Josephus, he asserts, was at pains to assign the credit for the crucifixion of Jesus to the Jews and to the Romans in equal measure, whereas the interpolators were at pains to blame the Jews and to whitewash Pilate. There is no indication in the other incidents in the context of the passage in the *Antiquities* that the Jews were in particularly harmonious accord with the Romans; on the contrary, they vigorously oppose Pilate in the passage just before the *Testimonium,* and they are expelled from Rome in the passage shortly thereafter (*Ant.* 18.81-84). That Josephus did not regard Pilate as a wise statesman is clear from the two incidents immediately preceding the *Testimonium* (*Ant.* 18.55-62). Indeed, Paul Winter more plausibly suggests that inasmuch as in the passage immediately before this Josephus gives two instances of Pilate's maladministration, this was the third in Josephus' original version;[45] as it is, the passage blames not Pilate but the leaders of the Jews.

Is there any hope of recovering the original working of the *Testimonium?* Kennard notes that even in the seventeenth century it is alleged that Thomas Gale of Cambridge had large fragments of Josephus which are not in the *textus receptus.*[46] Zeitlin, who regards the *Testimonium* as a forgery, suggests two reasons for Josephus' silence concerning Jesus: (1) We do not know how popular Jesus was in the Roman world at that time; and (2) the fact that Jesus' followers were accused of setting fire to Rome was a good reason for Josephus not to mention Jesus, since the early Christians were regarded as a Jewish dissenting party.[47]

The Language: "He Was the Messiah"

Ever since Osiander (and not Faber, as Schreckenberg would have it) first declared the *Testimonium* to be forged on the ground that if Josephus had written it he would have been a Christian, which he is not in any of his writings,[48] some have tried to use the references to Jesus in

190

the Slavonic version of the *War* as evidence of Josephus' attitude toward Christianity; but this is questionable, since the authenticity of this version is highly disputed. Inasmuch as Josephus nowhere else uses the word Χριστός, and in fact repeatedly suppresses the messianic aspects of the revolt against Rome because of the association of the Messiah with political revolt and independence, it would seem hard to believe that Josephus would openly call Jesus a Messiah.

Zeitlin remarks that in the works of neither Philo nor Josephus is there any mention of a Messiah or of messianic expectations (Zeitlin does not accept the statement that Jesus was the Messiah in *Antiquities* 18.63 as genuine) and that his omission was due not to fear of his benefactors, the Flavians, but rather to the fact that he did not share this belief.[49] But since Josephus declares himself a Pharisee (*Life* 12), it is hard to believe that he did not accept such a cardinal tenet of their beliefs. Ellis Rivkin, to be sure, on the basis of Josephus, concludes that neither the Pharisees nor the majority of the Jews were expecting the Messiah,[50] but such a view flies in the face of the overwhelming sentiment in the Talmud and the fact that aside from Hillel II in the fourth century (*Sanhedrin* 98b), no rabbi is cited as not believing in the coming of the Messiah.

As a Jew writing for a Roman public a work to defend his people, Josephus would hardly have sought to offend his Roman masters, to whom he was so deeply indebted for such things as citizenship, a pension, living quarters, and a library. In this connection, as Jay Braverman remarks, Josephus omits all direct reference to the prophecy in Daniel 9, despite the fact that he devotes more attention to Daniel than to any other prophet.[51] Josephus is deliberately ambiguous in *Antiquities* 10.276, where he says that "Daniel also wrote about the empire of the Romans and that it [ambiguous] would be made desolate by them [ambiguous]." As Braverman concludes with good reason, Josephus could not have afforded to be more explicit because of his Roman patrons. Similarly, Josephus (*Ant.* 10.210), in his comment on the stone in Daniel 2:34-35, 45, says that he does not think it proper to explain its meaning, "since I am expected to write of what is past and done and not of what is to be." He suggests that the reader who desires more exact information should turn to the book of Daniel itself. Similarly, Josephus tones down potentially anti-Roman material in his treatment of Nebuchadnezzar's dream (Daniel 2:44; cf. *Ant.* 10.203ff.); and in *Antiquities* 4.125, in his account of Balaam's prophecies, he speaks in the vaguest terms of the calamities that will befall cities of the highest celebrity, some of which had not yet been founded and among which his Jewish readers might well have recognized a reference to Rome. The reason for Josephus' evasiveness, as Ralph Marcus writes, is that the stone was regarded in current Jewish exegesis as a symbol of the Messiah who would put an end to the Roman Empire.[52] Again, as David Flusser remarks, Josephus (*Ant.* 10.276-77) could not speak of the common interpretation of the four empires in Daniel because of its anti-Roman character, but in *Antiquities* 15.385-87, where no danger could arise because there was no messianic context, he could give the common Jewish sequence of the four empires—Babylonian, Persian, Macedonian, and Roman.[53]

Felix Scheidweiler suggests that the passage originally read ὁ λεγόμενος Χριστός, just as it appears in *Antiquities* 20.200, where Jesus is referred to in the account of the death of his brother James.[54] The fact that Jerome (*De Viris Illustribus* 13) in his quotation of *Antiquities* 18.63 reads *credebatur esse Christus* would seem to indicate that Jerome's Greek text read "he was believed to be the Messiah" rather than "he was the Messiah," a reading similar to that in the Arabic version of Agapius and in the Syriac version of Michael the Syrian.

Walter Pötscher suggests that the original passage read that "he won over many of the Jews and many of the Greeks that [ὅτι] he was the Messiah." That Josephus did not accept Jesus as the Messiah is clear, he says, from the reference to Jesus as the "so-called" Christ (*Ant.* 20.200).[55] But the word here translated as "so-called" is λεγόμενος, which may very well mean merely "aforementioned." Moreover, Josephus elsewhere seems to avoid the use of the word Χριστός, even though he mentions numerous messianic figures in the last three books in the *Antiquities*. The very fact that he avoids the use of the word Χριστός elsewhere but employs it here (*Ant.* 20.200) in a passage the authenticity of which has not been seriously questioned seems significant.

Franz Dornseiff argues that the statement that Jesus was the Messiah does not make of Josephus a Christian, since many in his day called themselves messiahs.[56] But one may recall that Rabbi Akiva recognized Bar Kochba as the Messiah during the revolt of 132-35, an ascription in which he was opposed by others, and yet he was not read out of the Jewish fold, nor, so far as we know, were any other followers of Bar Kochba. Moreover, if a Christian had interpolated the *Testimonium,* he would probably have written "This *is* the Christ" not "This *was* the Christ." Dornseiff suggests that Josephus looked upon Jesus merely as a wonder-worker rather than as Christ, but in view of the usage of the word in the Septuagint, it is hard to believe that it would not be understood in the sense of "anointed," and hence as a reference to the King Messiah.

Samuel G.F. Brandon revives the theory of Eisler that Jesus was a political Messiah and that Josephus regarded him as such.[57] That

Josephus thought of the Messiah as a political figure seems likely, not merely because of the prophecy that from Judea would come a ruler of the world (*War* 6.310-15) but also because in Josephus' day this was the prevailing view, as can be seen notably in the great Rabbi Akiva's recognition of Bar Kochba as the Messiah in the revolt of 132. But it is precisely because of this that Josephus is opposed to the various charismatic figures who claimed to be messiahs, since the Romans would look upon such leaders as revolutionaries, as indeed they did look upon Jesus.

As J.C. O'Neill remarks, Josephus lists no less than ten leaders who gathered followings and might have been considered messiahs by adherents looking for the Messiah: Judas son of Ezekias (*Ant.* 17.271-72), Simon ex-slave of Herod (*Ant.* 17.273-76), Athronges the shepherd (*Ant.* 17.278-84), Menahem the Galilean (*War* 2.433ff.), Simon bar Giora (*War* 4.503ff.), Theudas (*Ant.* 20.47ff.), the Egyptian who led thirty thousand to the Mount of Olives (*Ant.* 20.167-71; *War* 2.261-63), Jonathan of Cyrene (*War* 7.437-38), Jesus son of Ananas (*War* 6.300-309), and the Samaritan who promised to show the sacred vessels of Moses (*Ant.* 18.85-89).[58] It is striking that in Josephus none of these calls himself or is called a messiah, either because as a superpatriot he could not tolerate the idea of a political rebel against Rome or because he did not believe in a personal messiah.

The silence with which Josephus passes over messianic beliefs as a background for the Jewish revolt against the Romans is particularly noteworthy. Inasmuch as the messianic background of the Bar Kochba rebellion of 132-35 is well authenticated, and since a messianic background for the rebellion of Loukuas-Andreas against Trajan (115-17) is very likely, as Victor A. Tcherikover has demonstrated,[59] it seems most likely that the messianic prophecy that Josephus applied to Vespasian and that is reported by Suetonius (*Vespasian* 4) and Tacitus (*Histories* 5.13) was applied by the revolutionaries to the Messiah. In particular, attention should be called to the fact that Menahem, the leader of the Sicarii (*War* 2.434), is described as returning to Jerusalem "like a veritable king" and as having been murdered while wearing royal robes (*War* 2.444). Such a description is appropriate for a leader with messianic pretensions. Again, as William Lane has noted, Josephus' account of pseudo-Messiahs in *Antiquities* (book 20) is complemented by rabbinic material.[60] Thus Josephus presents Elezar son of Deinaeus as a mere revolutionary, whereas the rabbis (*Midrash Rabbah* on Song of Songs 2:18) say that he prematurely tried to free the Jews, that is, one may presume, was a messianic pretender. Otto Michel notes that the messianic aspect of the apocalyptic revolutionary leader Simon bar Giora is obscured but not totally eliminated in Josephus.[61] This messianic aspect, as Lane remarks, is supported by his coins.[62] Apparently, as Abraham Schalit suggests, Josephus' silence regarding the role of messianism in arousing the Jewish masses to war was intended to represent the war as an action of the fanatical foreign element in order to exculpate the Jews as a whole in the eyes of the Roman administration.[63] Josephus was thus silent in order to conceal the Jewish hostility to the Romans, a hostility which is very apparent in the Talmud. In any case, if Josephus indeed wrote the passage calling Jesus "Messiah," one may wonder why he is so complimentary to him.

Samuel G.F. Brandon goes so far as to declare that Josephus recognized the emperor Vespasian as the predicted world-ruler, that is, the Messiah who would come forth from Judea, and hence that he could nct also have called Jesus the Messiah.[64] Similarly Marianus de Jonge, commenting on the fact that Josephus does not describe as messiahs any of the many messianic prophets who appeared in Palestine during the first century, concludes that, for Josephus, Vespasian is the central figure in his biblically inspired expectation for the future. It was this hope and the fact that he detested the Zealots that made it impossible for Josephus to evaluate fairly the expectations of his contemporaries.[65] In opposition to Brandon, however, one must note that Josephus, as a good Pharisaic Jew, could hardly have ascribed messianic status to Vespasian, inasmuch as the Messiah was generally regarded as the son of David. De Jonge himself concludes that Josephus did not give the oracle in *War* 6.312 a messianic interpretation and that he did not regard Vespasian as a messianic figure. He suggests the identification of Menahem as the Messiah (*War* 2.444-48) or the possibility of a belief in messianism without a belief in a personal Messiah.[66]

The most radical interpretation of the statement "he was the Messiah" is that of Jacob Zlotnik, who contends, largely on the basis of the *Testimonium,* that Josephus was not a Pharisee but a Jewish Christian, and indeed terms Bannus, the hermit with whom Josephus associated for three years, a Jewish Christian.[67] It is not likely that a Christian would have restricted his mention of Jesus to a single short reference (*Ant.* 18.63-64) in a long work and to a brief cross-reference, that a Christian would not have written "he was the Messiah" but "he is the Messiah," and that he would not have devoted approximately twice as much space to John the Baptist (*Ant.* 18.116-19) as to Jesus.

Josephus' Sources for the *Testimonium*

By the time Josephus completed the *Antiquities* in 93, the Gospel of Mark had been written and was already circulating in Rome, and that of Luke had recently been produced in Rome. There are a number of

194

parallels between Josephus and Luke, notably the mention of the census of Quirinius (*Ant.* 18.1-2; Luke 2:1-5) and the mention of Lysanias the tetrarch of Abilene (*Ant.* 15.92; Luke 3:1), though, as is well known, there are discrepancies. Of course, Josephus might have learned about the Christians in Jerusalem, where he had been born not long after the crucifixion of Jesus; moreover, he had been in Rome in 64, the year of the great fire which Nero had blamed upon the Christians.

Alfred Edersheim tries to connect the liberation of priestly friends at the instigation of Josephus (*Life* 13) with the liberation of Paul, who, like Josephus, had suffered shipwreck en route to Rome when he had been sent for trial a few years earlier by the procurator Festus;[68] but there is no evidence, even in Christian legend, linking Paul and Josephus, though one might suspect that their opponents, numerous for both, might have tried to link them.

Thackeray notes that Christianity had been gaining adherents at the court of Josephus' patron the emperor Domitian among members of his own family, including a niece and a cousin.[69] The persecution of the Christians understandably had created a stir, which may have led Josephus to include a mention of the group. But Josephus did not apparently regard the Christians as a "sect" of importance comparable to the Pharisees, Sadducees, Essenes, and Fourth Philosophy, since he does not mention them in his catalogs of such groups.

Both Justin Martyr and Tertullian, who wrote in the second and third centuries, assumed that there was an account of Jesus' trial in the Roman archives. In view of the Romans'—and especially Tiberius' —passion for bureaucratic details, one can assume that all administrators maintained careful records, which eventually must have been kept in Rome at the imperial court. Inasmuch as Josephus, as a ward of the Flavians, had easy access to the court, one can also assume that he was able to consult these records.

Josephus' Motives for Inserting the *Testimonium*

What motives, if any, can we establish for Josephus' insertion of a passage about Jesus? Richard Laqueur presents a now famous theory that Justus of Tiberias had charged that Josephus had misinterpreted the Bible, and that Josephus had taken the Septuagint as his basis, whereas by the end of the century a movement against the Septuagint was becoming strong in the rabbinical schools.[70] In his desperation, Josephus, the old fox who had alienated the Jews politically by his behavior in the war against Rome and who had offended them religiously by his use of the Septuagint, now turned to the Christians and inserted the

Testimonium to gain this small and devoted market, since for them the Septuagint was divinely inspired.

One might object that there is no evidence that Justus had charged Josephus with misinterpreting the Bible, and that since Domitian persecuted the Christians it would hardly have been politic for Josephus to seek to please them. Laqueur would have one believe that Josephus sought to sell copies to Christians, but there is no evidence that he needed any money, since, despite Laqueur, he apparently did not lose his comfortable pension and excellent living quarters under royal protection. Furthermore, why, if Josephus appended the work *Against Apion* to please the Jews, should he have risked offending them by inserting the *Testimonium* so as to gain a very small number of Christian readers? Again, Josephus' Jewish readers were Greek-speaking and continued to look to the Septuagint and would certainly not have objected to his use of the Greek Bible. Finally, Josephus frequently deviates from the Septuagint, where he has a different biblical text and midrashic tradition.

J. Spencer Kennard suggests that there might well have been interest in a movement whose followers had been accused by Nero of setting fire to Rome and which had won adherents in the imperial court of Domitian.[71] Josephus himself, he says, may have removed mention of Jesus from subsequent Greek editions in order to tone down the messianism, which would displease his Roman patrons; but while it is true that some scholars find evidence of two editions of the *Antiquities*,[72] there is no evidence that there were any changes made in the text of the *Testimonium*. In addition, why should Josephus have sought to tone down the messianism, since there was no revolt immediately pending at the time when he wrote the *Antiquities*?

The Arabic Version of the *Testimonium*

The most striking development in the study of the *Testimonium* since the translation of the Slavonic Josephus into a Western language in 1924-27[73] occurred when Shlomo Pines brought to the attention of the scholarly world—even the mass media showed great interest—two hitherto almost completely neglected works containing the *Testimonium,* one a tenth-century history of the world in Arabic by a Christian named Agapius and the other a twelfth-century chronicle in Syriac by Michael the Syrian.[74] Agapius does not have "if indeed we ought to call him a man"; he omits reference to Jesus' miracles; he omits completely the role of the Jewish leaders in accusing Jesus; he states not that Jesus

196

appeared to his disciples on the third day but that his disciples reported this; and, most important, he declares (at the end rather than in the middle of the passage) that "he was perhaps the Messiah" rather than that he was the Messiah. Michael's version is closer to the Greek, but he says, "He was thought to be the Messiah." Pines suggests that their versions are the product of Christian censorship applied to the original text, but in a less thoroughgoing form than in the case of the vulgate recension.

If it is unlikely that Josephus declared that Jesus was the Messiah, it seems hardly more likely that he would have stated that he was perhaps the Messiah; on such matters one either believes or does not believe. This may, of course, be due to the translation into Arabic. Since Agapius apparently used Syriac sources, and since the Syriac translation, as seen in the later chronicle of Michael, has "he was thought to be the Messiah" (as indeed we find in Jerome *De Viris Illustribus* 13), the original may well have read thus. A clue to the interpretation of Agapius may be found in what follows: "This is what is said by Josephus and his companions." Apparently Agapius used not only Josephus but other sources as well, and presumably combined them. That this is so may be seen from the fact that he proceeds to state that according to Josephus, Herod burned the genealogies of the tribes so that it would not be known that he was descended from undistinguished people—a fact that is not found in Josephus but is stated in Eusebius *Historia Ecclesiastica* 1.7.13. Indeed, Pines himself notes the relatively close correspondence between Agapius and Eusebius, *Historia Ecclesiastica* 1.10.2-6,[75] and it seems likely, as Pines himself admits, that Agapius derived his information not from Josephus directly but from a recension of Eusebius, and that the relatively minor divergences between them are due to the process of translation and paraphrase. As a believing Christian, Agapius would surely not have eliminated the passage about Jesus' superhuman nature, and hence one may assume that he is reproducing what he found. Pines leaves open the question whether Agapius' text is in the form in which Josephus originally wrote it or whether it had already been doctored by Christian copyists. But one may conclude that Agapius' excerpt is hardly decisive, since it contains several elements, notably changes in order, that indicate it is a paraphrase rather than a translation.

David Flusser suggests that Eusebius found in the library of Origen in Caesarea the original text of the *Testimonium,* which he changed to make it closer to the official Christian version so as to remove from himself the charge of heresy.[76] Eusebius based his changes on the Syrian version of church history. He concludes that the Arabic text is evidence

197

of a prior text of Josephus pertaining to Jesus and that the Christian falsifier made changes in converting the Jewish text of Josephus to a Christian text.

The value of Pines's work, as Schreckenberg has pointed out,[77] is that it makes more probable the view that the *Testimonium* once had a genuine but negative, or at best indifferent, statement about Jesus. As Daniélou has noted,[78] Pines's hypothesis is reasonable because Agapius' version is different in precisely those parts that Josephus as a Jew would not have written as they appear in our Greek text.

Ernst Bammel has suggested that the changes in Agapius' version indicate that it originated in an Islamic environment rather than in an earlier one. Christians were then confronted with the view that someone had died in place of Jesus, and that Jesus himself had escaped. He suggests that Agapius' new features were introduced in a period of debate, partly as a result of Agapius' own epitomizing activities. As to why the author did not include Jewish participation in the accusation of Jesus, he suggests that this was unnecessary because he had supplied the information in the two neighboring accounts. Bammel himself, however, remarks that "he was perhaps the Messiah" is too vacillating for a Christian to have made.[79] Pines has shown that Agapius used (Christian) Syriac rather than Arabic sources;[80] in any case, it seems hard to believe that a Christian, Agapius, or his Christian source (which ultimately seems to have been Eusebius) would have edited the text to make it more palatable to Muslim readers.

André-M. Dubarle compares Agapius and Michael with George Hamartolos ("George the Monk"), who lived in the ninth century, and George Kedrenos, who probably lived at the end of the eleventh and at the beginning of the twelfth century, as well as with the Chronicle of Pseudo-Simeon Magister (Ms. Parisinus 1712, Bibliothèque Nationale du Paris, fol. 76ʳ), and he notes many similarities as against the received text of the *Testimonium*.[81] Moreover, he cites a hitherto neglected Arabic witness in the Kitāb al-Kāfī of Gérasime of the thirteenth century, which omits "master of those who receive the truth gladly," though Dubarle admits that the changes may be due to the negligence of the copyist. He prefers to explain these changes by assuming that they depend actually on Eusebius. On this basis, as well as through other indirect witnesses of the passage, he reconstructs the original *Testimonium,* with the crucial passage reading: "People thought that he was the Messiah." He says that Josephus could well be responsible for every element in such a relatively favorable description of Jesus.[82] The accusing finger again seems to point in the direction of Eusebius as the one responsible for "adjusting" the text. Eusebius, one may recall, quotes the *Testimonium* in three slightly different forms, and there still may have been a fourth version, the one he found in the received text of Josephus.

Summary and Conclusions

Although the question of the authenticity of the *Testimonium Flavianum* has hardly been resolved, the following conclusions are proposed as most plausible:

1. One must start with the assumption that the *Testimonium* is authentic until proven otherwise, inasmuch as the manuscript tradition, late though it be, is unanimous in including it.

2. The fact that Josephus speaks of Jesus in *Antiquities* 20.200 in his reference to James the brother of "the aforementioned Christ," a passage whose authenticity has been almost universally acknowledged, indicates that Jesus had been mentioned previously.

3. The fact that so many church fathers who knew Josephus' works do not refer to the *Testimonium*, which would have been a mighty argument in polemics against Jews especially, until Eusebius, and the fact that a century elapses before it is again referred to, by Jerome, is a strong argument that the passage did not exist in the form in which it presently exists.

4. Origen's statement that Josephus did not admit "Jesus to be Christ" is a strong argument that Origen did have a passage about Jesus but that it was neutral.

5. The fact that there was a passage about Jesus in the *Antiquities* may help to explain the Talmud's silence about Josephus.

6. As a Jew, Josephus might well have acknowledged someone to be the Messiah without necessarily being excluded from the Jewish fold, but since the concept of the Messiah at this time had definite political overtones of revolution and independence, Josephus, as a lackey of the Roman royal house, could hardly have recognized Jesus as such; and indeed Josephus avoids the use of the term Messiah except here and in *Antiquities* 20.200 in connection with Jesus.

7. The modified versions of the *Testimonium* by Agapius in Arabic and by Michael in Syriac strengthen the view that the original *Testimonium* was not in the form in which we have it; Jerome's statement that "he was believed to be the Messiah" corroborates this.

Other Faith Images of Jesus: Some Muslim Contributions to the Christological Discussion

Willem A. Bijlefeld

Some reflections on certain aspects of the widely discussed topic of *The Islamic Jesus*[1] seem appropriate for this volume honoring Harvey K. McArthur, who once, when the occasion arose, expressed his awareness of the significance of the "Son of Mary" in and for the Muslim community,[2] and who through the years and in many ways has made the case that other people of faith should be taken seriously not only at the personal level but also in our (Christian) theological reflections.

The Wider Context of the Jesus References

The Qur'ān is clearly not concerned with (reconstructing) "the historical Jesus."[3] However, many Muslims state explicitly that *any* theology of the person of Christ is un-Islamic,[4] no matter what its specific details are. Consistent with both these considerations, the "faith image" language of the title points to the fact that one fails to do justice to the Qur'anic references to Jesus unless one interprets and evaluates them from within the primary context to which they belong: the Qur'anic message regarding God's sending of messengers and granting of the books of revelation. Two out of the six traditional Muslim articles of faith deal with these to some extent interrelated issues—Books and Messengers—and these two articles constitute the most common setting for Muslim references, admittedly often passing references, to the Injīl and to Jesus.[5]

Willem A. Bijlefeld is Director of the Duncan Black Macdonald Center for the Study of Islam and Christian-Muslim Relations; he is also editor of *The Muslim World*. Thus he and Harvey K. McArthur were colleagues at the Hartford Seminary Foundation for many years.

Understood in this way, the terminology of "faith images" affirms rather than challenges the intention of the provocative sentence with which Smail Balić opens his contribution "The Image of Jesus in Contemporary Islamic Theology." "If theology is discourse about God, then Islamic theology makes no assertions concerning Jesus Christ."[6] The subsequent discussion makes it clear that one of the author's main points is that any presentation of Jesus that fails to point consistently away from him to "the God of revelation" is in conflict with the Qur'ān and therefore unacceptable to Muslims, and that any such Christology from the Christian side forms a major obstacle for a fruitful Muslim-Christian dialogue:

> If Jesus is so interpreted that we no longer refer to the concept of God as found in revelation, then Christianity and Islam have nothing at all in common. . . . The Western theologians who distance themselves from the God of revelation open up a gulf which could make Muslim-Christian dialogue impossible.[7]

While some Christians seem to 'separate' Jesus from God, as Balić suggests, others make the impression of maintaining an "identity pure and simple" between Jesus and God,[8] and both extremes continue to constitute major obstacles on the road toward a greater mutual understanding between Muslims and Christians. Some may find it too simplistic to reduce the issue to the alternative of seeing Jesus either as a "destination" or as a "signpost," using Don Cupitt's language,[9] but the reference from Christ to God—the relation between Christology and theology—is indeed the fundamental issue. Far more consistently and explicitly one must come to terms with "the task of thinking about Christology in connection with God's relation to the world in general and especially in connection with his relationship to humanity in the course of its history." In the "Afterword" to his *Jesus—God and Man*,[10] from which these words are quoted, Wolfhart Pannenberg stresses—with a reference to Dietrich Wiederkehr—the urgency of the still unfinished task to "present the reality of Christ in the horizon of God's relation to the world."[11] Those who are outside this academic discipline may be surprised by this appeal to face the challenge of placing the whole christological discussion "within the context of the doctrine of God and this within the overall framework of a comprehensive dogmatics,"[12] but it appears to become an increasingly difficult task to the degree that Christology develops as a separate field of specialization and one monographic treatment of Christology after the other is forthcoming. In the meantime there is an immediate need for Christians living in a world in which one-sixth to one-fifth of the population is Muslim[13] to make it explicit—at every level of their accounting for their faith—what affirmations concerning Christ say about God's relationship to humanity and humanity's relationship to God, in both of which the issue of interhuman relationships is clearly also at stake.

Unless this double "theological contextualization"—of both the Qur'anic references to Jesus and of Christian affirmations regarding Christ—is taken seriously, Christian-Muslim discussions on Jesus will continue to be of marginal significance or even counterproductive, with regard both to understanding the other and to making ourselves understood. Christians' eclectic use of Qur'anic statements regarding Jesus has frequently led to a distorted view of Islam and its relation to Christianity, no matter whether the approach was sharply polemical or thoroughly irenical.[14] Often it was simply assumed that what the Qur'ān says about Jesus is as central to its kerygma and as important for the faith of Muslims[15] as the witness to Christ is in the New Testament and for the faith of Christians. Obvious parallels in Qur'anic and biblical statements regarding Jesus have been used as sufficient evidence for the thesis of a close affinity between Christianity and Islam, and apparent contrasts on this point have been used, with as much conviction, to substantiate the judgment that Islam is essentially anti-Christian.[16] It is the contention here, as indicated above, that only if both Muslim and Christian statements regarding Jesus are made consistently transparent as to what they say about God and God's way for and among us can Christians and Muslims begin to grasp some of the most fundamental beliefs that unite them and some of the basic questions to which different answers are given by as well as within the two communities of faith. We will return to this point in the final section, following a brief discussion of the Qur'anic Jesus and a review of three recent Muslim contributions to the christological discussion, by Mohamed Al-Nowaihi, Mahmoud Ayoub, and Ali Merad.

The Qur'anic Jesus

Many of the entries in Wismer's *The Islamic Jesus*[17] deal primarily or even exclusively with the Qur'anic data. The same holds true with regard to seven major studies in this field published in the West in the last two decades, of which five are devoted to Qur'anic material only.[18] Since in these works and in numerous other monographs and journal articles,[19] encyclopedic entries,[20] and indexes to the Qur'ān[21] very extensive and even exhaustive surveys of the Qur'anic verses dealing with Jesus are readily and widely available, there is no justification in repeating all these data once again. Therefore only a few references will be given in the following section.

Throughout the centuries of Christian writings about Islam and (presumably) to Muslims,[22] people have emphasized over and over again the Qur'anic recognition of Jesus' birth of the Virgin Mary,[23] the mention of his miracles (including raising people from the dead),[24] the use of such designations as Word of God, Spirit from Him, Sign, Mercy, Messiah,[25] the acknowledgment of him as prophet and apostle (especially to the children of Israel)[26] and as the recipient of the Injīl, "a light and guidance,"[27] and finally the reference to his being taken to heaven by God and his role at the end of time.[28] While these points have often been stressed by Christians as areas of significant agreement, controversies have normally focused on three other aspects of the Qur'anic Jesus narrative, commonly described as the Qur'anic denial of Jesus' death on the cross, his being the Son of God, and of the Trinity.[29] This dimension of the Qur'anic message will be surveyed briefly under two headings, somewhat related to these three points but with different emphases.

The claim of crucifixion. The single passage in the Qur'ān dealing explicitly with the evil intent to kill and crucify Jesus and the unjustified claim to have succeeded in triumphing over him is Sura 4:156-59.[30] The wider context, beginning with verse 153 or even 150, makes it clear that this whole section is a sharp criticism of the wrongdoings, false accusations, and unfounded claims of some Jewish people.[31] Their slander against Mary is mentioned in verse 156, followed directly by a reference to their (boastful) saying: "We have killed the Messiah Jesus,[32] son of Mary, apostle of God." Whatever answer one may give to the question whether it is justified to state on the basis of the next clause ("but they have not killed him and they have not crucified him") that the Qur'ān denies Jesus' death or—for many a significantly different issue—his death on the cross,[33] there can hardly be any disagreement concerning the decisive meaning of the whole passage: no matter how much evildoers may resist God, plotting and scheming against God,[34] rejecting signs and trying to overcome and silence messengers, the triumph and victory over all powers of evil are ultimately with God.[35] In this instance this reassurance is expressed in the words "God has lifted him [Jesus] to Himself. And God is mighty and wise" (v. 158). No matter how one interprets the meaning of the words "his death" in the concluding verse, this final reference to Jesus is also clearly seeking to honor him, stressing his importance on the last day: "And none is there among the People of the Scripture but he will believe in him [Jesus] before his death. And on the day of resurrection he will be a witness against them" (v. 159).

The necessary differentiation between God and Jesus. Mention has already been made of the oft-discussed Qur'anic rejection of the notion that God has or "has taken" any offspring, children, or a son—a criticism obviously directed in most instances against the Meccan polytheists,[36] but also used a number of times with reference to Christian statements regarding Jesus.[37] While many Christians have found this sufficient ground for their thesis that the Qur'ān consciously and deliberately denies the very heart and core of the Christian message, others have interpreted it as a response to an excessive, sectarian Mariology[38] and the resulting impression that Christians worshiped Mary and Jesus as gods besides God.[39] Many of the latter concluded, therefore, that the Qur'anic rejection of the notion of Jesus as Son of God is in no way a denial of the "orthodox" Christian notion of the divinity of Christ.[40] Within the scope of this essay it is not possible to deal with the danger of basing far-reaching theological conclusions on terminological differences that are not thoroughly probed as to their intended meaning, nor with the often farfetched and extremely uncritical attempts at harmonization of Qur'anic and biblical data, not infrequently accomplished by a totally irresponsible "Christianization" of the Qur'anic material.[41] Moreover, there is no need to take sides in this discussion, because the fundamental issue at stake in these Qur'anic "corrective denials"[42] is expressed in unambiguously clear language in a number of other texts. That basic issue is the Qur'anic insistence on the radical Otherness of God also with regard to and in relation to Jesus, and therefore the absolute necessity of an uncompromising differentiation between them.

The first two verses to be quoted stress in a significant manner the importance of Jesus who, however, was "nothing but a servant," "only an apostle":

He [Jesus] was nothing but a servant on whom We bestowed favor, and We made him a pattern for the children of Israel [Sura 43:59].

O People of the Scripture, do not exaggerate in your religion, nor say anything concerning God except the truth. The Messiah Jesus, son of Mary, was only an apostle of God, and His word which He conveyed to Mary, and a Spirit from Him. So believe in God and His messengers, and say not "three"—cease—that is better for you; God is only one God [Sura 4:171, beginning].

In Sura 5:116, a verse dealing with a conversation between God and Jesus in which Jesus needs to account for what he has taught people regarding himself and his mother, Jesus himself emphasizes the differentiation: "If I had said it, Thou wouldst know it. Thou knowest what is in my soul, but I do not know what is in Thy soul." Another expression of this same notion is found in Sura 5:17: "Who would have any power over God if He wished to destroy the Messiah son of Mary, and his mother, and those on earth, altogether." The last-mentioned verse opens with a clause repeated at the beginning of verse 72 in the same sura: "Unbelievers are those who say: 'God is the Messiah son of Mary.' " If the word order is taken literally, the issue here is not that Jesus should not be identified with God, but rather that God should not be identified with—and therefore, not be confined to and reduced to—Jesus.[43] Wherever one wants to lay the emphasis, the main issue is a recognition of the lordship of God also over Jesus, who humbly accepts his servanthood[44] and points the children of Israel to the One, "My Lord and your Lord,"[45] who alone should be worshiped and served.

Three Recent Muslim Contributions to the Christological Discussion: Mohamed Al-Nowaihi, Mahmoud Ayoub, Ali Merad

As the subtitle indicates, no attempt will be made to describe even in outline the whole field of contemporary Muslim writing about Jesus,[46] a topic to which one cannot do justice unless this material is placed against the background not only of relevant Qur'anic data—some of which were referred to above—but also of Muslim thinking and writing about Jesus during the past thirteen centuries.[47] Although by no means to be seen as the only aspect of that literature, Muslim polemics regarding Jesus Christ constitute at least in volume and notoriousness an important segment of it. Fritsch's study of 1930 remains also on this area a helpful and in general reliable short introduction to the issues raised and the criticisms expressed.[48] Besides the issues referred to in the previous section—the crucifixion, Jesus as the Son of God, and the Trinity—major points of controversy were (and to some extent continue to be) the reliability or corruption of the scriptures of Jews and Christians, the doctrines of redemption, atonement, reconciliation, and expiation,[49] and the "one-sidedness" of Jesus as a saint, whose example and instructions were insufficient as guidelines to cover all aspects of life and all needs of the society and whose task was often described as having been limited to the children of Israel.

The three contributions to be reviewed here take up, with a variety of emphases and points of view, three of the most widely debated issues: the ideas of redemption and atonement, the question of Jesus' death on the cross, and the notion of Jesus being more than just a human being.

Mohamed Al-Nowaihi, a distinguished Egyptian scholar deeply concerned with Muslim-Christian relations, read in the late 1960s at a conference of Muslims and Christians, held in Boston, a provocative paper entitled "Redemption: From Christianity to Islam."[50] Since the paper has not yet been published, extensive quotations from a privately distributed mimeographed copy seem in order.

Al-Nowaihi is fully aware of the fact that "no religion would appear to be more condemnatory of the idea of Redemption than orthodox Islam," not only because of various aspects of its understanding of God, but also because of "its refusal of the concept of original sin and of collective guilt and its declaration that every man is responsible for his own actions and has himself to expiate his sins, and its resulting denial of the need for vicarious sacrifice."[51]

Admitting that these tenets developed in classical theology are based on certain passages in the Qur'ān, Al-Nowaihi yet argues "that the Qur'an itself contains some other elements which, had they been developed, would have resulted in an attitude not so inimical to the concept of redemption." The first reference he gives is the Qur'anic narrative of the fall of Adam: "although it [the Qur'ān] nowhere specifically visits his sin upon his progeny, it does logically follow that the subsequent woes of man on earth sprang from that fall, and this in fact was the conclusion that was drawn by several classical writers and poets."[52] The second argument[53] is the one-sidedness of the traditional emphasis on God's "aloofness and indifference to the lot of man"—the Sufis are the great exceptions—while the Qur'ān itself

> asserts and reiterates God's concern for man. The God of the Qur'an is a very personal God, intimately involved in man's innermost heart.[54] The emphasis on the austere, aloof, forbidding image of Him was a later development, and was one that may be justly considered contrary to the ruling spirit of the Qur'an. . . . Again and again, in the most moving language, it expresses its sorrow and chagrin for the disobedience, blindness and crassness of man.

The third element in the Qur'ān discussed by Al-Nowaihi is the Qur'anic denial (Sura 4:157) that the Jews killed or crucified Jesus. Having mentioned the "orthodox" interpretation that God sent a substitute in the form of Jesus and that it was this person who was crucified,[55] the author continues:

But even according to this interpretation, this was not realized by the contemporaries of Jesus, who believed he was killed; moreover, he was, in any case, persecuted, renounced and defeated, and his message was rejected for a long time. It is true that the Qur'an avers that God will never abandon His prophets, but will accord them the victory on earth.[56] On the other hand, it states itself in several places that many prophets were killed by their peoples,[57] and, according to it, there was not one prophet who was not given the lie to, derided, vilified and ignobly treated by the people to whom he was sent.[58] Muhammad himself did not gain the victory till after long years of intense suffering and persecution. . . . So the promised victory of right over wrong must be understood to be eventual and not always immediate, nor even necessarily in the lifetime of the prophets themselves. Nor is it automatic: it demands much struggle and sacrifice on the part of the prophets. Hence all prophets may be considered in this sense Redeemers.[59]

Following a few observations on the notions of personal responsibility and communal guilt,[60] as well as the idea of intercession, the author deals with "the great festival" of Islam, "Id al-aḍḥā, the Anniversary of Sacrifice," celebrating Abraham's willingness to kill his son in obedience to God's commandments, and comments[61]:

Whence arises the need for such sacrificial atonement? It arises from man's basic wickedness. Some Quranic verses state that man is by his nature capable of both good and bad, hence he has free choice.[62] Still other verses, however, state that man is evil by nature: aggressive, unjust, ungrateful, quick to anger, greedy, avaricious, boastful, tendentious, impatient, vain when feeling safe and chicken-hearted in adversity.[63] It is only by the grace and mercy of God, through the guidance of the prophets He sends to mankind, that man is saved; alone, he would not have been capable of salvation.[64]

In the light of this Qur'anic evidence, Al-Nowaihi maintains, it is not surprising that

a few contemporary Muslim intellectuals—admittedly still few, but possibly pointing the way to an important change—do not view the Christian ideas with such abhorrence, but are becoming aware of the sheer beauty and nobility of the concept of Redemption. True, they do not accept these ideas as articles of creed—they are clearly against the orthodox Muslim credo. But they see in them a most uplifting and inspiring symbol. And this is not merely a symbol of a dreamed and so far unrealized urge in man. It is a symbol, but it stems from a record of facts—facts of certain individuals, in the long and tormented history of man, who were characterized by a tremendous love for their fellow-men and a chagrined concern over their ignorance, folly and crime, so much so that they willingly suffered great persecution and were even ready to pay the supreme penalty of martyrdom for the sake of humanity's salvation. The known history of man, for the most part a history of selfishness and brutality, is yet redeemed by such individuals, from Socrates to Solzhenitsyn. . . . The Redeemer, who atones for the sins of his fellow-humans by his own suffering and frequent death, may be the poet or artist . . . [or] the courageous Arab intellectual who is sick of the prevailing hypocrisy and all the crimes that are committed in the name of Arab nationalism, or Pan-Arabism . . . [or] else he is just the general Redeemer, vicariously atoning for the common sins of man.[65]

While "the crucifixion passage" in Sura 4 is discussed by Al-Nowaihi in a single paragraph, it is the focus of the second essay to be discussed. Mahmoud Ayoub's "The Death of Jesus, Reality or Delusion? A Study of the Death of Jesus in Tafsīr Literature."[66] At the end of the first, introductory section ("Jesus, 'The Word of Truth' ") the author summarizes the Qur'anic image of Jesus in a very significant passage that contains in a sense the conclusion of the article as a whole:

The Qur'ān presents a Christology of the human Christ, empowered by God and "fortified with the Holy Spirit."[[67]] It is a fully Islamic Christology based not on borrowed distortions of early Christian heresies, but on the Islamic view of man and God. There are, no doubt, some resemblances between the Qur'anic study of Jesus and early Christian sources[[68]]; these are at best, however, similarities of framework and story, not of theology or essential view. Islam differs from Christianity on two crucial points. First, it denies the divinity of Christ, but without denying his special humanity. Second, it denies the expiatory sacrifice of Christ on the Cross as a ransom for sinful humanity, but again denies neither the actual death of Christ nor his general redemptive role in human history.[69]

No summary of the next three sections ("Who Died on the Cross?" "Did Jesus Die?" "The Search for Meaning: Some Modern Attitudes") could possibly do justice to the exegetical material provided by Mahmoud Ayoub, and the few remarks about his essay offered here are in no way a substitute for a careful study of the whole article, which needs to be read in conjunction with his first contribution, "Towards an Islamic Christology," dating from 1976.[70] For present purposes it suffices, then, to quote a major section from the conclusion he reaches on the basis of his inquiry into the history of (Muslim) exegesis—both Sunni and Shī'ī—of Sura 4:156-59:

> The reproach of the Jews "for their saying: 'We have surely killed Jesus the Christ, son of Mary, the apostle of God,' " with which the verse starts, is not directed at the telling of an historical lie, or at the making of a false report. It is rather, as is clear from the context, directed at human arrogance and folly, at an attitude towards God and His messenger. The words identifying Jesus are especially significant. They wished to kill Jesus, the innocent man, who is also the Christ, the Word, and God's representative among them. By identifying Christ in this context, the Qur'ān is addressing not only the people who could have killed yet another prophet, but all of humanity is told who Jesus is.
>   The Qur'ān is not speaking here about a man, righteous and wronged though he may be, but about the Word of God who was sent to earth and who returned to God. Thus the denial of the killing of Jesus is a denial of the power of man to vanquish and destroy the divine Word, which is forever victorious. Hence the words, "they did not kill him, nor did they crucify him," go far deeper than the events of ephemeral human history; they penetrate the hearts and conscience of human beings. The claim of humanity (here exemplified in the Jewish society of Christ's earthly existence) to have this power against God can only be an illusion. . . . The words *wa lākin shubbiha lahum* ["it only seemed so to them"] do not disclose, therefore, a long-hidden secret of divine deception; rather they constitute an accusation or judgment against the human sin of pride and ignorance.[71]

Ali Merad's "Le Christ selon le Coran" has understandably evoked considerable discussion in the twelve years since it was published.[72] In order to highlight common elements as well as differences among the three Muslim contributions selected for this particular review, it seems justifiable to limit the discussion to the two major points of his presentation. The first issue is the author's emphatic affirmation of the Qur'anic denial of Jesus' death on the cross. In the last of five preliminary "general considerations" on Jesus in Qur'anic perspective,

Ali Merad deals briefly but explicitly with the issue.[73] The terminology of Sura 4:157—"they have neither killed him, nor crucified him"—leaves no place for any doubt, and every attempt to "soften" this denial is totally in conflict with classical orthodox doctrine as well as with the teachings of modern reformists. The author then returns to the same subject matter toward the end of his article, in a section entitled "The Mystery of the 'Death of Christ.' "[74] Once again linguistic evidence is said to be absolutely convincing with regard to the thesis that the Qur'ān denies Jesus' death on the cross and affirms his having been taken up by God to heaven. Moreover, this negation of Jesus' death at the hands of his enemies is in full accord with the logic of the Qur'ān and the constant structures of its teaching. The stories of Job, Moses, Joseph, and similar narratives, all point to and affirm a certain "custom of God" (*sunnat Allāh*), namely, the final triumph of faith over all powers of evil and adversity. The Jesus story is a clear confirmation of this same basic truth. Jesus' death would have meant a triumph of his opponents, while the Qur'ān clearly states their defeat.[75] The notion of Jesus' suffering unto death is thus rejected not only because Islam does not know the dogma of redemption, but also because Jesus' death would mean, in Qur'anic perspective, *"l'échec même de Dieu."* It is by this very denial of Jesus' death that the Qur'ān safeguards at the same time the honor of God and the dignity of human beings, for it is in Jesus that humanity reaches its supreme dignity.[76]

The last words constitute a good transition to a summary of Ali Merad's second major theme, "La Suréminence du Christ," the recognition of Jesus Christ as an exceptional event in world history.[77] The fact that the Qur'ān categorically denies the divinity of Jesus does not mean that it sees him as just another human being.[78] There is ample evidence in a different direction. The author mentions the Qur'anic message of Jesus' miraculous birth,[79] his designation as "Word of God"—meaning much more than "having been brought forth by His Word, His commandment"[80]—the use of the word Spirit (*rūḥ*) in connection with him,[81] the remarkable fact that the Qur'ān, while emphasizing for other messengers of God—including Muḥammad himself[82]—that they are mortal, natural human beings, does not apply the term *bashar,* "man," "a mortal," to Christ. With arguments based on Sura 3:45 (". . . Jesus, son of Mary, illustrious in this world and the hereafter, and one of those brought near . . .")[83] and on the Qur'anic recognition of Jesus' creative powers[84] (albeit "with the permission of God"), which elevate him to a rank never reached by any person, the author further substantiates his thesis of the "extraordinary mission of Jesus which has no precedent in the history of humanity."

Concluding Reflections

Although undoubtedly to most people far less perplexing than the variety present in "the thousand images" of Jesus found among Christians,[85] there are even in the small sample of contemporary Muslim writings referred to above a significant diversity of emphases and a few areas of real disagreement. The most obvious contrast is in the responses to the question whether the Qur'ān denies Jesus' death on the cross, leaves the possibility open, or even affirms it. We also noticed a significant difference of emphases in references to the notion of redemption: the "traditional" assertion that Islam has no place for this concept,[86] Mahmoud Ayoub's recognition of Jesus' "general redemptive role in human history," while denying the idea of his expiatory sacrifice, and Al-Nowaihi's even stronger emphasis on "the sheer beauty and nobility of the concept of Redemption," although in this case, too, coupled with the recognition that it is definitely not an article of the (orthodox) Muslim credo. Finally, while Al-Nowaihi stresses the fellow-humanness of Jesus, Mahmoud Ayoub and Ali Merad draw attention, with different nuances, to the Qur'anic recognition of the "special humanity" of Jesus and his uniqueness.[87]

It would make no sense to attempt to offer some "comparative notes" on Christian positions with regard to the second and third issue mentioned above: the centrality and meaning of the notion of redemption and the question of Jesus' being "more than man." Instead, let me conclude by indicating two important areas of basic agreement in the context of our subject matter, and a very crucial question to which the responses seem to differ significantly—fully aware that, on the one hand, there is no consensus, either "between us" or "among ourselves," with regard to the points of agreement, and that, on the other hand, the differences cannot simply be reduced to an over-against of Muslim and Christian reactions.

God's act. Both Qur'ān and Bible testify to the crucial importance of the divine initiative. "But for His guidance"[88] there would be no walking along the straight path, and in the "he loved us" is the ground for our loving him (1 John 4:10). Whatever else, then, Jesus may mean to Muslims and Christians, he is also the one who points to God as the Ultimate Subject, the One who acts, who takes the initiative, who in the sending of God's message and messengers makes an all-important move toward us. Many Christians undoubtedly want to move beyond this, referring to Hebrews 1:1 to stress the distinction between the many prophets and the one Christ, and perhaps suggesting—as has been done frequently—that the terms "sending down" and "coming down" point

211

to two radically different understandings of revelation in Islam and Christianity.[89] Whatever position one takes on that particular issue, the point made here still remains valid: no matter what verb of action we use, we face in Jesus Christ an act of God. This emphasis does not imply a "reduction" of Jesus to the status of "mere humanity," nor does it—a significantly different issue—settle for any Christian or for any situation the widely debated issue of the choice between a Christology "from below" and a Christology "from above."[90] But it does underscore the significance of the critical observation of Balić, referred to earlier, concerning any "Christian Christology" that deals with Jesus without referring from him to the One who sent him.[91] The question who Jesus Christ is should be answered first and most of all in terms of what God has done in and through him. In that sense Christ is a divine action word, an emphasis fully in line with what Claus Westermann called the "basic verb-dominated or historical structure of what the Old and New Testament say about God."[92] The Qur'anic *rasūliyya*[93] and the New Testament notion of "sending"—roots almost too common to continue to be recognized as meaningful—deserve ongoing attention, not only in the direction of further reflections as to what "sentness" implies as far as the human "possessing" of the divine gift and mandate is concerned,[94] but also in the direction of a heedful concern for the scriptural emphasis on the message granted to the "apostle" as something *received:* "Except as a divine mercy, it could not have been. It was 'the gift outright.' "[95]

An act of mercy. That the almighty and everlasting God is "the merciful Lord of Mercy"—using Kenneth Cragg's rendering of *al-rahmān al-rahīm*[96]—is clearly one of the main themes of the Qur'ān. With a variety of expressions and in numerous texts, the Qur'ān emphasizes that God's sending of messengers is a manifestation of God's mercy, a sign of God's grace.[97] As the Qur'ān is called "a Guidance and a Mercy," so is the book of Moses.[98] As God sent Muhammad as "a Mercy to all the worlds," so Jesus is described as "a Mercy from Us."[99]

In the New Testament and in the history of Christian theology, the Christ-event has been and is interpreted in several ways and with very different emphases. But in most descriptions of the meaning of Christ the idea is expressed in some way or another that Jesus is the grace of God manifested and realized on earth. Particularly in attempts to describe the significance of Jesus' suffering and death, this notion of God's grace (love, forgiveness) has often been juxtaposed with—and in a sense been qualified by—the ideas of divine justice (wrath, punishment). In his discussion of biblical perspectives on the meaning of

212

Christ's death and the notion of reconciliation, H. Berkhof suggested, that it seems "preferable in our time not to interpret Jesus' death primarily and exclusively with the, to us, rather foreign Pauline, juridical and cultic concepts . . . but rather with the Johannine concepts of love, obedience, and glorification."[100] These three key words seem to constitute a helpful vocabulary also for any attempt to articulate in Christian-Muslim conversations what is implied in the recognition of Jesus as an act of God's mercy—the sign, expression, manifestation, and realization of God's self-commitment to grace and compassion. While the way in which in the foregoing statement the name of Jesus is linked with the notion of God's commitment to mercy is peculiarly Christian, the idea of God's commitment to mercy is definitely present also in the Qur'ān: "Say: Unto whom belongs all that is in the heavens and on earth? Say: Unto God, who has willed upon Himself the law of grace," Sura 6:12 (see also v. 54) in Muhammad Asad's translation.[101] The recognition of "the darknesses" in which we find ourselves,[102] the acknowledgment of God's initiative in granting humanity divine guidance, and the belief that this act of God is a reflection and expression of mercy and that God's name is glorified in and through the obedience and humility of the one whom God sent—these interrelated elements seem to constitute a meaningful and promising starting point for Muslim-Christian reflections on Jesus. Such an approach enables Muslims and Christians to see what they share, but at the same time allows the different emphases and the basic differences to emerge—the former as well as the latter, far more clearly than when one starts from an uncritical assumption of consensus or a premature conclusion of irreconcilable differences based on various interpretations of such specific designations of Jesus as "Son of Mary," "Word," "Spirit," "Messiah," and "Son of God."

God with us. That God does not abandon humankind is one of the themes most frequently heard in Muslim discussions of Jesus' life. No matter how great the opposition and how radical the rejection on the side of humanity, ultimately the victory is with God.[103] The truth that God is with the messengers (and with the faithful in general) is exemplified in a special and vivid way in the story of Jesus' persecution and delivery. On the Christian side, the name "God with us," Immanuel, applied to Jesus only once in the New Testament (Matthew 1:23), became for countless people one of the most meaningful summaries of who Jesus is for them. What Jesus' life and person says about the meaning of the assurance that God is with us is perhaps one of the most crucial questions for Christians and Muslims to discuss whenever the conversation turns to the subject of Jesus Christ. Without denying the

213

validity and significance of other emphases, it is important to stress the notion of the 'inobtrusiveness'[104] of God's presence in the world and of the 'hiddenness' of God's power and triumph among us. God is not so present that people cannot fail to notice God's presence. It is much easier to overlook than to discover the "Imprints of His mercy"[105] all around us. God's acting and being among us remains "veiled,"[106] also in the Christ-event: "Gott ist ereignet, aber nicht in Vorfindlichkeit, sondern verhüllt. Er ist auch nicht in oder als Jesus von Nazareth vorfindlich, sondern verhüllt."[107] While Muslims and Christians commonly hold that God's glory and triumph over all powers of evil will ultimately become manifest, the question is whether the fact that so little of it is unmistakably visible and unambiguously clear at present is just a divinely permitted anomaly or whether it is exactly in this "veiling" that God is revealed and in the very act of condescension the divine glory is fulfilled. God does not overpower resistance by an overwhelming display of force or by a powerlessness which is only a disguise of God's strength, but in a way that gives the fullest meaning to Paul's statement that "power comes to its full strength in weakness only [2 Cor. 12:9]." This is not abandoning the notion of God's powerfulness for the sake of an emphasis on God's "weakness" and "powerlessness"[108] but a holding fast—as Berkhof suggested[109]—with equal emphasis on both the power of God *and* the way in which this power is realized and manifested. In one of his studies on Philippians 2:5-11, C.F.D. Moule wrote that he was inclined "to identify, rather than contrast, the so-called condescension with the so-called dignity," interpreting *harpagmos* not as "a thing to be snatched" but as "the act of snatching," and raising the possibility that the participial phrase in verse 6, usually interpreted in a concessive sense ("although he was in the form of God"), "might even, perhaps, have been intended, rather, in a causative sense: precisely *because* he was in the form of God he recognized equality with God as a matter not of getting but of giving."[110]

There is clearly, notwithstanding significant differences, some affinity between this emphasis in Moule's writing, Berkhof's language of the powerfulness of God which patiently leaves room for resistance and endures rejection and in that sense is not "self-defensive,"[111] and the notion of the "vulnerability of God," an emphasis sometimes especially associated with Kenneth Cragg.[112] Without a careful clarification of what is intended, the term vulnerability is in this context as questionable as the language of the weakness and powerlessness of God. In a sense we cannot "harm God," an expression which, as G.F. Hourani suggested, may well do justice to the intent of Sura 2:57 and 6:160: "They do not injure God, they injure themselves," or "They do not harm God, they harm only themselves."[113] But at the same time many Christians are convinced that God's love stops at nothing, that, in God's condescension, God does not keep out of harm's way, and that this is God's way of being with us and working among us. John Hick drew once again attention to H.H. Farmer's term "inhistorization" as pointing in a helpful way to the fact that in Christian experience God is known "as activity or operation rather than as substance" and that "God in Christ has not merely acted *upon* and *into* human history, . . . but has acted *within* and *through* man's life by influencing the course of our history from the inside."[114] The important and complex issue of the relation between revelation and history, touched upon earlier as far as a Muslim reaction is concerned,[115] may well be one of the most promising and fruitful areas for further discussion between Muslims and Christians, partly because of the variety of answers given particularly among Christians. There is an element of truth in the suggestion that at least major trends within the two traditions can be compared—applying Farmer's terminology to a context different from the one he was discussing—as a Muslim emphasis on God's acting "vertically," from above, *into* history, and a Christian emphasis on God's acting also "horizontally," *in* and *through* history.[116] The terms "external intervention" and "presence from within" have also been used to make the same point. Whatever degree of validity there may be in such typologies, a crucially critical issue is that we avoid creating the impression that it is a distinction between an emphasis on God's *acting* in(to) history on the Muslim side and a Christian emphasis on God's *presence* in Jesus Christ. Unless the "God in Christ" terminology is spelled out—consistent with, for example, 2 Corinthians 5:18-19—in unambiguously clear terms as a witness to God's act and action in Jesus Christ, we are in danger of obscuring rather than uncovering Christ's 'transparency unto God'; and unless the "presence" notion is articulated through a number of transitive verbs that play a significant role in the vocabulary of the New Testament, we are in danger of concealing rather than proclaiming the good news of God's "self-characterization" in and through the person, life, and work of Jesus Christ.

PART IV
Christological Perspectives in Contemporary Culture

CHAPTER 16

Jesus: Deacon of God and Persons

George Johnston

There is no lack of interest in Jesus among our contemporaries. Many of them carry a load of spiritual guilt, fear of their own *anima* or what they have heard about it through the psychological grapevine, or deep-seated fears about their own identity and even their own gender, sometimes a fear of death, though seldom perhaps a real fear of God. Our age has more than its share of alienation and profound loneliness, spiritual lethargy (called *accidie* in the medieval era), and a loss of direction in the revolutionary times that are not assuredly post-Nazi.

Refurbishing the Icon of Jesus

And so men and women will flock to Jesus, and especially to the cults that claim him—for example, Inspiration Inc., run successfully by Robert Schuller in California to promote a new Peale-ist form of optimism and tranquillity—for our environment is a vortex of disturbed and disturbing currents. People's concerns may be privatist and narcissistic, so that Jesus is made to serve as legitimatizer of a pathetic egoism by quoting the second love-commandment, "Love your neighbor as yourself," as if it sanctioned self-pride, self-respect, self-love as having his approval. A pop group like "Abba" will encourage this by reminding its devotees that such caring is in their own best interests: "Some day you may want your neighbor's help yourself." If the privatism is religious, Jesus will be dished up in evangelical clichés and advertised in trendy TV jingles as the Lamb upon his cross. He is not likely to be presented in the tail end of this century as a laughing radical who comes to men and women as a theological, pastoral, and demanding Teacher.

George Johnston taught New Testament at the Hartford Seminary Foundation and is now a member of the Faculty of Divinity, McGill University, Montreal.

Hence it becomes necessary to develop a new icon of Jesus by substituting *Liberator* for "Savior" and *sharing* for "love." Today's people in all five continents are desperate for true freedom. And it is not only individuals who are enslaved by their past, their lusts, ambitions, and errors. Bondage applies to the social systems of the First and Second Worlds, and the Third World too. If people are to be humanized and also godly, it will take a moral and religious revolution; and Jesus was in many ways a revolutionary.[1]

What Jesus had to say about human life needs to be applied to the local geography of ancient Galilee, Samaria, and Judea, but also to the Gaza Strip, the Golan Heights, the West Bank, and Lebanon by proper extension of his meaning, and then (because I am both Scot and Canadian) to the English home counties and the Scots regions, and to the bickering provinces of Canada, but also to the world of OPEC and the giant multinationals—which leaves nobody and no area out! The videotapes of Kenya and Zimbabwe-Rhodesia, of the boat-people refugees, of Ulster and Nicaragua, of Korea and Latin America, should be adequate evidence of the modern oversupply of bondage and liberating struggles. Where in our world would it be irrelevant to try applying the old Jewish ethic that Jesus endorsed, "Love your neighbor . . . and treat the resident aliens as members of your own family"[2]— and more than that, Jesus' own novel contribution, "Love your enemies"?[3]

One who observed the lilies of the field and the stormy squalls on the Galilean lake has something to say to citizens and legislators who are seeking ecological solutions for the planet Earth. Its habitat must be made safe for all the creatures who share it with humankind.

It is not likely that such a Jesus can be today elevated in Byzantine mosaics as the mystical Pantocrator. David Flusser in New Israel approves Hubert van Eyck's famous Ghent altarpiece because there, he says, Jesus the Son of man is shown as a human being who is divine[4]; and this would appeal to many. The thesis here is that we must refurbish the icon so that Jesus may appear as first-century Palestinian Prophet, as the supreme Jewish Teacher who has captured the imagination and the hearts of all the ages and must now be listened to afresh for what he has to say.

The task of so doing can be undertaken by:

1. those who wish to construct a theology of the New Testament, for Jesus did teach about God.
2. anyone who is ambitious to produce a *vita* of Jesus, for Jesus belongs within the kinship of historical humanity.

3. all who are engaged in contemporary religious dialogues
—Christians with Jews, Muslims with Christians, Buddhists with
Christians, and Christians with Marxists.
4. amateurs and professionals who chart the channels of Christian
education for the 1980s.

For all such people and for everyone else, the best icon is that of a
Deacon—of a young Jewish man who lived and taught graciously and
consistently as the servant of God and his neighbors.

The Deacon-Teacher as Herald

In the *Biblical Archeologist* for December 1976, Cobbey Crisler, an
American layman, tells how he tested sites beside the Sea of Galilee and
in Samaria near Nablus, ancient Shechem, and discovered that in
Palestine there are natural theaters with acoustical properties comparable to those of the Greek theater at Epidaurus. So, he writes, Jesus
could have embarked on a boat, as Mark 4:1 reports, at a spot near
Capernaum and addressed five to seven thousand people. Though for a
time Jesus had been permitted to speak inside the synagogues, often his
classrooms were in the dry, sunny air of the lovely hill country that
surrounds the lake.

Before he came to his lakeside platform there had been journeying:
from Nazareth south into Judea, to the banks of the river Jordan to see
and hear the man sent from God whose name was John. At the Jordan,
it is related, this young man Jesus was seized by God's Spirit and
commissioned to preach. Since his vocation focused directly on a
preaching mission, one can never divorce the Preacher from the
Teacher. And to appreciate fully the tenor and content of the teaching,
one must apprehend the substance of his homilies. They were almost
certainly in Aramaic.[5] Whether he was a scholastic homilist in the style
of John 6:30-58 is doubtful, though Peder Borgen argues that it
"represents the Church's understanding of Jesus' teaching."[6] What is
more certain is that he taught by using Oriental hyperbole, biting
humor, stories and poems, so that the modern exegete must be careful
not to ruin the poetry with unimaginative prose commentaries and
literalistic interpretations. His poetry employed traditional Hebrew
modes (e.g., parallelism) and meters, with assonance and rhyme.[7] T.W.
Manson in a magisterial study claimed that "strophic parallelism"
constituted Jesus' special contribution to the forms of Hebrew poetry.[8]

The initial message was a clarion call of momentous news: "The time
is fulfilled!" The *kairos,* he said, has come to its term—or, in Hebrew

221

terms, the *gēts* has arrived, God's own moment, a time freighted with fateful results for those who confess their commitment to God. It is the language of advent and delivery, of destiny and new birth, of hope and of new beginnings. If it promised thresholds and opportunities, it did not guarantee tranquillity or success. It cannot be compared to any secular news item, whether the landing on the moon or Signor Moro's abduction and murder, for it was news of God: "The time is fulfilled, and God's *basileia,* the *malkuth* of the Lord, his royal advent, is close by. Turn to him and believe! Welcome God into your life."

After 150 years of scholarly research, there is a need for such a new version of Mark 1:15, dropping from doctrine, sermon, and exposition the misleading phrase "the kingdom of God." Jesus' urgent call was directed to Israel's liberation to become more truly God's covenant-people and to be re-created in order to be worthy of the heritage in Abraham, Moses, Samuel, David, Isaiah, Amos, and all the prophets. This *basileia* was no abstract principle, no constitutional option, not even a piece of traditional Jewish theology—though it was of necessity communicated out of familiar biblical contexts (from the received scriptures and from the so-called intertestamental literature). It spoke of a hope and a faith for sensitive and godly men and women in Israel. But its heart was *divine activity.* It denoted the *power* and the *authority* proper to the living God—creator of the world and God of the ancestors, the source of promise that life can be remade and of grace that God is able and willing to meet human need. God's moment, in an hour of Israel's profoundest need, had brought this teaching Preacher onto the stage of history. Flusser correctly notes that Jesus' idea of "the kingdom of heaven" is one of three points at which the revolution Jesus intended breaks through.[9] "Revolution" may not be the most apposite expression, yet it reminds us that we are dealing, in Mark 1:15 and related sayings, with world-shattering tidings.

Jesus also presented himself as part of the demonstration that God's new advent had dawned; divine activity was mediated in time and space through this Teacher—and soon also through his student-disciples. [10] To communicate the message about the divine, Jesus frequently taught in parables (Mark 4:34a). A parable is a proclamation image, a story, a riddle. It is a verbal metaphor that uses normal everyday human elements, as contrasted with myths and fairy tales where so much is wholly imaginary (though not "untrue"). "A man went down from Jerusalem to Jericho. . . . A sower went out to sow. . . . A woman who owned ten coins lost one . . ."—that is the language of parables, and it was applied by Jesus to talk about the liberating activity of God and its implications (Mark 4:26, 30).[11]

Digging down to the bedrock of Jesus' career as teacher, one discovers that even prior to his gospel of sovereign liberation (the *basileia* theme), the secret of his life and the burden of his teaching was quite simply God. This is evident from the record of his prayer life and from his doctrine of God as Abba, Father—and even from the reserve with which he talked about God.[12] We shall get nothing right if we begin with *basileia* rather than Abba, the All-Merciful, the gracious Lord, the holy and mighty God, the God of the psalms and the prophets and the law.

Do that, then proceed to underline what he heralds about divine presence: about *coming, advent, drawing near to inaugurate a new era for Israel, arrival*. This can be illustrated from the parable of the sower, using the analysis and abbreviation of J.D. Crossan[13]—Mark 4:3, 4, 6b and 8: "Listen! A sower went out to sow, and as he sowed, some seed fell on the path, and since it had no root, it withered away. Some seed fell among thorns that grew up and choked it, so that it produced no grain. And the rest fell on good soil and produced a crop—thirty-fold, sixty-fold, and a hundred-fold."

The audience (and today's readers) was challenged to see and interpret a familiar picture. Gospel preaching is like seed-scattering, a chancy affair. But there will be a harvest. That was the norm of Judean farming. So too God has begun the work of a new spiritual springtime and, despite the inevitable losses, God is guaranteed to see its fruit. Read the "supernatural," then, out of the "natural." "Lend me your ears," shouts the Herald, "and I will lend you my eyes. Can you see the activity of God among you? Can you detect the presence of God at your door?"

The imperatives of Jesus summon people to try to perceive and to persevere, to go on asking, go on knocking, go on seeking, for it is God who will respond and answer. Indeed (as Crossan has put it), it is God who will be found, because men and women have, as it were, mislaid God, and they must do something about the situation. "Turn toward God; open up to the divine; take heart and believe in him and what he is up to in my coming among you as his Herald." In Matthew 13:44-45 there is a pair of parables that must have burst on the audience as tales of outrageous possibilities and almost incredible actions that defy conventional morality: "This business of the *basileia* is like a man who found treasure hidden in a field. He hid it again, went off and sold everything he possessed in order to buy that field! It's like a dealer in pearls who discovered a single pearl so valuable that he sold everything he possessed, and bought it."

Since metaphor is not allegory, one must not itemize the details of such stories and set down their spiritual equivalents. Rather, listeners were and are teased into discovery for themselves. Each has to see, each has to hear, and each must come to terms with the God whose herald Jesus is at the door. Jesus summed up the implications of what being liberated would mean by quoting in typical Jewish fashion the two great commandments of the law: to love God wholeheartedly, and similarly to love one's neighbor. But his moral teaching shows that he reinterpreted such loving in the most radical way. He was not much interested in loving God by performing cultic acts like sacrifices, prayers, and praises—the common stuff of much "religion." The service of God required a new kind of living, or an old way taken with the utmost seriousness. Space forbids discussion here of that new lifestyle of which Jesus as teacher was the expositor. Suffice it to say that this young Jew exemplified the lifestyle in his own character and in the manner of his living and dying.

The Deacon-Teacher as Warrior of the Spirit

If the mission of Jesus was encouraging news of divine presence to pardon and renew God's people, it was also part of a campaign to deliver that people (on certain conditions) from the dark forces of evil in the world. Part of the evidence that this was the case for Jesus, and for the subsequent church, is to be found in Mark's Gospel-book:

1. Men and women were possessed by unclean spirits which had to be destroyed (1:23; 5:1-13).
2. Demoniacs were restored to sanity, and many sick folk were healed (e.g. 1:31, 34; 7:29).
3. God's house, the temple in Jerusalem, had to be rid of corruption (11:11ff.)
4. The lord of the demons was Beelzebul (Satan, 3:22-27), and Jesus' enemies accused him of being an agent of Beelzebul. The counterclaim by Jesus was that God's Spirit governed him as the appointed warrior to bind and expel the evil one and his minions.

Much of Jesus' teaching bears on this war between good and evil.[14] Strangely enough, Jesus had very little to say directly about his own possession of God's Spirit.[15] The three or four authentic sayings are quite significant, and they focus on the Q word appended to the Beelzebul pericope at Luke 11:20//Matthew 12:28, "If it is by the finger [or, Spirit] of God that I expel demons, then God in his *basileia* [i.e., in his sovereign, liberating power] has come upon you unawares!" That "if" betokens no mere speculation; rather, it summoned the hearers to perceive the reality of a situation that had this Jesus working in it to heal minds and bodies. Could they recognize him as the human *locus* of

God's own royal grace? Jesus was concerned not just with the halfwits of Galilee and Judea and with the scum of village and town; he encountered plain ordinary sinners, some rich, many poor, who needed to be set free. Not all the oppressed and exploited became saints and wholesome Jews because they were poor and downtrodden; yet riches and secular cares, and not least religious complacency and self-conceit, often stifled the Teacher's gospel and their own responses. Reassurance and hope, it seems, came more readily to scoundrels and outcasts who discovered a new way to God and a thrilling return to decency because of Jesus (cf. Luke 7:36-50; 19:1-10; Mark 2:13-17).

Rigorous moral imperatives put substance into the repentance and faith of Mark 1:15,[16] and these were attached to the electrifying promises of Luke 6:20-26:

> Woe to you who now are rich. . . .
> Woe to you, full-bellied fat cats. . . .
> Woe to you that laugh now. . . .
> Woe to you who are now so popular. . . .
>
> It's all going to be turned upside down! . . .
>
> Happy are you poor folk. . . .
> Happy are you hungry ones. . . .
> Happy are you that weep now. . . .
> Happy are you who now are hated. . . .
>
> It's all going to be reversed.
> For with God you will have a great reward.

These future tenses must not be pushed too far ahead into some distant "eschatological denouement"—the end of an era or the end of the world or the second advent of Jesus. I have paraphrased Luke's "in heaven" by the words "with God," because God and God's beatifying grace need have no time reference. The reversal promised is always potentially *now*. As soon as Jesus announced it, it was true; and as soon as anyone turned in faith toward God, it became reality. Then and there the poor, the outcast, the disciple, or whoever, went into the *basileia,* as the Jewish idiom put it. God came into their lives anew, as liberator. They did not have to wait, except for the time when the entire world of humanity has come to believe. Matthew 21:31–32 makes the point. Future destiny had cast its gladness backward, to become a present tense of opportunity and responsibility—and, in this context only, of genuine spiritual tranquillity. For the emancipated the time had indeed

225

been fulfilled; they had found the precious pearl and the hidden treasure. No longer need they be captive to demons, "hodden doon" by bad habits, ancient fears, and godless anxieties. Yet few took the decisive step.[17]

Thus the revolutionary outcome of the divine campaign was that "many that are first shall be last, and the last first" (Mark 10:31),[18] for the secret remained hidden from the wise and prudent and was revealed to the childlike (Luke 10:21). Such men and women could take heart because God cares for them with an almighty love that called them to emulate the divine self (Matthew, 6:25-33; 5:45), not as kings and priests of a holy Jewish empire (Mark 10:35-44: Luke 12:32), but as witnesses and martyrs engaged like Jesus in the constant warfare against evil (Mark 13:9; Matthew 10:24-25; cf. John 16:2).

Much of this message was not brand-new in the time of Jesus, yet he was exceptional in the passion and devotion of his insight and his obedience to God. He was himself beset by storms, misunderstood and misrepresented. Even his inner circle was infiltrated (Mark 8:33; 14:10). But today one had better not repeat the obtuseness and errors of James and John, the sons of Zebedee (Mark 10:35ff.), or the enmity of the religious establishment. The warfare did not end at Calvary on April 7, A.D. 30, or on the succeeding Easter Day or at Pentecost. It still goes on, as noted at the beginning of this essay, and the Christian church is commissioned to set Jesus before the nations as Teacher and Liberator in whose spirit and with whose undying help his disciples and friends can carry on the divine campaign to bring true peace to earth.

The Teacher as Deacon of God and Persons

Refurbishing the icon of Jesus means that one should learn to see the smile on his face and the kindly look in his eye (Mark 10:25: Matthew 7:3). Compassion, not simply dire admonition, tempered his words (Matthew 7:26-27; Luke 16:23; Mark 10:22). Not that Jesus could never be stern or that he was a "soft touch." He could indeed be rigorous and stern in his ethical teaching, and devastating in his simplicity and directness. So caustic are some of the utterances ascribed to him, for example, about the hypocrisy of Pharisees, that some contemporary Jewish scholars exploit them to prove his defects and paint blots on his good name. It has even been suggested that he was sinful like the rest of us, and perhaps a sexual pervert. I admit I am prejudiced and on his side, but more convincing is the fact that not a shred of evidence exists to justify such accusations. In fact, it has ceased to matter in today's world whether this Jewish prophet was theoretically "sinless" or was a *guru* excelling all others in his wisdom and his perfect communion with

226

the unseen God. Enough that we should seek a predicate that will do justice to his message, his achievement, and his incredible spiritual influence. That predicate, I suggest, is Servant of God.

Even though one cannot demonstrate to the satisfaction of many critical scholars that Jesus interpreted his role in the light of the servant-poems of Second Isaiah, there is enough for me to indicate that he had discovered in service the keynote for a prophet's function in Israel. In the baptismal narrative of Mark 1:11 one can detect an echo of Isaiah 42:1. The programmatic passage, Luke 4:16-21, may represent his mind, though it is also likely to be a theological interpretation within the Lukan church. Mark 10:34-45 may go back to Jesus himself, because its message is unusual and distinctive: primacy means service; leadership is ministry (deaconship). "I myself came to serve" (Mark 10:45, where the original "I" has been altered piously to "the Son of man"; cf. Matthew 11:24-30). Humility in obedience, it may be said, is implicit in the doctrine of God as holy Parent and in the ethics of loving both friend and foe.

To this may be added the overwhelming documentation in the gospel traditions for Jesus' conviction that God had sent him and that he, in turn, had to send his representatives in a divine succession of ministry.[19]

All disciples are deacons, just as their Teacher was a deacon. He is the exemplar for women as well as men, and he seems to have had no intention of turning any of these deacons into "clergy." From this it follows that the teaching consists of his sayings and also, astonishingly, of his life. He is the model for all who respond to the news he came to herald, the prophecies he uttered as the word of God, in threat and in promise, the poems and parables he embroidered in the tapestry of his service to God, to his sisters and brothers.

It might have been much easier for many if Jesus' teaching had instead been concretized in a book or a philosophical system or a theological summa, for when the authentic core of it is uncovered, it is compounded of an awful demand and constraint: "Do as you would be done by. . . . Treat even your enemies as members of your clan. . . . Follow me, as I follow God. . . . Represent me among the people as I represented the Creator among the Jews and aliens of ancient Palestine, under the Romans long ago."

See what it means to rethink the icon of Jesus for this contemporary world, and to find that it is that of a Deacon-Teacher; consider what one lets oneself in for by choosing to be his pupil and his colleague!

CHAPTER 17

Existentialist Christology

John Macquarrie

When I speak of existentialist Christology, I have in mind the teaching about the person of Jesus Christ that one finds in such writers of recent times as Rudolf Bultmann, Fritz Buri, and Friedrich Gogarten. It could be claimed, however, that the sophisticated views of these scholars are no more than a modern counterpart to the oldest Christology of all, for what did the earliest disciples mean when they hailed Jesus as "Christ" or "Lord" or even "God"? Surely such language was, to begin with, confessional, situational, even emotive, rather than descriptive. The disciples were declaring their own attitude to Jesus. They were trying to express what he had come to mean for their own existence. This is especially obvious in the use of the title Lord. It is true that this word had many connotations, in the first instance from Old Testament usage and then as time went on from Hellenistic religion as well. But essentially the word Lord is a rank word, not a descriptive word. To call someone Lord is not to describe him but to indicate the relation that subsists between him and the speaker or the group to whom the speaker belongs. "The '*kyrios*' christology," writes Graham Stanton, "expresses the authority of the Lord over the individual and the Christian community and is often related to ethical statements."[1]

One might agree that these earliest acknowledgments of Jesus as Lord or Christ were not yet Christology in the strict sense. No doubt they were first used in the heat of the moment, so to speak—the moment of perception or conversion or recognition. Later they passed into liturgy, which recaptures and brings to life again the creative moment of faith. The confessions attributed to Peter (Mark 8:29) and Thomas (John 20:28) may or may not be accurately reported, but there certainly were such moments. The Christ hymn of Philippians 2:5-11 is from a later

John Macquarrie is Lady Margaret Professor of Divinity at Oxford University.

stage, when the confession of lordship has been stylized for liturgical use.

But Christology, as part of the theological enterprise, always needs something more—it needs reflection. That reflection is not yet present at the moment of the original confession of faith, but it is beginning to appear in liturgy, so far as this has a meditative character. Nevertheless, confession and liturgy provide the raw material for Christology and do not yet constitute Christology itself. Thus, I do not want to claim too much when I say that modern existentialist Christologies are a counterpart to the very earliest Christologies. It might be more accurate to say that existentialist Christology goes far toward recapturing the strongly personal, evaluative, confessional character of the earliest Christian responses to the person of Jesus Christ, and this is important when one remembers how quickly Christology took a metaphysical turn.

To be sure, the confessional and personal strains were never quite lost. One cannot explain the passion that went into the early christological controversies unless it is acknowledged that behind the disputes about metaphysical terminology there was the deeper issue of a right personal relationship to Jesus Christ. Yet that became more and more obscured. To say that Jesus is Christ or Lord or God was increasingly understood as descriptive language, to be explicated in terms of substance, nature, person, subsistence, and the like.

The existential strain in Christology was strongly reasserted for a time at the Reformation. Luther defined God in the Large Catechism in existential rather than metaphysical terms: "That to which your heart clings and entrusts itself is, I say, really your God."[2] The same approach colored his treatment of Christ, but it was Melanchthon who gave the almost classic statement:

> The mysteries of the Godhead are not so much to be investigated
> as adored. It is useless to labor long on the high doctrines of
> God, his unity and trinity, the mystery of creation, the mode of
> the incarnation. . . . To know Christ is to know his benefits, not
> to contemplate his natures and the modes of his incarnation.[3]

Both Luther and Melanchthon modified their early existential emphases, but they seem at this point to have injected into the Lutheran tradition an existential concern that has kept reappearing. Thus in the nineteenth century one finds Albrecht Ritschl condemning metaphysics and any theology that consists of a mixture of faith and metaphysics, and insisting that "we know the nature of God and Christ only in their worth for us."[4] His most forthright statement is:

If Christ, by what he has done and suffered for my salvation is my Lord, and if, by trusting to the power of what he has done for me, I honor him as my God, then that is a value-judgment of a direct kind. It is not a judgment that belongs to the sphere of disinterested scientific knowledge, like the formula of Chalcedon. Every recognition of a religious sort is a direct judgment of value.[5]

Wilhelm Herrmann and Martin Kähler were two other nineteenth-century German theologians whose thought was moving along similar lines,[6] and who may be considered forerunners of the explicitly "existentialist" Christology of the twentieth century.

Bultmann's clearest and most provocative statement of an existentialist Christology is to be found in his essay, "The Christological Confession of the World Council of Churches,"[7] published in 1951, that is to say, three years after the formation of the council. Bultmann had been asked by a conference of liberal Swiss theologians to comment on the statement adopted at Amsterdam that "the World Council of Churches is composed of churches which acknowledge Jesus Christ as God and Savior."

About the use of the term Savior he sees no special problem. The term is perhaps indefinite and nowadays has an archaic ring to it, but it is a functional term and refers to what Christ does in the Christian community. The difficult question arises when one speaks of acknowledging Jesus Christ as God—and Bultmann notes that in the christological confession under consideration it is this strong formulation of Christ as God that is put forward, not Christ as Son of God or Word of God or any other less direct formulation. This difficult question is whether the assertion that Jesus Christ is God speaks of his nature or of his significance. Is it a metaphysical assertion or a soteriological one? Or is it both? "Does the pronouncement have soteriological or cosmological character or both?"[8]

Bultmann's first step is to consider what grounds the New Testament offers for calling Jesus Christ "God." He finds that this way of speaking is hardly to be found in the sacred authors. "Neither in the Synoptic Gospels nor in the Pauline Epistles is Jesus called God; nor do we find him so called in the Acts of the Apostles or in the Apocalypse."[9] There are a few ambiguous passages in the deutero-Pauline literature, but Bultmann's conclusion is that "the only passage in which Jesus is undoubtedly designated or, more exactly, addressed as God is John 20:28, that is, at the end of the story of Thomas, where Thomas makes the confession 'My Lord and my God!' "[10] To be sure, Bultmann acknowledges that some of the other titles applied to Jesus in the New Testament (and he tends to stress the Hellenistic rather than the Old Testament provenance of these terms) do elevate Jesus into the divine sphere, perhaps as a cultic deity or world ruler, but not so as to put him on a level with God.

It is worth noting that some other New Testament scholars reach conclusions less negative than Bultmann's on this issue. Raymond E. Brown, for instance, claims that "in three clear instances and in five instances that have a certain probability, Jesus is called 'God' in the New Testament."[11] The three allegedly clear instances include Thomas's confession, cited by Bultmann, together with Hebrews 1:8 (in which a psalm is addressed to Jesus, "Thy throne, O God, is for ever . . .") and John 1:1 ("The Word was God"). However, Brown claims that it is the neglect of some of the more marginal but probable instances that makes Bultmann's treatment of the question exaggeratedly negative. So whereas Bultmann says, "It is only with the Apostolic Fathers that free unambiguous reference to Jesus Christ as 'our God' begins,"[12] Brown is more cautious in observing that "the use of *theos* of Jesus which is attested in the early second century was a continuation of a usage which had begun in New Testament times."[13]

Even accepting Brown's more moderate position, one would still have to say that God as a direct appellation of Jesus is rare in the New Testament. What may be of greater importance here is that the clearest instance, the utterance of Thomas, is strongly confessional and existential. Furthermore, we find Brown asserting that most of the other instances which he cites come from a liturgical background.[14]

If then we agree that Jesus Christ is rarely called explicitly God in the New Testament, and that when and if this does happen the context is confessional or liturgical rather than dogmatic, we are prepared for Bultmann's statement of his "existentialist" Christology. The question is whether these exalted ways of speaking of Jesus are descriptions of him in the sense of objectifying statements about his being, or whether they express his significance for the believer. To quote Bultmann: "Do they speak of his *physis* or of the *Christus pro me?* How far is a christological pronouncement about him also a pronouncement about me? Does he help me because he is God's Son, or is he the Son of God because he helps me?"[15] Bultmann answers these questions in a strongly existentialist sense. Christ is God in the sense that in him I encounter God's word or God's act. So he can write,

The formula, "Christ is God," is false in every sense in which God can be understood as an entity which can be objectivized, whether it is understood in an Arian or Nicene, an orthodox or a

231

liberal sense. It is correct, if "God" is understood here as the event of God's acting.[16]

In this passage Bultmann would seem to be imposing a veto on any dogmatic, speculative, or metaphysical Christology—in his view these are all "objectifying," and that is always with him a bad word. In another essay he seems to allow the possibility of holding beliefs about the nature of Jesus Christ, though these would be very secondary in importance. He writes: "To have faith in Christ does not mean to hold particular opinions about his nature, although one can certainly have such opinions."[17] But although this might seem to suggest that speculative Christology is permissible, we read a little farther on: "What is meant by christology?" and we get the answer: "It is not the theoretical explanation of experiential piety; it is not speculation and teaching about the divine nature of Christ. It is proclamation, it is summons."[18]

It is important to notice, however, that Bultmann is not trying to flee from the problem of how the divine and the human come together in Jesus. He rejects the Chalcedonian formula as objectification and, moreover, as impossible for our modern thought. But he equally rejects the suppression of the problem of Christ's person by the liberals who humanized him, and he thinks that the "Amsterdam people" (as he contemptuously calls them) are essentially no different from the liberals, because they too have suppressed the problem, though in the opposite direction. But Bultmann himself wants to maintain the paradox of the eschatological event—the event of the man Jesus of Nazareth, which is also the event of God's acting. The use of the word event here is important. "Christ's lordship, his deity, is always only an event at any given time."[19] That is to say, Christ's deity is not an eternal property of his person, nor is the confession of it an eternal dogmatic truth. Confession of his deity is a confession of his significance in the moment of encounter—the eschatological moment, in Bultmann's sense of the phrase. This also explains why Bultmann always held that Jesus' personality is unimportant and that discipleship does not consist in personal attachment or devotion to him. Jesus is the vehicle of the Word, first in his own preaching but then, more important, in the kerygma in which he became the preached, and for which his own preaching was only a preparation. It is in the hearing and proclaiming of the kerygma that God speaks and acts and the event of Christ's lordship takes place.

There is much that is attractive in Bultmann's Christology. It stays close to faith and does not wander into airy speculation and scholastic distinctions. In this regard we can see it as standing solidly in the Lutheran tradition, and it would be as fair to call it Lutheran as

232

existentialist. It belongs, too, in the prophetic tradition and visualizes discipleship in primarily ethical terms, as obedience to the word that meets us and makes its demand for love through Jesus Christ. We might say that it is a Christology stripped down to the most basic essentials, demythologized and deontologized.

Yet one must also raise several critical questions.

1. On what ground does one recognize the ultimacy of Jesus Christ or acknowledge that the kerygma brings us to face the word of God? Bultmann may well be right in making commitment to the reality that meets us in Christ, the beginning point for Christology, but how easily we commit ourselves to that which is not ultimate, though we represent it as such. How does one guard against idolatry in such a commitment, save by reflection at the ontological level? Bultmann is very much afraid of "objectifying," of digressing from the existential relation of faith into a possibly idle and uncommitted speculation. But surely there can be ontological reflection that does not degenerate into this. If one has decided that something is ultimate (a "word of God"), then in view of the grave danger of idolatry or superstition or fanaticism, one must think out the question of what constitutes this ultimacy. Therefore one cannot avoid the question about Christ's relation to the Father. Bultmann may well set aside Chalcedon (though he does so in much too dismissive a fashion), but there is still a principle of incarnation that needs to be thought out insofar as he holds that a divine reality (God or God's word or act) impinges on us through a human reality (Jesus Christ or his word or the kerygma in which he is proclaimed).

2. The question must also be asked whether a word can bear all the weight that Bultmann places upon it. We have seen that the personality of Jesus is of no importance—it is entirely absorbed into the word. Preaching is the center of everything. Jesus himself preaches the word. Whether one could say that he *is the Word* seems doubtful. He appears instead as the bearer of the word, though this is the description that was traditionally applied to the Blessed Virgin. But then he becomes the one who is preached and is taken up into the kerygma. The risen Christ is identified with the word of preaching, which ever and again renews the eschatological moment. It has all become verbal. God has become a word, and God's act is the act of speaking. We have to ask at this point whether Christianity has been too narrowly confined to the speaking and hearing of language. This may arise from the fact that Bultmann seems to have no place for liturgy and worship, only for preaching. Even the sacraments are simply *verbum visibile*. But is not this a truncated version of Christianity, which thinks of it as a word to be heard and understood and obeyed, not as a wider reality that seeks to embrace and transform the whole human nature?

3. Following on this, one must ask whether the reduction of Jesus Christ to the bearer of a word does justice to his person or to that tradition of Christian spirituality that has prized incorporation into Christ, devotion to Christ, mystical communion with him, and so on. Bultmann, like many other German Protestant theologians before him, has no sympathy for mysticism. Equally, he is impatient of pietism —and rightly so, when this becomes a mere sentimental attachment to Jesus. But there is an important tradition of Catholic sacramental spirituality that cannot be so lightly set aside. One can understand the protest of the Jesuit L. Malevez:

> We are no longer confronted either by the ontological reality or the spiritual presence of the ever-living Christ. All that concerns us is the message of which he is the instrument. . . . How can the Christian reader of Bultmann help exclaiming in his surprise, "They have taken away my Lord, and I do not know where they have laid him?"[20]

4. A related point concerns the possibility of growing and deepening in the Christian life. Like Kierkegaard, Bultmann denies that faith is a permanent possession. It needs to be renewed from one situation to another. In a sense this is surely correct. Yet Bultmann's view of the matter seems far too episodic. Christ's lordship, we are told, is only an event of the moment. No doubt there may be many moments, but presumably most of a person's life is lived in the intervals between those moments of high decision. Incidentally, Bultmann teaches the same episodic view of the believer's relation to God.[21] But surely one must make allowance for continuity as well as discontinuity, for what is called the "practice of the presence" of God or Christ, for steady growth in discipleship.

5. Finally, although Bultmann has no use for pietism and mysticism, he seems to suffer himself from what is the worst defect of pietism—its individualism. The *pro me* features prominently in Bultmann, and one cannot find in his works the *pro nobis*. Let us recall the sentence already quoted: "Does he help me because he is God's Son, or is he the Son of God because he helps me?" Bultmann may be right in thinking that soteriology affords the right way into the question of Christ's person, but what is required is a much broader and firmer base than individual experience of salvation. It is enormously presumptuous to imply that Christ is the Son of God because he helps *me*—even where the "me" is Rudolf Bultmann! It is not enough to substitute for this even the collective Christian experience of salvation. One is brought back to the question of whether an existentialist (or functional or soteriological)

234

approach to Christology does not demand to be ontologically deepened or, to put it in another way, whether consideration of *what Christ does for us* must not lead into the question of *who Christ is.*

Bultmann is the outstanding example of a theologian who has expounded an existentialist Christology, but he does this mainly on the grounds of his New Testament scholarship. It may be useful therefore to consider the views of two systematic theologians who have also followed the existentialist path in Christology: Friedrich Gogarten and Fritz Buri.

Gogarten's Christology is in many ways very close to Bultmann's, but he relates it more definitely to the development of Western thought. What characterizes the modern age is the supersession of metaphysics by history.

> This historical approach is the expression of a profound change
> which has taken place since the beginning of the modern age in
> the relation of man to the world and to himself. This change
> means nothing more and nothing less than that by it the world
> has for man become his own world.[22]

In the ancient world and the medieval world there was an unchanging metaphysical framework that formed, as it were, the stage on which history took place. Everything was already determined, and there was no place for human responsibility and creativity. But now the situation is reversed. Human beings make history. Metaphysical systems themselves are swallowed up in history and are seen to be products of history. So the problem for the modern theologian is to take Christology out of its traditional metaphysical setting and express it in historical terms.

Like Bultmann, Gogarten dissociates himself from nineteenth-century liberalism. He is not concerned with reconstructing the "historical Jesus." Rather, it is a question of reading the existential significance of Jesus' history in such a way that it illuminates our own history and presents a possibility of existence. In that sense he can declare that "the word of Jesus is the word of God."[23] But, more clearly than Bultmann, Gogarten understands that to say this is to speak of an intimate relation between God and the Father. Moreover, he claims that this has a finality about it which distinguishes Jesus from the line of Hebrew prophets, who also spoke the word of God. This relation is not for us expressible in outmoded metaphysical terms, though Gogarten is more respectful to the early councils than Bultmann. Jesus' special relation to God consists in the fact that he was the first human being to accept full responsibility before God, and so the first also to be delivered from the idolizing of the powers of the world.[24] Gogarten, of course, was deeply impressed by

235

Paul's teaching in Galatians that the Christian has come of age and been delivered by Christ from the tutelage of law and subordination to worldly powers. He brought the old world to an end and inaugurated the kingdom of God in which human beings can be free responsible co-workers with God. This is also associated by Gogarten with the idea of secularization. Secularization is in fact historicization, coming to grips with human responsibility before God in time.

It will be seen, then, that Gogarten does to some extent provide the sketch of an ontology of history, so that his existentialist Christology does begin to take up some of the questions left unanswered by Bultmann. But there are considerable obscurities in Gogarten's theology. Is liberation for historical responsibility in the world really the existential significance of Jesus? And even if Jesus conceived that responsibility as a responsibility before God, is that how it is being understood today? Here we strike on the ambiguities of a so-called secular Christianity, though Gogarten himself is not unaware of them. He writes in one place: "The difference between modern historical thought and Jesus' understanding of history is that virtually nothing remains of responsibility before God."[25] Again, when everything has been historicized and all metaphysical systems (including, one must suppose, theism) have been recognized as products of history, are we not plunged into a thoroughgoing relativism that threatens Gogarten's own positions? He might not be too worried about the undermining of theism, for, like Bultmann, he thinks of God as a call to existential responsibility rather than an object of thought. But what about the claim for Jesus' finality and the difference between him and the prophets who came before him? Must not Jesus be seen in a much more relative way, as an inaugurator who was important for his own time but whose significance will increasingly diminish as human beings "come of age" and take over their own responsibility, no longer understood as a responsibility before God?

With Fritz Buri there is something different again. Perhaps it should be said that here Buri is considered in his existentialist phase, for both before and after that phase his theology has had a somewhat different character. In some ways he is more thoroughly existentialist than Bultmann. He does not agree with the criticisms of those who have complained about the lack of an ontology in Bultmann, and says: "Bultmann has good reason for foregoing an ontology of faith. The analogical thinking that he hinted at cannot be carried through in the form of an ontology or metaphysic but is only manifested in the actualization of faithful existence."[26] Buri says this because, like Bultmann, he thinks that any ontology must involve an illegitimate objectifying of that which is nonobjectifiable and unconditioned, namely, personhood, responsibility, the voice that calls to responsibility (God). He seems also more existentialist than Bultmann in denying Jesus the decisive place as act or word of God which Bultmann assigns to him. For Buri, "there is no difference in principle between philosophy of existence and theology of existence."[27] An authentic responsible existence is achievable apart from Christ. Nevertheless, Christ remains as a still powerful symbol of such an existence, and Christian theology still has the task of unpacking in existential terms that symbol and the several doctrines derived from it.

> There must be an enormous depth and inexhaustible fullness of possibilities of understanding and realization of human life in the eschatological christology of the New Testament, that through all changes, additions, deviations and distortions, it has been understood continually as the revelation of the redeeming grace of God. On theological, existential and ethical grounds, Christ Jesus is of immense significance for a christology of existence . . . he represents the prototype of a christology of existence. Therefore, the christology of existence conceives its task to be to transfer Jesus Christ from the historical past into the historicality of present existence by means of the transforming application of his self-understanding of existence.[28]

But is there not an inconsistency in Buri at this point? Unlike Bultmann, he sought to demolish the difference between Christian faith and philosophy of existence. But in the passage just quoted, the claims made for Jesus Christ are surely such that he cannot be just an optional symbol of authentic existence.

There is no doubt about the strengths of existentialist Christology. They go back to the New Testament and have kept reappearing in the history of theology, especially Lutheran theology in the past four centuries. But I hope that I have made apparent some of the weak points also. A purely existentialist Christology is neither adequate nor self-consistent, and that is why I have advocated an existential-ontological approach.[29]

CHAPTER 18

Two Christic Paradigms:
Focuses of a Theological Revolution

George A. Riggan

Until the advent of Ayatollah Ruhollah Khomeini, many intellectuals would have scorned the suggestion that an adequate interpretation of the dynamics of a revolution requires the examination of its theological aspects. We have been led to expect responsible consideration of political, economic, and social transformations in accounts of revolutions, yes. But theological transformations, no! Even now reports of the Iranian revolution tend to present its theological aspect as an idiosyncratic vestige of an age that has largely passed. By examining the reported behavior of those responsible for the emergence in biblical literature of the Christ figure as a cosmic presence, this study intends to suggest that theological transformations are properly to be sought among the basic phenomena generally characteristic of social revolutions.

Our attention focuses, therefore, on the praxis of the tiny minority of first-century Jews who accepted Jesus as in some sense the historic self-disclosure of God. I shall infer both the fact of the Christic revolution and its sociotheological character from the literary evidence of their disruptive behavior and the transformed self-world perception in terms of which they accounted for their actions. Thus theology as here understood has to do with the experience of *having gods* as that experience bears on social revolution, and deals with the *god idea* and the *Christ idea* only insofar as those ideas facilitated and interpreted behavior expressive of a profound shift in the faith commitments communally shared in a revolutionary situation.

George A. Riggan is Riley Professor of Systemic Theology, Emeritus, at Hartford Seminary.

In answer to his own question, "What is it to have a god?" Martin Luther long ago observed: "Whatever your heart clings to and confides in [or conversely, fears most], that is really your god. . . . To have a god is simply to trust and believe in one with our whole heart."[1] On this assumption, which I share with Luther, human life is as inevitably theological as it is social, political, economic, technological, and psychological. We all have gods. When the theological is thus understood, the preliminary function of theology as an academic discipline becomes descriptive, and its methods become sociological and historical. Luther's further comments in the same context, however, clearly imply that theology has also a normative function. "Confidence and faith of the heart alone," he continued, "make both God and an idol. If your faith and confidence are right, then likewise your god is the true God. On the other hand, if your confidence is wrong, then you have not the true God."

Since our perceptions of significant reality are variously shaped in dynamic interaction with the particular physical and cultural environments within which respectively we mature as persons, and since in the nature of the case no human perception can be proved to be isomorphic with the reality it intends, how can the members of any community of faith know that together they have made God and not an idol? Or, to rephrase this essentially theological question without resort to traditional theological language, how can they know that the most profound faith and confidence of a community are fixed on realities that actually undergird its security in the present and its hopes for the future? How can they know that the self-perception and hopes to which it has committed itself in action are realistic?

If we distance ourselves from the trust and hope expressed in our most profound and persistent commitments to action, we can express the theological question another way: How can we test the validity of the statements in which whatever is actually our deepest faith comes to social expression (whether in the language of traditional religions or in the language of skeptical secularisms)?

Theological constructions are not necessarily invalidated by the fact, stressed by Feuerbach, that they are projections of human consciousness, for as Peter Berger has observed, the scientific application of mathematics is also a projection upon reality of certain structures of human consciousness, an application that has proved to be powerfully predictive of behavior in the world "out there."[2] The fact that the sciences have advanced by employing projective techniques hardly requires that modern science be regarded as an illusion. That theological projections, in the precise meaning here intended, might constitute a parallel case is far from obvious, but the possibility may well merit examination.

Certainly in contrast to verification of scientific projections, the validation of theological projections is at least tenuous indeed, because of their all-encompassing scope. In any case, our projected pictures or models of realities, whether scientific or theological, should never be confused with the realities to which they point, for our projections and the cultural infrastructures upon which they are based evolve in the continuing interchange between our distinctively human consciousness and its changing environment. Yet, to rephrase a statement Berger has made about a religious view of the world, if a theological view of the world is consciously posited, the human beings who make theological projections may themselves constitute an evolving image of a reality that *includes* both the world and humankind, so that human ejaculations of meaning into the universe point, however accurately or erratically, to an all-encompassing meaning in which humanity itself is grounded.[3]

The raising of explicit questions as to what are the proper norms for fateful commitment, that is, the question of normative sociotheology, is a species-specific trait that will probably engage us as long as severe crises continue periodically to threaten the security and hopes of the several communities with which by faith and trust persons in every age identify themselves.

However, we are here engaged in a task of descriptive theology, not in an explicit quest for dependable norms of communal faith. It is the limited purpose of this essay to show that, by recognizing in the person of Jesus the self-disclosure of the cosmic Christ,[4] a minority within the Jewish community of the first century of our Common Era signaled the emergence of a new and revolutionary sociotheological paradigm that struck the majority as a threat to the very foundations of Jewish society.

The term paradigm, as it is here applied sociotheologically, refers to *a set or a series of events interpreted by a community as exemplifying its very nature and destiny, and thus determining the praxis by which alone it can hope to realize that destiny through successive generations.*[5] Praxis, within this context, includes not only the overt behavior of the community, but also the sociopolitical, ecological, and metaphysical assumptions implicit and explicit in the fundamental concepts by which that community traditionally extrapolates and seeks to perpetuate its self-perception and the norms of behavior inferred from the particular set of exemplary events.

To appreciate the revolutionary character and the shocking impact of the emergent paradigm in which Jesus appears as the Christ figure, we need first to examine the cluster of events traditionally celebrated in Jewish literature as determining the character and destiny of the Jewish

240

people, paying particular attention to the role of the Christ figure within that paradigmatic cluster.

Paradigmatic Events in the History of Israel

Israelites in every age have reached profound agreement that the rehearsal and prolongation of certain events exhibit Israel's true character, obligations, and destiny among the nations. Jews of the first century, claiming descent from the migrant Abraham, counted among those events the *exodus* of enslaved Hebrews from Egypt, their desert *sojourn* and tribal *federation* under the law delivered by Moses at Sinai, their *conquest* of Palestine, the *conduct of domestic and foreign policy* under the finely balanced authority of David and Nathan, the *building, destruction, and rebuilding* of the temple in Jerusalem.

By continual rehearsal of these events, Jews of the period identified themselves symbolically as participants in the original experience. Thus they both maintained an exceedingly strong sense of their communal identity and powerfully reinforced observance of the praxis they deemed appropriate to the destiny toward which they understood those events to point. When members of the small sect, later to be called Christians, initiated ritual rehearsal of the death of Jesus as the crowning episode within this cluster of historic occasions, bitter conflict flared inevitably, for the dominant majority saw clearly that inclusion of the crucifixion would transform the structure and the dynamics of the entire paradigmatic cluster, and hence revolutionize the praxis inherent in its prolonged rehearsal. A brief review of the events in sequence makes intelligible the majority's rejection of a crucified savior of Israel.

The exodus has since become a universal symbol of liberation, but to most Jews of Jesus' time it was all that and infinitely more. To them it signified the miraculous election of a few enslaved Hebrews to become a numerous and powerful people, providentially destined to a prominent role among the nations. If the second cataclysmic eruption of Thera (Santorini), ca. 1470 B.C., did indeed destroy the Minoan civilization on the Isle of Crete (biblical Caphtor) some sixty miles to the south, as some scholars now argue;[6] if the ash from that eruption accounts for the migration of the Minoans (the biblical Philistines) from Crete to Palestine; if the same monstrous vulcanism and its tsunamic flooding also make credible the biblical memory[7] that Hebrews crossed the sea over a temporary land-bridge on which Pharaoh's army drowned shortly thereafter, as other scholars argue,[8] the persistence of a profound sense of providential election among Israelites is no cause for wonder. Whether in actual fact or only in imagination, they nevertheless remembered the melting earth, the thunderous shock wave, the dark-

241

ened sun, and the monstrous wave of the advancing tsunami as mighty acts of the war god Yahweh—awesome signs of their salvation by Yahweh's unmerited favor.

By their adoption of the Sinaitic law as a basis for their federation in covenant with Yahweh, the desert tribes of Israel met the need for a differentiating code of conduct—a need characteristic of a people who deem themselves to be specially chosen. The Torah delivered by Moses was singular in its time for its stringent demands for ethnic purity, for its emphasis upon communal justice, and especially for its concern for the weak, the disadvantaged, and the poor within the community. Responsive to the latter concern, the prophets in the period of the monarchy vigorously pressed the cause of the weak and the oppressed, in the name of Yahweh.

The prevailing understanding of Torah, however, was ethnocentric. The prophets after Moses frequently portrayed war and peace among the nations as covert functions respectively of the observance or the flaunting of the Torah within Israel. In his account of the Assyrian conquest of Northern Israel, for example, Isaiah portrays Assyria as the unwitting instrument by which Yahweh is about to punish Israel's domestic aversions from the Torah. In the same ethnocentric perspective, he envisions the fall of Assyria as Yahweh's coming judgment upon Assyria's failure to recognize the author, and honor the limits, of her mission against Israel (Isaiah 10).

The adoption and firm establishment of monarchical government and the rapid expansion of Israel's hegemony under the genius of Nathan and David, together with the erection of the temple in Jerusalem under Solomon, climaxed the events in the startling transformation of an obscure tribe enslaved in Egypt into a populous and cultured people ruling Palestine.

The Yahwistic paradigm of ethnic imperialism. The perception of the events in this astonishing rise to power as a paradigm of human historical existence was peculiar to the people of Israel. The central figures in this paradigm are Yahweh and Israel. All other peoples become bit players in this dramatization of history. Yahweh is the theological construct by which this community rationalized its obstinate faith that it had been chosen for the dominant role among all the peoples. Yahweh emerges as the invariant and invisible presence shaping the miracles of Israel's life and destiny, prospering humble obedience to Torah, punishing even by the might of foreign armies the breaches of the covenant binding Yahweh to the chosen people of Israel.

According to the Yahwistic paradigm, ethnic monism is the proper condition of the human species, and ethnic and linguistic pluralism the

242

ironic consequence of the hubris that led to the attempted erection of the Tower of Babel. Ethnic homogeneity, it follows, is the manifest goal of history. As perceived through this paradigm, the course of history is not determined out of the past. Rather, its course is eschatological, a future-oriented movement toward the conversion of all peoples to Jewish orthoprax worship of Yahweh, centering in the temple at Jerusalem. The eventual coming of the kingdom of God comprises Israel's responsible and benevolent hegemony over all peoples on earth. Thus the prevailing interpretation of Israel's formative experiences yielded a paradigm of ethnic imperialism.

The essential logic of this paradigm evidences ambivalence alike toward the self, toward human community, and toward the cosmic matrix out of which human life arises. On the one hand, the paradigm bespeaks a confidence that the humane behavior commanded by Torah is thoroughly grounded in a universe all elements of which—the physical and biological as well as the social and interpersonal —constitute a single moral order. Hence the paradigm fed the egocentric expectation that long life, good health, numerous offspring, and material prosperity immediately and inevitably reward the righteous individual. The book of Job is the classic literary challenge to the view, still prevalent in New Testament times, that personal misfortune evidences personal unrighteousness. Likewise in the social sphere, the ethnocentric and moralistic reading of its paradigmatic experiences fed the conviction that Israel's fortunes were precise functions of its loyalty or disloyalty to its covenant with Yahweh.

The essential logic of this imperialistic paradigm betrays, on the other hand, the paradoxical conviction that the ultimate factor in human history is not moral integrity but arbitrary power. Yahweh was originally the war god of desert tribes. The naked sanction of ethnic purity, even into New Testament times, was death by stoning. Under Yahweh's aegis, Israel conquered Palestine by force, sometimes being deliberately ruthless toward its victims. If Yahweh's presumed preference for Israel above all other peoples displays a feeling for the weak and oppressed, it also betrays the yearning of the weak and oppressed to wreak vengeance upon the strong, and it displays the impulse of the strong to serve their own narrow advantage rather than the common good of humankind. The ideological development of Yahwism constituted a communal commitment to imperialistic praxis in one form or another.

The figure of the messiah in the paradigm of ethnic imperialism. The exultant hopes aroused by David's conquest of Palestine projected the figure of the Messiah into a central role in the Yahwistic paradigm. David's astonishing victories would seem to have been impossible had

243

Israel not shifted from amphictyonic alliance to monarchial government under his leadership. By accepting David as Yahweh's Messiah, king by divine appointment, Israel submitted for the first time to the levy of taxes, the conscription of labor, the drafting of people for service in the army, and compulsory participation in battle.

The title messiah in its Hebrew form, *mašiaḥ*—as also in the Aramaic, *mešiḥa*, and the Greek *christos*—is simply a verbal adjective meaning "anointed." Our English equivalent derives from a Hellenized spelling of the Aramaic, *messias*. From David onward, anointment with oil at the hands of a prophet or priest was the indispensable legitimation of a king's claim to the throne of Israel. Priests, and seemingly prophets also, were anointed for office and thus were in some sense messiahs.[9] But thanks to David's political and military success, the unqualified phrase "messiah of Yahweh" in Hebrew literature is exclusively a synonym for the king, or for the whole Davidic dynasty, until in 587 B.C. Israel's hope in the monarchy as the chief instrument for the achievement of world empire was diminished as Nebuchadnezzar, impatient with repeated Israeli rebellion, destroyed Jerusalem with its temple and led Zedekiah and his people into ignominious exile. Still the expectation of a messiah in the lineage of David persisted into New Testament times.

Prophets and kingly messiahs led an uneasy coexistence in ancient Israel. By his anointment of David for kingship (ca. 1000 B.C.) and his prophetic proclamation of the covenant by which Yahweh raised David to the throne, the prophet Nathan legitimized the very institution of kingship. Eminent prophets throughout the monarchic period served as a check upon royal lust for absolute power, as guardians of the Yahwistic ethos against secularizing tendencies of royal government, and as the public voice of conscience. Indeed, for 150 years following David's enthronement, prophets were king-makers, using their power of anointment to make or break royal dynasties. As the pretensions of royalism began to whimper out under the blows of successive foreign invasions, Jeremiah came to regard the prophet himself, rather than the king, as the agent through whom Yahweh was acting to reform Israel and to move it toward its eschatological hegemony over all nations. He declared in effect that the oracle of Yahweh spoken through the true prophet causes the events of history to happen: "Behold, I have put my words in your mouth. See, I have set you this day over nations and over kingdoms, to pluck up and to break down, to destroy and to overthrow, to build and to plant [Jer. 1:9-10, RSV]." In the period of Persia's restoration of Jerusalem and the temple, Zechariah briefly aroused hopes that *two* messiahs (literally, "two sons of oil," Zechariah 4:14), Zerubbabel as king and Joshua as high priest, would be the co-agents through whom Yahweh would soon make public Yahweh's and Israel's until now cryptic imperium over Persia and all other peoples. Yahweh failed to honor Zechariah's oracle, and Darius dashed Israel's hopes by stripping the puppet Davidic dynasty of political power and by bending Joshua the high priest to his own imperial ends. This messianic fiasco marked the end of the Davidic dynasty and the passing of prophecy as a significant literary genre in Israel.

The prolonged Maccabean revolt, first against Grecian and later against Roman occupation, focused Israel's messianic expectation upon the figure of the high priest and upon the reconstructed temple. But the Hasmonean priest-kings proved to be a sorry lot of messiahs. Corrupt and weakened by internecine struggles for power, the Hasmoneans were no match for Pompey's legions, who crushed their revolt and tightened the Roman grip upon Israel.

Still the Yahwistic paradigm shaped the expectations and fired the imaginations of most Israelites. Under it, daily life was constrained by a fanatic stress upon ethnic purity, perceived as the precondition of Israel's assumption of its destined role among the nations.

In the evolving Yahwistic paradigm, the temple in Jerusalem emerged as the apparent hub of the universe. It not only served as the central cult site, but also functioned as the financial center of the province of Israel and as the focus for such remnants of theocracy as the Romans permitted the Israelis. A focus of political aspiration, it could serve in time of war as a citadel.

Mesmerized by the Yahwistic paradigm, radical groups still yearned for a priestly messiah or for a royal messiah in the succession of David. The power of the paradigm among a radical minority is most intensely exhibited in the literature originating within the Qumran community to describe its faith and praxis. This literature sets forth an expectation of two messiahs, one royal, the other priestly—both presumably destined to lead Israel into a cataclysmic war in which all humankind will be destroyed, saving only righteous Jews and those who convert to their cause. The wider prevalence of the Yahwistic paradigm in the New Testament era is evidenced in the fanatic zealotry of the actual Jewish wars, leading finally, in A.D. 70, to the destruction of the second temple by the Romans and the dispersion of the Jewish population.

The Historical Critique of the Yahwistic Paradigm

When current events no longer fit into a paradigmatic structure, the paradigm itself will sooner or later be called into question. That holds whether the paradigm be scientific and the events amenable to human control, or sociotheological and the events beyond scientific control. The virtual extinction of Northern Israel by Assyria, and the subsequent destruction of the temple and the Babylonian exile of Judah, precipitated in the "suffering servant" passages of Second Isaiah (Isaiah 52:13 —53:12), the classic literary challenge to the assumption, fundamental in the Yahwistic paradigm, that Israel's fortunes are precise functions of her loyalty or disloyalty to her covenant with Yahweh. That challenge greatly influenced the later development both of rabbinism and of Christianity. But the "suffering servant" concept does not in itself evidence the acceptance of a new paradigm of understanding and praxis in Israel.

The failure of royal messiahs in the Assyrian and Babylonian crises, together with the tyranny and eventual failure of the Hasmonean royal-priestly messiahs during the Greco-Roman occupation of a restored Judah, precipitated in the Parables of Enoch the classic literary repudiation of all traditional Israeli messiah figures.[10] In all previous Hebrew literature the term *mašiaḥ* designates some human agent through whom God blesses Israel, whether king, priest, prophet, Cyrus the Persian, or a future heir in the dynastic succession of David. The Parables of Enoch, second of five basically independent sections in the composite apocryphon of Enoch, employs the equivalent term, *christos,* to designate a preexistent heavenly being. In this usage, *christos* names a figment of a perfervid Jewish imagination, a purely ideal figure who will destroy heaven and earth, send sinners to everlasting punishment, abolish the kingdoms of this world, and establish the righteous in a new heaven and earth where this figure will reign at God's right hand forever. Three other titles, long current in the literature, are here also applied as proper names of this ideal figure. The "righteous [one]" (*dikaios=tsaddiq*), a descriptive name often given to people in the Old Testament, here becomes the Righteous One, a proper noun designating an abstraction, the ideal prototype of all human righteousness. The term (God's) "elect" (*bachir*) is widely applied in the Old Testament to Moses, David, Israel, the Servant; here the Elect One serves as the specific title of the figure who in the author's fantasy will deliver Israel. Daniel's metaphor for Israel triumphant, "one like a son of man [Dan. 7:13]," here becomes the Son of man, the proper name of the imaginary individual who will have everlasting dominion over a new heaven and earth after the eschatological judgment.

Projections of the human imagination are integral to paradigms, whether they be scientific or sociotheological. However, the messianic projections in the Parables of Enoch do not of themselves constitute a paradigm of human existence, for they make no claim that their realization was, or could be, sought in actual human praxis. Instead they signify a quietistic withdrawal from action and reality. When in the New Testament the same titles—Christ, the Righteous One, the Elect One, and the Son of man—are applied as proper names for Jesus of Nazareth, the situation has radically changed.

Jesus' Life and Crucifixion as a Paradigmatic Event

The very notion of a crucified Christ (*Christos, Mašiaḥ*) was a scandalous offense, if not to a majority of the first-century Israelite community, then certainly to a significant minority committed to a paradigmatic praxis the ultimate goal of which was ethnic imperialism. Yet an influential minority of Jews and gentiles of that century entered boldly upon a revolutionary way of life for which the paradigm was their understanding of the action, the teaching, and the consequent crucifixion of Jesus of Nazareth.

In the literature precipitated by this sociotheological revolution, there is no biography of Jesus, no news accounts of his crucifixion or of the events leading up to it. As with the Yahwistic paradigm, so also with the revolutionary Christic paradigm, wc havc access to the founding events only through a literature enjoining a particular praxis perceived as requisite for human salvation. Each praxis bases its claim to acceptance upon the assumption that the founding events, as understood in the particular case, truly exemplify the human situation as it really exists. In response to the intent of the literature itself, therefore, our highest priority is an examination of the distinctive features of each Christic paradigm as a guide to living. Since the alternate paradigm itself claims events in the life of Jesus as its empirical foundation, certain of those events emerge inevitably in an examination of the paradigm. But those events are remembered, selected, and presented for their paradigmatic function long after their occurrence, rather than in a strictly historical sequence and setting.

The Christic Paradigm of Integrated Ethnic Pluralism

The letters of Paul, written some fifteen to twenty years after the crucifixion of Jesus, constitute the oldest literary deposit reflecting the praxis and ideology of the primitive Christian community. Since Paul himself was a major contributor to the shaping of specifically Christian behavior and thought, we need to draw cautiously upon a later work by Luke, the Acts of the Apostles, for a fuller picture of the paradigmatic shift in which Paul figured so prominently.

Too often discounted is the fact, startling upon reflection, that Paul's first intimate experience with Christians came in mixed congregations of Jews and gentiles. Only later was he instructed in the Christian faith by leaders of the sect in Jerusalem. The subsequent formal approval by the

Jerusalem church of his mission to the gentiles clearly evidences a paradigmatic shift. That is to say, Paul had eventually won communal support within a Jewish minority for abandoning an ethos of imperialistic ethnic superiority and for deliberately adopting an ethos and praxis of integrative ethnic pluralism. The organic unity of the pan-ethnic Christian community and the maintenance of that unity in praxis are the burden of two of his most important pastoral letters (1 Corinthians and Galatians). Making few demands upon believers for his personal support, he vigorously promoted among the gentile churches a substantial collection for the church in Jerusalem. This offering of tribute was for Paul a symbolic act expressive of Christian unity, an acknowledgment that this emerging and potentially universal community had its origins in the experience of Israel, an ironic fulfillment of the faith that Yahweh's Christ would bring Israel to prominence among the peoples of the earth.

This was an ironic fulfillment, because the Christ proclaimed by this sect of the Nazarene was no figure of military and political power, but Jesus crucified. In the service of this Christ, Paul brought the collection to Jerusalem, by this time a hotbed of Zealotry. For reasons of security and of symbolic meaning, he was accompanied to Jerusalem with the gift by a caravan of other Christians, among whom were two uncircumcised Greeks. Paul's reputation for tolerance of uncircumcision had preceded him. His opponents spread the rumor that he had defiled the temple by bringing the two Greeks with him into an area of the temple forbidden to the uncircumcised. He was mobbed, then arrested by the Roman tribune for disturbing the peace. Protesting the impending use of the lash, he successfully appealed as a Roman citizen for a hearing before Caesar, and thus was brought eventually to Rome and to martyrdom.

In a variety of vivid but loosely constructed concepts, Paul expressed his perception of the system of realities within which his promotion of integrative ethnic pluralism was an appropriately responsible action, worthy of the risk of martyrdom. Those concepts derive inevitably from his own Jewish background, but their meanings shift with the perception of the crucified Jesus as the promised Christ who should redeem Israel. As might be expected, the ideological transformations by which he justified his praxis were therefore no less scandalous to his opponents than his revolutionary behavior itself.

One may reasonably infer that *Christ the Lord,* in Paul's usage, is a synonym for the *Spirit of God* as it has taken shape in the life of Jesus.[11] In any case, the Christ (Messiah), traditionally a precisely human medium of God's saving power, becomes for Paul metaphorically the preexistent *Son of God,* who by submitting to human birth, crucifixion,

248

and exaltation is revealed as the Lord of all creation (Philippians 2:5–11). Jesus Christ, biologically the son of David, is designated Son of God with power by the Holy Spirit through his resurrection from the dead (Romans 1:2–4). The spiritual renaissance coincident with the exaltation of Jesus convinced Paul that God works through compassionate, self-sacrificing resistance, rather than through punitive and imperialistic aggression, to overcome dehumanizing distortions in the interrelated processes of history. Thus in his view Jesus Christ by his crucifixion has overthrown the existing establishment (*kosmos*) and is bringing a new order into being. The old era is passing, the new age is dawning.

To accept Jesus as the Christ, according to Paul, is to die to the old establishment and to be born into the new. The believer dies with Christ and is raised with him to newness of life, a life that is hidden except to faith in Christ until the new age has fully come. What Paul says of himself he would hold to be true of all believers, insofar as he and they are faithful: "I have been crucified with Christ; it is no longer I who live, but Christ who lives in me, and the life I now live in the flesh I live by faith in the Son of God, who loved me and gave himself for me [Gal. 2:20, RSV]." He holds that the very recognition of God as Father (*Abba*) is an act of God himself within the believer (Romans 8:15-16). Indeed, the inarticulate yearnings of the believer's heart constitute a prayerful dialogue in which God as immanent Spirit speaks to the divine self through the transformed medium of the human unconscious (Rom. 8:26-27). The organic union of all believers is a Christic manifestation. In Christ all distinction among persons is transcended through systemic interdependence (1 Corinthians 14). The whole will never be under the imperium of any one of its parts. "For as many of you as were baptized into Christ have put on Christ. There is neither Jew nor Greek, there is neither slave nor free, there is neither male nor female; for you are all one in Christ Jesus. And if you are Christ's, then you are Abraham's offspring, heirs according to promise [Gal. 3:27-29, RSV]."

Paul's attitude toward Torah is a sore subject among those who reject or fail to understand the paradigm to which he was eventually converted by the Christ-event.[12] Within that new paradigm the ritual content of Torah is sharply distinguished from its moral content. Paul was tolerant of the idiosyncratic customs characteristic of ethnic groups, except as their practice undercut what he perceived to be the organic unity of humankind in Christ. That tolerance alone proved to be offensive enough to ethnic purists. For many, that offense is compounded by Paul's view that the deliberate effort to obey the ethical imperatives of Torah is a self-defeating enterprise.

For Paul, as for many sensitive Jews of his time, the commandments to love the source of life with all one's soul, mind, and strength, and to be concerned for the well-being of the neighbor as for one's own welfare comprised the essence of Torah. But the endeavor to obey those imperatives *because they are commanded* is really to love neither God nor self nor neighbor. The situation thus perceived is heteronomous, and its inherent goal is not love but sheer obedience. However, to accept these two commandments as the proper imperatives of one's own being, and hence to seek obedience in order to be such a lover, is no less self-defeating, for to love God and neighbor *in order to become what one ought to be* is to place the self before all others in the moral enterprise. By a similar analysis one can approach the Pauline understanding that *agape* is a charisma, the highest of all spiritual endowments, by which the self becomes the agent through whom the transcendent reality (Christ) affirms both the self and the neighbor. Thus Paul understood that in the praxis of *agape* the Christian becomes, so to speak, an element in a living feedback loop through which God's love returns enriched upon itself.

In Paul's perception, Torah as a system of imperatives brings to despair, and beyond despair it points to faith in Jesus Christ. Heteronomy and autonomy yield to Christonomy. This does not mean that the ethical imperatives of Torah are abrogated. That which remains eternally imperative when viewed as law becomes descriptive of those truly in Christ, for Christ himself fulfills in them all that is essentially imperative. Because for Paul the ethical demands of Torah constitute its essence, the open possibility of its charismatic fulfillment in Christ meant that all peoples are potentially children of Abraham and heirs equally of the promise, whether or not they observed circumcision, the dietary laws, and other ritualistic customs of Jewry.

The Gospel According to Mark, acknowledged to be the first of the gospel genre, was written in a time of persecution somewhat later than the letters of Paul. It preserves oral traditions promulgated among gentile Christians and shaped by their needs. Basically Mark rehearses events in the life of Jesus, taken by his intended readers as paradigmatic, in order to delineate and reinforce a characteristically Christian praxis, demanding renunciation, bearing one's cross, losing life in order to save it, and becoming a slave to other Christians, with special concern for the poor.

Mark relates the divine sonship of Jesus to the descent of the Holy Spirit at the time of Jesus' baptism by John. He places the ministry of Jesus principally in Galilee, a province notorious among Judeans for its ethnic tolerance. Mark mentions the teaching of Jesus often, but gives little of its content, stressing Jesus' proclamation that the eschatological kingdom of God is actually present. Mark's narrative employs Jesus' alternate presence with and withdrawal from his followers to maintain a mounting dramatic tension as the followers muddle through to an eventual understanding of what it means to be a true disciple. In the narrative Jesus' actions themselves become a proleptic and enigmatic manifestation of the kingdom of God, and his cryptic identity becomes that of the preexistent Son of man. The drama reaches its climax not in Galilee but in Jerusalem. Jesus' symbolic cleansing of the temple brought two conflicting ways of life into head-on collision and led finally to the enigma of his crucifixion. The narrative tension between presence and withdrawal escalates at his death, the final withdrawal.

If years later the mere rumor that Paul had brought two uncircumcised Greeks into temple territory forbidden to them aroused a mob against Paul, precipitating his arrest and eventual martyrdom, we can well understand that Jesus' symbolic challenge of the whole temple regime would bring the fury of the establishment down on him. Yet though the three synoptic writers agree on the critical importance of the cleansing of the temple, the full import of the episode is no longer entirely clear. That Jesus challenged the commercialization of the temple and profiteering within it seems evident. "Is it not written, 'My house shall be called a house of prayer for all [peoples] (*ethnesin*)'? But you have made it a den of robbers [Mark 11:17, RSV]." Moreover, the narratives of Matthew and Luke, following Mark, include the brief quotation from Isaiah 56:7, (RSV): "My house shall be called a house of prayer." But only Mark completes the quotation with the phrase "for all peoples," stressing thereby the original context in which foreign converts to Judaism are assured of welcome in the temple.

We cannot know whether Jesus' excoriation of the temple regime was also a protest against the narrow ethnocentrism later rejected by Paul and by leaders of the Christian sect in Jerusalem. That Mark himself considered the temple episode a rejection of priestly if not ethnic arrogance is obvious from the one awesome phenomenon he attributes to the death of Jesus on the cross: "And the curtain of the temple was torn in two, from top to bottom [Mark 15:38, RSV]." A curtain wall in the temple marked the line beyond which gentile men and women were forbidden; another curtain farther on marked the line beyond which Jewish women were forbidden. Still another marked the line beyond which even Jewish men were forbidden, except the high priest who once a year might pass through into the holy of holies.

The denouement of the authentic Markan narrative makes no appeal to resurrection appearances of Jesus to resolve the tension of his final withdrawal. We read instead of a young man who confronted the women in the otherwise abandoned tomb and bade them: "But go, tell his disciples and Peter that he is going before you to Galilee; there you will see him, as he told you [Mark 16:7, RSV]." The whole tenor of

Mark's Gospel is an exhortation to discipleship oriented to the expected presence (Parousia) of Jesus. And that expectation first centers not in the stronghold of Jewish ethnicity but in Galilee.

The Gospel According to Matthew is at once a denunciation of the ethnic arrogance current in Israel of the first century and a commission to citizens of a pan-ethnic Israel of the Spirit. Its message is addressed to readers thoroughly familiar with the literature and customs of first-century Judaism.

Matthew employs the preaching of John the Baptist to disparage biological descent from Abraham as the sufficient basis for membership in Israel. "Do not presume to say to yourselves, 'We have Abraham as our father'; for I tell you, God is able from these stones to raise up children to Abraham [Matt. 3:9, RSV]." By means of John's preaching, the narrative calls instead for spiritual kinship with Abraham. "Bear fruit that befits repentance. . . . Even now the axe is laid to the root of the trees; every tree therefore that does not bear good fruit is cut down and thrown into the fire [Matt. 3:8, 10, RSV]." Further, Matthew's narrative utilizes the action and the sayings of Jesus (the latter from a source Q[uelle], shared with Luke but unknown to Mark or neglected by him) to intensify the ethical demands of Torah while disparaging the idiosyncratic aspects of ethnic Judaism.

In Mark's narrative, Jesus is identified as the Christ and Son of God at his baptism. Matthew presses the identification back to his birth; he is born king of the Jews (Matthew 2:2). The narrator first assures us that Jesus' biological conception fulfills traditional expectations of the Messiah; he is descended from David and thus from Abraham. Yet, since according to Matthew biological descent from Abraham does not of itself make a true Israelite, he tells us that Jesus was conceived also by the Holy Spirit. Wilhelm Wuellner has pointed out to me that Matthew uses the detailed genealogy of Jesus as an ingenious literary device to pull the reader into the Gospel story in a way that also emphasizes spiritual descent from Abraham. Matthew summarizes the lineage of Jesus by reporting that there are fourteen generations from Abraham to David, fourteen from David to the deportation to Babylon, and fourteen from the deportation to the Christ. The careful reader will note, however, that in the third of the three sets of fourteen generations, Jesus is but the thirteenth generation. We are led to infer that readers of the Gospel constitute the Christic fourteenth generation, provided they love their enemies and pray for those who persecute them, thus giving evidence that they too are children (*huioi*) of God (cf. Matthew 5:45).[13]

Matthew's expansion of Mark's brief reference to the temptation of Jesus further dramatizes the shift away from the ethos of ethnic

252

imperialism. Given the political and religious climate in Judea of the first century, we may reasonably suppose that, by having Jesus quote Deuteronomy 8:3 in repudiating the first temptation, the narrator declares in effect that Jesus is no Moses redivivus leading Israel by a succession of miracles toward territorial conquest. By placing the second temptation in the temple setting and quoting Deuteronomy 6:16, with its reference to the episode at Massah (Exodus 17:7), the narrative effectively declares that Jesus is no priestly Messiah exploiting religion in the interest of ethnic dominance. The third temptation makes clear that in the mind of the narrator the dream of world conquest by royal armies is no less satanic; the kingdom over which Jesus reigns is not a kingdom like David's.

In the Matthean narrative, as in the Markan upon which it depends, Jesus' cleansing of the temple precipitates the events leading to his crucifixion. Matthew, however, elaborates the Markan post crucifixion scene by inserting two resurrection appearances of Jesus, the first to the women at the tomb, the second to the eleven apostles in Galilee, some of whom were doubtful about what they had seen. In this closing scene, Matthew's Gospel reaches its climactic charge to its readers in words ascribed to the risen Christ: "All authority in heaven and on earth has been given to me. Go therefore and make disciples of all [peoples] (*ethne*), baptizing them in the name of the Father and of the Son and of the Holy Spirit, teaching them to observe all that I have commanded you; and lo, I am with you always, to the close of the age [Matt. 28:18–20, RSV]." Jesus, the paradigm of the authentic Christ, is declared to be present among all peoples in the praxis of which he is the exemplar.

The Gospel According to Luke replicates about 70 percent of Mark's Gospel. Besides the sayings of Jesus from the Q source, it is worth noting for this discussion that Luke's Gospel shares exclusively with Matthew's the disparagement of biological descent from Abraham, ascribed to John the Baptist, as well as the expanded version of the temptation of Jesus. Thus the dramatic tension in Luke's narrative arises also from the confrontation of two sharply conflicted modes of human conduct and their respective ideologies. Ideologically, however, Luke is exceptional in portraying Jesus as the sole bearer of the Spirit prior to Pentecost. Incidentally, his version of the genealogy of Jesus goes back to "Seth, the son of Adam, the son of God [Luke 3:38, RSV]"; and he employs the voice of an angel to announce even before his birth that Jesus will be called "holy, the Son of God [Luke 1:35, RSV]."

The originality of Luke's narrative of that praxiological conflict is best seen, however, when his Gospel is studied in conjunction with the Acts of the Apostles, generally taken to be also his work. Where Mark and

Matthew end their narratives with attention centered in Galilee, Luke's narrative brings the apostles back from Galilee into Jerusalem to await Pentecost. He opens the narrative of Acts with an account of Pentecost as an earnest of the outpouring of the Spirit upon all flesh, as prophesied by Joel (Joel 2:28–32)—an outpouring that marks for the narrator the end of an era and the opening of a radically new age. In his account of Pentecost he dramatizes the ethnic transcendence of the Christian life by an ingenious literary device. He places in the scene devout Jews from every nation under heaven, *apo pantos ethnous ton hupo ton ouranon,* each in the tongue in which he was born, spoken by ecstatic Galilean Jews.

In the unified literary structure of Luke-Acts, the plot of the conflict between the actors, respectively representing the two opposed theological paradigms for living, approaches passionate climax three times before its final resolution. The setting in each instance is in Jerusalem. In the first instance the clash results in the crucifixion of Jesus; in the second instance, in the martyrdom of Stephen. In the third, the prolonged struggle brings about the mobbing and arrest of Paul and his arrival in Rome as a prisoner in chains. "The plot of Luke-Acts is resolved when in Acts 28 Paul breaks the structure of antagonism by ceasing to go to the Jews, preaching henceforth only to gentiles."[14]

The Gospel According to John, addressed to gentiles, relates the paradigmatic episodes of the Christ-event with notable divergencies from the chronology and locale specified in the synoptic Gospels. It differs from them also in that its message is rather more an ideological apologia than a praxiological exhortation, though it remains something of both.

The Christ is identified in the prologue of the Gospel as the Logos of God, the divine logic of the creative process, incarnate in the human flesh of Jesus for the renewal of moribund humankind. The narrator portrays *agape,* God's gracious love as manifested in the sending of the Son, as the dynamic of the kingdom of heaven on earth. That love brings believers into organic union one with another in Christ, even as it constitutes the organic unity in which God and Christ exist. This Johannine transformation of the Christic motif, however, does not fulfill its potential for a universally comprehensive ontology in which at the deepest level believer and unbeliever share common ground, for the dramatic conflict between living actors in the narrative concretizes a universal opposition between mutually exclusive symbolic abstractions suggesting a dualism that remains unresolved: darkness against light, love against hate, life against death. Though the function of these oppositions in the creative process remains ambiguous, their meaning at the existential level is clear. Not to trust in Jesus as the Christ is to reject

254

the abundant life he offers, for he is the way, the truth, and the life.

In the Johannine Gospel, however, opposition to Jesus by the living actors in the narrative is not confined to the reactionary leaders in the Israelite establishment; he is persecuted, rejected, and crucified by "the Jews," the people of Israel as a whole. Thus the narrative communicates a reverse discrimination of gentile Christians against Jews. As an ideological account of the Christian paradigm it is infected by the disease of ethnic imperialism of which Christian praxis originally professed to be the cure.

The letter to the Colossians, with supporting evidence from Ephesians, is here selected to illustrate one terminal development of the Christic paradigm of ethnic pluralism within the canon of New Testament literature. In the Christic hymn imbedded in Colossians 1:15–20, the ideological evolution of the paradigm climaxes in the declaration that all things whatsoever are systemically interrelated in Christ. Thus the oneness of things in Christ is seen as more than pan-ethnic; it embraces all creation without exception.

Here the Christ is identified as the image of the invisible God, the firstborn of all creation. It is generally agreed that in this context *image* and *firstborn* are titles of sovereignty deriving from the ancient ideology of kingship. Thus the employment of the metaphors implies the sovereignty of Christ over all creation. To insist, however, that as here used the metaphors carry no ontological implication is to impose orthodoxy upon the obvious ambiguity of the text—an ambiguity evidenced in the long history of controversy as to its meaning. The influence of Philo or of the Stoics cannot be excluded, and nothing in the text itself prohibits the inference that though born, not made, Christ is an invariant aspect of the created order.[15] The politics of dogmatic interpretation, insistent that in all Christian literature *theos* and *kosmos* are elements of a radical dualism, tend to blind us to the possibility that Colossians advances neither theocosmic dualism nor pantheism, but an innovative panentheism.

Postponing for the moment the discussion of a possible panentheistic interpretation, the text clearly declares that all things in heaven and on earth, visible and invisible, were created in Christ, by him, and for him. He is at once the source, the agent, and the goal of their continuing existence. We commonly think of all institutions of the human social order as created by humankind. Colossians affirms that, no matter what their proximate agency, thrones, dominions, principalities, and powers are among the things created in, by, and for Christ.[16] He precedes all things both in time and in dignity. In him all things stand together (Colossians 1:17).

Possible warrant for a panentheistic interpretation can be found in the declaration that in Christ "all things hold together." The use of the verb *synesteken* (stand or hold together), from which the Greek noun *systema* and our term system derive, implies that all creatures constitute a group of interdependent and interacting elements of an indivisible whole whose functions transcend the mere sum of the functions of its constituent parts. Thus interpreted, the term *Christos* in this cosmology symbolizes and personifies the presumed fact that all created novelties —in their becoming, in their continued existence, and in their perishing —constitute not a chaos, but a cosmos; and the further presumption that every part of the cosmos systemically interrelates with every other. Let one portion miss the goal inherent in its design, and all parts are at least remotely modified, as indeed is the whole in which it exists.[17]

This bold paradigmatic assumption is of course subject to no more than provisional verification or falsification in praxis; it is never capable of conclusive proof. But then "the notion implicit in the word universe [also] expresses an act of faith, for it [likewise] projects system far beyond the evidence."[18]

Parenthetically, although it challenges the radical dualism of *theos* and *kosmos,* this interpretation is quite compatible with the orthodox concern for monotheism. The conception of God as the Father of Christ can here be understood as symbolizing the aboriginal nexus of possibilities preceding every novel event, a nexus infinitely richer than the sum total of possibilities ever actualized in any particular phase of cosmic evolution. Thus the metaphor, "God the Father," is at least remotely analogous to Alfred North Whitehead's conception of the primordial nature of God, rich in potentiality, ever deficient in actuality.[19] God the Father, the invisible God, denotes in this conception the awesome, inexplicable wonder we face when we look profoundly into the antecedents of any emergent novelty.

The symbol "Christ the Son of God" personifies in like manner the invariant aspect of the creative process in its continuous movement from potentiality to actuality, namely, its systemic character. Thus the symbol of the cosmic Christ is roughly analogous to Whitehead's conception of the consequent nature of God, the dynamic principle of concrescence. In this context, therefore, the father-son metaphor does not compromise monotheism but rather denotes a dipolar theism. It points in personalistic metaphors to the polar tension between potentiality and actuality in the successive phases of the evolutionary process.

In this panentheistic interpretation, the coherence of all things in Christ means that all systemic phenomena are seen as theophanies. One New Testament author expressly proposes that love (*agape*) is a theophany: *Ho theos agape estin!* (1 John 4:16). God as manifest at the level of interpersonal relations is love. Thus qualified, the subject of this proposition may become the predicate. Love is God as manifest at the level of interpersonal relations. The theological cosmology of Colossians implies, subject to such careful qualification, a series of epiphanies ranging in amplitude through every level of the total cosmos. Every occurrence of physical, chemical, psychological, social or spiritual bonding; every instance of cohesion, however minute and seemingly insignificant; every linkage, whether sensible or intelligible; every assimilation into a concrescent whole; the biosphere, every ecological system, each living organism, including every human being; every social construct, including every government, every gang, every conspiracy; every cultural construct, including languages, ideologies, value systems; every instance of either erotic or of altruistic love—insofar as it is a holding of things together, each and every one by implication is here claimed to be a theophany, that is, a spatio-temporal appearance of the cosmic Christ. Christ, in some degree of amplitude, is physically present in every object, incarnate in all living flesh.

Though every human being incarnates Christ, the human family is nevertheless in bondage, seduced into serving the elements of the cosmos (*stoicheia tou kosmou*) rather than the indivisible whole of which they are organic parts (Colossians 2:8, 20; see also Galatians 4:3, 9).

Contrary to much recent scholarship, the *stoicheia tou kosmou* are not figures of an esoteric mythology, but, as Walter Wink has shown, the elemental constituents of the actual cosmos.[20] Thus Colossians 2:8 warns not against philosophy as such, which is an intrinsic element of human cultural experience, but against praxis based upon philosophies that reduce the cosmos to "nothing but" the lowest common denominator of its constituent elements (as if a professed lover cherished the object of his or her affection for sexuality alone). Colossians 2:20 counts religiosity as among the inherent elements of the human cosmos and warns not against ritual, celebration, and ethnic traditions as such, but against religion and ethos pursued as ends in themselves—against fanatic, xenophobic, or merely empty formalism, be it Jewish or pagan.

In like manner the apostle Paul, in Galatians 4:3, reckons the Jewish Torah as among the elements of the universe.[21] But in that context he implies that to face the law as a person capable of fulfilling its demands out of one's own resources isolates one from the indispensable support of the full community of being in Jesus Christ. His upbraiding of the Galatians for turning "back again to the weak and beggarly [elements] whose slaves you want to be once more [Gal. 4:9, RSV]," condemns religiosity in which human relation with the elements of the universe is distorted by the superstitious fantasy to which religions are so easily and so often perverted.[22]

The supreme healing and reconciling incarnation of the cosmic Christ, according to Colossians, is the crucified carpenter of Nazareth: "For in him the whole fulness of deity dwells bodily [Col. 2:9, RSV]." His crucifixion liberates the human family from the perversions of religion (Colossians 2:13-14). Though they crucified him, he despoiled and exposed the principalities and powers of the perverse religious establishment, even as a conquering general might expose naked captives in a triumphal march through the streets of Rome. His cross, indeed, was their undoing (Colossians 2:15). While the text stresses the role of the religious establishment in the crucifixion, all human institutions (e.g., thrones), indeed, all subsystems within the creation, are implicated in the defection, and all are subject to the reconciliation initiated by the blood of the cross (Colossians 1:15-20; cf. Romans 8:22). However indispensable in a human cosmos, government too readily becomes entrapment; bondings, bondage; authorities, authoritarianism; managerial hierarchies, imperialisms. Speaking mythically, Christ himself becomes the victim of the monstrous distortions among the systems that constitute his living body.

The praxis implicit in this theological paradigm is resistance of pernicious distortions within the subsystems of creation—resistance perceived as in the service of the indivisible and surpassingly personal whole of which human life is a flowering. Parenthetically, Ephesians 6:12 implies that the struggle is not against the particular persons wielding power in a system, but against the perverted systems of power as such. The subversion of subsystems appears, of course, to be the inevitable risk of a divine creativity in which creatures have a relative independence one of another and within the total creative process. The subverted principalities and powers are seen to hold sway by the threat of death; the human family is seen to submit out of fear of death. Hence this praxis involves a proleptic participation in the death and burial of Christ in baptism, and resurrection with him to a new life beyond the fear of death. Whatever the full meaning of resurrection in the narratives circulating after Jesus' crucifixion, the behavior of early Christians in the face of devastating persecutions evidences a quality of life that they themselves regarded as a resurrection, a sharing of Christ's immortality, here and now (Colossians 2:12-13; cf. Romans 6:3-5). "When Christ who is our life appears, then you also will appear with him in glory [Col. 3:4, RSV]."

Since the early days of the Christian social revolution, the paradigm of an integrated ethnic pluralism has been more admired than practiced. Institutionalized Christianity soon ceased to be an open, integratively transforming movement of the human spirit and became instead a dogmatically repressive, proselytizing sect. The crucifixion largely

258

ceased to be a symbol of resistance to the perverse powers of this world. It became instead a model for enduring exploitation in this life in the hope of joyful freedom in the next. Resurrection largely ceased to be a metaphor of liberation for abundant life in overcoming the perversions of the actual world. It became instead a rationalization of a compulsive escape from the fear of physical death into a world of fantasy. Institutional Christianity adopted the accoutrements of imperial power and even resorted at times to capital punishment to enforce observance of its ethos.

So-called theocracies, long recognized for the fraud they are, have given way in most of the world to a separation of church and state. But integrated ethnic pluralism is no more the prevalent praxis in modern secular states than in world religions. Indeed, contemporary national-isms are openly and covertly committed to the paradigm of ethnic imperialism. Each clings to the myth of absolute sovereignty in its internal affairs. All betray in praxis the conviction that the ultimate determinant of human relations is not moral suasion but coercive physical power, economic or military. From this perspective, the cosmos is not an indivisible system of which the human family is a living part, but an alien object subject to our dominion through ever-expanding technological control.

The relative merit of competing scientific paradigms is finally deter-mined not by the number of their adherents at a particular time but by their respective capacity to resolve the riddle of perplexing observations and to open new avenues of scientific investigation. Theological para-digms likewise are eventually brought up against the enigmas and ironies consequent upon their praxis. Nevertheless, a radical shift in praxis, whether based upon scientific or upon existential commitments, can be exceedingly difficult, because perception of the consequences of praxis is to a large extent paradigmatically determined.

If the human family continues a praxis dominated by the paradigm of competition and ethnic imperialism, the foreseeable escalation of physical violence raises grave questions as to the merits of the paradigm itself. Shall access to diminishing supplies of fossilized energy be determined by inflation and by eventual resort to the neutron bomb against civilian populations? Shall we let our ethnic xenophobia prolong the escalation of nuclear overkill? And shall the pressure of the human population upon finite resources be resolved by a rapid technological rape of the global ecology until plague and famine take over? Can we trust the future of land and water use to competition among special-interest groups? Or will mounting evidences of interdependence move us toward a paradigmatic revolution long since begun but never consummated? Will the holding together of all things encourage us to overtures of trust and mutual cooperation based on a perception of an indivisible cosmos of which we all are children? Is the cosmos really our enemy to be conquered, or is it our Mother and our Father, "our help in ages past, our hope for years to come, . . . and our eternal home"? What embodiment of the cosmic Christ shall we serve, then: the Nazarene or Caesar?

Notes

PREFACE

1. Webster's New Collegiate Dictionary (Springfield, MA: G.&C. Merriam Co., 1979), p. 196.
2. Ibid., p. 849.

CHAPTER 1:
CHRISTOLOGICAL PERSPECTIVES:
THE CONTEXT OF CURRENT DISCUSSIONS

1. Adolf von Harnack, *What Is Christianity?* trans. Thomas Bailey Saunders (New York: Harper & Bros., 1957), p. 128.
2. Ibid., p. 144.
3. Ibid., p. 184.
4. E.g., Jon Sobrina, *Christology at the Crossroads: A Latin-American Approach,* trans. John Drury (Maryknoll, NY: Orbis Books, 1978); or Hans Küng, *On Being a Christian,* trans. Edward Quinn (New York: Doubleday, 1976).
5. Richard Heirs and David Holland, eds., *Jesus' Proclamation of the Kingdom of God* (Philadelphia: Fortress Press, 1971).
6. See *The Mystery of the Kingdom of God,* trans. Walter Lowrie (New York: Macmillan, 1950); and *The Quest of the Historical Jesus,* trans. F.C. Burkitt (New York: Macmillan, 1968), chaps. 19, 20.
7. William Wrede, *Das Messiasgeheimnis in den Evangelien* (Göttingen: Vandenhoeck & Ruprecht, 1901).
8. English ed.: Martin Kähler, *The So-called Historical Jesus and the Historic, Biblical Christ,* trans. and ed. Carl E. Braaten (Philadelphia: Fortress Press, 1964).
9. Still the most thorough form-critical analysis is Rudolf Bultmann's *History of the Synoptic Tradition,* trans. John Marsh (New York: Harper & Row, 1976).
10. See, e.g., Karl Barth's "The Strange New World Within the Bible," in *The Word of God and the Word of Man,* trans. Douglas Horton (London: Hodder & Stoughton, 1928), pp. 28–50. It was that "strange new world" which lay at the center of Barth's then "new theology," still frequently labeled as neoorthodoxy.
11. This small book has now gone through many publications; it was first published in 1936 by Hodder & Stoughton (London).
12. Some recent studies include C.F.D. Moule, *The Origin of Christology* (Cambridge: Cambridge University Press, 1977); I.H. Marshall, *The Origins of New Testament Christology* (Downers Grove, IL: Inter-Varsity Press, 1976);

Walter Kasper, *Jesus the Christ,* trans. V. Green (New York: Paulist Press, 1976).

13. Reginald H. Fuller, *The Foundations of New Testament Christology* (New York: Charles Scribner's Sons, 1965); Ferdinand Hahn, *The Titles of Jesus in Christology,* trans. Harold Knight and George Ogg (New York: World, 1969); see also Oscar Cullmann, *The Christology of the New Testament,* trans. Shirley C. Guthrie and Charles A.M. Hall (Philadelphia: Westminster Press, 1964).

14. Rudolf Bultmann, *Theology of the New Testament,* trans. Kendrick Grobel (New York: Charles Scribner's Sons, 1951), 1:3.

15. See Bultmann, *History of the Synoptic Tradition,* op. cit.

16. Rudolf Bultmann, *Jesus and the Word,* trans. Louise Pettibone Smith (New York: Charles Scribner's Sons, 1958), p. 12.

17. See Rudolf Bultmann, "Christology of the New Testament," in *Faith and Understanding,* ed. R. Funk (New York: Harper & Row, 1969), pp. 262–85.

18. See Fuller, op. cit.; and Hahn, op. cit.

19. Harvey McArthur, "From the Historical Jesus to Christology," *Interpretation* 23, no. 2 (1969): 190–206.

20. Originally published under the German title "Das Problem des historischen Jesus," in *Zeitschrift für Theologie und Kirche* 51 (1954): 125–33; English trans. in *Essays on New Testament Themes,* trans. W.J. Montague (Naperville, IL: Alec R. Allenson, 1964), pp. 15–47.

21. James M. Robinson, *A New Quest of the Historical Jesus* (Naperville, IL: Alec R. Allenson, 1959).

22. Günther Bornkamm, *Jesus of Nazareth,* trans. Irene and Fraser McLuskey, with J.M. Robinson (New York: Harper & Bros., 1960).

23. Bultmann, "Christology of the New Testament," op. cit., p. 283.

24. Bornkamm, op. cit., esp. pp. 25–26, 171ff.

25. Ernst Fuchs, "Jesus' Understanding of Time," in *Studies of the Historical Jesus,* trans. A. Scobie (London: SCM Press, 1964), pp. 104–65.

26. Willi Marxsen, *The Beginnings of Christology: A Study in Its Problems,* trans. Paul J. Achtemeier (Philadelphia: Fortress Press [Facet Books]. 1969).

27. Ibid., p. 19.

28. See Hans Conzelmann, *Jesus,* trans. J. Raymond Lord (Philadelphia: Fortress Press, 1973); Reginald Fuller, *The New Testament in Current Study* (New York: Charles Scribner's Sons, 1962), p. 33; Ferdinand Hahn, "The Quest of the Historical Jesus and the Special Character of the Sources Available to Us." in *What Can We Know of Jesus?* trans. Grover Foley (Philadelphia: Fortress Press, 1969), pp. 44–48; Norman Perrin, *Rediscovering the Teaching of Jesus* (New York: Harper & Row, 1967), pp. 15–49; that same principle of dissimilarity provides the chief criterion for Herbert Braun's reconstruction of the ministry of Jesus in *Jesus of Nazareth,* trans. Everett Kalin (Philadelphia: Fortress Press, 1979). See also chapter 3 above.

29. Marxsen, op. cit., p. 21 (italics added).

30. Ibid., pp. 32–33.

31. Bultmann, *Theology of the New Testament,* op. cit., 1:30ff. See, e.g., Mark 8:38 and other synoptic passages where the apocalyptic use of the title appears always as a third-person reference.

32. See, e.g., Moule, op. cit., pp. 11ff.

33. H.B. Sharman, *Son of Man and Kingdom of God* (New York: Harper & Bros., 1943).

34. Philipp Vielhauer, "Gottesreich und Menschensohn in der Verkündigung

Jesu," in *Aufsätze zum Neuen Testament* (Munich: Chr. Kaiser Verlag, 1965), pp. 55–91.

35. Hans Conzelmann, *An Outline of the Theology of the New Testament,* trans. John Bowden (New York: Harper & Row, 1969), p. 6; see also Conzelmann, *Jesus,* op. cit., pp. 43ff.

36. See esp. Norman Perrin, "The Son of Man in Ancient Judaism and Primitive Christianity: A Suggestion," in his *A Modern Pilgrimage in New Testament Christology* (Philadelphia: Fortress Press, 1974), pp. 23ff.

37. H. Riesenfeld, *The Gospel Tradition and Its Beginning* (London: A.R. Mowbray, 1957); see also the much more detailed study of Birger Gerhardsson, *Memory and Manuscript,* trans. Eric J. Sharpe (Lund: G.W.K. Gleerup, 1961). An even earlier suggestion of this approach can be seen in Nils Dahl, "Anamnesis: Memory and Commemoration in Early Christianity," originally a lecture given at Oslo in 1946 and now published in a recent collection of Dahl's essays, *Jesus in the Memory of the Early Church* (Minneapolis: Augsburg, 1976), pp. 11–29.

38. See esp. Vincent Taylor, *The Life and Ministry of Jesus* (Nashville: Abingdon Press, 1955), pp. 13–50; see also T.W. Manson, *Studies in the Gospels and Epistles* (Philadelphia: Westminster Press, 1962), esp. pp. 3–12, 20–27, 40 45.

39. The overall results of Joachim Jeremias' studies are clearly apparent in his *New Testament Theology,* trans. John Bowden (New York: Charles Scribner's Sons, 1971), pp. 61ff.

40. Cullmann, op. cit., pp. 283ff.

41. Werner Georg Kümmel, *The Theology of the New Testament,* trans. John E. Steely (Nashville: Abingdon Press, 1973), pp. 71–73.

42. Moule, op. cit.

43. Ibid., pp. 1–10.

44. Ibid., p. 5.

45. Ibid., pp. 138–41.

46. Marshall, op. cit.

47. Martin Hengel, *Judaism and Hellenism,* trans. John Bowden (Philadelphia: Fortress Press, 1974).

48. Martin Hengel, *The Son of God,* trans. John Bowden (Philadelphia: Fortress Press, 1976).

49. Ibid., pp. 63–66.

50. Rudolf Bultmann, *Jesus Christ and Mythology* (New York: Charles Scribner's Sons, 1958).

51. Van Harvey, *The Historian and the Believer* (New York: Macmillan, 1966), esp. chap. 8, where Harvey discusses the issue of "once-for-allness" with respect to the event of Jesus. See further Schubert Ogden, *Christ Without Myth* (New York: Harper & Bros., 1961), in which the author argues that Bultmann was inconsistent in not carrying his demythologizing program through to the historical Jesus.

52. Wilhelm Bousset, *Kyrios Christos,* trans. John E. Steely (Nashville: Abingdon Press, 1970).

53. See Rudolf Bultmann, *Primitive Christianity in Its Contemporary Setting,* trans. R.H. Fuller (Cleveland: World, 1956). See also his *Theology of the New Testament,* in which Bultmann's discussion of pre-Pauline and Pauline Christianity assumes the presence of this formative Hellenistic background; see esp. 1:63, the opening paragraph.

54. Bultmann, *Primitive Christianity,* op. cit. pp. 176–77.

55. Bousset, op cit., pp. 8–9.

56. W.D. Davies, *Paul and Rabbinic Judaism* (1948; reprint ed., New York: Harper & Bros., 1967).

57. Ibid., pp. 150ff.

58. See Krister Stendahl, *Paul Among Jews and Gentiles* (Philadelphia: Fortress Press, 1976); this collection of essays includes his now famous article "The Apostle Paul and the Introspective Conscience of the West," originally published in *Harvard Theological Review* 56 (1963): 199–215.

59. Hengel, op. cit.

60. E.P. Sanders, *Paul and Palestinian Judaism* (Philadelphia: Fortress Press, 1977).

61. That view is essentially taken in Samuel Sandmel, *Judaism and Christian Beginnings* (New York: Oxford University Press, 1978).

62. Hahn, *The Titles of Jesus in Christology,* op.cit., pp. 103ff.

63. Ibid., pp. 89ff.

64. Bultmann, *Jesus and the Word,* op.cit., pp. 12ff.

65. Rudolf Bultmann, *Kerygma and Myth,* ed. H.W. Bartsch (New York: Harper & Bros., 1961), p. 42.

66. Conzelmann, *Jesus,* op.cit., p. 94.

67. Willi Marxsen, *The Resurrection of Jesus of Nazareth,* trans. Margaret Kohl (Philadelphia: Fortress Press, 1970), pp. 138–48.

68. Bultmann, *Kerygma and Myth,* op. cit. p. 41 (italics mine).

69. See, e.g., Conzelmann, *Jesus,* op. cit., pp. 94–95.

70. Wolfhart Pannenberg, *Jesus—God and Man,* trans. Lewis Wilkins and Duane Priebe (Philadelphia: Westminster Press, 1968).

71. Ibid., pp. 108–14.

72. Küng, *On Being a Christian,* op. cit., p. 351; Küng's italics.

73. Ibid., p. 352.

74. John Hick, ed., *The Myth of God Incarnate* (Philadelphia: Westminster Press, 1977).

75. Ibid., p. ix.

76. See note 51, above.

CHAPTER 3:
THE CRITERION OF DISSIMILARITY:
THE WRONG TOOL?

1. Reginald H. Fuller, *A Critical Introduction to the New Testament* (London: Duckworth, 1966), pp. 94–98; Norman Perrin, *Rediscovering the Teaching of Jesus* (New York: Harper & Row, 1967), pp. 39–47.

2. Rudolf Bultmann, *History of the Synoptic Tradition* (Oxford: Blackwell, 1972), p. 205.

3. Hans Conzelmann, *Jesus,* trans. J. Raymond Lord (Philadelphia: Fortress Press, 1973), p. 16.

4. Morna D. Hooker, *The Son of Man in Mark* (Montreal: McGill University, 1967), pp. 6–7; F. Gerald Downing, *The Church and Jesus,* Studies in Biblical Theology 2/10 (London: SCM Press, 1968), pp. 111–30; Morna D. Hooker, "Christology and Methodology," *New Testament Studies* 17 (1970/71): 480–87;

R.S. Barbour, *Traditio-Historical Criticism of the Gospels: Some Comments on Current Methods* (London: SPCK, 1972), pp. 1–27; D.G.A. Calvert, "An Examination of the Criteria for Distinguishing the Authentic Words of Jesus," *New Testament Studies* 18 (1971/72): 209–19; Morna D. Hooker, "On Using the Wrong Tool," *Theology* 75 (1972): 570–81; R.T. France, in *History, Criticism, and Faith,* ed. C. Brown (Downers Grove, IL: Inter-Varsity Press, 1976), pp. 108–17; Eric Mascall, *Theology and the Gospel of Christ,* (London: SPCK, 1977), pp. 87–97; I. Howard Marshall, *I Believe in the Historical Jesus* (London: Hodder & Stoughton, 1977), pp. 201–3.

5. "On Using the Wrong Tool," op. cit. Mascall merely repeats Hooker's arguments in this article. Marshall repeats some of them.

6. "The Dissimilarity Test," *Scottish Journal of Theology* 31 (1978): 41–50. I am greatly indebted to this article.

7. E.g., Hooker, "On Using the Wrong Tool," op. cit., p. 575.

8. E.g., Ibid., p. 576.

9. E.g., Calvert, op. cit., pp. 212, 214; France, op. cit., p. 112.

10. Hooker, "Christology and Methodology," op. cit., p. 481; "On Using the Wrong Tool," op. cit., p. 574.

11. Hooker, "On Using the Wrong Tool," op. cit., p. 576.

12. Calvert, op. cit., p. 219; Hooker, "Christology and Methodology," op. cit., p. 486; France, op. cit., p. 114. Already Oscar Cullmann had made the same point in "Unzeitmässige Bemerkungen zum 'historischen Jesus' der Bultmannschule," in Helmut Ristow and Karl Matthias, eds., *Der historische Jesus und der kerygmatische Christus* (Berlin: Evangelische Verlagsanstalt, 1961), pp. 266–80, esp. p. 277; also Oscar Cullmann, *Salvation in History* (New York: Harper & Row, 1967), p. 18.

13. Raymond E. Brown, *The Birth of the Messiah: A Commentary on the Infancy Narratives in Matthew and Luke* (New York: Doubleday, 1977), pp. 29–32 and elsewhere.

14. I would argue in general for adaptation rather than creation. Nearly all the principal synoptic messianic titles, Christos, Kyrios, Son of God, Son of David, Son of man, have *some* roots in the authentic Jesus material, even though none of them was used directly as a self-designation by Jesus himself.

15. E.g., France, op. cit., p. 110.

16. These statements summarize the findings of various participants in the New Quest (Käsemann, Fuchs, Bornkamm, Conzelmann). It is gratifying that John A.T. Robinson, after a period in which he one-sidedly (though in the British situation understandably) emphasized the human side of Jesus, has most recently taken up this God-sidedness of Jesus from Fuchs and others; see J.A.T. Robinson, *Can We Trust the New Testament?* (Grand Rapids, MI: Eerdmans, 1977), pp. 104–7.

17. See, e.g., A.M. Hunter, *Paul and His Predecessors* (London: SCM Press, 1961).

18. The debate on pre-Lukan elements in the kerygmatic speeches of Acts continues. A reasonable position is that of Eduard Schweizer, "Concerning the Speeches in Acts," in *Studies in Acts,* ed. Leander E. Keck and L. Louis Martyn (Nashville: Abingdon, 1966), pp. 208–16. As they stand, the Acts speeches are Lukan compositions, but they enshrine pre-Lukan and primitive christological materials.

19. As happens in Hooker's treatment of the Son-of-man material in *The Son of Man in Mark,* op. cit.

20. Leander E. Keck, *A Future for the Historical Jesus* (Nashville: Abingdon Press, 1971), p. 262.

21. It is incorrect to say that Bultmann sees the eschatological emphasis as "wholly future" (ibid.). It is a future that decisively qualifies the present. The kingdom is "schon im Anbruch" (Rudolf Bultmann, *Theology of the New Testament* [London: SCM Press, 1952], 1:7).

22. E.g., "Christology," p. 486.

23. As far as I am aware, the only critic to eliminate implicit 1:7 as well as explicit Christology from the authentic Jesus material is Howard M. Teeple, "The Origin of Son of Man Christology," *Journal of Biblical Literature* 84 (1965): 211–50, esp. p. 227.

24. As when I overconfidently eliminated the logion Matthew 5:17 from the Jesus material, in *A Critical Introduction to the New Testament,* op. cit., p. 96.

CHAPTER 4:
DID JESUS HAVE A DISTINCTIVE USE OF SCRIPTURE?

1. In *Interpretation* 23, no. 2 (April 1969): 190–206.

2. F.W. Dillistone, *C.H. Dodd: Interpreter of the New Testament* (Grand Rapids, MI: Eerdmans, 1977), pp. 242–43.

3. C.H. Dodd, *According to the Scriptures* (London: Nisbet & Co., 1952), p. 110.

4. Kurt Aland et al., eds., *The Greek New Testament* (New York: United Bible Societies, 1966). I have used for this purpose the first edition (1966) in preference to the third (1975), since the latter uses boldface type only for direct quotations. In only one case (John 7:42), however, where the quotation was evidently regarded as too free to count, does this affect only the first, allusive use.

5. Matthew Black, "The Christological Use of the Old Testament in the New Testament," *New Testament Studies* 18 (1971–72): 11–14.

6. Joachim Jeremias, *New Testament Theology* (London: SCM Press, 1971), pp. 29–37.

CHAPTER 5:
JESUS AND ISRAEL:
THE STARTING POINT FOR NEW TESTAMENT CHRISTOLOGY

1. For this distinction, see C.F.D. Moule, *The Origin of Christology* (Cambridge: Cambridge University Press, 1977), pp. 1–10.

2. See P.W. Schmiedel, "The Gospels," in *Encyclopaedia Biblica* 1 (1881 –83).

3. Morna D. Hooker, "Christology and Methodology," *New Testament Studies* 17 (1970/71): 480–87. But cf. Fuller's discussion in chapter 3 above.

4. Cf. H.R. Balz, *Methodische Probleme in der neutestamentlichen Christologie* (Neukirchen-Vluyn: Neukirchener Verlag, 1967).

5. Moule, op. cit., pp. 46ff.

6. This argument of Moule's is complementary to, but not identical with, the case so forcefully made by James Denney in *The Death of Christ,* 5th ed. (New York: Armstrong, 1907), that soteriology takes logical precedence over Christol-

ogy; the early church first asked what it was that Jesus had done, and the answers to that question prompted the further question about who Jesus was.

7. Particularity is inherent not only in the life of Jesus, but also in his teaching; he taught his disciples to love their neighbors, not humankind.

8. Moule, op. cit., pp. 129, 131.

9. T.W. Manson, *The Teaching of Jesus* (Cambridge: Cambridge University Press, 1943), pp. 171–236; C.H. Dodd, *According to the Scriptures* (London: Nisbet & Co., 1952); Johannes Munck, *Paul and the Salvation of Mankind* (Richmond: John Knox Press, 1959); Joachim Jeremias, *Jesus' Promise to the Nations* (London: SCM Press, 1958).

10. George B. Caird, *Jesus and the Jewish Nation* (London: Althone Press, 1965).

11. See, e.g., the tradition alluded to in Romans 4:13, that Abraham was promised the world as his inheritance.

12. Matthew 15:24 is an editorial addition to the version of Mark, which makes explicit what was implicit in the saying about giving the children's bread to dogs.

13. The letter of James is addressed specifically to "the twelve tribes in the Dispersion," but it is less certainly intended for gentiles.

14. C.H. Dodd, *Historical Tradition in the Fourth Gospel* (Cambridge: Cambridge University Press, 1975), pp. 112–20, 216–17, 430.

15. E.g., to sin according to the pattern of Adam's transgression (Romans 5:12, 14) and to die as Adam died (1 Corinthians 15:22).

16. Similarly, in 1 Corinthians 15:22 Paul does not say "in Adam all died" but "in Adam all die," because he is thinking of Adam not as a figure of ancient history but as a contemporary phenomenon. When he comes to speak of Adam in the individual, primeval sense, he calls him explicitly "the first man," but also defines him as "the image of the man of dust" (15:45–48).

17. It is a curious and persistent illusion that this opening paragraph has as its referent the preexistent Wisdom or Logos. However exalted and from whatever sources the language, our author leaves us in no doubt that the events alluded to have happened in "these last days" and that the person being talked about from start to finish is the man Jesus.

CHAPTER 6:

THE CHRISTOLOGICAL FOUNDATION OF EARLY CHRISTIAN PARENESIS

1. Martin Dibelius, *Die Formgeschichte des Evangeliums,* ed. G. Bornkamm (Tübingen, 1919, ²1933, ⁶1971); idem, *Der Brief des Jakobus,* ed. H. Greeven, Kritisch-exegetischer Kommentar 15, 11th ed. (Göttingen, ⁷1921, ¹¹1964); idem, *Geschichte der urchristlichen Literatur* (Berlin, 1926), reprinted in *Theologische Bücherei* 58, ed. F. Hahn (Munich, 1975), pp. 140ff.

2. Alfred Seeberg, *Der Katechismus der Urchristenheit* (Leipzig, 1903), reprinted in *Theologische Bücherei* 26, ed. F. Hahn (Munich, 1966). Compare also idem, *Die beiden Wege und das Aposteldekret* (Leipzig, 1906); and idem, *Die Didache des Judentums und der Urchristenheit* (Leipzig, 1908).

3. C.H. Dodd, *Gospel and Law: The Relation of Faith and Ethics in Early Christianity* (Cambridge, 1951).

4. E.G. Selwyn, *The First Epistle of St. Peter* (London, 1946, ²1947), pp. 64–115, 365–466.

267

5. Martin Dibelius, *An die Kolosser, Epheser, an Philemon,* Handbuch zum Neuen Testament 12 (Tübingen, 1913), pp. 91–92; ³1953 (ed. H. Greeven), pp. 48–50; K. Weidinger, *Die Haustafeln: Ein Stück urchristlicher Paränese,* Untersuchungen zum Neuen Testament 14 (Leipzig, 1928); J.E. Crouch, *The Origin and Intention of the Colossian Haustafel,* Forschungen zur Religion und Literatur des Alten und Neuen Testaments 109 (Göttingen, 1973); W. Schrage, "Zur Ethik der neutestamentlichen Haustafeln," *New Testament Studies* 21 (1974/75): 1–22; L. Geppelt, *Der Erste Petrusbrief,* Kritisch-exegetischer Kommentar 12/1 (Göttingen, 1978), pp. 163–79.

6. A. Vögtle, *Die Tugend- und Lasterkataloge im Neuen Testament,* "Neutestamentliche Abhandlungen" 16/4–5 (Münster, 1936); S. Wibbing, *Die Tugend- und Lasterkataloge im Neuen Testament,* Beihefte zur *Zeitschrift für die neutestamentliche Wissenschaft* 25 (Berlin, 1959); E. Kamlah, *Die Form der katalogischen Paränese im Neuen Testament,* Wissenschaftliche Untersuchungen zum Neuen Testament 7 (Tübingen, 1964).

7. K. Wengst, *Tradition und Theologie des Barnabasbriefes,* Arbeiten zur Kirchengeschichte 42 (Berlin, 1971), pp. 58–70.

8. W. Schrage, *Die konkreten Einzelgebote in der paulinischen Paränese* (Gütersloh, 1962).

9. Compare James 3:1; as is clear from 3:13–18, one must think especially of the (Christian) teacher of wisdom. Passages such as 1 Thessalonians 4:1–2, Philippians 4:9, and 1 Corinthians 4:16–17 indicate that the specific reference is to Christian instruction.

10. Developed catechetical instruction prior to baptism arose only after the New Testament period, but the beginnings of this custom are evident in Hebrews 6:1–2.

11. This matter has been explored most notably by Dibelius, op. cit. (1919), pp. 66ff.; ²1933, pp. 234ff.

12. This was dealt with by Harvey K. McArthur, *Understanding the Sermon on the Mount* (New York, 1960). Compare also William D. Davies, *The Setting of the Sermon on the Mount* (Cambridge: Cambridge University Press, 1964).

13. Note esp. 1 Thessalonians 4:1–9; 5:(1–11, 12–14)15–22; Galatians 5:14—6:10; Philippians 4:4–9; Romans 12:9—13:14; Colossians 3:5—4:6; Ephesians 4:17—6:10; Hebrews 13:1–9, 17; 1 Peter 2:11—4:11 (5:1–11); James 1:3—5:11. At this point the parenetic tradition in the Pastorals and the apostolic fathers is ignored.

14. Note the survey provided by Dibelius, *Geschichte der urchristlichen Literatur,* op. cit., pp. 140ff., and also material in the appropriate monographs and commentaries.

15. See 1 Thessalonians 4:9b; Galatians 5:14; Romans 12:9; 13:8–10; Colossians 3:14; Ephesians 5:2; 1 Peter 1:22; 2:17; 4:8; James 2:8 (cf. 1:25; 2:12).

16. For this, see pp. 73–76 of this study.

17. In addition there are the incomplete patterns and, apart from the lists of virtues and vices and the household codes, the beginnings of church regulations (e.g., James 5:12–20; 1 Peter 5:1–4).

18. An unmistakable reference to general *(usuelle)* parenesis appears in 1 Corinthians 6:9–11. For a concrete *(aktuelle)* application of parenesis, see Philippians 1:27—2:18 (also 3:17–21) and Romans 14:1—15:13.

19. See H. Schlier, "Vom Wesen der apostolischen Ermahnung," in *Die Zeit der Kirche,* Gesammelte Aufsätze 1 (Freiburg im Breisgau, 1956), pp. 74–89. For the Pauline understanding of instruction, see esp. O. Merk, *Handeln aus*

Glauben: Die Motivierungen der paulinischen Ethik, Marburger theologische Studien 5 (Marburg, 1968).

20. This is most clearly illustrated in the Jewish-Christian Kerygmata Petrou, which is the oldest layer in the pseudo-Clementines. See E. Hennecke and W. Schneemelcher, *Neutestamentliche Apokryphen II* (Tübingen, ³1964), pp. 63–80 (Eng. trans. 1965, pp. 102–27). But this perspective is present also in the traditional material in the Gospel of Matthew, as is indicated by such passages as Matthew 5:18–19. The evangelist himself had adopted basically this position, as is demonstrated by Matthew 5:17, 7:12, and 22:40, but he understood the Torah so clearly from the perspective of Jesus' message that the words of Jesus he records portray a totally new interpretation.

21. Decisive for this development was a Hellenistic Jewish-Christianity that recognized the mission to the gentiles as its responsibility; see Galatians 2:1–10 and Acts 15:1–35. See also my discussion in *Das Verständnis der Mission im Neuen Testament*, Wissenschaftliche Monographien zum Alten und Neuen Testament 13 (Neukirchen-Vluyn, ²1965), pp. 48ff., 65ff.

22. The most obvious evidence of this dependence on the ethical tradition of the Hellenistic popular philosophy is Philippians 4:8, but one must note the connection of verse 8 with verse 9 (corresponding to 1 Thessalonians 5:21).

23. See, e.g., Philipp Vielhauer, *Geschichte der urchristlichen Literatur* (Berlin, 1975), pp. 53ff.

24. A significant methodological observation is that the parenetic materials varied considerably with respect to content and arrangement. This is evident from the writings of early Christianity. In the New Testament writings, traditional materials have not been taken over without considerable change. In fact, the sections are filled with passages that come from the final author. Nevertheless, the traditional materials incorporated by the early Christian writers stand out from their style of extended argument, since the traditional material was formulated in brief sentences, strung together, and occasionally illustrated by vivid examples. (Only the letter of James is a partial exception to this generality, because it was so clearly tied to the parenetic tradition.)

25. Reference may be made to Romans 12:1–2 (which clearly refers back to 6:3ff.; 8:4ff., 12ff.; Galatians 5:1, 13, 16–17 (with reference back to 3:26—4:7; 4:21–31); 1 Thessalonians 4:3, 7–8 (for the motif of "holiness" and its connection with baptism, see 1 Corinthians 6:11); Colossians 3:10–12 (cf. 2:11–13); Ephesians 4:20–24; 5:8–14 (cf. 2:4–10); 1 Peter 1:22—2:3; James 1:(17)18–21; 2:7.

26. See the passages listed in note 15. In Ephesians 5:2 the connection between God's act of love and the parenetic instruction is specifically underlined.

27. The expected parousia is mentioned explicitly in 1 Thessalonians 5:1–11; Philippians 4:5b; Colossians 3:4 (cf. 4:5b); Ephesians 6:8–9; James 5:7–11. It is assumed in 1 Corinthians 6:9, 10; Galatians 5:21; 6:9–10; Romans 13:11–12; Ephesians 5:5; 1 Peter 4:7.

28. In the letter of James, such passages as 2:5, 8–9; 3:17–18; and 4:5, but also 1:17–18; 1:21; 2:7, and 4:7–11, have an important significance, since it is apparent there which is the decisive element in the interrelation between the so frequently mentioned "faith" (see the concordance) and actual deeds ("works"). The statement in James 4:17 is very close to that of Romans 14:23. Similarly, the argument of James 2:20–26 is an attempt (in some ways not too satisfactory) to formulate a safeguard against a misuse of Paulinism. Paul makes

his own position clear in Galatians 5:6 when he speaks of faith working through love. In any event, the author of the letter of James follows a Jewish tradition that arose after the Old Testament period when he uses Genesis 22:1–14 to explain Genesis 15:6 and employs the somewhat unfortunate motif of the "working together" of faith with works (v. 22). This reveals that he has a very limited conception of faith (cf. also 2:18ff.) and as a result real difficulties arise in the question of the relation between actual deeds and faith.

29. Otherwise, Paul speaks of the kingdom of God only in 1 Corinthians 15:24, 50.

30. See H. Merklein, *Die Gottesherrschaft als Handlungaprinzip: Untersuchung zur Ethik Jesu,* Forschungen Zur Bibel 34 (Würzburg, 1978), pp. 217ff.

31. Romans 13:9 and James 2:11; cf. Mark 10:19 and pars.

32. This is especially true of such statements as Romans 12:14, 17; James 1:5–6; 1:22–23; 4:9–10.

33. See, e.g., Romans 12:11–13; Galatians 5:25; 6:1–2; James 5:13–20; Colossians 3:16–17 (Ephesians 5:19–20).

34. Naturally, the contrast with pagan lifestyles is everywhere taken for granted. Relevant in this context is a passage such as Ephesians 5:8–14, with its stress on the contrast between the light and the darkness and its exhortation "walk as children of light." See also Romans 13:12–14.

35. See Galatians 4:1–7, 21–31; 5:1, 13; James 1:25; 2:12. The "law of liberty" in the letter of James centers on the love commandment as interpreted in the preaching of Jesus.

36. I call attention to my study "Neutestamentliche Grundlagen einer christlichen Ethik," *Trierer Theologische Zeitschrift* (1977): 31–41.

37. From this emphasis emerged the reference to the "spirit of Christ." Frequently the writers speak simply of the "Spirit" or "Holy Spirit."

38. In addition to the passages mentioned in note 27, see 1 Thessalonians 4:6 and also the summons to make "the most of the time" in Colossians 4:5.

39. Compare 1 Thessalonians 4:1; 5:18; Philippians 2:5; 3:1; 4:1–2, 4; Colossians 3:18, 20; Ephesians 4:21 *(bis);* 6:1; 1 Peter 3:16.

40. See the literature referred to in note 5.

41. See Romans 12:11.

42. The household code seems archaic in comparison with Colossians 3:5–17 and must therefore be older coming from at least as early as the time of Paul.

43. Apart from a passage such as James 2:1, the introduction in 1:2–12 demonstrates clearly that the entire following parenesis should be understood out of the situation of the Christians who live in the midst of temptation which they are expected to overcome.

44. See J.N.E. Kelly, *The Epistles of Peter and of Jude,* Black's New Testament Commentaries (London, 1969), pp. 64ff.; Geppelt, op. cit., pp. 110ff.; N. Brex, *Der erste Petrusbrief,* Evangelisch-Katholischer Kommentar zum Neuen Testament 21 (Zurich-Neukirchen, 1978), pp. 72ff.

45. 1 Peter 1:23 is closely related to James 1:21.

46. Hebrews 10:26–39 is specific, concrete parenesis *(actuelle paränese)* referring back to 5:11—6:8, and Hebrews 11:1—12:3 is a homiletic development on the theme of 11:1. From this perspective the author makes a reference in Hebrews 12:4–11 to the necessary "chastisement," and only then does he continue the parenetic theme. Hebrews 10:19–25 and 12:12–17 provide the introduction and transition to the general *(usuelle)* parenesis in 13:1–8, 17,

which comes after certain basic issues have been raised in 12:18–29 and then again in 13:9–16.

47. The author's special ecclesiological interest is clear, along with his christological motif. See Ephesians 4:4–6 and above all 4:7–16.

48. Connections with Colossians are undeniable; the author of Ephesians must have known Colossians. See C.L. Mitten, *The Epistle to the Ephesians* (Oxford, 1951), and note especially the extended list of parallel passages on pp. 279ff.

49. The theme of spiritual armor appears already in 1 Thessalonians 5:8, though in brief form. For the early history of this motif, see K.G. Kuhn, *Theologisches Wörterbuch zum Neuen Testament* 5 (Stuttgart, 1954), pp. 297 –300 (Eng. trans.: pp. 296–300).

50. Ephesians 4:32 deals with the gracious activity of God in Christ, 5:1–2 with Christ's self-giving, and 5:14 with the illumination that comes through Christ. The specifically Christian motivation for the exhortation to slaves in 6:5–8 agrees substantially with Colossians 3:22–25.

51. In addition to the commentaries and recent investigations, see J.P. Sampley, *And the Two Shall Become One Flesh: A Study of Traditions in Ephesians 5:21–33*, Society for New Testament Studies Monograph Series 16 (Cambridge, 1971); K. Niederwimmer, *Askese und Mysterium: Über Ehe, Ehescheidung und Eheverzicht in den Anfängen des christlichen Glaubens*, Forschungen zur Religion und Literatur des Alten und Neuen Testaments 113 (Göttingen, 1975), pp. 124ff. (The hypotheses in the field of comparative religions are somewhat problematic.)

52. See esp. Ephesians 1:1–14; 2:11–22; 3:1–7.

53. The deutero-Pauline letters were the first to express the distinction between head and body in the sphere of ecclesiology. Paul himself used only the concept of the body of Christ, in which all believers and baptized people belong, along with Christ. (It was from this concept that Paul derived his picture in 1 Corinthians 12:14–27 of the Christian community as an organism in which all the parts function harmoniously together.) See also 1 Corinthians 6:15; 12:12–13; Romans 12:4–5. Originally in Colossians 1:18, Christ was identified as the "head" of creation (cf. 2:10), but the writer of the letter has expanded the reference in 1:18 to "[head] of the church" and thus linked to the second strophe (1:18–20; cf. 2:9–19). The letter to the Ephesians builds on this ecclesiological usage; see Ephesians 1:22; 4:15; 5:23. Still in Ephesians it is assumed that "the body" (i.e., the church) will penetrate the entire world until it absorbs all things, and so all will be subordinated to Christ as head (1:10; cf. 1:23).

54. The statement that Christ has loved "us" appears in still earlier tradition; cf. Galatians 2:20. In Ephesians this is interpreted to mean that he loved "the church." The writer stresses in other passages the church as a preexistent reality; cf. 1:3–14.

55. The idea of Jesus as Savior appears in the earliest tradition only in Philippians 3:21, and there it is related to him as the returning Lord who brings salvation to completion (Paul generally used *soteria* in a similar fashion). It is first of all in Ephesians 5:23 that "Savior" is used to characterize the work of the earthly Jesus. For the usage in early Christianity, see Martin Dibelius and Hans Conzelmann, *Die Pastoralbriefe,* Handbuch zum Neuen Testament 13 (Tübingen, ⁴1966), pp. 74ff.

56. "Sanctification" is accomplished "through the water-bath in the word,"

that is, through baptism (cf. 1 Corinthians 6:11; 1 Thessalonians 4:3, 7–8). Its purpose is to bring the church through to the end of time pure and spotless. See H. Schlier, *Der Epheserbrief* Düsseldorf, ⁶1966), pp. 256ff.

57. Unmistakably, a motif from Christology, or ecclesiology, is here transferred to the sphere of anthropology, but as verses 28 and 29 indicate, the two spheres are fully integrated.

58. In early Christianity the command of love for the neighbor, Leviticus 19:18, which was interpreted by Jesus in terms of love for the enemy, was related primarily to the mutual love within the congregation, but without eliminating the dimension of love for the enemy. The command to love others "as yourself" is applied in Ephesians 5:28 in a very specific fashion.

59. This perspective, so crucial for the life together in the Christian community, was prepared for by such earlier statements as Galatians 3:28, 1 Corinthians 12:13, and Colossians 3:11.

60. This is valid just from the perspective of syntax, since the verb is missing in Ephesians 5:22. The participle in verse 21, understood as an imperative, is decisive. See D. Daube, "Participle and Imperative in I Peter," in Selwyn, op. cit. (²1947), pp. 467–88.

61. See J. Gnilka, *Der Epheserbrief,* Herders Theologischer Kommentar 10/2 (Freiburg im Breisgau, ²1977), p. 289.

62. This is not unusual, but in the New Testament it cannot automatically be taken for granted. See E. Schweizer, *Theologisches Wörterbuch zum Neuen Testament* 7 (Stuttgart, 1966), pp. 123–38 (Eng. trans., pp. 124–38).

63. For Ephesians 5:32 and the idea of "mystery," see Günther Bornkamm, *Theologisches Wörterbuch zum Neuen Testament* 4 (Stuttgart, 1942), pp. 809–34 (Eng. trans. pp. 802–28).

64. Here there is an implicit reference to the missionary dimension of the marriage partnership, just as in 1 Peter 3:1 there is reference to the missionary function of a believing wife toward her non-Christian marriage partner.

CHAPTER 7:
CHRISTOLOGICAL PERSPECTIVES IN THE PREDICATES OF THE JOHANNINE *Egō Eimi* SAYINGS

1. See Virgil P. Howard, *Das Ego Jesu in den Synoptischen Evangelien* (Marburg: Alwert Verlag, 1975). Pp. 10–27 discuss the occurrences of "I" in Greek, Hebrew, Aramaic, and the Septuagint; pp. 28–75 discuss the use of "I" in the history of religions, with special reference to the *egō eimi* phrase.

2. I have included only passages in which *egō eimi* occurs in that order and without any intervening words. Other lists differ slightly, e.g., Rudolf Schnackenburg, *Das Johannesevangelium,* 3 vols. (Freiburg: Herder, 1965ff.), 2:59 (vol. 1 in English [New York: Herder & Herder, 1968]), and Moulton and Geden, *A Concordance to the Greek Testament,* 2d ed. (Edinburgh: T. & T. Clark, 1899), ad loc.

3. Three of the passages in John's Gospel are not regarded as "significant": 4:26; 8:18; 9:9.

4. On these passages, see Dean Alford, *The Greek Testament,* 4 vols., new ed. (Boston: Lee & Shepard, 1877); and Marcus Dods, *The Expositor's Greek Testament* (New York: Dodd, 1905), vol. 1. This appears to be the view also of

Chrysostom (see *Homilies on St. John,* Nicene and Post-Nicene Fathers, First Series, vol. 14 [New York: Christian Literature Co., 1890]), although his comment on 8:58 may be an exception ("As the Father uses the expression 'I am,' so also does the Christ").

5. This position has been developed especially by D. Daube ("The 'I Am' of the Messianic Presence," in his *The New Testament and Rabbinic Judaism* [London: Athlone, 1956], pp. 325–29), E. Stauffer (*Jesus and His Story* [New York: Knopf, 1960]), H. Zimmermann, ("Das Absolute *Egō Eimi* als die neutestamentliche Offenbarungsformel," *Biblische Zeitschrift* 4 [1960]: 54–69, 266–76), and Philip B. Harner (*The "I Am" of the Fourth Gospel* [Philadelphia: Fortress Press, 1970]). It appears in the commentaries of W. Bauer (*Das Johannesevangelium,* 2d ed. [Tübingen: J.C.B. Mohr, 1977]), R.H. Strachen (*The Fourth Gospel,* 3d ed. [London: SCM Press, 1941]), C.K. Barrett, (*The Gospel According to St. John* [London: SPCK, 1955]), R.H. Lightfoot (*St. John's Gospel* [Oxford: Clarendon Press, 1956]), Raymond E. Brown (*The Gospel According to John,* Anchor Bible 29, 29A [New York: Doubleday, 1966, 1970]), and John Marsh, (*Saint John,* Pelican New Testament Commentaries [Harmondsworth: Penguin, 1968]). They do not all agree on precisely which occurrences of the absolute phrase carry this special force. This position had been taken earlier, e.g., H.J. Holtzmann on John 8:24 (see his *Evangelium, Briefe und Offenbarung des Johannes,* 2d ed. [Freiburg: J.C.B. Mohr, 1893]).

6. I believe this is the position of Rudolf Bultmann, *The Gospel of John* (Philadelphia: Westminster Press, 1971). On 8:58 he explicitly rejects the suggestion that the *egō eimi* equals "I am God" or that it reflects Old Testament usage. But on 6:20 he says the phrase is "the traditional formula of greeting by the deity." On 13:19 he says that "the Revealer" is to be supplied as predicate. In the extended note on 6:35 he states that a sacred formula is not intended in 4:26; 1:18, 23; 18:5, 6, 8.

7. Oscar Cullmann, "Der johanneische Gebrauch doppeldeutiger Ausdrücke als Schlüssel zum Verständnis des vierten Evangeliums," *Theologische Zeitschrift* 4 (1948): 360–72.

8. See note 5.

9. See Rudolf Bultmann, "Die Bedeutung der neuerschlossenen mandäischen und manichäischen Quellen für das Verständnis des Johannesevangeliums," *Zeitschrift für die neutestamentliche Wissenschaft* 24 (1925): 100–146. See also Rudolf Bultmann "Der religionsgeschichtliche Hintergrund des Prologs zum Johannesevangelium," *Eucharisterion,* Studien zur Religion und Literatur des Alten und Neuen Testaments, new series, 19 (Göttingen: Vandenhoeck & Ruprecht, 1923), pt. 2, pp. 1–26; and idem, *The Gospel of John,* op. cit.

10. See the translations of M. Lidzbarski (*Ginza: Der Schatz oder das grosse Buch der Mandäer* [Göttingen: Vandenhoeck & Ruprecht, 1925]; *Das Johannesbuch der Mandäer* [Giessen: Töpelmann, 1915]; *Mandäische Liturgien,* Abhandlungen der Königliche Gesellschaft der Wissenschaften zu Göttingen, new series 17/1 [1920]) and Ethel S. Drower, ed. (*The Canonical Prayerbook of the Mandaeans* [Atlantic Highlands, NJ: Humanities Press, 1959]).

11. While Bultmann has been the leader in defense of the Mandaean theory, he has been supported by other scholars, e.g., W. Bauer. H. Becker, who was a student of Bultmann's, goes so far as to reconstruct a hypothetical Gnostic *Vorlage* which was utilized by the evangelist (see H. Becker, *Die Reden des Johannesevangeliums und der Still der gnostischen Offenbarungsrede* [Götting-

en: Vandenhoeck & Ruprecht, 1956; actually completed in 1941], pp. 129–36). Hans Conzelmann appears to provide some agreement with Bultmann (see Hans Conzelmann, *An Outline of the Theology of the New Testament* [New York: Harper & Row, 1969], pp. 330f.), but his statement is too brief and cautious for a clear judgment.

12. K. Rudolph's presentation (*Die Mandaeer*, Forschungen zur Religion und Literatur des Alten und Neuen Testaments 92, 93 [Göttingen: Vandenhoeck & Ruprecht, 1960, 1961]) is still the nearest approach to a definitive study of the Mandaeans available. The critics of Bultmann insist that there is need for a major critical study of Mandaean literature indicating the various chronological layers. This would be of enormous value, but it may be an impossible task until new sources are discovered.

13. Ernst Percy, *Untersuchungen über den Ursprung der Johanneische Theologie* (Lund: Gleerup, 1939). See the comments of Jan-A. Bühner, *Der Gesandte und sein Weg im 4. Evangelium* (Tübingen: J.C.B. Mohr, 1977), pp. 29–30.

14. C.H. Dodd, *The Interpretation of the Fourth Gospel* (Cambridge: Cambridge University Press, 1953), pp. 115–30. See the comments of Bühner, op. cit., pp. 49–51, and Bühner's criticism of Dodd's *Tendenz*.

15. See the comments of Bühner, op. cit., pp. 30–32, 34–35.

16. Eduard Schweizer, *Egō Eimi*, 2d ed. (Göttingen: Vandenhoeck & Ruprecht, 1965). Schweizer's position is of special interest, since he had been a student of Bultmann's and the first edition of *Egō Eimi* was in many respects a continuation of Bultmann's analysis.

17. Eduard Schweizer, *Church Order in the New Testament* (Naperville: Allenson, 1961), esp. p. 118 and nn. 445, 447.

18. See the summary of Bühner's study, op. cit., pp. 422–33. It is hoped that the near future will see major discussion of the views Bühner has supported.

19. Ibid., pp. 156–57.

20. In fact, the current tendency is away from stress on Gnostic sources for the Johannine tradition.

21. See note 12.

22. It is perhaps in opposition to this claim that Dodd stresses that in John the Revealer reveals to humankind the demand for "love, trust and obedience directed to Him . . ." (op. cit., p. 114). It should be made explicit that Dodd does not deny the possibility that some motifs may have appeared, in different forms, in John and in gnosticism, e.g., the *anthropos* figure (ibid., pp. 111–12).

23. L. Morris, *The Gospel According to John*, New International Commentary on the New Testament (Grand Rapids: Eerdmans, 1971), p. 47, appears to support this view.

24. Howard, op. cit., pp. 1–9, presents the evidence.

25. See William Barclay, *The Gospels and Acts* (London: SCM Press, 1976), p. 118. For other discussions of the "historicity" issue, see E.C. Hoskyns, *The Fourth Gospel*, rev. ed. (London: Faber & Faber, 1947), pp. 58–85 ("The Historical Tension of the Fourth Gospel"); Dodd, op. cit., pp. 444–52 ("Appendix: Some Considerations upon the Historical Aspect of the Fourth Gospel"); Strachen, op. cit.; Morris, op. cit., pp. 40–49 ("History and Theology"); Schnackenburg, op. cit., 2:67–70; Brown, op. cit., 1:xli–li; and V. Taylor, *The Names of Jesus* (New York: St. Martin's Press, 1953), pp. 132f.

26. This is a major theological watershed, and consciously or unconsciously, those who deal seriously with the Christian tradition must make their own decisions before they can proceed. The issue will reappear below in Section 4,

"Contemporary Significance."

27. On the variant reading at John 11:25, see B.M. Metzger, *A Textual Commentary on the Greek New Testament* (London and New York: United Bible Societies, 1971), p. 234.

28. See S.S. Smalley, *John: Evangelist and Interpreter* (Exeter: Paternoster Press, 1978); and Schnackenburg, op. cit., 2:60–61.

29. See Schnackenburg, op. cit., 2:60.

30. See Brown, op. cit., 1:499–501 and the bibliography noted there. See also Dodd, op. cit., pp. 170–78.

31. See Brown, op. cit., 2:674–79; and Barrett, op. cit., pp. 392ff. An extended discussion of the "Vine" as Israel appears in the Midrash Rabbah on Leviticus 26:42 (section 36/2, which is on pp. 457–59 of the Socino translation). Similar but more abbreviated comments are frequent in rabbinic thought.

32. Although Morris, op. cit., p. 170, says, "No satisfying explanation of this has been put forward," speaking of the double "truly" in the fourth Gospel. This may mean that he does not accept what most would regard as the obvious explanation.

CHAPTER 8:
LOGOS ECCLESIOLOGY IN JOHN'S GOSPEL

1. R.E. Brown, "Johannine Ecclesiology," *Interpretation* 31 (1977): 379–80.

2. Rudolf Schnackenburg concludes that the contrasts between prologue and Gospel are so great as to show that the prologue was originally a logos hymn that has been transformed into a Gospel introduction (*The Gospel According to St. John* [New York: Herder & Herder, 1968], 1:224–49). Although R.E. Brown does not go that far, he stresses the contrasts in attitudes toward the logos (*The Gospel According to John,* Anchor Bible [New York: Doubleday, 1966], 1: 19). So when he looks for the origins of the logos idiom, he makes no mention of the later chapters of the Gospel (1:518–24).

3. At a meeting of the RSV translation committee in June 1978, I objected to this practice but failed to win support for my case. The evidence below may justify my conviction that there are passages other than the prologue in which logos merits capitalization.

4. The significance of an image may be measured by the number of allusions and associations it arouses in the mind. "The inner world of experience and memory exhibits a structure which is causally determined by significant associations rather than by causal connections in the outside world. To render this peculiar structure, therefore, requires a symbolism or imagery in which the different modalities of time—past, present, and future— . . . are always inextricably and dynamically associated and mixed up with each other" (H. Meyerhoff, *Time in Literature* [Berkeley: University of California Press, 1955], pp. 23–24).

5. S. Pancaro, *The Law in the Fourth Gospel* (Leiden: E.J. Brill, 1975), p. 2.

6. Susan Sontag, *Against Interpretation* (New York: Farrar, Straus & Giroux, 1966), pp. 5–7.

7. In many cases I will use the transliterated term logos where I think it conveys important theological overtones but in other cases use the ordinary translation *word.*

8. "This 'word,' however, is not merely the teaching of Jesus nor the works of

Jesus, but the very person of Jesus as the manifestation of the Father" (J.F. Forestell, *The Word of the Cross* [Rome: Biblical Institute, 1974], p. 192).

9. It is such associations as these that give to Johannine thought "a feeling of unfathomable depth," and this feeling in turn "makes any attempt to convey his thought in another tongue so formidably difficult" (G. Vann, *The Eagle's Word* [London: Collins, 1961], p. 19).

10. Pancaro, op. cit., pp. 7–8.

11. In many respects the function of this narrative in John is comparable to the "recognition scene" in Mark 8:22—9:1. Readers are enabled to discern the hidden nexus between the Messiah's identity and the necessity of suffering on the part of both Messiah and followers.

12. R.E. Brown provides a convenient summary of the use of *menein* to describe this intimate union. Jesus' followers abide in life, love, and truth, and simultaneously the same three realities abide in them. This same subtle reciprocity is indicated by the disciples' abiding in the logos, and by the logos abiding in them. Op. cit., 1:511–12.

13. Pancaro, op. cit., pp. 403–51.

14. This use of logos illustrates a point made by Vann: "The prophetic vision is many-levelled, mingling past or present with future, the temporal with the eternal, the literal and the metaphorical, history with symbol. . . . In the fourth gospel there are no parables because the whole gospel is a parable" (op. cit., p. 12). A similarly pluralistic use of logos may be found in the Apocalypse. Cf. Paul S. Minear, *I Saw a New Earth* (Washington: Corpus Books, 1968), pp. 222–23.

15. For the distinctively Johannine concept of the world, see my "Evangelism, Ecumenism, and John Seventeen," *Theology Today* 35 (1978): 7ff.

16. See my "The Audience of the Fourth Evangelist," *Interpretation* 31 (1977): 339–54.

17. See my "'We Don't Know Where . . .' John 20:2," *Interpretation* 30 (1976): 125–39.

18. See my *To Die and to Live* (New York: Seabury Press, 1977), chap. 5.

19. E.C. Hoskyns, *The Fourth Gospel* (London: Faber & Faber, 1947), p. 156.

20. C.K. Barrett, *The Gospel of John* (London: SPCK, 1955), p. 126.

21. Pancaro, op. cit., p. 427.

22. In the following summary, I have profited from the essay of Amos N. Wilder, "Eschatological Imagery and Earthly Circumstance," *New Testament Studies* 5 (1958–59): 244ff.

23. Harvey K. McArthur, *The Quest Through the Centuries* (Philadelphia: Fortress Press, 1966), p. 143.

CHAPTER 9:

ATTEMPTS AT UNDERSTANDING THE PURPOSE OF LUKE-ACTS:
CHRISTOLOGY AND THE SALVATION OF THE GENTILES

1. Ward Gasque, *A History of the Criticism of the Acts of the Apostles* (Tübingen: J.C.B. Mohr, 1975), p. 21.

2. Ibid., p. 84, my trans.

3. Ibid., p. 91.

4. Ibid., p. 99.

5. Ibid., p. 175.

6. Ibid., p. 191. See also the balanced discussion by Cadbury himself in Henry J. Cadbury, *The Making of Luke-Acts* (London: SPCK, 1961), pp. 299–316.

7. Gasque, op. cit., p. 194.

8. Hans Conzelmann and Andreas Lindemann, *Arbeitsbuch zum Neuen Testament* (Tübingen: J.C.B. Mohr, 1975), pp. 270–71.

9. Ernst Haenchen, *The Acts of the Apostles* (Philadelphia: Westminster Press, 1971), p. 102.

10. Horst R. Moehring, "The Census in Luke as an Apologetic Device," in *Studies in New Testament and Early Christian Literature,* ed. David E. Avnc (Leiden: E.J. Brill, 1972), esp. pp. 158–60.

11. Werner Georg Kümmel, *Introduction to the New Testament* (Nashville: Abingdon Press, 1975), pp. 162–64.

12. Ibid., p. 163.

13. Jacob Jervell, *Luke and the People of God* (Minneapolis: Augsburg, 1972), esp. pp. 41–74.

14. C.K. Barrett, *Luke the Historian in Recent Study* (London: Epworth, 1961).

15. Gasque, op. cit., pp. 260ff.

16. Jervell, op. cit., p. 175.

17. Ibid., p. 41.

18. Ibid., p. 43.

19. Ibid., p. 10.

20. Ibid., esp. pp. 153ff.

21. Ibid., p. 159.

22. Ibid., p. 161.

23. Ibid., p. 173.

24. Samuel Sandmel in *The Interpreter's Dictionary of the Bible,* ed. G.A. Buttrick (Nashville: Abingdon Press, 1962), 2:592.

25. Hans Conzelmann, *Die Apostelgeschichte,* Handbuch zum Neuen Testament 7 (Tübingen: J.C.B. Mohr, 1963), p. 93.

26. Karl Paul Donfried, "A Short Note on Romans 16," *Journal of Biblical Literature* 89 (1970): esp. 443–46.

27. Haenchen, op. cit., p. 574.

28. E.g., vv. 17ff., 20ff., 23. See Jacob Jervell, "The Divided People of God," in his *Luke and the People of God,* pp. 41–74.

CHAPTER 10:
CHRISTOLOGICAL *Tendenz*
IN COLOSSIANS 1:15–20:
A *Theologia Crucis*

1. "Making peace through the blood of his cross [1:20]."

2. See the history of research on the "hymn" in Hans-Jakob Gabathuler, *Jesus Christus, Haupt der Kirche—Haupt der Welt: Der Christushymnus Colosser 1:15–20 in der theologischen Forschung der letzten 130 Jahre,* Abhandlungen zur Theologie des Alten und Neuen Testaments 45 (Zurich, 1965).

3. "Kein anderer paulinischer Brief enthält so viele Aussagen über die vorzeitliche Stellung und kosmische Bedeutung Christi." Ernst Percy, *Die Probleme der Kolosser- und Epheserbriefe* (Lund: Gleerup, 1946), p. 68. Cf. Allan D. Galloway, *The Cosmic Christ* (London: Nisbet & Co., 1951).

4. Percy, op. cit. C.R. Bowen, "The Original Form of Paul's Letter to the Colossians," *Journal of Biblical Literature* 43 (1924): 197.

5. "It may be said that the center of interest has shifted from the work of Christ to the person of Christ . . . the soteriological interest is subordinated to the cosmological." Francis W. Beare, "Introduction and Exegesis of the Epistle to the Colossians," in *Interpreter's Bible* (Nashville: Abingdon Press, 1955), 11:144.

6. Eduard Lohse, "The Letter to the Colossians and Pauline Theology," in *Colossians and Philemon,* trans. W.R. Poehlmann and Robert J. Karris, Hermeneia, 1st Eng. ed. (Philadelphia: Fortress Press, 1971), p. 178; quotations from this work in this essay are used by permission of Fortress Press.

7. Ibid., p. 55 (italics added).

8. Ibid., p. 43 (italics added).

9. Ibid., p. 61.

10. Ibid., p. 60.

11. Ibid., p. 40, n. 63.

12. Ibid., p. 40 (italics added).

13. Ibid., p. 41 (italics added).

14. Ibid., p. 131 (italics added). See also Eduard Lohse, "Christusherrschaft und Kirche im Kolosserbrief," *New Testament Studies* 11 (April 1965): 207: "This new creation which is described in mythological language in the hymn of the first chapter would be understood by the author of the letter not as a metaphysical drama, but as an historical event." See also Eduard Lohse, "Christologie und Ethik im Kolosserbrief," in *Apophoreta: Festschrift für Ernst Haenchen,* Beihefte zur *Zeitschrift für die neutestamentliche Wissenschaft* 30 (Berlin; 1964): 168: "While the Epistle to the Colossians speaks of the cosmic meaning of the Christ event, it also emphasizes its historical character and preaches Christ not only as the Lord over all but also as our Lord."

15. Percy, op. cit., p. 202. Cf. Eduard Schweizer, "Christ in the Letter to the Colossians," *Review and Expositor* 70 (April 1973): 451–67, who notes that the author has modified the meaning of the pre-Pauline hymn by emphasizing the centrality of the cross and the historical character of the body of Christ as a historical church related to the world.

16. Lohse, *Colossians and Philemon,* op. cit., p. 64, n. 15, correctly observes, "The pre-Christian past of the community is described in phrases which remain general without making possible any closer knowledge of particular circumstances."

17. As will be noted below, scholarly consensus sees Colossians 1:15–20 as a pre-Pauline composition adopted by the author.

18. Lohse, *Colossians and Philemon,* op. cit., p. 128–30, suggests they are a pre-Gnostic Jewish group.

19. This interpretation of Θρησκείν τῶν ἀγγέλων is persuasively advanced by F.O. Francis, "Humility and Angelic Worship in Col. 2:18," *Studia Theologica* 16 (1962): 109–34.

20. The author's proclamation of Christ as God's mystery is likely motivated by the prior claim of the Errorists to be the exclusive possessors of the divine

mystery. See the reference to the prevalence of "mystery" language at Qumran, below.

21. J.B. Lightfoot, *Saint Paul's Epistles to the Colossians and to Philemon* (London: Macmillan, 1892), p. 74, n. 1.

22. Ibid., pp. 73–113, 349–419.

23. "The Community Rule X"=1QS X, in G. Vermes, *The Dead Sea Scrolls in English* (Baltimore: Penguin, 1962), pp. 88–89.

24. Ibid., p. 42. Vermes notes that their solar calendar was referred to as "the laws of the Great Light of heaven" (p. 43). See also the reference in the Damascus Document to the "Book of the Divisions of the Times into their Jubilees and Weeks," p. 109.

25. The covenanters of Qumran employed three separate terms to refer to the divine "mystery" or "hidden things": נסותרות, סוד, and רז. See Wayne G. Rollins, "The Christology of Colossians" (Dissertation, Yale University, 1959), p. 284. Lohse, *Colossians and Philemon,* op. cit., p. 74, n. 44. C.C. Caragounis, *The Ephesian Mysterion: Meaning and Content,* Coniectanea Biblica, N.T. Series 8 (Lund: Gleerup, 1977).

26. CD 3:14–16, in T.H. Gaster, *The Dead Sea Scriptures* (New York: Doubleday, 1956), p. 64.

27. See 1QS 11:5–8.

28. 1QS 4:18; 5:24; cf. 9:2; 11:21. The scrolls also speak of the "mysteries of sin," "the mystery to come," the "iniquitous mysteries" (IQH 5:36), and the "hostile mysteries of Belial" (1QS 5:24).

29. Lohse, *Colossians and Philemon,* op. cit., pp. 88 and 188, n. 11. Lohse is inclined to interpret these parallels as evidence of affinities between Qumran and the author of Colossians. One suspects Lohse's judgment may be colored by his contention that Colossians is deutero-Pauline.

30. For τέλειος and τελειότης in Colossians, see Rollins, op. cit., p. 289. Lohse, *Colossians and Philemon,* op. cit., p. 89, n. 154, cites linguistic parallels with Qumran. The Manual of Discipline refers to one who is barred from the community as one who "shall not be reckoned among the perfect." Cf. Vermes, op. cit., p. 74.

31. Cf. Colossians 1:12–14. The author maintains over against the Errorists that deliverance from the powers of darkness is a fait accompli for the Christian. Cf. Vermes, op. cit., p. 76.

32. Colossians 2:20–23. Cf. ibid., p. 46.

33. Colossians 2:11ff.; 3:11. Vermes correctly proposes that although circumcision is not mentioned in the Qumran scrolls, its practice can be taken for granted; ibid., pp. 44–45.

34. Cf. Millar Burrows, *More Light on the Dead Sea Scrolls* (New York: Viking Press, 1958), pp. 381–82.; cf. Colossians 2:18; 1QS XI in Vermes, op. cit., p. 41.

35. Cf. Vermes, op. cit., p. 42. A highly developed angelology is evident at Qumran.

36. Cf. Burrows, op. cit., pp. 89ff., and Colossians 2:18 for reference to the Errorists being "puffed up" and "disqualifying" others.

37. Lohse, "Christusherrschaft," op. cit., p. 203.

38. Colossians 2:20–21. vs. 1:3–8.

39. Colossians 2:18 vs. 1:3, 12.

40. Colossians 2:18–23 vs. 3:14–16.

41. Colossians 3:11; cf. 2:19; 3:14.

42. Colossians 2:8, 18, 23 vs. 2:3 and 1:24–26.

43. Lohse, *Colossians and Philemon,* op. cit., pp. 25, 27, 30, 34–35.

44. Ibid., p. 40, n. 63.

45. Lohmeyer, for example, proposes two seven-line strophes, each preceded by a unit of three lines; Masson suggests five strophes (cf. Lohse, *Colossians and Philemon,* op. cit., p. 42, n. 69); James M. Robinson, "A Formal Analysis of Colossians 1:15–20," *Journal of Biblical Literature* 76 (1957): 270–87, rearranges the material to create two strophes of three lines each plus two additional pairs of lines. Eduard Schweizer, "Die Kirche als Leib Christi in den paulinsichen Antilegomenon," *Theologische Literaturzeitung* 86 (1961): 241–56, reconstructs two strophes and a median strophe, excising editorial interpolations. Most recently, W. McCown, "The Hymnic Structure of Col. 1:15–20," *Evangelical Quarterly* 51 (1979): 156–62, sees vv. 17–18a as a refrain between two stanzas of equal length (15–16 and 18b–19).

46. Lohse, *Colossians and Philemon,* op. cit., p. 44.

47. Ibid., pp. 44–45. Some italics are added at "in him," vv. 16, 17, and 19; "through him" and "for him," v. 16; and "toward him," v. 20. The designations of verses and strophe divisions are also added.

48. Cf. ibid., pp. 45, 46, n. 100.

49. Rollins, op. cit., pp. 197–228.

50. Martin Dibelius, *An die Kolosser, Epheser, an Philemon,* 3d rev. ed. by D. Heinrich Greeven, *Handbuch zum Neuen Testament* 12 (Tübingen: J.C.B. Mohr, 1953), p. 10; cf. Lohse, *Colossians and Philemon,* op. cit., p. 42, n. 69.

51. On Christ as κεφαλη', cf. Rollins, op. cit., pp. 331–410; Lohse, *Colossians and Philemon,* op. cit., p. 54.

52. Lohse, *Colossians and Philemon,* op. cit., p. 44, repudiates the notion that an early Christian hymn "would have consisted of regularly constructed verses and strophes," though he supplies little evidence, if any, for this supposition. Aside from the quasi-hymnic prologue in John, there is no evidence of a bi-strophic hymn in the New Testament.

53. See note 45 above. Robinson regards earlier reconstructions as "impossible" and absurd strophic arrangements (op. cit. p. 274). Having warned against "procrustean beds," he does not seem to have avoided them himself.

54. Käsemann describes this as a shift toward the "eschatological," so Lohse, *Colossians and Philemon,* op. cit., p. 55, n. 169.

55. Cf. the quasi-hymnic ὅς construction in 1:13–14, preceding Strophe A, which is also largely the construction of the author and is likewise designed to provide a context of interpretation for Strophe A.

56. Ernst Käsemann, "A Primitive Christian Baptismal Liturgy," in *Essays on New Testament Themes,* Studies in Biblical Theology 41 (London: SCM Press, 1964), p. 158., notes that the ἐις αὐτόν expresses an "eschatological orientation which then receives concrete expression in the soteriological statements of the second stanza."

57. This cosmology-centered consciousness becomes evident in the thought of the developed Gnostic systems of the second century A.D.

58. The phrase "things above" occurs in 3:1, where, as we will propose below, the author is employing irony. His argument is that the Colossians, who have claimed to be "raised in Christ" and to seek the "things above," are actually doing the opposite. In the verse immediately preceding, he observes that the ascetic attempts of the Errorists to be severe to the body have resulted in the

opposite effect, namely, preoccupation with the flesh. The author's point in the parenetic chapters 3 and 4 is that anyone who *truly* seeks the "things above" "where Christ is" will be engaged in the work below on earth, spreading the gospel and building up the "body of Christ."

59. Cf. Rollins, op. cit., on "Christ in Whom the Whole *Plēroma* Dwells Bodily," pp. 111–70.

60. The verb ἀποκαταλλάξαι, here and in Ephesians 2:16, is a distinctively Christian term (although καταλλάσειν, without the prefix, occurs in Koine literature commonly). The force of the ἀπο-prefix is intensive, in this instance characterizing the Christ event as a restorative act, reclaiming a lost condition. There is little doubt that in the author's judgment this restorative event, described in Strophe B, was of preeminent importance.

61. Contrary to Lohse, *Colossians and Philemon,* op. cit., p. 178, who maintains that "nothing is said about Christ's victory over the constraining power of sin, law, and death," it is clear that for the author reconciliation implies "forgiveness of sins" (1:14; 2:13), freedom from *dogmata* (2:20) and from the condemnation effected by the law (2:14), and victory over the power of death (2:12–13; 3:3–4).

62. Thomas Kingsmill Abbott, *A Critical and Exegetical Commentary on the Epistle to the Ephesians and to the Colossians,* International Critical Commentary (New York: Charles Scribner's Sons, 1956), renders the phrase "by Him, I say" (p. 221). Dibelius-Greeven, op. cit., p. 20, attaches the phrase to the following allusion to earth and heaven: "Irdisches wie Himmlisches durch ihn!"

63. See "4" under material on 1:18b–20 (Strophe B), above.

CHAPTER 11:
CHRISTOLOGICAL PERSPECTIVES IN THE BOOK OF REVELATION

1. Scholars tend to treat the book of Revelation as a unit: George B. Caird, *A Commentary on the Revelation of St. John the Divine,* Harper's New Testament Commentaries (New York: Harper & Row, 1966), p. 6; Werner Georg Kümmel, *Introduction to the New Testament,* 14th rev. ed., trans. A.J. Mattill, Jr. (Nashville: Abingdon Press, 1966), pp. 456–58; E.S. Fiorenza, *The Apocalypse* (Chicago: Franciscan Herald Press, 1976), pp. 12, 38.

2. Raymond E. Brown, *Gospel According to John,* Anchor Bible 29 (New York: Doubleday, 1966), pp. xxxiv–xxxix.

3. With slight variations as to where the apocalyptic core ends, many scholars note a comparable division in the book: J.M. Ford, *Revelation,* Anchor Bible 38 (New York: Doubleday, 1975), p. 27; S. Giet, *L'Apocalypse et L'Histoire* (Paris: Ophrys, 1957), p. 146; J.A.T. Robinson, *Redating the New Testament* (Philadelphia: Westminster Press, 1976), p. 226; and H. Sahlin, *Die Bildersprache* (Schweden: Adr. Djakneg, 1927), pp. 3–4.

4. John F. Whealon, "New Patches on an Old Garment: The Book of Revelation," *Biblical Theology Bulletin* 11, no. 2 (April 1981): 54.

5. Ibid., pp. 57–58. Ford (op cit., p. 56) wants to date it as early as possible in order to relate it to John the Baptist and his circle; she therefore puts it at A.D. 68, prior to Mark's Gospel. Robinson (op. cit., pp. 252, 256) also sets it in A.D. 68 to accord with his theory that the whole New Testament was completed prior to A.D. 70.

6. Whealon, op. cit., p. 58. Revelation (as a whole) is dated A.D. 90–95 by

Kümmel (op. cit., p. 329) and R.H. Charles (*The Revelation of St. John, International Critical Commentary* [Edinburgh: T. & T. Clark, 1920; reprinted 1975], 1:xxii) and A.D. 91–96 by *The Jerome Biblical Commentary* (ed. R.E. Brown, J.A. Fitzmyer, and R.E. Murphy [Englewood Cliffs, NJ: Prentice-Hall, 1968]), J.L. D'Aragon ("The Apocalypse" in ibid., p. 469), Caird (op. cit., p. 6), A. Farrer (*The Revelation of St. John the Divine* [Oxford: Oxford University Press, 1964], pp. 31–35), W.J. Harrington (*Understanding the Apocalypse* [Washington: Corpus Books, 1969], p. 7); and Willi Marxsen (*Introduction to the New Testament*, trans. G. Buswell [Philadelphia: Fortress Press, 1974], pp. 277–78).

7. That is also why the book was attributed to John the apostle; an author without apostolic credentials would have no clout in the early church. The book itself claims Johannine authorship in 1:1, 4, 9; and 22:8. As Whealon (op. cit., p. 5) implies, this claim is made only in the Christian section. Charles (op. cit., 1:xxii) lists impressive linguistic evidence to show that the book could not have been written by John the evangelist. Fiorenza (op. cit., p. 19) and Kümmel (op. cit., p. 331) agree. Some scholars claim that "the author of the Apocalypse has left us his real name": Caird, op. cit., p. 10; Charles, op. cit., 1:2; Kümmel, op. cit., p. 321; and Marxsen, op. cit., p. 276. John was such a popular name in early Christian circles that this could be true; unless the author were an apostle, like Paul, the use of his real name would have kept his book out of the canon. Ford (op. cit., pp. 28–38), often so astute about this book, tries with little success to show that it was written by John the Baptist and/or one of his disciples.

Where was the book written? Revelation 1:9 (RSV) says "on the island called Patmos." The other most likely locale is Ephesus, just over the horizon from Patmos. Farrer (op. cit., p. 5) notes that the first mention of the work was in Justin Martyr's dialogue with Trypho the Jew at Ephesus. Ford (op. cit., p. 3) also favors this locale. Kümmel (op. cit., pp. 328–29) prefers Asia Minor. There is no way of knowing whether both sections were written in the same place or whether the Christian section and final compilation were written in one of the places noted above, while the apocalyptic core was composed elsewhere.

8. *The Interpreter's Dictionary of the Bible*, ed. G.A. Buttrick et al. (Nashville: Abingdon Press, 1962), 3:362.

9. Harrington, op. cit., p. 175. Cf. Whealon, op. cit., p. 5; J. Ellul, *Apocalypse*, trans. G.W. Schreiner (New York: Seabury Press, 1977), p. 85.

10. Harrington, op. cit., pp. 154–55.

11. A. Feuillet, "Quelques énigmes des chapîtres 4 à 7 de l'Apoc.," *Esp. Vie* 86 (1976): 471–79, as cited in *New Testament Abstracts* 21, no. 2 (1977): 48.

12. R. Bouckham, "The Eschatological Earthquake in the Apocalypse of John," *Novum Testamentum* 19 (March 1977): 224–33 as cited in *New Testament Abstracts* 22, no. 2 (1978): 166.

13. I do not agree with the article in the *Theological Dictionary of the New Testament* (hereafter referred to as *TDNT*), ed. G. Kittel, trans. and ed. G.W. Bromily (Grand Rapids: Eerdmans, 1964–78), 5:127, which identifies the Word of God in Revelation with Jesus of Nazareth.

14. The sharp sword is also mentioned in Revelation 19:15, 21. See Isaiah 11:4; Psalms of Solomon 17:26–27, 39; and 1 Enoch 6:2, and the discussion in Harrington, op. cit., pp. 112, 227–31.

15. "The white anger of God" is a phrase cited by one of my classmates at Bryn Mawr College; although I cannot locate the exact reference in French

literature, it seems appropriate here. The wrath of the Lamb is also mentioned in Revelation 6:16 and 14:10. Caird (op. cit., p. 90) correctly notes that this wrath is inconsistent with the picture of Christ in the Gospels—and incorrectly concludes that these references are interpolations.

16. W.F. Arndt and F.W. Gingrich, *A Greek-English Lexicon of the New Testament,* 4th ed. (Chicago: University of Chicago Press, 1974), p. 107; J. Jeremias in *TDNT* 1:341; *The Jerome Biblical Commentary,* op. cit., pp. 468–69; R. Bultmann, *Theology of the New Testament,* trans. K. Grobel (New York: Charles Scribner's Sons, 1951), 2:174; Charles, op. cit., 1:140–41, 151; Caird, op. cit., p. 174; Fiorenza, op. cit., p. 46; H.J. Richards, *What the Spirit Says to the Churches* (New York: P.J. Kenedy & Sons, 1967), p. 63; *Interpreter's Dictionary of the Bible,* 4:59. Perhaps this identification is the reason Vischer tried to show that τὸ ἀρνίον is an interpolation throughout (noted by Charles [op. cit., p. 141], who thinks Vischer does not prove his point).

17. W.F. Moulton and A.S. Geden, eds., *A Greek Concordance to the New Testament,* 4th ed. (Edinburgh: T.& T. Clark, 1963), p. 107.

18. All Greek quotations in this essay are from K. Aland et al., eds., *The Greek New Testament* (Stuttgart: United Bible Societies, 1974).

19. Arndt and Gingrich, op. cit., p. 45; *TDNT* 1:338–39. Note that in the LXX, Exodus 12 uses πρόβατα in both accounts.

20. In John 21:15, ἀρνίον represents the community: Arndt and Gingrich, op. cit., p. 107; Ford, op. cit., p. 119; *TDNT* 1:341. There is similar usage in the LXX at Isaiah 40:11 and Jeremiah 11:19, and also in Psalms of Solomon 8:28 and Josephus. The Lamb also stands for the Hebrew community in Revelation 5:12, 13; 6:1; and for Hebrew martyrs in 7:14, 12:11, and 13:8.

21. Brown, op. cit., 1:59; Ford, op. cit., p. 30.

22. Ford, op. cit., p. 16.

23. See also ibid., p. 85; Caird, op. cit., p. 73; V. Taylor, *The Names of Jesus* (New York: St. Martin's Press, 1953), p. 86.

24. This coat-of-arms stands at the entrance to City Hall in Jerusalem, which I visited in 1967.

25. Reginald H. Fuller, *The Foundations of New Testament Christology* (New York: Charles Scribner's Sons, 1965), pp. 33, 162–63; Charles, op. cit., 1:143; Ferdinand Hahn, *The Titles of Jesus in Christology,* trans. Harold Knight and George Ogg (New York: World, 1969), pp. 244–46; Kittel, op. cit., 8:389–90, 481; Richards, op. cit., p. 60.

26. Revelation 5:12 notes that the Lamb is worthy to open the scroll; Revelation 21:27 speaks of the Lamb's book of life. These concepts almost certainly echo Daniel 12:1–4. Revelation 5:9, 12, and 13:8 speak of the Lamb as slain; 7:14 and 12:11 mention his blood. Revelation 17:14 affirms that the Lamb will conquer.

27. Charles, op. cit., 2:4–5. Also in Revelation 14:4, where there is a classical Jewish reference to first fruits. Other symbols relating the Lamb to messianic eschatological fulfillment:

The Marriage Supper of the Lamb: Revelation 19:7, 9, and 21:9—based on Isaiah 25:6. Harrington (op. cit., pp. 225–27) comments that this is "a common figure for the kingdom." This association of the Messiah and the messianic banquet underlies Mark 14:25//Matthew 26:29//Luke 22:18.

The Lamb as the Temple: Revelation 21:22. Charles (op. cit., 2:170–71): The Lamb will be the ark of the covenant. Richards (op. cit., p. 107) calls this "purely Israel." This association of Messiah and temple underlies John 2:19–21.

The Lamb as the Lamp: Revelation 21:33—probable reference to the feast of lights. This association underlies John 8:12.

28. *TDNT* 3:165–66.

29. Based on a study of all references to the throne of God in the Bible, as noted for the Old Testament in *Analytical Concordance to the Bible,* ed. R. Young (Grand Rapids: Eerdmans, n.d.), pp. 984–85. For the New Testament see Moulton and Geden, op. cit., pp. 462–63. The same reticence is shown in the Nicene Creed, where like the guest of honor at a dinner, Christ "sitteth on the right hand of God the Father."

30. Ford, op. cit., p. 21.

31. See the discussion in J. Jeremias, *New Testament Theology,* trans. John Bowden (New York: Charles Scribner's Sons, 1971), pp. 62–68.

32. Arndt and Gingrich (op. cit., p. 842) note that the term is occasionally used in Judaism as "an honorary title for the Messiah." See also Werner Georg Kümmel, *The Theology of the New Testament,* trans. John E. Steely (Nashville: Abingdon Press, 1973), p. 110; Hahn, op. cit., pp. 281–83, 288; Fuller, op. cit., pp. 31, 88; Taylor, op. cit., pp. 52–54; and *TDNT* 8:361–62.

33. See, e.g., Psalm 27.

34. Schweizer in *TDNT* 18:389.

35. Daniel is the first extensive work in the Judeo-Christian apocalyptic genre: *The Jerome Biblical Commentary,* op. cit., pp. 342–43; G. Fohrer, *Introduction to the Old Testament,* trans. D.E. Green (Nashville: Abingdon Press, 1968), p. 479. The best article on the apocalyptic genre is in *Interpreter's Dictionary of the Bible,* op. cit., 1:157–61. The Jewish apocalyptic core of Revelation contains the characteristic "dualistic, cosmic and eschatological belief in two opposing cosmic powers, God and Satan . . . and in two distinct ages—the present, temporal and irretrievably evil age under Satan . . . and the future, perfect and eternal age under God's own rule" (ibid., p. 157). It also contains all the distinguishing secondary features of the Danielic apocalyptic genre: a series of visions, pseudonymity, angelology and demonology, animal symbolism, numerology, predicted woes, and astral influences.

36. Ford (op. cit., p. 16) notes that the title is only used in the Danielic sense in Revelation. For the background of this expression in Canaanite, Babylonian, Egyptian, and classical Greek usage—which may or may not be relevant to the biblical concept—see *TDNT* 8:335–38, 408–19.

37. Oscar Cullmann, *The Christology of the New Testament,* trans. Shirley C. Guthrie and Charles A.M. Hall (Philadelphia: Westminister Press, 1959), p. 140; C.F.D. Moule, *The Origin of Christology* (Cambridge: Cambridge University Press, 1977), p. 23; Fuller, op. cit., pp. 34–37; *TDNT* 8:421–23; Kümmel, *Theology of the New Testament,* op. cit., p. 78; and Moule, op. cit., p. 23.

38. Arndt and Gingrich, op. cit., p. 459.

39. Ibid., pp. 459–60; *TDNT* 3:1040, 1058, 1086; Fuller, op. cit., pp. 50, 68; Cullmann, op. cit., pp. 196, 202; Hahn, op. cit., pp. 88–89; Kümmel, *Theology of the New Testament,* op. cit., p. 113. Charles, op. cit., 1:212, cites its use in polite conversation in the LXX: Genesis 19:2, 23:6, 31:35; Daniel 10:16ff.; Zechariah 1:9, 4:4, 13.

40. Moule, op. cit., p. 35.

41. In the phrase "Lord of lords," Revelation 17:14 and 19:16, both terms are probably sociological.

42. Cullmann, op. cit., pp. 200–201; Fuller, op. cit., p. 68; Hahn, op. cit., pp. 71–72; *TDNT* 3:1082; Taylor, op. cit., p. 39. Matthew Black, "The Christological Use of the Old Testament in the New Testament," *New Testament Studies* 18 (1971–72); 10: the Aramaic equivalent of Adonai and κύριος is Μαρ.

43. κύριος ὁ Θέος ὁ παντοκράτωρ is one of the apocalyptist's favorite titles for God, repeated in Revelation 11:17; 15:3; 16:7; 19:6; and 21:22. κύριος refers to God in Revelation 7:11; 11:4, 15; 15:4; 18:8; and 22:5–6 (2x). The *Trisagion* is from Isaiah 6:3.

44. Hans Conzelmann, *History of Primitive Christianity,* trans. John E. Steely (Nashville: Abingdon Press, 1973), p. 69; *TDNT* 9:496.

45. I saw the statue and its inscription when visiting Olympia in 1978.

46. *Interpreter's Dictionary of the Bible,* op. cit., 3:360–61.

47. Arndt and Gingrich, op. cit., p. 895. They note that it is always a title in the New Testament.

48. Black, op. cit., p. 3; Cullmann, op. cit., p. 111; Hahn, op. cit., p. 164; *TDNT* 9:498.

49. Ford, op. cit., pp. 13–14. I disagree with Hahn (op. cit., p. 167), who sees here a reference to the Parousia.

50. In the New Testament, only here and in Revelation 12:10. In the Old Testament, a standard term; Ford (op. cit., p. 13) cites 1 Samuel 2:10; 12:3, 5; and Charles (op. cit., 1:294) notes Psalm 22.

51. There is no significant manuscript evidence for the omission of any of these interpolations. See *Novum Testamentum Graece,* ed. C. Tischendorf (Graz: Akademische Druck U. Verlagsanstalt, 1965; reprinted from the 8th ed. of 1872), vol. 2, ad loc.; *Novum Testamentum Graece,* ed. E. Nestle and K. Aland (Stuttgart: Wurttembergische Bibelanstalt, 1964), ad loc.

52. Whealon, op. cit., p. 55; Charles, op. cit., 1:331; Ford, op. cit., p. 193. (Ford notes that both Weiss and Wellhausen also considered this a gloss.)

53. Whealon, op. cit., p. 55; Charles, op. cit., 2:128–30; Ford, p. 311.

54. Ford, op. cit., p. 349.

55. Ford, op. cit., p. 237. Charles (op. cit., 2:18) says the phrase is merely out of context. Whealon (op. cit., p. 55) calls it a parenthesis.

56. Whealon, op. cit., p. 55; Charles, op. cit., 2:66.

57. Arndt and Gingrich, op. cit., p. 494.

58. Charles, op. cit., 2:66.

59. Whealon, op. cit., p. 55.

60. Ibid. Both Ford (op. cit., p. 333) and Whealon (op. cit., p. 55) consider this a gloss.

61. Whealon, op. cit., p. 55; Charles, op. cit., 1:287.

62. Whealon, op. cit., pp. 55, 58. As Whealon points out, this theme was stressed in Revelation 1:1, 3, 7, and will be developed further in 22:12, 20. I find it was also announced to six of the seven churches—all but Smyrna—in Revelation 2:5, 16, 25; 3:3, 11, 20.

63. Tischendorf (op. cit., p. 1044) follows Codex Alexandrinus in omitting Χριστοῦ from his text, thus bringing the benediction even closer to Romans 16:20 (rsv): "The grace of our Lord Jesus Christ be with you." Romans 16:27 adds the Amen.

64. There are seven letters to seven churches in the canon of the New

Testament: Revelation to the churches at Ephesus, Smyrna, Pergamum, Thyatira, Sardis, Philadelphia, and Laodicea; Paul to the churches at Rome, Corinth (two letters), Galatia, Philippi, and Thessalonica (2 letters). Philemon is addressed to an individual. Ephesians is the work of the later editor of Paul's letters. The authenticity of much of Colossians is uncertain. The Pastorals are clearly much later.

I am indebted to John Knox, under whom it was my privilege to study at Union Theological Seminary. Other Pauline echoes: Revelation 1:5 calls Jesus ὁ πρωτότοκός τῶν νεκρῶν; cf. Romans 8:29. In Revelation 2:23 Jesus searches the mind and heart; cf. Romans 8:27.

65. The saying is also used in Matthew 11:15; 13:9; Luke 14:35; Mark 4:23 and 7:16 (where it may be a gloss).

66. Moulton and Geden, op. cit., p. 880.

67. Ariel's song, "The Tempest," Act I, scene 2, lines 400–401, in *The Complete Works of William Shakespeare*, ed. G.L. Kittredge (New York: Ginn & Co., 1936).

68. Ford (op. cit., pp. 402–3) and *TDNT* (8:371) stress that this title is used here of the exalted Christ Jesus.

69. As this sentence suggests, I disagree with Moule (op. cit., pp. 20–22), who finds a corporate significance in Jesus' use of the terms, and also with Hahn (op. cit., p. 171), who feels that this title "failed to absorb the motif of exaltation." I find a strong sense of exaltation in its use in Acts 7:56 and Hebrews 2:5–8.

70. See Matthew 16:27, δεῖ αὐτὸν . . . πολλὰ παθεῖν, where parallels Mark 8:31 and Luke 9:22 replace αὐτὸν with τὸν υἱὸν τοῦ ἀνθρώπου; or Matthew 16:13, τὸν υἱὸν τοῦ ἀνθρώπου, where Mark 8:27 and Luke 9:18 read με . . . εἰναι. See *TDNT* 8:401–2; Kümmel, *Theology of the New Testament,* op. cit., p. 77; Hahn, op. cit., p. 22; Cullmann, op cit., pp. 137–38.

71. Fuller, op. cit., p. 120; Arndt and Gingrich, op. cit., pp. 842–43.

72. See, e.g., Isaiah 41:4. ὁ κύριος refers to God 65 percent of the time in the apocalyptic core, 33 percent in the Christian document; to Christ (i.e., Messiah) 20 percent in the apocalypse (including two glosses), 62 percent in the Christian document. Thus the usage is almost exactly reversed in the two sections of Revelation. (Figures are based on data given in Moulton and Geden, op. cit., p. 574.)

73. *TDNT* 1:336–38.

74. As noted above, Μαρ is the Aramaic equivalent of Κύριος. Paul gives the petition in Aramaic in 1 Corinthians 16:22. This is essentially a eucharistic prayer: Caird, op. cit., p. 288; Cullmann, op. cit., p. 211; Hahn, op. cit., pp. 95, 100–102.

75. This prayer is also used in Greek in Revelation 22:21 (another Pauline echo, see note 73). *The Greek New Testament,* op. cit., p. 895n., shows that Χριστοῦ has been added after Ἰησοῦ in Revelation 22:21 by the Vulgate and the Old Syriac version and various minuscules.

76. In this section, Χριστός occurs in 1:1, 2, 5, always with Ἰησοῦς.

77. Conzelmann, op. cit., p. 69.

78. R.E. Brown, *The Birth of the Messiah* (New York: Doubleday, 1977), p. 373.

79. Tischendorf, op. cit., pp. 614, 651.

80. Whealon in a memo to the author.

CHAPTER 12:
THE MESSIAH AS SON OF GOD:
PETER'S CONFESSION IN TRADITIO-HISTORICAL PERSPECTIVE

1. John 6:66–69 presents a close parallel to the synoptic accounts, but there the true textual reading is "the Holy One of God" (so RSV and other modern translations), not "Christ, the Son of the living God" (KJV).

2. For a discussion of the theological significance of the epithet, see Walter Eichrodt, *Theology of the Old Testament*, trans. J.A. Baker (Philadelphia: Westminster Press, 1961), 1:213–14. The importance of the motif "at a fairly early stage," as Eichrodt observes, is indicated in the oath formula "As Yahweh lives" *(ḥay yhwh)*.

3. See Th. De Kruijf, *Der Sohn des Lebendigen Gottes: Ein Beitrag zur Christologie des Matthäusevangeliums*, Analecta Biblica 16 (Rome, 1962).

4. Paul echoes this Hoseanic passage in Romans 9:25–26. It is worth noting that at the very beginning of his discussion of the interrelationship of the Jewish and Christian communities in the elective purpose of God he sets forth his premise that Israel enjoys certain divinely given benefits, the first being election to the rank of a son (huiothesía), Romans 9:4.

5. Odil Hannes Steck, "Theological Streams of Tradition," in *Tradition and Theology in the Old Testament*, ed. Douglas A. Knight (Philadelphia: Fortress Press, 1977), pp. 183–214, esp. pp. 193–94, 199–212.

6. Gerhard von Rad, "Das judäische Königsritual," *Theologische Literaturzeitung* (1947): cols. 213–14., reprinted in his collection of essays, *The Problem of the Hexateuch and Other Essays* (New York: McGraw-Hill, 1966), chap. 10; see also his *Old Testament Theology* (New York: Harper & Row, 1962), 1:318–24. The royal enthronement ritual is also discussed by Sigmund Mowinckel in *The Psalms in Israel's Worship* (Nashville: Abingdon Press, 1962), 1:61–76, esp. pp. 62–65.

7. In the preceding presentation of Voegelin's view I have cited freely my own summary in a review essay, "Politics and the Transcendent: Eric Voegelin's Philosophical and Theological Analysis of the Old Testament in the Context of the Ancient Near East," *Eric Voegelin's Search for Order in History*, ed. Stephen A. McKnight (Baton Rouge: Louisiana State University Press, 1978), pp. 62–100.

8. For objection to a structural evaluation of Mesopotamian and Egyptian culture, owing to the ambiguity and fragmentary character of sources, see A. Leo Oppenheim, *Ancient Mesopotamia: Portrait of a Dead Civilization* (Chicago: University of Chicago Press, 1964), pp. 171ff. John Bright, *History of Israel*, 2d ed. (Philadelphia: Westminster Press, 1972), rightly questions whether Israel adopted wholesale the ancient Oriental views associated with the institution of kingship (pp. 221–23).

9. See Mircea Eliade, *Cosmos and History: The Myth of the Eternal Return* (New York: Harper Torchbook, 1959), "The Symbolism of the Center," pp. 12–17; see also *The Sacred and the Profane* (New York: Harper Torchbook, 1959), chap. 1 on "sacred space."

10. Scandinavian scholars have attempted to give a royal interpretation to both Psalm 8:5–6 and Genesis 1:26–28, but in these texts the language is "democratized." On this subject see Bernhard W. Anderson, "Human Dominion over Nature," *Biblical Studies in Contemporary Thought*, ed. Miriam Ward

(Somerville, MA: Greeno, Hadden & Co., 1975), pp. 27–45, esp. pp. 37–43.

11. See Niek Poulssen, *König und Tempel im Glaubenszeugnis des Alten Testaments,* Stuttgarter Biblische Monographien 3 (Stuttgart: Verlag Katholisches Bibelwerk, 1967).

12. The technical term, *berît ôlam,* "covenant in perpetuity," is not used here as in 2 Samuel 23:5. See Psalm 89:28, 34, where the meaning of Nathan's oracle is expounded in terms of an unalterable covenant.

13. The word *miškan* does not imply dwelling place in the sense of a "home," but carries the archaic meaning of a tabernacle or "encampment" in which Yahweh's "covenant presence" is made known. See Frank M. Cross, "The Priestly Work," in *Canaanite Myth and Hebrew Epic* (Cambridge, MA: Harvard University Press, 1973), p. 299.

14. J.B. Pritchard, *Ancient Near Eastern Texts* (Princeton: Princeton University Press, 1969), p. 265.

15. See the translations in the *Jerusalem Bible,* the *New American Bible,* and the *New International Version.* The *Revised Standard Version* translates, "Your divine throne endures for ever and ever," and the *New English Bible* renders, "Your throne is like God's throne, eternal."

16. On Isaiah's reinterpretation of the Davidic-Zion tradition, see Walther Zimmerli, "Prophetic Proclamation and Reinterpretation," in *Tradition and Theology in the Old Testament,* pp. 82–87.

17. For more extended treatments of Second Isaiah's reinterpretation of Israel's traditions, see my essays "Exodus Typology in Second Isaiah," *Israel's Prophetic Heritage: Festschrift for James Muilenburg* (Harper & Bros., 1962), pp. 177–95; and "Exodus and Covenant in Second Isaiah and Prophetic Tradition," in *Magnalia Dei: The Mighty Acts of God* (New York: Doubleday, 1976), pp. 339–60.

18. von Rad, *Old Testament Theology,* 1:323–24.

19. Son of David: Matthew 1:1, 20; 9:27; 12:23; 15:22; 20:30–31; 21:9, 15; 22:41–46. Son of God: Matthew 3:17; 4:3, 6; 8:29; 11:27; 14:33; 16:16; 17:5; 26:63; 27:40, 43; 27:54; 28:19.

20. After completing this essay, my colleague J.J.M. Roberts shared with me his paper, given at the meeting of a professional symposium in Japan, on "Zion in the Theology of the Davidic-Solomonic Empire." This paper, to be published soon, throws lights on the Zion tradition from the side of texts of the Ancient Near East.

CHAPTER 14:
THE TESTIMONIUM FLAVIANUM:
THE STATE OF THE QUESTION

1. Alexander Berendts and Konrad Grass, ed. and trans., *Flavius Josephus: Vom Jüdischen Kriege Buch I-IV, nach der slavischen Übersetzung deutsch herausgegeben und mit dem griechischen Text verglichen,* 2 vols. (Dorpat, 1924–26, 1927).

2. Robert Eisler, *Iēsous Basileus on Basileusas,* 2 vols. (Heidelberg, 1929 –30); Eng. trans.: abridged and corrected by Alexander H. Krappe, *The Messiah Jesus and John the Baptist According to Flavius Josephus' Recently Discovered "Capture of Jerusalem" and the Other Jewish and Christian Sources* (London, 1931).

3. Heinz Schreckenberg, *Bibliographie zu Flavius Josephus,* Arbeiten zur Literatur und Geschichte des hellenistischen Judentums 1 (Leiden, 1968).

4. Heinz Schreckenberg, *Bibliographie zu Flavius Josephus: Supplemente 1966–77, Nachträge und Gesamtregister* (Leiden, 1978).

5. See note 2 above, pp. 36ff., in both the original and the translation.

6. Appendix K in Josephus, vol. 9: *Jewish Antiquities, Books XVIII–XX,* Loeb Classical Library (London, 1965), pp. 573–75. Some of the items are discussed in my *Scholarship on Philo and Josephus 1937–62* (New York, 1963), pp. 42–43.

7. *Journal of Historical Studies* 1 (1968–69): 289–302, and 2 (1969–70): 292–96; revised and reprinted in Emil Schürer, *The History of the Jewish People in the Age of Jesus Christ (175 b.c.–a.d. 135),* revised and edited by Geza Vermes and Fergus Millar, vol. 1 (Edinburgh, 1973), pp. 428–30.

8. André-M. Dubarle, "Le témoignage de Josèphe sur Jésus d'après des publications récentes," *Revue Biblique* 84 (1977): 38–58.

9. See Heinz Schreckenberg, *Die Flavius-Josephus-Tradition in Antike und Mittelalter* (Leiden, 1972), p. 26.

10. Ibid., p. 28. See also Heinz Schreckenberg, *Rezeptionsgeschichtliche und Textkritische Untersuchungen zu Flavius Josephus* (Leiden, 1977), pp. 114–15.

11. Schreckenberg, *Die Flavius-Josephus-Tradition,* op. cit., p. 16; and Schreckenberg, *Rezeptionsgeschichtliche,* op. cit., pp. 114–15.

12. Despite the obvious importance of the Latin version, since it antedates by half a millennium the earliest extant Greek manuscript, it has not been edited, except for the first five books of the *Antiquities* and the treatise *Against Apion* since 1524, when Frobenius, who did not have the Greek original at hand, did so. The main manuscript of the Latin version, the *Ambrosianus papyraceus,* dates from the ninth century, two centuries before the earliest of the Greek manuscripts. A critical edition of the *Testimonium* in the Latin version remains a *desideratum.*

13. See Schreckenberg, *Die Flavius-Josephus-Tradition,* op. cit., pp. 70ff.

14. István K. Horváth, "Egy Origenes-hely problematikájához" (On the Problem of a Passage in Origen), *Antik Tanulmányok (Studia Antiqua)* 9 (1962): 92–96.

15. Louis Préchac, "Reflexions sur le 'Testimonium Flavianum,'" *Bulletin de l'Association Guillaume Budé,* 1969 pp. 101–11.

16. Zvi Baras, "*Testimonium Flavianum:* The State of Recent Scholarship," in Michael Avi-Yonah and Zvi Baras, *Society and Religion in the Second Temple Period,* vol. 8 of *World History of the Jewish People* (Jerusalem, 1977), pp. 310–11.

17. So Schreckenberg, *Die Flavius-Josephus-Tradition,* op. cit., p. 90.

18. Eduard Norden, "Josephus und Tacitus Über Jesus Christus und eine messianische Prophetie," *Neue Jahrbücher für das klassische Altertum, Geschichte und deutsche Literatur* 16 (1913): 637–66; reprinted in Abraham Schalit, *Zur Josephus-Forschung,* Wege der Forschung 84 (Darmstadt, 1973), pp. 27–69.

19. Henry St. John Thackeray, *Josephus the Man and the Historian* (New York, 1929; reprint ed., 1967), pp. 140–41.

20. Jacques Moreau, *Les plus anciens témoignages profanes sur Jésus* (Brussels, 1944).

21. Clyde Pharr, "The Testimony of Josephus to Christianity," *American Journal of Philology* 48 (1927): 137–47.

22. Horváth, op. cit.,

23. Albert A. Bell, Jr., "Josephus the Satirist? A Clue to the Original Form of the *Testimonium Flavianum*," *Jewish Quarterly Review* 67 (1976): 16–22.

24. Bell notes that Hegesippus' treatment of the Paulina-Mundus story (*De Excidio Hierosolymitanae urbis* 2.12.1) is a parody of the annunciation (Luke 1:26–38).

25. Ernst Bammel, "Zum Testimonium Flavianum (Jos. Ant. 18.63–64), " in Otto Betz, Klaus Haacker, Martin Hengel, eds., *Josephus-Studien: Untersuchungen zu Josephus, dem antiken Judentum und dem Neuen Testament, Otto Michel zum 70. Geburtstag gewidmet* (Göttingen, 1974), pp. 9–22.

26. An attempt has been made to find a hidden reference to Josephus in a minor talmudic tractate, *Derekh Erez Rabbah* 5 (*Pirke Ben Azzai* 3, ed. Higger, p. 183), by Nehemiah Brüll, "Eine talmudische Nachright über Josephus," *Jahrbücher für Jüdische Geschichte und Literatur* 4 (1879): 40–42; and by Hayim Leshem, "Flavius on the Antiquity of the Jews Compared with the Greeks" (in Hebrew), *Mahanaim* 112 (1967): 92–95. The passage notes that when four great sages, Joshua ben Hananiah, Akiva, Gamaliel, and Eleazar ben Azariah, went to Rome toward the end of Domitian's reign to protest Domitian's decision to kill all the Jews in the Roman Empire, they visited a nameless "philosopher." In view of the fact that Josephus seems to have been the only Jew in Rome who continued to have influence with Domitian, being an adopted Flavian, it would be reasonable to expect that envoys called upon him for his aid. Josephus must have been eager, because of the many accusations against him, to prove his loyalty to the Jewish people, as he did in his last written works, namely, the *Antiquities* and especially *Against Apion*. However, Josephus is not presented in his own extant writings as a philosopher (though the term may be used in an imprecise sense); moreover, the philosopher in the talmudic story is a pagan. Ernest Wiesenberg, "Related Prohibitions: Swine Breeding and the Study of Greek," *Hebrew Union College Annual* 27 (1956): 213–33, attempts to identify Josephus as the old man (Talmus, *Baba Kamma* 82b, *Sotah* 49b, *Menahoth* 64b) who was learned in Greek wisdom and who gave the advice to send up a pig instead of cattle for the sacrifices in the temple during the civil war between Hyrcanus and Aristobulus. But the term old man is in the Talmud (*Kiddushin* 32b) a synonym for a wise man, and this incident occurred in 63 B.C., a full century before the birth of Josephus (unless we follow the Jerusalem Talmud in placing it in the time of Titus). Finally, there is no particular reason for identifying the old man as Josephus, except for his Greek learning, which, despite Josephus' own statement (*Ant.* 20.263) praising his knowledge in this field, was hardly restricted to Josephus.

27. Wolfgang Trilling, *Fragen zur Geschichtlichkeit Jesu,* 2d ed. (Düsseldorf, 1967), pp. 53–56.

28. Morton Smith, "Palestinian Judaism in the First Century," in *Israel: Its Role in Civilization,* ed. Moshe Davis (New York, 1956), pp. 67–81, notes that the Pharisees hardly figure in Josephus' account in the *War* (2.162–63), but that in the *Antiquities,* written some twenty years later, the Pharisees take first place in the discussion of the Jewish sects. It is in the *Antiquities,* he remarks, that the claim is first made that Palestine is ungovernable without Pharisaic support. This shift is due, he says, to a desire to win support from the Romans for the Pharisees against the Sadducees. But the Sadducees had for all practical purposes lost power with the destruction of the temple in 70; hence, when

Josephus wrote the *War* in 75–79, the Pharisees were clearly on their way to becoming the dominant party in Palestine. Smith's position has been adopted by Jacob Neusner, "Josephus' Pharisees," in *Ex Orbe Religionum: Studia Geo Widengren Oblata* (Leiden, 1972), pp. 224–44; idem, "Josephus' Pharisees: The Real Administrators of the State," in his *From Politics to Piety: The Emergence of Pharisaic Judaism* (Englewood Cliffs, NJ, 1973), pp. 45–66; idem, *The Rabbinic Traditions About the Pharisees Before 70* (Leiden, 1971), 1:137–41, 3:175–79; idem, "The Rabbinic Traditions About the Pharisees Before 70 A.D.: The Problem of Oral Tradition," *Kairos* 14 (1972): 57–70; and Shaye J.D. Cohen, *Josephus in Galilee and Rome: His Vita and Development as a Historian* (Ph.D. diss., Columbia University, 1975).

29. William L. Dulière, "Inventaire de quarante-et-un porteurs du nom de Jésus dans l'histoire juive écrite en grec," *Novum Testamentum* 3 (1959): 180–217.

30. Eisler, op. cit.

31. Thackeray, op. cit., p. 140.

32. George C. Richards, "The Testimonium of Josephus," *Journal of Theological Studies* 42 (1941): 70–71.

33. Felix Scheidweiler, "Das Testimonium Flavianum," *Zeitschrift für die neutestamentliche Wissenschaft* 45 (1954): 230–43.

34. Franz Dornseiff, "Zum Testimonium Flavianum," *Zeitschrift für die neutestamentliche Wissenschaft* 46 (1955): 245–50.

35. Thackeray, op. cit., p. 145.

36. Bammel, op. cit.

37. Moreau, op. cit.

38. Solomon Zeitlin, "The Hoax of the 'Slavonic Josephus,'" *Jewish Quarterly Review* 39 (1948–49): 171–80; and *The Rise and Fall of the Judaean State: A Political, Social, and Religious History of the Second Commonwealth* (Philadelphia, 1967), 2:152.

39. Ch. Martin, "Le 'Testimonium Flavianum': Vers une solution définitive," *Revue Belge de Philologie et d'Histoire* 20 (1941): 409–65.

40. J. Spencer Kennard, Jr., "Gleanings from the Slavonic Josephus Controversy," *Jewish Quarterly Review* 39 (1948–49): 161–70.

41. Zeitlin, op. cit.

42. André Pelletier, "L'originalité du témoignage de Flavius Josèphe sur Jésus," *Recherches de Science Religieuse* 52 (1964): 177–203; idem, "Ce que Josèphe a dit de Jésus (Ant. XVIII 63–64)," *Revue des Études juives* 124 (1965): 9–21.

43. Théodore Reinach, "Josèphe sur Jésus," *Revue des Études juives* 35 (1897): 1–18.

44. Haim Cohn, *The Trial and Death of Jesus* (in Hebrew) (Tel-Aviv, 1968; Eng. trans.: New York, 1971), pp. 308–16.

45. Paul Winter, "Josephus on Jesus," *Journal of Historical Studies* 1 (1968): 289–302; revised in Emil Schürer, *The History of the Jewish People in the Age of Jesus Christ (175 b.c.–a.d. 135)*, rev. and ed. Geza Vermes and Fergus Millar (Edinburgh, 1973), 1:428–41.

46. Kennard, op. cit.

47. Zeitlin, op. cit.

48. Lucas Osiander, *Epitomes historiae ecclesiasticae centuria I, II, III* (Tübingen 1592–1604), cent. 1, 1.22, cap. 7, p. 17. Cf. Tanaquil Faber (Tannegui

LeFèvre) (Lefèbre), *Flavii Josephi de Jesu Domino testimonium suppositum esse diatriba* (Saumur, 1655); and Schreckenberg, *Bibliographie zu Flavius Josephus,* op. cit., p. 23.

49. Solomon Zeitlin, "The Essenes and Messianic Expectations: A Historical Study of the Sects and Ideas During the Second Jewish Commonwealth," *Jewish Quarterly Review* 45 (1954–55): 83–119.

50. Ellis Rivkin, prolegomenon to *Judaism and Christianity, I: The Age of Transition,* ed. William O.E. Oesterley (reprinted.: New York, 1969), pp. xliv–xlv.

51. See Jay Braverman, *Jerome's Commentary on Daniel: A Study of Comparative Jewish and Christian Interpretations of the Hebrew Bible,* Catholic Biblical Quarterly Monograph Series 7 (Washington, D.C., 1978), pp. 109–11.

52. Ralph Marcus, ed. and trans., *Josephus,* vol. 6: *Jewish Antiquities, Books IX–XI,* Loeb Classical Library (London, 1937), p. 275, note c, on *Ant.* 10.210.

53. David Flusser, "The Four Empires in the Fourth Sybil and in the Book of Daniel," *Israel Oriental Studies* 2 (1972): 148–75.

54. Scheidweiler, op. cit.

55. Walter Pötscher, "Iosephus Flavius, Antiquitates 18,63f. (Sprachliche Form und thematischer Inhalt)," *Eranos* 73 (1975): 26–42.

56. Dornseiff, op. cit.

57. Samuel G.F. Brandon, *The Fall of Jerusalem and the Christian Church: A Study of the Effects of the Jewish Overthrow of* A.D. *70 on Christianity* (London, 1951; 2d ed., 1957), pp. 185–205. See Eisler, op. cit.

58. J.C. O'Neill, "The Silence of Jesus," *New Testament Studies* 15 (1968): 153–67.

59. Victor A. Tcherikover, Prolegomena, in *Corpus Papyrorum Judaicarum,* vol. 1 ed. Victor A. Tcherikover and Alexander Fuks (Cambridge, MA, 1957), pp. 89–93.

60. William L. Lane, *Times of Refreshment: A Study of Eschatological Periodization in Judaism and Christianity* (Th.D. diss., Harvard University Divinity School, 1962), pp. 283–84.

61. Otto Michel, "Studien zu Josephus: Simon bar Giora," *New Testament Studies* 14 (1967–68): 402–08.

62. Lane, op. cit., pp. 283–84.

63. Abraham Schalit, "Josephus Flavius," *Encyclopaedia Judaica* 10 (1971): 251–65.

64. Samuel G.F. Brandon, "Testimonium Flavianum," *History Today* 19 (1969): 438.

65. Marianus de Jonge, "χρίω, χριστός, ἀντίχριστος, χρῖσηα, χριστιανός: "Philo and Josephus," in Gerhard Kittel, *Theolgisches Wörterbuch zum Neuen Testament* (Stuttgart, 1973), 9:511–12 (pp. 520–21 in the English translation).

66. Marianus de Jonge, "Josephus und die Zukunftserwartungen seines Volkes," in *Josephus-Studien: Untersuchungen zu Josephus, dem antiken Judentum und dem Neuen Testament, Otto Michel zum 70. Geburtstag gewidmet,* ed. Otto Betz, Klaus Haacker, and Martin Hengel (Göttingen, 1974), pp. 205–19.

67. Jacob Zlotnik, "Josephus Flavius" (in Hebrew), *Sinai* 13 (1949–50): 19–35, 185–93.

68. Alfred Edersheim, "Josephus," *A Dictionary of Christian Biography,* ed. William Smith and Henry Wace (London, 1882), 3:441–60.

69. Thackeray, op. cit., p. 128.

70. Richard Laqueur, *Der jüdische Historiker Flavius Josephus: Ein biograph-*

ischer Versuch auf neuer quellenkritischer Grundlage (Giessen, 1920), pp. 274ff. In this theory Laqueur had been anticipated by Francis C. Burkitt, "Josephus and Christ," *Theologisch Tijdschrift* 47 (1913): 135–44.

71. Kennard, op. cit.

72. E.g., Laqueur, op. cit., and Eisler, op. cit., 1:146. The hypothesis is rejected by Hans Lewy, review of Eisler, in *Deutsche Literaturzeitung* 51 (1930): 481–94; and by Heinz Schreckenberg, "Neue Beiträge zur Kritik des Josephustextes," *Theokratia* 2 (1970–72): 87n., and idem, *Die Flavius-Josephus-Tradition,* op. cit., pp. 63, 176–77. Schreckenberg's argument is that our Josephus manuscripts appear to be descended from one archetype rather than from two. The studies of the text of Josephus as transmitted by the church fathers support the view that the polarization of the two text families from the third century onward must be attributed to a different choice of alternate readings rather than to two different editions. But as Cohen, op. cit., has properly remarked, this means only that our manuscript tradition, which as we have noted is quite late, provides no proof for a second edition, not that it provides evidence against it. Moreover, as Hilarius Emonds in *Zweite Auflage im Altertum: Kulturgeschichtle Studien zur Überlieferung der antiken Literatur* (Leipzig, 1941), a work that curiously has no references to the alleged second edition of Josephus, has remarked, ancient book production afforded ample opportunity for changes and corrections. However, the absence of any specific reference in Josephus to a second edition would place the burden of proof on those who argue that there was one.

73. Berendts and Grass, op. cit.

74. Shlomo Pines, *An Arabic Version of the Testimonium Flavianum and Its Implications,* Publications of the Israel Academy of Sciences and Humanities, Section of Humanities (Jerusalem, 1971).

75. Ibid., pp. 54–63.

76. David Flusser, "The Evidence of Josephus on Jesus" (in Hebrew), in his *Jewish Sources in Early Christianity: Studies and Essays* (Tel-Aviv, 1979), pp. 72–80.

77. Schreckenberg, *Rezeptionsgeschichtliche,* op. cit., pp. 9–12.

78. Jean Daniélou, "Flavius Josèphe: Qu'a-t-il écrit sur Jésus?" *Le Dossiers de l'Archéologie* 10 (1975): 56–57.

79. Ernst Bammel, "A New Variant Form of the *Testimonium Flavianum,*" *Expository Times* 85 (1974): 145–47.

80. A thorough study of the Syriac sources utilized by Agapius would be welcome.

81. André-M. Dubarle, "Le témoignage de Josèphe sur Jésus d'après la tradition indirecte," *Revue Biblique* 80 (1973): 481–513.

82. André-M. Dubarle, "Le témoignage de Josèphe sur Jésus d'après des publications récentes," *Revue Biblique* 84 (1977): 38–58.

CHAPTER 15:
OTHER FAITH IMAGES OF JESUS:
SOME MUSLIM CONTRIBUTIONS TO THE CHRISTOLOGICAL DISCUSSION

1. Notwithstanding the strict language limitations, Don Wismer's *The Islamic Jesus: An Annotated Bibliography of Sources in English and French* (New York: Garland, 1977), offers an extremely useful introduction to the literature.

2. Harvey K. McArthur, "Son of Mary," *Novum Testamentum 15* (1973): 38.

3. Describing the Qur'anic stories of the prophets as "sidelights, fragments and intimations," legends "to incite and stimulate the pious mind," Smail Balić remarked: "Islam did not arise out of the history of a covenant with God, as is the case with Judaism. An intimate connexion between God and man based on interaction in history is unknown to Islam." ("The Image of Jesus in Contemporary Islamic Theology," in *We Believe in One God: The Experience of God in Christianity and Islam,* ed. Annemarie Schimmel and Abdoldjavad Falatūri [New York: Seabury Press, 1979], pp. 2–3). In the same volume, in "Experience of Time and History of Islam," Falatūri observed (pp. 65–66) that since according to the Qur'ān divine guidance "remains or should remain forever unaltered by time or history . . . there is no reason to conceive of revelation as something temporal or historical," explaining in this way, e.g., the lack of chronological order in the Qur'anic lists of prophets. See on Islamic concepts of history, especially Mazheruddin Siddiqi, *The Qur'anic Concept of History* (Karachi: Central Institute of Islamic Research, 1965); and Yvonne Haddad, *Contemporary Islam and the Challenge of History* (Albany: State University of New York Press, 1981). The view that the Qur'ān does not seek to present a historical account of either the prophets or "the peoples of the past" has important implications also for the interpretation of the Jesus references.

4. "No relationship can be set up between the person of Christ and Muslim theology" (Balić, op. cit., p. 1).

5. For such statements in two of the Islamic "catechisms" available in English translation, see Kenneth Cragg and Marston Speight, *Islam from Within: Anthology of a Religion* (Belmont, CA: Wadsworth Publishing Co., 1980), pp. 140–41; and Arthur Jeffery, ed., *A Reader on Islam* (The Hague: Mouton & Co., 1962), pp. 459–60.

6. Balić, op. cit., p. 1.

7. Ibid., pp. 1–2, 7. See below, note 91.

8. The issue for Christians is how they can do justice to Jesus' unity with God without suggesting identity or, at least in Pannenberg's terminology, without confusing "Trinitarian identity" with "identity pure and simple" or "undifferentiated identity." See Wolfhart Pannenberg, *Jesus—God and Man,* trans. L.W. Wilkins and D.A. Priebe, 2d ed. (Philadelphia: Westminster Press, 1977), pp. 407 and 160. In his discussion of the christological starting point of Christian theology, Carl Heinz Ratschow clearly states that faith in God *is* faith in Jesus, but warns that this is not a matter of identification: "Wir haben es nicht damit zu tun, dass dieser Mann mit Gott selbst identifiziert wird und dieser Mann also in seinem So-Sein Gottes Unmittelbarkeit wäre." *Der angefochtene Glaube* (Gütersloh: Gütersloher Verlagshaus Mohn, 1957; 1st paperback ed., 1978), p. 91. On this point and on many other issues raised below, see also Antonie Wessels, "Speaking About Jesus Christ in Dialogue with Muslims," *Theological Review Near East School of Theology* 1, no. 2 (November 1978): 3–17 (esp. 15).

9. Don Cupitt, "One Jesus, Many Christs?" in *Christ, Faith, and History,* ed. S.W. Sykes and J.P. Clayton (Cambridge: Cambridge University Press, 1972), p. 142.

10. Pannenberg, op. cit., pp. 399–410; translated from the fifth German edition.

11. Ibid., p. 406.

12. Ibid.

13. Figures for the world total of Muslims range from approximately 650

million to over 950 million, with 850 million as a widely accepted estimate.

14. An allusion to Siegfried Raeder's assertion that there are only two methods for a theological assessment of the faith of other people, namely, *"die eklektische und die fundamentale,"* of which the former, either in its polemical or in its irenical form, focuses on the obvious contrasts and the apparent similarities, while the latter seeks to move beyond these to the basic point where the denial as well as the affirmation of the gospel find their origin ("Sura 55: Schöpfung und Gericht: Versuch einer religionswissenschaftlichen Deutung und theologischen Kritik," in *Prophetie in Bibel und Koran* [Breklum: Breklumer Verlag, 1974], pp. 50–52).

15. Jacques Jomier warned several years ago that the role Jesus plays in the life of many Muslims and Muslim communities must not be overestimated (*The Bible and the Koran* [Chicago: Henry Regnery Co.; New York: Deselee, 1964], p. 84). Seriously misleading, e.g., is the remark of Gaston Zananiri, *L'Église et l'Islam* (Paris: Spes, 1969), pp. 40–41: "Mahomet cite Jésus plus que n'importe quelle autre figure religieuse." The frequency of the Qur'anic references to Jesus, Noah, Abraham, and Moses is (in verses dealing with them) 93, 131, 245, and 502, respectively (Youakim Moubarac, *Abraham dans le Coran* [Paris: J. Vrin, 1958], p. 28).

16. Hermann Stieglecker devoted eighty pages of his *Die Glaubenslehren des Islam* (Munich: Schöningh, 1960) to Muslim views of Jesus, defending the thesis: "Obwohl die Muhammedaner dem Propheten Isa und seiner Mutter Maryam grosse Ehren zubilligen, so tut sich trotzdem gerade hier die tiefe Kluft zwischen Islam und Christentum auf, es ist das die unüberbrückbare Kluft zwischen dem Isa der Muslim und dem Jesus der Christen" (p. 258).

17. Note 1.

18. The five are Henry Michaud, *Jésus selon le Coran* (Neuchâtel: Delachaux et Niestlé, 1960); Heikki Räisänen, *Das Koranische Jesusbild* (Helsinki: Finnische Gesellschaft für Missiologie und Ökumenik, 1971); Claus Schedl, *Muhammed und Jesus* (Vienna: Herder, 1978); Geoffrey Parrinder, *Jesus in the Qur'ān* (1965; reprint ed., New York: Oxford University Press, 1977); and —because of its wide impact—the appendix "The Qur'ān and Christ," in R.C. Zaehner, *At Sundry Times* (London: Faber & Faber, 1958), pp. 195–217. The two studies dealing with Jesus in Islam (and not just in the Qur'ān) are Michel Hayek, *Le Christ de l'Islam* (Paris: Éd. du Seuil, 1959); and Olaf H. Schumann, *Der Christus der Muslime* (Gütersloh: Gerd Mohn, 1975).

19. Wismer, op. cit., gives a useful list of "major and minor general sources" on pp. 293–95. For additional literature see some of the titles referred to in this article in notes 3, 8, 16, 18, 19, 20, 36, 38, 40, 41, 46, 47, 48, 66, and 117, as well as, e.g., Johan Bouman, *Gott und Mensch im Koran* (Darmstadt: Wissenschaftliche Buchgesellschaft, 1977), pp. 39–68 ("Jesus und die Prophetengeschichte"). Of the "popular" Christian booklets on Islam, note especially Ernest Hahn, *Jesus in Islam: A Christian View* (Vaniyambadi: Condordia Press, 1975); W. Höpfner, "Jesus im Koran und im Neuen Testament," in *Der moslemische Jesus und wir* (Breklum: Breklumer Verlag, n.d.), pp. 13–20; Ulrich Parzany, *Jesus der Moslems, Jesus der Christen* (Wuppertal: Aussaat Verlag, 1968); and F.L. Bakker, *Jezus in de Islam* (Den Haag: J.N. Voorhoeve, 1955).

20. In particular the entry " 'Īsā" in the first edition of the *Encyclopaedia of Islam* (2:524–26, Duncan Black Macdonald) and in the new edition (4:81–86, Georges C. Anawati).

21. The most useful indexes in general are those in the Qur'ān translations by J.H. Kramers (*De Koran* [Amsterdam: Elsevier, 1956; 5th reprint, 1976], "'Īsā," p. 675), Regis Blachère (*Le Coran* [Paris: G.-P. Maisonneuve-Max Besson, 1957], "Jésus," p. 719), and D. Masson (*Le Coran* [Paris: Gallimard, 1967], "Jésus," p. 1068).

22. An early example of a Christian discussion of the Qur'anic references to Jesus is found in the twelfth-century letter from the Melkite bishop Paul to some Muslim friends, published—with translation—in Paul Khoury, *Paul d'Antioche, Evêque Melkite de Sidon (XIIes.)* (Beirut: Impr. Catholique, n.d.), pp. 59–83 of the Arabic section, French trans. pp. 169–87.

23. Sūra (hereafter the traditional spelling, Sura, is used) 3:42–47; 19:16–22; 21:91; 66:12. See also Sura 3:59 and, esp. on Mary, 3:42–43. The designation "Son of Mary," used twenty times for Jesus, is often interpreted as implying that Jesus had no human father.

24. Sura 3:49; 5:110. See also Sura 3:46; 19:29–33.

25. *Word,* Sura 3:45 (see also v. 39); *Word and Spirit,* 4:171 (supported by the Spirit, 2:87, 253; 5:110); *Sign,* 21:91; 23:50; *Mercy,* 19:21; *Messiah,* used 11 times in 9 verses and read by many Muslims as "simply a title or an address," not to be interpreted in a Christian theological sense; see, e.g., Balić, op. cit., p. 7.

26. For examples of passages in which Jesus' name occurs in a list of prophets, see Sura 3:84; 4:163–65; 33:7. His function as apostle *(rasūl)* to the children of Israel is mentioned in, e.g., Sura 3:49 and 61:6.

27. Sura 5:46, 110; 57:27.

28. Sura 4:159. Indirectly Sura 43:61 may refer to his eschatological role also.

29. See the text at notes 30–45, below.

30. Sura 3:54 is most likely an indirect reference to the failure of the plans of those opposing Jesus, and God's "restraining the hands" of the Jews so that they could not harm Jesus (5:110) may well be understood as applying also to the crisis of the crucifixion attempt.

31. Including the demand to see God face-to-face, the making of the calf (v. 153), the breaking of the covenant, and the killing of the prophets (v. 155). On this last issue, see below, note 57.

32. Muhammad Asad, *The Message of the Qur'ān, Translated and Explained* (Mecca: Muslim World League, 1964), 1:176 (the complete translation has now been published: Gibraltar: Dar al-Andalus, 1980), renders the verse as follows: "Behold, we have slain the Christ Jesus, son of Mary, [who claimed to be] God's apostle." His emphasis that this statement should not be read as if it contains the enemies' recognition of Jesus as apostle of God seems valid, and even the cautious words of Hahn (op. cit., p. 23) that "it is possible, though improbable, that the Jews may have admited (reluctantly?) that they slew a messenger of God," may give rise to wrong speculations.

33. The texts used most frequently to substantiate the thesis that the Qur'ān acknowledges the fact of Jesus' death are Sura 19:33; 3:55; 5:117. Parrinder, op. cit., pp. 107–8, leaves the possibility open that Sura 5:17 and 75 can be read also as references to the death of Jesus, and solves the problem of what he sees as the contradictory message of Sura 4 by the pretentious and odd statement that "it might be suggested that the Muslim teachings of 'abrogation' *(nāsikh)* could apply to 4:156/157, in view of the numerous contrary verses" (p. 121). Not less than 130 entries in Wismer's *The Islamic Jesus* (op. cit.) deal with the Ahmadiyya as well as the "orthodox" views of the crucifixion of Jesus; see the

index, p. 297, under "Crucifixion denied" (this wording seems inaccurate as far as the Ahmadiyya is concerned). See also below, note 55.

34. Sura 3:54 (cf. above, note 30); 8:30; 13:42. See also below, note 75.

35. From the many texts that express the assurance of the victory of God (and God's apostle, and the believers), note Sura 5:56; 9:32 (61:8); 58:22.

36. Sura 16:57, 62; 17:40; 37:149, 153; 43:16–18; 52:39; 53:21–22. Most probably also Sura 37:152; 61:100–1012; 72:3. Although this is more questionable, Sura 10:68; 18:4–5; 43:81; and the much discussed Sura 112 can be seen as in first instance referring to the polytheists as well. The thesis that the last mentioned sura contains "the earliest, indirect denial that Jesus is the Son of God in the Qur'ān" was recently once again defended by Arne Rudvin, "The Gospel and Islam: What Sort of Dialogue Is Possible?" *Al-Mushir* 21 (1979): 98. Rudvin announces in that context his forthcoming article "Some Reflections on 'Jesus in the Qur'ān and the Bible' in the light of the Muslim Veneration of Muhammad," to be published also in *Al-Mushir*.

37. Sura 2:116; 4:171; 9:30–31; 17:111; 19:35.

38. See, e.g., Josef Henninger, *Spuren christlicher Glaubenswahrheiten im Koran* (Schöneck/Beckenried: N.Z.M.W., 1951), pp. 54–55, esp. nn.50 and 50a (chaps. 2–5, pp. 7–56, deal with Jesus in the Qur'ān).

39. Arne Rudvin makes an interesting case against interpreting Sura 5:116 as a 'confused' reference to the Trinity or as a "rejection of a heretical Christian understanding of the Trinity, conceived in terms of a Holy Family, comprising God, Jesus and Mary," and sees it as a condemnation of the worship of the Madonna and Child (*Al-Mushir* 21 [1979]: 102, 118). In that case the only direct critical references to the doctrine of the Trinity are Sura 5:73 ("They have disbelieved who say: God is the third of a trinity") and 4:171.

40. A 'classical' example is Ignazio di Matteo, *La Divinità di Cristo e la Dottrina della Trinità in Maometto e nei Polemisti Musulmani* (Rome: Pontificio Instituto Biblico, 1938), who maintains that the Qur'ān denies neither the divinity of Jesus Christ nor the Trinity (only a "tritheism") (chaps. 1 and 3, pp. 3–13, 43–49). A far more careful statement of the idea that the Qur'ān rejects a heretical Christianity only is found, e.g., in W. Montgomery Watt, "The Christianity Criticized in the Qur'ān," *The Muslim World* 57 (1967): 197–201. See also my editorial in that same issue, "The Danger of Christianizing Our Partners in the Dialogue," *The Muslim World* 57 (1967): 176. (Hereafter *The Muslim World* will be referred to as *M.W.*)

41. A clear instance is the twelfth-century Bishop of Sidon's suggestion that Sura 90:3 contains a recognition of the idea of God the Father and God the Son (Khoury, op cit., p. 179, Arabic section, p. 72). A more subtle, contemporary example of a Christian interpretation of the Qur'ān is found in the work of Julius Basetti-Sani: "For a Dialogue Between Christians and Muslims," *M.W.* 57 (1967): 186–96; and *The Koran in the Light of Christ* (Chicago: Franciscan Herald Press, 1977).

42. The wording chosen simply emphasizes that there is a positive confession implied in the Qur'anic negations and that Christians need to hear what the Qur'ān affirms also in its denials and rejections of Christian notions.

43. The confinement-language was used in the rejection of the statement that "God was (is) Jesus" by (among others) Ibn al-'Arabī; see Wismer, op. cit., pp. 10, 122–23 (nos. 24, 326, 330).

44. Sura 4:172: "The Messiah does not despise it to be a servant of God, nor

do the angels who are near unto Him." See below, note 83. Stressing the necessity to do justice to the different christological conceptions within the New Testament itself, Heikki Räisänen drew attention to "the emphatic subordination of Jesus to God" in Luke, obviously without in any way claiming "that Qur'anic Christology is somehow identical with that of Luke." "The Portrait of Jesus in the Qur'ān. Reflections of a Biblical Scholar," *M.W.* 70 (1980): 127–29.

45. Sura 5:117; 43:64.

46. See Wismer, op. cit., pp. 73, 120–21, 188 (nos. 191, 324, and 508, with a total of twenty-three cross references); Schumann, op. cit., pp. 111–212, 226–41; and Irene West, "What Is Islam Today Saying About Christ and Christianity?" in *The Christian Faith and the Contemporary Middle Eastern World,* Asmara Conference Report (New York: Commission on Ecumenical Mission and Relations, U.P.C. in the U.S.A., 1959), pp. 31–36.

47. Wismer, op. cit., subject index, "Hadith," pp. 298–99, lists several of the most important titles. Special attention should be given Hayek, op. cit., pp. 49–271, esp. pp. 137–214. See also Elsa Sophia von Kamphoevener, *Islamische Christuslegenden* (Zurich: Verlag der Arche, 1963); and Mahmoud M. Ayoub, "Towards an Islamic Christology, I: An Image of Jesus in Early Shī'ī Muslim Literature," *M.W.* 66 (1976): 163–88.

48. Erdmann Fritsch, *Islam und Christentum im Mittelalter: Beiträge zur Geschichte der Muslimischen Polemik gegen das Christentum in arabischer Sprache* (Breslau: Müller & Seiffert, 1930). A still-valuable source of factual information is M. Steinschneider, *Polemische und apologetische Literatur in arabischer Sprache zwischen Muslimen, Christen und Juden* (Leipzig: Abh. für die Kunde des Morgenlandes, bd. 6, no. 3, 1877). Focusing on a work attributed to al-Ghazālī, but placing it in the wider context of Muslim polemical literature on this subject, is Franz-Elmar Wilms, *Al-Ghazālī's Schrift wider die Gottheit Jesu* (Leiden: E.J. Brill, 1966).

49. The notion of vicarious suffering is not mentioned in the Qur'ān in the context of Christian interpretations of the meaning of the death of Jesus. However, the Qur'ān states emphatically that "every soul earns only to its own account; no soul laden bears the load of another" (Sura 6:164; 17:15; 35:18; 39:7; 53:38, in the translation of Arthur J. Arberry, *The Koran Interpreted* [London: Oxford University Press, 1964]). See also below, note 60.

50. Mohamed Al-Nowaihi, who was professor of Arabic Language and Literature at the American University in Cairo, passed away on February 13, 1980.

51. Mohamed Al-Nowaihi, "Redemption: From Christianity to Islam," unpublished paper, pp. 2–3. See, e.g., Isma'il R. Al Faruqī, *Islam* (Niles, IL.: Argus Communications, 1979), pp. 9–10 ("In the Islamic view, human beings are no more 'fallen' than they are 'saved.' Because they are not 'fallen,' they have no need of a savior. But because they are not 'saved' either, they need to do good works—and do them ethically—which alone will earn them the desired 'salvation' "), and Fālatūri's remark in Balić, op. cit., p. 65, that "the Koran recognizes no original sin and no corresponding redemption, so that the Koran presents no salvation history comparable to the Christian tradition." H. Lazarus-Yafeh also comes to a basically negative answer in "Is There a Concept of Redemption in Islam?" in *Types of Redemption,* ed. R.J. Zwi Werblowsky and C. Jouco Bleeker (Leiden: E.J. Brill, 1970), pp. 168–80.

52. Al-Nowaihi, op. cit., p. 3.

53. Ibid., p. 4. In the sections on Al-Nowaihi and Mahmoud Ayoub, note numbers in brackets are renumbered footnotes of the authors discussed.

54. "Sura 50:16; 58:7. These and the following Quranic references are given as examples only, and not meant to be exhaustive. . . ."

55. In a footnote Al-Nowaihi refers to Kenneth Cragg's translation of M. Kamel Hussein, *City of Wrong* (New York: Seabury Press, 1959), p. 222, where one finds Hussein's remark that "no cultured Muslim believes in this nowadays." Al-Nowaihi himself points to Sura 3:169 (martyrs are not "dead") as giving a clue to the right interpretation of 4:157. It is of interest to note that instead of using the common "proof texts" (see above, note 33) a *fatwa* by the Chief Qadi of Kenya, Sheikh Abdalla Saleh Farsy listed the following Qur'anic verses to substantiate his pronouncement that Jesus had actually died: Sura 3:144 and 21:34; *The Truth* (Nairobi), December 8, 1978, p. 2.

56. "Sura 37:171–73; 14:14–15."

57. "Sura 2:87, 91; 3:181." [For a fuller discussion of this issue see my "A Prophet and More Than a Prophet?" *M.W.* 59 (1969): 22.]

58. "Sura 15:11; 36:30."

59. Al-Nowaihi, op. cit., pp. 4–5.

60. Al-Nowaihi points to Sura 74:38 and 31:33 in connection with the notion of personal responsibility and finds some notion of communal guilt reflected in places such as Sura 17:16 and 33:67.

61. Al-Nowaihi, op. cit., p. 6.

62. "Sura 90:10; 91:8."

63. "Sura 96:6–7; 14:34; 33:72; 100:6–7; 18:54; 21:37; 17:83; 70:19–21."

64. "Sura 12:53; 4:83."

65. Al-Nowaihi, op. cit., pp. 6–8.

66. *M.W.* 70 (1980): 91–121.

67. "Sura 2:87, 253."

68. "See, e.g., the Infancy Gospel of Thomas and the Protevangelium of James, in Edgar Hennecke, *New Testament Apocrypha,* trans. and ed. R. McL. Wilson, vol. 1 (Philadelphia: Westminster Press, 1963)."

69. *M.W.* 70 (1980): 94. Quotations in this essay from *The Muslim World* are used by permission.

70. See above, note 47.

71. *M.W.* 70 (1980): 117.

72. *Revue de l'Occident Musulman et de la Méditeraneé* 5 (1968): 79–94.

73. Ibid., p. 82.

74. Ibid., pp. 89–93.

75. Besides Sura 3:54 (above, note 34), the author mentions 61:14 linked with 22:40 (Jesus' disciples are "helpers of God," and God "helps him who helps Him").

76. *Revue de l'Occident Musulman et de la Méditeraneé* 5 (1968): 91; see also ibid., p. 89, on the Qur'anic exaltation of Christ as possibly standing for a form of glorification of the human race, with a reference to Sura 17:72.

77. Ibid., pp. 88–89. "Tout, dans le Coran, nous oriente vers une conception du Christ comme un événement exceptionnel dans l'histoire du monde, événement chargé du significations exceptionnelles."

78. Ibid., p. 84.

79. Ibid., p. 85.

80. Ibid.

81. Ibid., pp. 86–87, with references to Sura 4:171; 21:12 and 66:91 [should be: 21:91 and 66:12], and drawing attention to the somewhat parallel statements about Adam, 16:29; 38:73; 32:9.

82. Ibid., p. 87, mentioning Sura 17:93; 18:110; 41:6.

83. Ibid., p. 89. The author observes that the word *wajīh*, "illustrious" or "highly honored," implies, according to the commentators, the notion of sainthood and the privilege of intercession, as a gift of grace. The term *muqarrabūn*, "those who are nearest [to God]," used in Sura 3:45, also occurs in 4:172 (above, note 44), and Ali Merad emphasizes (ibid., p. 87) that the designation of Jesus as *ʿabd* ("servant") in that text is intended to stress not his humanity but his dependence on God.

84. Ibid., p. 89, observing that the attributes of creation and raising from the dead (*yakhlūq-yuḥyi*, Sura 3:49) are not ascribed to any other prophet and therefore place Christ above other messengers.

85. An expression Joseph Blank borrowed from a Marian hymn of Novalis and applied to the great variety of images of Jesus in modern (Christian) exegesis ("The Image of Jesus in Contemporary Exegesis," in Balić, op. cit., p. 9).

86. Above, note 51.

87. See above, note 69. Since we focused attention on Mahmoud Ayoub's remarks concerning the crucifixion passage in Sura 4, very few references were made to his discussion of "the special humanity" of Jesus, a significant issue in both his contributions "Towards an Islamic Christology." See, e.g., *M.W.* 66 (1967): 166 (on *wajīh*, Sura 4:171; see note 83, above), 168 (the unique place of Jesus in Shīʿī piety), 186–88 ("Thus we see that . . . the Jesus of the Qurʾān and later Muslim piety is much more than a mere human being, or even simply the messenger of a Book"). In *M.W.* 70 (1980): 93, the author refers in his discussion of the uniqueness and purity of Jesus to the oft-quoted tradition (see, e.g., Wismer, op. cit., pp. 23, 60–61, 243, 246, nos. 54, 151, 641, 645): "Every child born of the children of Adam Satan touched with his finger, except Mary and her son, peace be upon them both."

88. See above, note 64 and, as additional references, Sura 7:43 and 2:64.

89. Annemarie Schimmel gave the following formulation of the Book-Person comparison in its extended form (including references to the Virgin Mary and the Prophet Muhammad), in a discussion of the *ummī* ("illiterate") designation of the Prophet: "For just as Mary had to be a virgin, an immaculate vessel to contain and to give birth to the 'word made flesh,' so Muhammad had to be free from secondary intellectual pollutions in order to be a pure receptacle for God's word that was to be 'made a book' in the Koran: 'incarnation' and 'inlibration' (a term coined by Harry Wolfson) stand in phenomenological relation to each other." "The Prophet Muhammad as a Centre of Muslim Life and Thought," in Balić, op. cit., p. 37. The Book-Person parallelism that found widespread acceptance through Wilfred Cantwell Smith's remarks (see Wismer, op. cit., pp. 227–28, nos. 611, 613) was proposed several times by Nathan Söderblom at least as early as 1920 and for the last time in his Gifford Lectures of 1931 (Tiele-Söderblom, *Kompendium der Religionsgeschichte*, 5th ed. [Berlin: Grabow, 1920], sec. 5b, "Allah und sein Prophet," and *The Living God* [London: Oxford University Press, 1933], p. 327). Heinrich Frick elaborated it in his well-known comparison of the three holy nights, *Vergleichende Religions-wissenschaft* (Berlin: De Gruyter & Co., 1928), p. 68. While there is an element

of truth in the parallelism, one should be careful not to draw the dividing line between the Muslim and the Christian concepts of revelation too sharply; see, e.g., Abdus Salaam Madsen, "The Quranic Concept of Revelation with Reference to the Biblical Concepts (A Semantic Essay)," *Review of Religions,* 73, January-February 1978): 1–16, and the last paragraph of the present article.

90. From the many "introductions" to the meaning and implications of these terms, I mention only Pannenberg, op. cit., pp. 33–37, 400–406.

91. Above, note 7. Much further goes Seyyed Hossein Nasr's warning that "un chrétien qui croit sans restriction à la Trinité est plus proche de la conception islamique de la Divinité qu'un chrétien qui dilue la notion de Trinité au profit d'un unitarianisme qui a vite fait de sombrer dans l'humanisme" (in *Les Musulmans,* Verse et Controverse 14, ed. Youakim Moubarac [Paris: Beauchesne, 1971], p. 53). The author denounces any "tampering" with God's revelation by adjusting our theological formulations to the mood of the time—and the Trinitarian understanding of God is as much God's gift to Christianity as the emphasis on God's unity is the divine gift to Islam.

92. Claus Westermann, *What Does the Old Testament Say About God?* (Atlanta: John Knox Press, 1979), p. 96.

93. Kenneth Cragg gave a sensitive introduction to the issues involved in *The House of Islam* 2d ed. (Belmont, CA: Dickenson Publishing Co., 1975), pp. 18–25 ("Muhammad and the Rasūliyyah"). See also his theological reflections on "Islam and Incarnation," in *Truth and Dialogue in World Religions: Conflicting Truth Claims,* ed. John Hick (Philadelphia: Westminster Press, 1974), pp. 126–39.

94. A term used by Kenneth Cragg, *The Event of the Qur'ān* (London: Allen & Unwin, 1971), p. 39, dealing with the Qur'ān as the gift to be possessed: "In the possessing is the whole clue to Muhammad."

95. Ibid.

96. Ibid., pp. 73–77.

97. Cf. the remark of Fazlur Rahman: "God's mercy reaches its logical zenith in 'sending Messengers,' 'revealing Books,' and showing man 'the Way,' " *Major Themes of the Qur'ān* (Minneapolis: Bibliotheca Islamica, 1980), p. 9.

98. Sura 7:203 (10:57; 12:111; 16:64; 17:82; 27:77; 31:3; 45:20) and 6:154 (28:43; 45:12), respectively.

99. Sura 21:107 and 19:21.

100. H. Berkhof, *Christian Faith,* trans. S. Woudstra (Grand Rapids: Eerdmans, 1979), p. 305.

101. Muhammad Asad's translation, *Message of the Qur'ān,* op. cit.

102. Sura 57:9 speaks about God's sending down clear signs on Muhammad "that He may lead you from the darknesses into the Light."

103. See above, notes 35 and 56.

104. In the sense in which Isaiah 42:2 speaks about God's servant who "will not call out or lift his voice high, or make himself heard in the open street."

105. An expression found in Sura 30:50, *āthār rahmat Allāh.*

106. In Paul of Antioch's "Letter" (above, notes 22 and 41) we find an illustration of the Christian use of Sura 42:51, relating the notion of God's speaking "from behind a veil" to the mystery of the "veiled" presence of God's Word in Jesus Christ. Khoury, op. cit., pp. 179–80; Arabic section, pp. 72–73.

107. Ratschow, op. cit., p. 78.

108. Dietrich Bonhoeffer, *Letters and Papers from Prison* (London: Collins,

1959), p. 122: "God is weak and powerless in the world, and that is exactly the way, the only way, in which He can be with us and help us."

109. *Christian Faith,* op. cit., pp. 133–40.

110. C.F.D. Moule, "The Manhood of Jesus in the New Testament," in *Christ, Faith and History,* op. cit., p. 97.

111. Berkhof chose the expression "the defenseless superior power"—as the English translation renders the Dutch clause "de weerloze overmacht"—to avoid the "marginally biblical" notion of Omnipotence and to emphasize through the adjective defenseless the notion of God's acceptance, with all its consequences, of an over-against: in the creation of humankind, in God's dealing with Israel, in God's silence when humanity seems to triumph in the event of Jesus' crucifixion, in the way the Spirit works with the means of proclamation and persuasion, and in the life of those who have heard the commandment not to avenge themselves, turning the other cheek in a preparedness to suffer. *Christian Faith,* op. cit., pp. 134–35; in the Dutch original, *Christelijk Geloof,* 2d ed. (Nijkerk: G.F. Callenbach, 1974), p. 318.

112. Among others, Hans Jochen Margull, "Verwundbarkeit: Bemerkungen zum Dialog," *Evangelische Theologie* 34 (1974): 410–20, pointed to the significance of the notion of the vulnerability of God in the writings of Kenneth Cragg, mentioning his 1956 study *The Call of the Minaret* (New York: Oxford University Press) (no specific page references are given by Margull, but the section referred to may well be pp. 297–301, where Cragg writes with a reference to John 1:29, "Here, the mercy of God accomplishes the forgiveness of the world within the pattern of suffering which is the necessity of the Divine nature") and particularly Cragg's article "The Qur'an and the Contemporary Middle East," *Journal of Ecumenical Studies* 11 (1974): 1–12. From among later references to the same issue in Cragg's writings, I mention his discussion of "the Christian criteria of transcendence," which excludes the notion of an "utter immunity" of God ("The Art of Theology: Islamic and Christian Reflections," in *Islam: Past Influence and Present Challenge,* ed. Alford T. Welch and Pierre Cachia [Edinburgh: Edinburgh University Press, 1979], pp. 290–91), and his preface to *We Believe in One God,* op. cit., pp. viii–ix (". . . the Christian criteria of God as love, vulnerable to man in evil and thereby self-consistently ultimate in redemption and grace").

113. G.F. Hourani, "Zulm an-nafs in the Qur'ān, in the Light of Aristotle," in *Recherches d'Islamologie,* receuil d'articles offert à Georges C. Anawati et Louis Gardet (Louvain: Éditions Peeters, 1977), pp. 144–47.

114. John Hick, "Christ and Incarnation," in *God and the Universe of Faiths,* rev. ed. (Cleveland: World [Fount Paperbacks], 1977), pp. 152–53. See below, note 116.

115. Above, note 3.

116. Herbert H. Farmer, "The Bible: Its Significance and Authority," in *The Interpreter's Bible* (Nashville: Abingdon Press, 1952), 1:6. Farmer's "inhistorization" seems, therefore, far preferable to his other suggestion, "'inhumanization" (ibid., p. 12). Alexander Altmann's statement about Franz Rosenzweig's understanding of God is of interest also in this context: "For him God remains wholly outside history. He need not 'become,' for He 'is.' Providence, therefore, can not mean the self-realization of God. It means the law of God as expressed in revelation. God who is the first will also be the last. He will be the One above all, not the One in all" (*Studies in Religious Philosophy and Mysticism* [Ithaca: Cornell University Press, 1969], p. 291).

CHAPTER 16:
JESUS:
DEACON OF GOD AND PERSONS

1. See David Flusser, *Jesus* (New York: Herder & Herder, 1969), pp. 56, 65, 70–71, 75, 89.

2. Leviticus 19:18, 33–34 (NEB): "You shall love your neighbor as a man like yourself. . . . When an alien settles with you in your land, you shall not oppress him. He shall be treated as a native born among you, and you shall love him as a man like yourself, because you were aliens in Egypt."

3. Matthew 5:44. Enemies today would include hijackers, kidnappers, managers, union bosses, and even civil servants in many sectors of society. "Love" in Semitic idiom meant, of course, to care unselfishly and to exercise goodwill.

4. Op. cit., p. 103.

5. Much has been contributed to the study of Jesus' Aramaic in the past century by such scholars as Dalman, Burney, Lagrange, Schlatter, T.W. Manson, Black, Boismard, and Fitzmyer, and most recently by the study of material from the Dead Sea caves.

6. Peder Borgen, *Bread from Heaven* (Leiden: E.J. Brill, 1965), p. 57.

7. See, e.g., Mark 9:43–48; Luke 11:31–32; 12:24–28; 13:18–21; 15:3–10; Matthew 13:44–46.

8. T.W. Manson, *The Teaching of Jesus* (Cambridge: Cambridge University Press, 1943), p. 56.

9. Op. cit., p. 65.

10. See Luke 10:24 and Mark 6:7ff.

11. Many parables related specifically to the theme of liberation (i.e., God's Βασιλεία or kingship); in the Q material of Matthew and Luke there are eight; in passages found only in Luke there are at least fifteen, edited, of course, and set in Lukan contexts according to congregational and mission interests and needs; in passages found only in Matthew there are nine. Recent students who have enriched our understanding of these parables and of Jesus' message as a whole include Harvey K. McArthur, whom we delight to honor, Sally McFague, Kenneth Bailey, William Doty, Robert Funk, Willi Marxsen, and Norman Perrin. A notable contribution has been made also by J.D. Crossan, and I am indebted to them all.

12. I learned this from reading T.W. Manson's *The Teaching of Jesus*, op. cit.

13. John D. Crossan, *In Parables* (New York: Harper & Row, 1973), pp. 31–44.

14. In opposition to Joachim Jeremias, Crossan asserts that Jesus' parables are "the cause of the war and the manifesto of its inception" (op. cit., p. 32).

15. See my essay "Spirit," in *A Theological Word Book of the Bible,* ed. Alan Richardson (New York: Macmillan, 1951).

16. See Matthew 5:20, 46–47; Luke 6:27–28, 35; Matthew 6:15 (M); Mark 11:25; Matthew 18'35 (M); Luke 15:25–32 (L).

17. Cf. Mark 12:34 and Matthew 25:10.

18. Other texts to be noted are Matthew 6:21, 24; Mark 10:17–25; Luke 18:9–12.

19. See Mark 9:37 (with parallels at Matthew 18:5 and Luke 9:48); Matthew 10:40; Luke 10:16; and, to supplement these synoptic sources, John 12:44–45; 13:20; 17:18–19; and 20:21.

CHAPTER 17:
EXISTENTIALIST CHRISTOLOGY

1. Graham Stanton, "Incarnational Christology in the New Testament," in *Incarnation and Myth*, ed. M. Goulder (London: SCM Press, 1979), p. 155.

2. "The Large Catechism," in *The Book of Concord*, trans. and ed. Theodore G. Tappert (Philadelphia: Fortress Press, 1959), "The First Commandment," sec. 3.

3. Philipp Melanchthon, *Loci Communes* (1521), Plitt-Kolder edition (Erlangen, 1890); my trans.

4. Albrecht Ritschl, *The Christian Doctrine of Justification and Reconciliation*, trans. H.R. Mackintosh and A.B. Macaulay (Edinburgh: T. & T. Clark, 1900), p. 212.

5. Ibid., p. 398.

6. Wilhelm Herrmann, *The Communion of the Christian with God*, trans. J.S. Stanyon and R.W. Stewart (London: Williams & Norgate, 1909); Martin Kähler, *The So-Called Historical Jesus and the Historic Biblical Christ*, trans. C.E. Braaten (Philadelphia: Fortress Press, 1964).

7. In Rudolf Bultmann, *Essays: Philosophical and Theological*, trans. J.C. Greig (London: SCM Press, 1955), pp. 273–90; Quotations from this work in this essay are used by permission of SCM Press and Macmillan Publishing Company, Inc.

8. Ibid., p. 275.

9. Ibid.

10. Ibid., p. 276.

11. Raymond E. Brown, *Jesus, God and Man* (New York: Macmillan, 1967), p. 28.

12. Bultmann, op. cit., p. 276.

13. Brown, op. cit., p. 29.

14. Ibid., p. 36.

15. Bultmann, op. cit., p. 280.

16. Ibid., p. 287.

17. Rudolf Bultmann, *Faith and Understanding,* trans. L.P. Smith (London: SCM Press, 1966), pp. 276–77.

18. Ibid., p. 277.

19. Bultmann, *Essays,* op. cit., p. 286.

20. L. Malevez, *The Christian Message and Myth*, trans. Olive Wyon (London: SCM Press, 1958), pp. 124, 144.

21. Cf. John Macquarrie, *Thinking About God* (London: SCM Press; New York: Harper & Row, 1975), pp. 179–90.

22. Friedrich Gogarten, *Demythologizing and History*, trans. N.H. Smith (London: SCM Press, 1955), pp. 25–26.

23. Ibid., p. 69.

24. Friedrich Gogarten, *Christ the Crisis*, trans. R.A. Wilson (London: SCM Press, 1970), p. 196.

25. Ibid., p. 157.

26. Fritz Buri, *How Can We Still Speak Responsibly of God?* trans. C.D. Hardwick and H.H. Oliver (Philadelphia: Fortress Press, 1968), p. 37.

27. Fritz Buri, *Theology of Existence*, trans. H.H. Oliver and G. Onder (Greenwood, SC: Attic Press, 1966), p. 21.

28. Ibid., p. 83.

29. Cf. John Macquarrie, *Principles of Christian Theology,* 2d ed. (New York: Charles Scribner's Sons, 1977), pp. 272ff.

CHAPTER 18:
TWO CHRISTIC PARADIGMS:
FOCUSES OF A THEOLOGICAL REVOLUTION

1. *Luther's Large Catechism,* trans. J.N. Lender, (Minneapolis: Augsburg Publishing House, 1935), "The First Commandment," sec. 1.

2. Peter L. Berger, *The Sacred Canopy: Elements of a Sociological Theory of Religion* (New York: Doubleday, 1969), p. 181.

3. Ibid., p. 180.

4. The proclamation of Jesus as the cosmic Christ incarnate is implicit, as will become apparent, in numerous sources in the New Testament; it is most explicit in John 1:1–18 and in Colossians 1:15–20.

5. This restricted application of the term paradigm in the context of theology is indebted to an analogous use of the term in the history of the sciences, introduced by Thomas S. Kuhn in his influential work *The Structure of Scientific Revolutions* (Chicago: University of Chicago Press, 1962), and to clarification and slight modification of the term in the postscript of the second edition of that work (1970). Account is also taken of the views of Ian Barbour, *Myths, Models and Paradigms* (London: SCM Press, 1974). Barbour provides a critical review of the widespread discussion of Kuhn's use of the term as it bears on the relation of theory to observation in the sciences; adopts his own use of the term paradigm to refer to *a tradition transmitted through historical exemplars;* and shows its adaptability to the study of religion as conventionally understood. I have broadened its reference beyond conventional religion to include the existential faith commitments of peoples, whether expressly acknowledged as religions or not.

6. Compare J.V. Luce, *Lost Atlantis: New Light on an Old Legend* (New York: McGraw-Hill, 1969); and Bruce C. Heezen, "A Time Clock for History," *Saturday Review,* December 6, 1969, pp. 87–90.

7. It is of interest that Amos 9:5–7 connects both the Philistine migration from Caphtor and the Hebrew exodus from Egypt with vulcanism and tsunamic inundations.

8. Compare John Lear, "The Volcano That Shaped the Western World," *Saturday Review,* November 5, 1966, pp. 57–66.

9. Anointment for the priesthood seems to have been regularly practiced; see Exodus 30:30, Leviticus 4:3; 16:32. There are two references to the anointment of prophets, Elisha (1 Kings 19:16) and Isaiah (Isaiah 61:1).

10. The Parables of Enoch comprise chapters 37–71 of the pseudepigraphal *Book of Enoch.*

11. Compare the expressions in the context of 2 Corinthians 3:17.

12. Compare Samuel Sandmel, *Anti-Semitism in the New Testament* (Philadelphia: Fortress Press, 1978), pp. 8ff.

13. Compare also Matthew's interpretation of the parable of the wheat and tares, in which he distinguishes the "sons of the kingdom" from the "sons of the evil one."

14. Norman R. Petersen, *Literary Criticism for New Testament Critics* (Philadelphia: Fortress Press, 1978), p. 87.

15. For an opposing view, see G. van der Leeuw, *Religion in Essence and Manifestation* (London: Allen & Unwin, 1938), chaps. 11–13.

16. The notion that the Θρόνοι, κθριότης, ἄρχαι, and ἐξουσίαι of Colossians are angelic figures of an esoteric mythology is the misguided consequence of a curious contemporary tendency to mythologize certain literal New Testament concepts. Compare Walter Wink, "The 'Elements of the Universe' in Biblical and Scientific Perspective," *Zygon* 13 (1978): 225–33.

17. Compare Romans 8:18–23.

18. See under the word "system" in *Webster's Third New International Dictionary, Unabridged* (Springfield, MA: G.&C. Merriam Co., 1961).

19. Alfred North Whitehead, *Process and Reality: An Essay in Cosmology* (New York: Macmillan, 1929), p. 374.

20. Wink, op. cit., pp. 225–48. Wink, however, is not accountable for my treatment of the passages in question.

21. Paul elsewhere makes plain that despite the handicap of existence under Torah as an end in itself, the law is good (Romans 7:13). In numerous instances he makes clear that the ethical demands of the law are graciously fulfilled under existence in Christ.

22. Compare Wink, op. cit., p. 231.